CHRISTOCENTRIC COMMENTARY SERIES

A COMMENTARY ON THE EPISTLE TO THE

HEBREWS

—⁓—

JESUS – Better Than Everything

James A. Fowler

ciy

PUBLISHING
P.O. BOX 1822
FALLBROOK, CALIFORNIA 92088-1822

A COMMENTARY ON THE EPISTLE TO THE HEBREWS

—⚭—

JESUS – Better Than Everything

~ Christocentric Commentary Series ~

Copyright ©2006 by James A. Fowler

ISBN-10 – 1-929541-07-4
ISBN-13 – 978-1-929541-07-2

Published by **C.I.Y**. PUBLISHING
P.O. BOX 1822
FALLBROOK, CALIFORNIA 92088-1822

Printed in the United States of America

Scriptural quotations are primarily original translations from the Greek text of the New Testament, but otherwise from the New American Standard Bible, copyrights 1960, 1962, 1963, 1968, 1971, 1972, 1973, 1975, 1977, 1995 by the Lockman Foundation, LaHabra, California.

CHRISTOCENTRIC COMMENTARY SERIES

Cognizant that there are a plethora of New Testament Commentary series available on the market, the question might legitimately be asked, "Why another series of New Testament commentaries?" Although many capable commentators with varying theological perspectives have exegeted the text of the New Testament over the years, seldom do they bring with them into their studies a Christocentric understanding that the Christian gospel is solely comprised and singularly centered in the Person of the risen and living Lord Jesus Christ. The *Christocentric Commentary Series* will exegete and comment on the text of the New Testament from the perspective that the totality of what Jesus came to bring to the world of mankind is Himself – nothing more, nothing less. Having historically died on the cross and risen from the dead, He is not confined to the parameters of the "Historical Jesus," but as the Spirit of Christ He continues to live as He spiritually indwells those who are receptive to Him by faith. This recognition of the contemporary experiential dynamic of Christ's life in the Christian will form the distinctive of the *Christocentric Commentary Series*, bearing out Paul's Christ-centered declaration, "I have been crucified with Christ; it is no longer I who live, but Christ lives in me; and the life I now live in the flesh I live by faith in the Son of God, who loved me and gave Himself up for me" (Gal. 2:20).

All legitimate exegesis of the scriptures must pay close attention to the context in which the texts were originally written. The historical context of a text's *sitz im leben*, the "setting in life" of the author and recipients, is particularly important, for otherwise the interpretation will simply read into the text the presuppositions of the commentator and become *eisegesis* instead of *exegesis*. The *CCS* will carefully consider the historical context as well as the textual context of the scriptures.

Whereas the *CCS* is not intended to be a devotional commentary series or a detailed technical commentary citing all contemporary scholarship, our intent is to steer a middle course that maintains non-technical explanation that is academically viable. Although reference will be made to words from the Hebrew and Greek languages, those words will be converted to Roman lettering, allowing those who do not know the original languages to pronounce them. Citations, quotations, and endnotes will be kept to a minimum.

A diversity of interpretive formats will be utilized in the *CCS*. Some volumes will employ a verse-by-verse exegetical format (cf. *Hebrews* and *Galatians*), whereas others will provide comment on contextual passages (cf. *The Four Gospels* and *Revelation*). Regardless of the interpretive format, the *CCS* will render a "literal interpretation" of the scripture text, that is, in accord with the intended literary genre of the author.

As most biblical commentaries are utilized by pastors and teachers, or studious Christians seeking to understand the scriptures in depth in order to share with others, we join the Apostle Paul in the desire to "entrust these to faithful men (and women) who will be able to teach others also" (II Tim. 2:2). In so doing, may you "do all to the glory of God" (I Cor. 10:31).

TABLE OF CONTENTS

JESUS

Better Than Everything

An Introduction to the Epistle to the Hebrews

The Epistle to the Hebrews has suffered from anonymity. There is anonymity of both author and recipients because these details are not included in the text of the letter. Such anonymity makes the document suspect in the minds of some for it provides no specificity of its intended meaning within a given context. The anonymity of writer and reader allows the epistle to be abstracted and generalized without a specific *sitz im leben* (setting in life) to provide historical context and a basis for specific amplification and application of the meaning of the words. Anonymous text allows for a dilution of meaning in interpretation of the text, or allows an expositor to run rampant with personal presuppositions imposed upon or applied to the text. In other words, anonymity can diminish *exegesis* (interpretive meaning drawn out of the text) and/or facilitate *eisegesis* (interpretive meaning read into the text). In either case, whether subtractive or additive, such interpretation cannot and does not take into account the full intent of the original author to his recipients, and thus diminishes the value and meaning of the text for subsequent generations of readers.

This has certainly been the case in the interpretation of the Epistle to the Hebrews. The letter has suffered from neglect and misuse. The regrettable consequence of the anonymous authorship of this literature has been the reluctance of some Christians to accept it as fully authentic and authoritative. Even in the early church it was little used and cited. Hebrews has suffered from a subtle skepticism throughout Christian history because of its unknown authorship, and contemporary interpretation continues to neglect this important portion of inspired scripture. But perhaps of greater consequence is the fact that the Church through the ages has therefore suffered from the lack of understanding of the unique message of this letter in its assertion of the radical supremacy of the Christian gospel over Judaic religion, and religion in general.

The Epistle to the Hebrews is not the only document of antiquity that is devoid of the details of origin and destination. Within the New Testament literature itself there are other examples of literature without statement of authorship or destination. John's epistles, for example, do not contain his name or any designation of his readers, but these have been reconstructed with what evidence is available (particularly in the case of First Epistle of John) to provide a meaningful historical context for interpretation. The same can be accomplished for the Epistle to the Hebrews, as we will set about to do.

The task of a biblical expositor is to consider the evidence available concerning the historical context of a document, draw a conclusion based on that evidence, and interpret the text accordingly. Biblical scholarship, with its ever-skeptical approach, has been very cowardly in drawing conclusions about the authorship of Hebrews, thus assuring that the text can have only nebulous interpretive meaning. What, then, is the evidence for authorship, destination and dating of this epistle, in order to give it specific historical context? What is the most legitimate conclusion that can be drawn based on that evidence?

Authorship

The primary objections to Pauline authorship have traditionally been explained as: (1) the absence of Paul's name in the epistle, (2) the apparent second-hand knowledge referred to in 2:3, and (3) the style, grammar and vocabulary of the epistle which seems to differ from other Pauline writings.

The absence of Paul's name or signature was explained as early as A.D. 200 in the *Hypotypos* of Clement of Alexandria (c. 155-215). Though that eight volume outline of Christian thought has not been preserved, a portion of that document was quoted by Eusebius in his *Ecclesiastical History*:

> He (Clement of Alexandria) says that the Epistle to the Hebrews is the work of Paul, and that it was written to the Hebrews in the Hebrew language; but that Luke translated it carefully and published it for the Greeks, and hence the same style of expression is found in this epistle and in the Acts. But he says that the words, "Paul the Apostle", were probably not prefixed, because, in sending it to the Hebrews, who were prejudiced and suspicious of him, he wisely did not wish to repel them at the very beginning by giving his name. ...Paul, as sent to the Gentiles, on account of his modesty did not subscribe himself an apostle of the Hebrews, through respect for the Lord, and because being a herald and apostle of the Gentiles he wrote to the Hebrews out of his superabundance.[1]

The reason for the absence of Paul's name is hereby explained early in church history as a sensitivity of the "Apostle to the Gentiles" in writing to Hebrew peoples, who were his kinsmen. The absence of his name does not exclude Paul from authorship any more than the absence of John's name excludes his authorship of the epistles attributed to him.

The contested statement in Hebrews 2:3, "After it (the word of salvation) was at first spoken through the Lord, it was confirmed to us by those who heard," seems to evidence a second-hand knowledge of the gospel, and Paul certainly argues vehemently for the right of apostleship through a first-hand knowledge of Jesus Christ in Galatians 1:11–2:10. But the words can just as accurately be interpreted by explaining that Paul was admitting that he was not one of the original twelve disciples who traveled with the historical Jesus, and therefore was not privileged to directly hear the words that Jesus spoke in that context. This does not in any way diminish his apostleship that he argued for in Galatians, such argument for his apostleship to the Gentiles obviously muted in this correspondence to Jewish Christians.

The argument of differing style, grammar and vocabulary is not all that conclusive either, especially since this epistle was being written to any entirely different audience and with an entirely different purpose than any of Paul's other epistles. Many of the vocabulary differences, where Paul employs words not used in other writings (*hapax logomena*), are in the context of his contrasting Jesus with Jewish history and theology, of which he was obviously quite knowledgeable and would not have been so apt to use in writing to Gentile congregations. The stylistic differences of the Greek text were explained by Clement of Alexandria (see above) as due to Luke's translation from Hebrew to Greek.

Having considered the objections to Pauline authorship, it is incumbent upon us to now present the evidence that exists that points to Paul as the most likely author of this letter.

The papyrus fragment identified as P^{46} is the oldest extant manuscript of the Pauline epistles. This Greek manuscript from Alexandria in Egypt is dated around A.D. 200, and there are no earlier available manuscripts of Paul's epistles. By acceptable criteria of textual criticism, the oldest manuscripts, i.e., those closest to the date of the original writing, must be given greatest import or weight in textual considerations. Since P^{46}, the earliest manuscript containing the Pauline corpus of literature, includes the Epistle to the Hebrews immediately following Paul's Epistle to the Romans and attributes authorship of the epistle to the Hebrews to Paul, this ascription must be granted a predominating weight of evidence in the critical consideration of authorship.

We have already noted that the eight volume *Hypotypos* of Clement of Alexandria, written c. A.D. 200, clearly indicated that Paul was the author of the Epistle to the Hebrews, giving explanation of the absence of his name in the epistle and explanation of the variation in grammatical style of the Greek text (see quotation from Eusebius above).

Origen (185-253), in his *Commentary on the Gospel of John*, wrote that "the Apostle Paul says in the Epistle to the Hebrews: 'At the end of the days He spoke to us in His Son'." (Heb. 1:2).[2] Origen clearly attributes Pauline authorship to the Epistle to the Hebrews, from which he quotes.

The early Alexandrian scholars of the Eastern Church consistently regarded Paul as the author of this epistle. The scholars of the Western Church in Rome were more skeptical of Pauline authorship until Jerome (c. 340-420) and Augustine (396-430) supported the thesis of Paul's authorship. From the Sixth Synod of Carthage (419) until modern times, the Roman Catholic Church affirmed Pauline authorship of the Epistle of the Hebrews. The Protestant reformers, on the other hand, revived the questioning of Paul's authorship, with Martin Luther the first to propose Apollos as the author and John Calvin speculating that Clement of Rome or Luke may have been the author. Scholastic speculations of authorship of this epistle have abounded since the Reformation, often with arrogant unwillingness to accept early tradition or to counter prevailing skepticism of scholarship.

As additional evidence it should be noted that the author mentions Timothy (13:23), who was Paul's closest colleague in ministry, mentioned often in other Pauline epistles (Rom. 16:21; II Cor. 1:1; Phil. 1:1; 2;19; Col. 1:1; I Thess. 1:1; 3:2,6; Philemon 1:1). The author appears to have previously visited the group of people to whom he was writing, and hoped to revisit them (13:19,23), consistent with the fact that Paul had visited the church in Jerusalem on several occasions (Acts 21:11-31; Rom. 15:25; Gal. 1:18). The mention of the "saints of Italy" (13:24) would be consistent with Paul's imprisonment in Rome, and his desire to send greetings on behalf of the

Italian Christians to the Jewish-Christian recipients of this letter.

The evidence is certainly not sufficient to dismiss or deny Paul as the most likely author of this epistle to the Hebrews. In fact, we must be honest enough to admit that the preponderance of the evidence leads to Pauline authorship. All other proposed authors of this epistle (Silas, Philip, Mark, Priscilla, etc.) are merely speculative assignments, "shots in the dark" to suggest another name other than Paul. The name of Apollos was not even suggested until the 16th century by Martin Luther. There is no way to compare the literary criteria of grammar, vocabulary and style with other writings of these speculatively proposed authors for many of them have no other literature to compare with. What a convenient way to preclude Pauline authorship and preempt having to deal with the grammatical issues by assigning authorship to unpublished persons.

Though one must "swim against the tide" of several centuries of skeptical academic scholarship in the textual criticism of Protestant biblical studies, the evidence is quite sufficient to assert that the Apostle Paul was the most likely author of this Epistle to the Hebrews.

Recipients

The text does not indicate who the first readers were, again leaving us with an anonymity of original recipients. So, what internal and external evidence can be presented to make an assignment of destination?

Based upon the abundance of references to Jewish religion and the old covenant, particularly the Levitical priesthood and temple practices, this document has been referred to as "the Epistle to the Hebrews," at least since the latter part of the second century AD. It is reasonable to assume that the original readers were Christians from a Jewish background, even though the quotations from the Old Testament seem to be from the Greek translation of the Septuagint (*LXX*), which would be consistent with Paul's bilingual knowledge of the Old Testament and his frequent utilization of the *LXX* among Gentiles.

It appears that the author was addressing a particular community of Christians with whom he was personally acquainted. He was aware of their having endured persecution (10:32,33; 12:4), as well as their present situation (5:12; 6:9; 13:17), and intended to revisit them (13:19,23). The author and the readers were mutually acquainted with Timothy (13:23).

The mention of "Italy" (13:24) in the closing comments of the epistle has caused some to conclude that the recipients were Jewish Christians residing in Rome, who were being greeted by fellow Italians living in the location from whence this epistle was written. That same reference can be interpreted to mean that the location of origination was Italy, however, and that the author is sending greetings to the readers from the Italian Christians where he is located. Although other destinations such as Alexandria, Caeserea, Ephesus, Corinth, and Antioch have been suggested, the most likely location of the residence of the original readers is Jerusalem.

Who else would have had such attachment to Jewish history and theology, such close ties with temple worship and its sacrifices, such pressure to relapse to Judaic religion, than the Hebrew saints in Jerusalem? Consider also that in subsequent Christian history no church claimed that this letter had been written to them, a practice of all the other churches who sought to make a "claim to fame" as the recipients of an apostolic letter from Paul. The church at Rome did not claim this letter. The churches at Alexandria, Ephesus, Corinth or Antioch did not claim this letter. No church claimed to be the recipients of this letter in the history of the early church. The explanation for this phenomenon is simple: within a few years after this epistle was written the church at Jerusalem ceased to exist. Jerusalem was destroyed in A.D. 70 Palestine was devas-

tated and its inhabitants decimated. There was no church in
Jerusalem to lay claim to being the recipients of this epistle
after A.D. 70 This serves as an important historical evidence to
the Jerusalem church having been the likely recipients of this
letter.

It is most reasonable to assume that Paul was imprisoned
in Rome in the mid-60s of the first century (as we know from
Luke's account in the Acts of the Apostles 28:16-31), and he
had a good social and spiritual perspective of what was going
on in the Roman persecutions of Christians under Emperor
Nero (who died in A.D. 68), as well as the Roman attitudes
toward the Palestinian Jews. He also knew the attitudes of the
Palestinian Jews with their intense nationalist patriotism, their
religious absolutism, their racist superiority, and he could fore-
see that a violent war was about to erupt in Palestine between
the Romans and the Jews.

The Christian Jews in Palestine had lost their leaders
(13:7), and Paul, though he knew he was the Apostle to the
Gentiles (Acts 9:15; Rom. 1:5; Gal. 1:16; 2:7), never lost his
heart for his Jewish kinsmen (Rom. 9:3). It is likely that he
decided to write this letter to encourage (13:22) the Jewish
Christians in Jerusalem to be confident in their endurance
(10:35,36) by emphasizing the superiority of Jesus over all
religion. The Palestinian Christians were being pressured to
revert to Judaism, to join the patriotic cause of militaristic
defense against the Roman empire. Christianity did not seem
to be going anywhere except among the Gentiles, and even
then Paul was on death-row in Rome. Some of the Christians
were not even assembling together anymore (10:25), were
becoming casual about sin (10:26; 12:10-16), and were in danger of apostasizing (6:4-6; 10:26-31).

Paul writes to encourage these Palestinian Christians not to
take the easy way out and revert to religion again, in particular
Judaism, with its religious practices and nationalistic patriotism. He explained that the old covenant of God's working with

and through the Jews, was obsolete and would soon disappear in destruction (8:13) – as it soon did in A.D. 70 The old covenant was only intended to pre-figure and set-up the new covenant of all that God intended to do in His Son, Jesus Christ. Jesus is the fulfillment of all the old covenant pictures and types, the fulfillment of all God's intents and promises (II Cor. 1:20) for His people. "Don't go back to religion," Paul is saying. "Go outside the camp" (13:13), repudiate Judaism, perhaps even consider leaving Jerusalem and Palestine (as many of them did, and survived the Roman slaughter of 70 A.D.). To reject Christ and go back to Judaic religion (any religion) is fatal and final, Paul indicates (10:29-31). Paul was telling the Palestinian Christians that there was a polarity of either/or, either Christ or Judaism, but you cannot have both. Like oil and water, Christianity and religion do not mix!

J. Barmby explains that

> when the Epistle to the Hebrews was written, the time had come for a complete and final severance from the ancient order. For now the predicted judgment was impending on Jerusalem, the temple was about to be destroyed forever, the whole sacrificial system connected therewith to cease, and the nation to be scattered through the world without a home in Palestine. Full time was it now for Christ's followers fully to perceive that from the old dispensation, never more than provisional, the glory was passed away; to come entirely out of the once holy but now doomed city; to lean no longer on the tottering fabric of the temple, lest their very faith should be shattered in its downfall.[3]

If, as the evidence suggests, Paul wrote this epistle to the church in Jerusalem which was undergoing persecution (not only by the Romans, but even more by the Palestinian Jews - cf. 10:32-36), then this epistle was one of the last, if not the last, that Paul wrote. Why is this important? Because if the Epistle to the Galatians was the first of Paul's extant epistles, and the Epistle to the Hebrews was the last, then we can observe the total consistency of Paul's thinking throughout his ministry. Galatians and Hebrews are two of the clearest New

Introduction

Testament epistles exposing the radical uniqueness of Christianity as set against the old covenant and Judaic religion. All of Paul's other writings must then be interpreted in the context of Galatians and Hebrews, as they form the *alpha* and *omega* of the Pauline corpus, serving as the "bookends" of Pauline theology.

Date of Writing

There is also no direct indication of the date of writing in the text of this epistle. Most scholars have concluded that it was written prior to the fall of Jerusalem in A.D. 70 since there is no reference to that catastrophic historical event, and one would certainly expect such had it been written to Christian readers of Jewish background after that event. The writer's repeated references to Jewish rituals using present tense verbs (7:8; 9:6-13; 13:10,11) also seems to indicate a date when such practices were still being performed in the temple at Jerusalem prior to its destruction. The only other referent point for dating this document is that Clement of Rome was apparently acquainted with this epistle by approximately A.D. 95.

It is quite likely that Emperor Nero's "urban renewal project" had just occurred in Rome, when in A.D. 64 Nero had apparently arranged to burn a large section of Rome in order to clear the way for his building campaign which would memorialize him in its lasting grandeur. "Nero fiddled while Rome burned" was the scuttlebutt that prevailed at the time, and the phrase remains as a lasting indictment to that imperial crime. The Christians, regarded as but a sect of the Jews at the time, became Nero's scapegoat of blame for setting the fire, igniting an incendiary wave of suspicion and persecution against the Christians, as well as the Jews.

Paul, under house arrest in Rome, might well have observed the glow of the flames and smelled the smoke from the fire. Hearing that the Christians had been blamed for setting the fire, Paul may have "seen the handwriting on the wall," so to speak, and realized that the days ahead would be difficult times for Christians and Jews. Paul was also well aware of the growing sentiment of resentment against Rome in Palestine, with the feverish swell of nationalistic patriotism being incited by the Zealot party within Judaism, advocating their alleged God-given right as the "chosen people" of God to operate as a sovereign nation in the line of David within the Palestinian land that they regarded as their "promised land." But Paul may have had a much better perspective of the might and power of the Roman army than the Palestinian peoples had in their blind fervor for self-rule. He may have had grave concerns of the outcome if the Roman military were to move into Palestine to put down an insurrection of revolt against Rome by the Jewish nationalists. Aware of attitudes both in Rome and Palestine, Paul may have decided that this was a timely opportunity to encourage his Christian brothers in Jerusalem by writing an epistle to the Church there, encouraging them to remain faithful to Jesus Christ and not to succumb to the political and religious influences that were being brought to bear upon them at that time.

The best conclusion, based on the evidence, seems to indicate that this letter was written by Paul from Rome to the Hebrew Christians in Jerusalem in the middle 60s of the first century, perhaps in A.D. 64 or 65 just prior to Paul's likely execution at the hands of the Romans.

Interpretive Considerations

Be forewarned that the Epistle to the Hebrews contains what is perhaps the most radical message in the New Testament. It may upset the applecart of your religious understanding. No other book in the New Testament so categorically asserts that God's arrangement with men in the Old Testament is no longer valid, making that point by declaring that Jesus is better than every feature of the old covenant. To drive the point home the readers are warned that if they revert to the Judaic religious practices of their past, having participated in the new covenant realities of Jesus Christ, they will forfeit all opportunity to participate in the eternal realities of Jesus Christ again.

With at least eighty-six direct references to the Old Testament within this letter, and with constant attention drawn to the Jewish people and their religion, it is important to consider the correlation of this document to the Old Testament. Some have indicated that a thorough understanding of the Old Testament is essential to understanding the Epistle to the Hebrews. Though it is true that an understanding of the historical background and ritualistic practices of the old covenant and the Hebrew peoples provides a valuable context for interpreting this document, it is perhaps even more important to realize that a thorough understanding of the Epistle to the Hebrews is essential to a proper understanding of the Old Testament from a Christian perspective. If the "Old Testament is the New Testament concealed, and the New Testament is the Old Testament revealed," as has often been explained as the basis for Christian hermeneutics, then the revealing of the gospel, especially in the book of Hebrews, should serve as the starting-point to consider how the gospel was concealed in the clues of the prefiguring of the Old Testament. The failure to interpret the Old Testament from this perspective has led to much confusion and misemphasis in Christian teaching, allowing the Old Testament to serve as the priority literature even in the lives of new covenant Christians. When this happens Christianity is perverted into religious forms of Christianized Judaism, which is the very thing that this epistle warns against and condemns. The Epistle to the Hebrews is the best antidote to such religious perversion, serving as the necessary commentary on the Old Testament, and interpreting the history, worship and prophecy of the Old Testament as it points in its entirety to Jesus Christ.

Clyde F. Whitehead explains,

> The Hebrews epistle deals with most of the important things that were associated with the old dispensation. The writer's objective is to show that the Mosaic law has been replaced by something that is far 'better.'[4]

J. Barmby, writing in the *Pulpit Commentary*, comments,

> its main purport is to show, from the Old Testament Scriptures themselves, that the Mosaic dispensation was from the first only preparatory for and prophetic of a higher one to come which was entirely to supersede it, and that Christ had come as the one only true High Priest for all mankind, the true fulfilment of all ancient ritual and prophecy, the satisfaction of all human needs, to renounce whom would be to renounce salvation.[5]

The Epistle to the Hebrews is pivotal to understanding the old covenant literature of the Old Testament. It is equally as pivotal to understanding all of the rest of the new covenant literature of the New Testament. This epistle might well have been placed as the first book in the New Testament canon arrangement, providing the bridge that explains the preliminary purpose of God in the old covenant and the superlative fulfillment of God's purpose in the new covenant, i.e., in Jesus Christ.

Over and over the author of the Epistle to the Hebrews uses the word "better" to describe the spiritual reality afforded in Jesus Christ. Christians have a "better hope" (7:19) within a "better covenant" (7:22; 8:6) with "better promises" (8:6). "God has provided something better for us" (11:40) by the "better sacrifice" (9:23) of Jesus Christ, that we might enjoy the "better possession" (10:34). This theme provides the basis of our entitling this study, "Jesus – Better Than Everything."

Introduction

R.B. Yerby writes,

Along with the other New Testament writers, the author of Hebrews saw the total and overwhelming superiority of the new and better age that dawned at Calvary. Like them he saw that all of the people, and events, and institutions of the former dispensation were merely shadows of the better things that God reserved for this present age, and for the eternity of the new heavens and new earth. Like them he realized that after Calvary the natural types and figures had served their purpose and were vanishing away, having been replaced forever by the eternal and spiritual realities.[6]

Those who fail to understand the better reality of the new covenant in Jesus Christ as plainly expounded in the Epistle to the Hebrews, tend to have a false hope for a reversionary return to the physical and external rituals of old covenant Jewish religion. This has become a popular theological interpretation in Western Christendom. Yerby responds to such by noting,

Hebrews...perhaps more than any of the books of the Bible, stands as a monumental source of frustration and embarrassment to those who teach that God plans to return one day to the natural trappings and embellishments of the old Jewish economy, to the natural land and city, the natural law and ordinances, the natural kingdom and throne, and the natural temple and sacrifices.[7]

Like Paul, we should be 'afraid of' anyone who teaches that God's program calls for a future return to the bondage of those weak and beggarly elements of Old Testament Judaism (Gal. 4:9-11).[8]

Proper understanding of the Epistle to the Hebrews will reveal the logical absurdity of any expectations that God is going to renew the Jewish religion, re-establish a physical kingdom, reinstitute the Jewish priesthood, reinstate the animal sacrifices, rebuild the Jewish temple, or restore the physical land. Such expectations are the very backward reversions to religion that this epistle warns against, by explaining that all such external and physical religion has been superseded in the spiritual reality of Jesus Christ.

Christocentric Emphasis

In the Epistle to the Hebrews we are inculcated to "consider Jesus" (3:1; 12:3) as the spiritual reality that God has made available for all men. The ontological dynamic of the living Lord Jesus by His Spirit is the essence of Christianity. This Christocentric emphasis is at the heart of all of the inspired literature of the New Testament, and is certainly the focal point of this letter.

Jesus is better than all religion because He is personal. The personal, living God sent His Son as the God-man to personally redeem and restore mankind. Only by the dynamic Person and life of Jesus Christ can man be restored to function as God intended in a personal faith/love relationship with God. To revert to religion is to settle for impersonal things, events, places and practices which can never satisfy.

Jesus is better than all religion because He is the singular, exclusive, ultimate and final revelation of God to man. He is the sum of all spiritual things (cf. Eph. 1:10), allowing for no religious syncretism or admixture. Though religion regards such an assertion as "the scandal of singularity and exclusivism," Jesus is the only "mediator between God and man" (I Tim. 2:5). "No man comes unto the Father, but by Me" (John 14:6). "There is no other name under heaven whereby a man must be saved" (Acts 4:12).

Jesus is better than all religion because of the completeness and permanency of His finished work (John 19:30). Whereas religion is limited, temporary and repetitive, the life of Jesus is eternal and forever. As a "priest forever" (5:6), Jesus is "eternal salvation" (5:9) within the "eternal covenant" (13:20).

Jesus is better than all religion because He is the provision and sufficiency for practical experiential behavior that glorifies

God. The impracticality of religious belief-systems, moralities, and rituals are most unsatisfying, but "through Jesus Christ we are equipped in every good thing to do God's will" (13:20).

The writer of the Epistle to the Hebrews exalts Jesus Christ as the essence of the Christian gospel. Christianity is not religion; Christianity is Christ! Jesus is better than all religion.

ENDNOTES

1   Eusebius, *Ecclesiastical History.* VI,14,2. A Select Library of Nicene and Post-Nicene Fathers of the Christian Church. Second Series. Grand Rapids: Wm. B. Eerdmans Pub. Co. 1982. pg. 261.

2   Origen, *Commentary on the Gospel of John.* Menzies, Allan (ed.), The Ante-Nicene Fathers, Vol. X. Grand Rapids: William B. Eerdmans. 1986. pg. 328.

3   Barmby, J., *The Pulpit Commentary.* Vol. 21. Grand Rapids: William B. Eerdmans Pub. Co., 1950. pgs xix, xx of introduction to Hebrews.

4   Whitehead, Clyde F., *Israel Vs. Israel: The Great Paradox of Scripture.* Sevierville: Covenant House Bks., 1993. pg. 219.

5   Barmby, *op. cit.*, pg xx of introduction.

6   Yerby, R.B., *The Once and Future Israel.* Sterling: Grace Abounding Ministries. 1988. pg. 126.

7   *Ibid.,* pg. 125,126.

8   *Ibid.,* pg. 75.

JESUS

The Better Revelation of God

Hebrews 1:1 – 2:4

This epistle does not have a traditional epistolary introduction or prologue as do other Pauline epistles. Explanation for the absence of such was made by Clement of Alexandria (c. A.D. 200), noting that Paul avoided the inclusion of his name at the beginning of the letter so that the message he had to share would not be detracted from by any previous biases or prejudices of the recipients who were suspicious of his association with, and inclusion of, the Gentiles. Paul, therefore, gets right to the point of demonstrating and documenting that Jesus Christ is the better revelation of God to men. He will do so by asserting that Jesus is better than the prophets (1:1-3), and better than the angels (1:4-14), and thus provides a better incentive to continue to be receptive to the dynamic of Christ's life (2:1-4).

The saints in the church at Jerusalem were wavering in their stand with Christ. They were in danger of drifting (2:1) back to Judaic religion, of slipping away from their moorings in the supremacy and sufficiency of Jesus Christ. From the very outset of this letter Paul proceeds to affirm the superiority of Christ over the religion of Judaism, and thus to demonstrate that the reality of Jesus is better than any and all religion.

1:1 In the original Greek language the letter begins with two "poly" prefixed words referring to *"many parts and many ways,"* The revelation of God in the old covenant was multi-

portional and multifarious, or to use "poly" words, polyparti-
tive and polymodal. ***"Of old*** (long ago) ***God was speaking to
the fathers in the prophets"*** in multiple portions and by multiple means. Over a period of several millennia God revealed
Himself partially and progressively throughout the Hebrew
history recorded in the Old Testament. Paul begins this letter
to the Palestinian Jews by reminding them of the multiple
occasions and multiple dimensions by which God spoke and
made Himself known in old covenant history, but the point he
is making is simply to set up the logical contrast of how Jesus
Christ is the singular, undivided and complete and final self-
revelation of God to mankind. The multiple preliminary prefiguring of God's actions in Jewish history, as He spoke to the
fathers through the many Hebrew prophets, is used by Paul to
create the explanation of the better revelation of God in the
singularity of His self-revelation in His Son. The "fathers" are
not necessarily restricted to the "patriarchs" of Genesis, but are
the ancestral forefathers of previous generations of Hebrew
peoples (cf. 3:9; 8:9).

Jesus was not just another in a long line of Hebrew
prophets. He was not merely a spokesperson for God. Jesus
was the singular and unique God-man, the Son of God incarnated in the humanity of a man. As such, He provided the only
provision of God for the needs of mankind, superior to all previous and prior revelatory pronouncements about God in the
old covenant. Jesus did not come to tell us more about God, or
to give mankind more information about God's attributes and
God's intentions. No, Jesus came *as* God – the self-revelation
of God. His every act was invested with the very Being of
God, and the very Being of God was fully operative in every
act. The self-revelation of God in Jesus necessarily implies the
oneness of His Being and act. Jesus was not the "virtual reality" of God, "as if" He were God in action; nor was He the
"remote action" of God, manipulated from a position of tran-
scendence to produce a secondary and mediated action of God.

No, Jesus was the real action of the very reality of God, the ontological dynamic of the very essence of God operational in the man, Jesus. I do not believe that this in any way overstates the point Paul sought to make in his contrast with the prior prophetic pronouncements of God in the past.

The participial form of the verb Paul uses about "God having spoken" in this first verse may have been intended to be contrasted with the aorist indicative form of the same verb in the second verse. That "God has spoken to us in the Son" expresses a more definite and deliberate act of God, perhaps even the punctiliar action that emphasizes the singularity and superiority of God's revelation of Himself in the Son, as contrasted with polymorphous expression of the prophets in the old covenant. The better expression and revelation of God is in the Son. Such revelation is not just a proclamation, but an incarnation, a personified self-revelation.

The use of "old" (Greek *palai*) in this initial verse of the epistle establishes a theme that will be employed throughout, contrasting the old covenant arrangement of God's preparatory dealing toward mankind with the new covenant arrangement of God's permanent and eternal action for man in Jesus Christ. Paul wants to dissuade the Jewish Christians from reverting to the old covenant religion of Judaism after they have already participated in the better spiritual realities of the new covenant in Jesus Christ.

1:2   The Pauline perspective of history is always divided by not only the old covenant and the new covenant, but by the correlative concept of the "past" and the "last." The old is "past," even obsolete (8:13), and the "last" in the sequence (Greek word *eschatos* from which we transliterate the word "eschatology") is the new reality that God has made known in His Son, Jesus, Who is the "last Adam," the *Eschatos* Man (I Cor. 15:45); God's "last word" for mankind – singularly, completely, decisively and finally. Eschatology is often mistakenly

19

understood to be the study of the future and that which is yet to transpire. Properly understood, eschatology is the study of "last things," and God's last and final arrangement for man is in Jesus Christ. In the first proclamation of the early church, Peter commenced by saying that Joel's prophecy of the "last days" (Joel 2:28) was fulfilled by the Pentecostal manifestation of the Spirit of Christ (Acts 2:17). Now Paul commences with the same theme that *"in these last days God has spoken to us in His Son."* The "last days" are not future. Rather, they began in the past when God historically revealed Himself incarnationally in the Son, and they continue throughout the new covenant "day of salvation" (cf. II Cor. 6:2) unto the "last time" (cf. I Peter 1:5) of the future. Although Jewish eschatology was always future-focused, Christian eschatology is focused on Christ, the fulfillment of God's "last things", and must necessarily be based on what Christ has already accomplished on our behalf in His "finished work" (John 19:30), all the while recognizing the perpetuity and continuum of His eternal work into the future. Christian eschatology will always recognize the "already" and the "not yet" of God's "last things" in Jesus Christ.

Writing to the Jewish Christians in Jerusalem, Paul wanted to emphasize the inaugurated and realized eschatological realities in Jesus Christ. The Jews in Palestine in the middle of the seventh decade of the first century (mid A.D. 60s) were anticipating a hoped-for future of deliverance from Rome and consequent self-rule. The Zealot theme of patriotic Jewish nationalism was at a crescendo. They were confident this would reestablish the Davidic kingdom which they considered to be their God-given right of self-rule in the Palestinian land that they regarded as given to them by God. Paul did not want the Jewish Christians to accept the false hopes for a physical utopian kingdom being offered by the Jewish religionists, but wanted them to base their hope in Jesus Christ alone (cf. I Tim. 1:1).

Although this letter primarily contrasts old covenant and new covenant, Judaism and Christianity, it is important to note that there is both continuity and discontinuity in the connection and contrasts. Continuity is evident in that it is "God who spoke to the fathers in the prophets" (1:1), and the same "God who has spoken in His Son" (1:2). Judaism and Christianity are historically linked, and God's action in the old covenant must not be regarded as irrelevant or of no value by those who participate in the new covenant. Though the previous revelation of God was temporary and preparatory as a pictorial prefiguring, it was nonetheless foundational and necessary, having been enacted by God. Paul's point is that the old arrangement has been superseded by all that is new and better in Jesus Christ. So it is that he commences by noting the diverse and fragmentary modality of the prophetic proclamation of God in the old covenant as contrasted with the superior, singular modality of God's self-revelation in the Son, Who Himself declared, 'I AM the way, the truth, and the life; no man comes unto the Father but by Me" (John 14:6).

It is *"the Son whom God appointed heir of all things."* A son is always a primary heir prior to any eligibility (if any) of servants. Later in the epistle (3:5,6) Paul will note that Moses was a "servant," whereas Jesus was the "Son." In the distinctly Messianic second Psalm, we discover the prophetic pointer to the Messianic Son inheriting all from His Father: "He said to Me, 'Thou art My Son... Ask of Me, and I will surely give the nations as Thine inheritance'" (Psalm 2:7,8). Jesus, the Son, was foreordained of God to be the heir of all things, i.e., everything God has to give. The prophets were not the heirs of all things of God. The Jewish people were not the heirs of all things, even though they thought they had an exclusive right to all the things of God. This may be the contrastual point Paul was making when he wrote that the "Son was appointed heir of all things." The Jews had long considered that they had an exclusive right to the fulfillment of all God's promises, that the divine inheritance was all theirs. Particularly, they laid claim to the promises of God to Abraham pertaining to land (Gen. 12:7; 15:7; 17:8), nation (Gen. 12:2; 17:4,5; 18:18), blessing (Gen. 12:2,3; 18:18), and posterity (Gen. 13:15,16; 15:5; 22:17), believing these to be their divine right of inheritance in physical fulfillment. When this epistle was written the Palestinian Jews were zealously mobilizing to claim their inheritance of land, nation and blessing by attempting to oust the Romans from Palestine. In that context Paul writes that "the Son has been appointed heir of all things." Does that mean that Jesus is the heir and fulfillment of all God's promises and intents? Yes, for as Paul wrote to the Corinthians, "For as many as may be the promises of God, in Him (Jesus Christ) they are yes..." (II Cor. 1:20) – affirmed, confirmed, fulfilled. The mistake of the Jewish people was to interpret God's promises only as physical, racial and national promises, rather than figurative and spiritual promises which were to be fulfilled in the Son, Jesus Christ. So Paul explains to the Jewish Christians of Jerusalem that "Jesus was appointed by God as heir of all things." All things? Yes, all things pertaining to God's intentions to give Himself to mankind in His Son in order to restore the necessary divine presence that allows man to be man as God intended. Jesus is "heir of all things" because God has only one "only-begotten" Son, Who is the one heir of all that is His. But those who are incorporated into the one heir, "in Christ" as Paul uses the phrase, are then "joint-heirs with Christ" (Rom. 8:17). As such, Christians "inherit the promises" (Heb. 6:12) and "receive the promises of eternal inheritance" (Heb. 9:15). Christians are thus "heirs of all things" in Christ, "blessed with every spiritual blessing in heavenly places in Christ" (Eph. 1:3), having been "granted everything pertaining to life and godliness" (II Pet. 1:3), so that "all things belong to us" (I Cor. 3:21-23). Paul wanted the Christians in Jerusalem to realize that they were the heirs of "all things" of God in Jesus Christ, and did not need to fight for such militarily in insurrection against Rome, as they were being pressured to do by the Jewish nationalists. Why is it then that Zionist interpretations still influence Christian thinking today, still advocating that the Jewish people are to be the "heirs of all things," and that the promises of God to Abraham are yet to be fulfilled physically for the Jews in the future? This can be nothing less than a failure to understand the point Paul is making throughout this epistle to the Hebrews, if not an abominable attempt to recreate the aberrant religious model of physical, racial and national privilege that Paul was attempting to deny by directing the Jerusalem Christians to Christ alone, and to the recognition that He is "the heir of all things," which things Christians participate in "in Him."

Paul proceeds to explain to his readers that this Son is the one *"through whom also He made the ages."* In other words, Jesus was preexistent with God, one in Being with God, and active in the divine creation of all created existence. Paul had explained this in other writings, noting that "through Christ are all things, and we exist through Him" (I Cor. 8:6), for "by Him all things were created...by Him and for Him" (Col. 1:16). John likewise explained that "all things came into being by Him (Jesus, the Word), and apart from Him nothing came into being that has come into being" (John 1:3), for "the world was made by Him" (John 1:10). Jesus, as God, created "all things" and is the heir of "all things." He is the beginning and the end (Rev. 21:6; 22:13) of all things, the origin and the objective of all divine things, for He is divine Being in action. Etiology and teleology merge in the divine action of the Son. This is the point that Paul is seeking to drive home to these Christians of Jewish heritage, that the popular Jewish perspective of God as a singular and isolated monad is insufficient to explain God's actions and intents. A Trinitarian perception of God as Father, Son and Holy Spirit is required to understand the better revelation of God's self-revelation of Himself in the Son.

It was *as* God that Jesus was instrumental in the creation of the universe, of time and space. The word Paul employs here is not *kosmos*, the Greek word for "world", but *aionas*, the Greek plural for "ages" (cf. Heb. 11:3). Though these two words can be used synonymously for divine creation in general, there may be an emphasis on Christ's creative action in both the old age and the new age, and that to establish that "at the consummation of the ages (which He Himself had created) He was manifested to put away sin by the sacrifice of Himself" (Heb. 9:26), so that those "in Him" might participate in "the powers of the age to come" (Heb. 6:5). Jesus' divine action in the physical creation of time and space is reenacted in the re-creation of man spiritually by His redemptive and restorative work. "If any man is in Christ, he is a new creature" (II Cor. 5:17), a participant in the "new creation" (Gal. 6:16). Despite the attempts of the Jewish nationalists in Judea to create a "new thing" in Palestine, Paul would tell the Christians to be content with the creative acts of Jesus Christ, who had already constituted them "a holy nation" (I Pet. 2:9) in Him.

Paul has explained that the better revelation, the final revelation of God, presently available "in these last days" was incarnationally, redemptively and restorationally enacted in the self-revelation of Himself in the Son, Who is the divine creative source of all things and the divinely ordained heir of all things, so that all of God's Being in action is in Him. He will continue to explain this unitive and Trinitarian basis of divine action in the next sentence.

1:3   *"He* (Jesus) *is the radiance of His (God's) glory."* As the "I AM" (cf. John 8:58; 10:9,11; 11:25; 14:6), Jesus is the eternally present tense emanation of divine glory. "The Word was made flesh, and we beheld His glory" (John 1:14), and the eternal Word continuously radiates divine glory as God. It is not that the Son merely reflects the glory of God like a mirror.

24

That would be to separate the Son from the divine source. No, Jesus radiates, emanates and expresses divine glory as the self-generating God. Through the prophet Isaiah, God declared, "I am the Lord..., I will not give My glory to another" (Isa. 42:8; 48:11). God cannot dispense His glory as if it were a detached commodity. His glory is in Himself, and God is glorified when His all-glorious character is expressed unto His own glory. Again, He is subject and object, source and recipient, of His own glory. "Crowned with glory and honor" (Heb. 2:7,9) as the God-man, Jesus glorified the Father by expressing divine character at all times as a man, and then prayed that He might "be glorified with the glory that He had with the Father before the world was" (John 17:5), in order to continue as the Glorified One to express and emanate divine glory as God.

It seems that religion is always attempting to find God's glory in something other than the Christic expression of such, believing that God's glory "shines from" determined manifestations or successful results. Some have thought that God's glory was only in their belief-system, their denomination, or their worship patterns. The particular religious situation that Paul addresses in writing to the Jerusalem Christians was that the Jewish religion conceived of God's glory either as the Shekinah glory observed by the high priest once a year in the Holy of Holies of the temple, or in considering themselves as "God's chosen people" to be the glory of God. Paul explains that the living Lord Jesus is "the radiance of God's glory," allowing the invisible character of God to be made visible by generating such out of His own Being. Jesus is "the image of the invisible God" (II Cor. 4:4; Col. 1:15), and only by His presence and activity (Being in action) can Christians "do all to the glory of God" (I Cor. 10:31), having beheld "the light of the knowledge of the glory of God in the face of Christ" (II Cor. 4:6), in order to be "transformed into the same image from glory to glory" (II Cor. 3:18).

In what some have regarded as a synonymous or parallel statement to the previous, but which is surely a deeper amplification of Jesus' deity, Paul explains that the Son is ***"the express image of God's essence."*** This is a difficult phrase to translate, as is evident in the many English translations: "exact representation of His nature" (NASB), "express image of His person" (KJV), "bears the very stamp of His nature" (RSV), "exact representation of His being" (NIV). It seems inadequate to indicate that Jesus is the "representation" of God, for the point that Paul seems to be making is that Jesus is the very "reality" of God. The word that Paul uses, the Greek word *charakter* (from which we get the English word "character"), was used in the engraving of an imprint to stamp an image on a coin, thus eliciting the translations of "representation," "image," "stamp," "imprint," etc. What we must avoid is any translation that implies that Jesus is a separated, secondary, instrumental stamp or imprint that is in any way less than God. The second noun in the phrase is no less difficult to translate: the Greek word *hupostasis* refers to the underlying reality of essence, substance or constitution. Since the Greek language has a clear word for "nature" (*phusis*), it is preferable not to translate this word in the same way, but to translate it as "essence" or as "substance" (as the KJV translates the same word in Heb. 11:1).

What is Paul attempting to convey in this phrase? Apparently the same thought as he expressed to the Colossians, that "in Him (Jesus) all the fullness of deity dwells" (Col. 2:9). Or as Jesus said, "He who has seen Me, has seen the Father" (John 14:9), for "I and the Father are one" (John 10:30), essentially and purposefully. Perhaps to counter the tendency of Judaism to make God into a monad, Paul wanted to emphasize to the Jewish Christians in Jerusalem that Jesus is the very embodiment of deity, the self-existent, self-generating essence of God. All that God is, Jesus is, and Jesus is the better revelation of God, superior to the Jewish prophets because He is the very essence and Being of God in action.

Christian theologians have long struggled to express this inexplicable oneness of Father and Son (and Spirit). Sometimes they have referred to the "hypostatic union" (from *hupostasis*) of the persons of the Godhead, or to the consubstantial oneness of God as "three in one". Other explanations have referred to the ontological coinherence of Father and Son in perichoretic oneness (based on the Greek word *perichoresis*, meaning the interpenetration of Being), or of the *homoousion* of the singular sameness and oneness of Being in Father and Son. Simply put, Paul wanted to tell the Jewish Christians that "Jesus is God," a foundational premise of Christianity that they may have been in danger of denying as they endured the pressure of Judaism in Jerusalem. But from Paul's perspective, to reject Jesus would be to reject God.

Continuing his extended statement concerning Jesus, Paul writes that the Son *"upholds all things by the word of His power."* This is not a portrayal of Jesus as an "Atlas figure" holding up the planet in his hand. The statement conveys more than the words of the popular song, "He's got the whole world in His hand." Though inclusive of the idea of God's providential sustenance of the created order, it appears that Paul's meaning is closer to what he wrote to the Colossians, that "in Him (Jesus) all things hold together" (Col. 1:17). "All things" of God (which He is the co-creator of and heir of - cf. 1:2) are continually borne and carried by the Son. Jesus bears the responsibility to express the dynamic of God's empowering in all things. He was "declared the Son of God with power by the resurrection from the dead" (Rom. 1:4), and thus serves as the divine agent of expressing the divine dynamic and empowering of all the activities of God, including "the power of God for salvation to every one who believes" (Rom. 1:16). The Palestinian Jews were preparing to make a power-play against Rome, but Paul tells the Christians that the real power of God is invested in Jesus, on Whom they should rely instead of military might.

In his continuing explanation of the divine work of the Son, Paul wrote, ***"Having made cleansing for sins,*** He (Jesus) sat down at the right hand of the Majesty on high." The Jewish religion was obsessed with the cleansing of bodies, hands, feet, food, utensils, etc., always seeking a ceremonial purification. Once a year, on the Day of Atonement, the high priest entered the Holy of Holies of the temple to effect a "cleansing of their sins before the Lord" (Lev. 16:30; cf. Exod. 30:10). Paul's objective in this Epistle to the Hebrews is to categorically declare that Jesus is the fulfillment of the type of the high priest (Heb. 2:17; 4:14; 7:24-28), having dealt with the sins of mankind (Heb. 8:12; 10:12,17,18) once and for all (Heb. 7:27; 9:12,25,26; 10:10-12) by His own atoning sacrifice in death. The redemptive cleansing is complete and permanent in Christ. By His "finished work" (John 19:30) the penalty for sins is removed, and the sanctifying catharsis of the power of sin in Christian lives is operative.

Therefore, Paul declares, ***"Jesus sat down at the right hand of the Majesty on high."*** In the Jewish temple the responsibilities of the priests were never finished. "Every priest stands daily ministering and offering time after time the same sacrifices, which can never take away sins" (Heb. 10:11), but Jesus "having offered one sacrifice for sins for all time, sat down at the right hand of God" (Heb. 10:12). There is a repeated allusion throughout this epistle (Heb. 1:3; 8:1; 10:12; 12:2) to Psalm 110:1 and David's comment that "the Lord says to my Lord, 'Sit at My right hand...'" There was no place to sit in the Jewish temple because the job was never done, and this is true of religion in general as it requires ever-repetitive rituals and exercises in an attempt to please God. Jesus, on the other hand, "accomplished the work which the Father gave Him to do" (John 17:4), and exclaimed from the cross, "It is finished!" (John 19:30). That is why He sat down, not because

He was tired or exhausted, but because as *Christus Victor* He
had triumphed over evil, cleansed mankind from their sins,
and could thus assume the place of honor and authority at the
right hand of Majesty. The figure of Jesus being "at the right
hand of God" does not diminish His equality and essential
oneness with God, but represents pictorially His authority and
divine reign. "All authority is given to Me in heaven and
earth" (Matt. 28:18), Jesus declared. Despite this declaration,
religion always wants to attribute authority to a holy book, to a
tradition, to an organization, or to a person. All divine authority is vested in Jesus based on His "finished work" which effectively and remedially dealt with men's sins in order to restore
God's intended Being in action in man. That is why Paul can
tell the Ephesians that all Christians are "seated in the heavenlies with Christ" (Eph. 1:20; 2:6), resting (Heb. 4:1-11) in
Christ's "finished work." Why, then, would any Christian consider reverting back to religion and its ceaseless activities,
"standing up" for this or that, fighting the pseudo-enemies in
never-ending power plays? Why would the Christians of
Jerusalem want to join the nationalists and their religious
defense to "stand up" against Rome, and engage in a militaristic power-play? That was Paul's question to the Jewish
Christians to whom he wrote. Why not participate in the victory already won by the Lord, Jesus Christ, rather than seek a
triumph over the Romans? Meanwhile, religion always strives
for a "right-hand position" with Christ, just as the mother of
James and John sought such for one of her sons (Matt. 27:38;
Lk. 23:33), but the religionists are never willing to "be seated"
and rest in Christ's victorious sufficiency. They always want to
"stand up" and do battle, forgetting that Christ's work is finished by God's grace. This was the temptation that the
Jerusalem Christians faced – to forget the triumphant and completed work of Jesus, and revert to the Judaic activistic cause
of the day – a fatal and permanent relapse according to Paul
(cf. Heb. 6:4-6; 10:29-31).

1:4   Though still a part of the previous sentence, Paul commences to explain that not only is Jesus better than the prophets, He is also better than the angels. This theme necessitates some background concerning the Jewish conception of angels and their relationship to God in order to fully appreciate Paul's argument.

The conception of God as a transcendent monad in Jewish theology fostered an elaborate development of angelology. Whenever there is alleged to be a great distance or a vast separation between God and man, religion often employs the explanatory medium of angels to serve as intermediaries to fill in that great gap, and to provide an explanation of an indirect access to God via such angelic go-betweens or liaisons. This is evident in Islamic theology and their tradition of angelic delivery of the Koran to Mohammed. It is also part of Mormon theology with the delivery of the tablets to Joseph Smith by the angel, Moroni. Such was certainly the case in the Judaic understanding of the first century. Angels were regarded to be the agents of everything God did. They were thought to be hierarchically formed into the "army of God," controlling the destiny of the people and nation of Israel (and the Jews of Palestine were confident that angelic intervention would assure the victory of their revolt against Rome). There were angels assigned to every act of God and every object of creation: guardian angels for every individual, prosecuting angels for every violation of God's Law, death angels who could terminate life. An angel was identified with every physical element such as fire, wind (cf. 1:7), thunder, lightning, rain, snow, dew, as well as mountains, the sky and the sea. The movement of the stars was thought to be controlled by the angels. One rabbinic source stated that "every blade of grass has its angel." On a practical level, despite their monotheistic assertion of the one Jehovah God, their worship was not that far removed from animism or the nature-religions with their innumerable nature-gods.

Jewish interpretation of Old Testament history inserted angelic involvement throughout. When God said, "Let us make man in our image" (Gen. 1:26), they explained that God was speaking to the angel assembly who would serve as His divine assistants in creation. Prayer was understood as angelic intercession whereby angels carried the prayers of God's people into the unapproachable presence of God, and returned to implement God's answer. Though the narrative in Exodus 19 and 20 does not refer to angels delivering the Law-tablets to Moses, this became the Jewish explanation, as is apparent in both the Old and New Testaments. Moses, himself, had explained that "the Lord came *from Sinai*...and He came from the midst of ten thousand holy ones (angels?); at His right hand there was flashing lightning for them" (Deut. 33:2). The psalmist, David, mentions that "the chariots of God (angels?) are myriads, thousands upon thousands; the Lord is among them as *at Sinai*" (Psalm 68:17). These references to the involvement of angels at Mount Sinai when Moses received the Law are reiterated in the New Testament when Stephen's recitation of Jewish history notes that "the *angel* was speaking to him (Moses) on *Mount Sinai*" (Acts 7:38), and that the Jewish people "received the law as ordained by *angels*" (Acts 7:53). That this was also Paul's understanding is evident in his Epistle to the Galatians: "It (the Law) was added because of transgression, having been ordained through *angels* by the agency of a mediator, until the seed (Jesus) should come to Whom the promise had been made" (Gal. 3:19).

It is in the context of this Jewish perception of angels that Paul writes that Jesus, the Son, **"has become as much better than the angels,"** as He is superior to the prophets (1:1-3). The self-revelation of God in the Son supersedes previous revelations of God through both the prophets and the angels. It is not Paul's primary objective to counteract the erroneous reverence that the Jewish people may have had concerning angels. Paul apparently shared the belief about the intermediary

31

actions of angels on Mount Sinai (Gal. 3:19; Heb. 2:2). His primary objective was not to attack Jewish angelology, but to assert the superiority of the revelation of God in Jesus Christ above any revelatory participation by angels. In so doing he will necessarily counter some of the presuppositions that formed the foundation of an exaggerated Jewish angelology. The self-revelation of God in the Son posits that the transcendent God has acted to intervene incarnationally in human history, taking the form of a man (Phil. 2:7,8). God in Christ is not a separated and detached deity, a transcendent monad, unknown and to be feared. Rather, God has made direct contact and identification with humanity in order to facilitate a direct and immediate access and union with Himself for those "in Christ." Such a revelation of God in the Son allows the transcendent God to have a direct and immanent indwelling in mankind by His triune spiritual presence in the spirit of man (cf. Rom. 8:16). "The Lord is the Spirit" (II Cor. 3:17), and "the one who is joined to the Lord is one spirit with Him" (I Cor. 6:17). Paul wanted the Jewish Christians in Jerusalem to understand the superiority of God's revelation which is Christ, and to reject the temptation to revert to an inadequate view of a far-removed transcendent God Whose action was enacted by angelic intermediaries because He was unapproachable without direct access. Jesus is better than angels because those "in Christ" have direct and immediate access with God in spiritual union with Christ, and the operation of God's grace in the living Lord Jesus empowers all that God desires to continue to express in and through the Christian.

When was it that Jesus "became so much better than the angels" according to Paul's statement in this verse? It does not appear that Paul is referring to the incarnation of God in Jesus at His birth, but rather to the resurrection exaltation of Jesus, which will be supported in the following verses. The preexistent Son of God *"inherited a more excellent name than the angelic beings"* when He "was declared the *Son of God* with power by the *resurrection* from the dead" (Rom. 1:4). When God *"raised* Him from the dead, and seated Him at His *right hand* in the heavenlies, far above all rule and authority and power and dominion, and every *name* that is *named*...and put all things (including angels) under his feet, and gave Him as head over all things to the church" (Eph. 1:20-22), Jesus became "heir of all things" (1:2), having been "bestowed with the *name* that is above every *name*" (Phil. 2:9). "Through the *resurrection*," Jesus "is at the *right hand* of God, having gone into heaven, after *angels* and authorities and powers had been subjected to Him" (I Peter 3:22), writes Peter. What Paul is saying here is that by His resurrection-victory (cf. I Cor. 15:57) *Christus Victor* is confirmed as the revelation of God Himself, superior to all angels. Though eternally the Son of God, He was "born as a child; a son given to man" (Isa. 9:6) whose name would be called "Mighty God, Eternal Father, Prince of Peace" (Isa. 9:6), such "excellent name" made explicit by His resurrection when He was "declared the Son of God with power" (Rom. 1:4) to enact the entirety of God's grace initiative among men.

1:5 Continuing his argument Paul asks the Jewish Christians, *"For to which of the angels did He ever say, 'THOU ART MY SON, TODAY I HAVE BEGOTTEN THEE'?"* This rhetorical question contains within its wording an implied negative answer. Never to any angels was such a divine declaration made. Employing the first of seven Old Testament quotations to bolster his argument of the superiority of Jesus over angels, Paul utilizes this series of quotations to demonstrate that "all the promises of God" (II Cor. 1:20) are fulfilled in Jesus Christ as "the heir of all things" (1:2). This first quotation is from the second Psalm, understood by the Jews to be a Messianic Psalm referring to God's anointed Messiah who would be decreed God's Son in a special way, and be given the nations as His inheritance (Psalm 2:7,8). Paul had previously used these very same words of Psalm 2:7 when he expounded the gospel in Antioch of Pisidia, declaring that "God has *fulfilled this promise*...in that He *raised* up Jesus, as it is written in the second Psalm, 'THOU ART MY SON; TODAY I HAVE BEGOTTEN THEE'" (Acts 13:33). Clearly Paul considered the statement of this Messianic Psalm to have been fulfilled in the resurrection of Jesus, whereby Jesus was "declared the Son of God with power" (Rom. 1:4), a "more excellent name" (1:4) than any angels, and was "begotten" of God. The word "begotten" is the Greek word meaning "to be born," and it is used of Moses' physical birth in 11:23, but here it is obviously to be understood figuratively as Jesus' being brought out of death into life in resurrection. In His resurrection Jesus was "the first-born from the dead" (Col. 1:18; Rev. 1:5), having experienced spiritual death on behalf of all fallen humanity in order to allow the spiritual life of God to conquer death for all, that "He might be the first-born among many brethren" (Rom. 8:29) who would experience such spiritual birthing to life "in Him." By His victorious resurrection Jesus is the more excellent Son, begotten of God unto eternal life for all mankind. No angel qualifies for such a name or place, so Paul is asking the Jerusalem Christians why they would even consider going back to the inferior religious revelation of angels.

"And again," Paul adds to reinforce his argument of Jesus having inherited the "more excellent" name and place of Sonship, and then he proceeds to quote from II Samuel 7:14, *"I WILL BE A FATHER TO HIM, AND HE SHALL BE A SON TO ME."* The original context of this statement was God's statement to David through Nathan, the prophet, indicating that He would provide a descendant of David who would build a temple. Though this was an obvious physical reference to his son, Solomon, who did build the temple in Jerusalem, the Davidic offspring who would extend the Davidic kingdom was often applied to the expectation of the Messiah in Jewish

thought, and that in conjunction with the similar statements of
Psalm 89:1-4; 26-29. Paul certainly connected the resurrection
of Jesus with the promised Davidic kingdom as is evident in
that same message in Antioch of Pisidia cited above, where he
declared that God's *raising up* Jesus from the dead was the
bestowal of "the holy and sure blessings of *David*" (Acts
13:34). In the opening of his Epistle to the Romans the same
link is made concerning God's Son, "Who was born a descendant of *David*, according to the flesh, Who was declared the
Son of God with power by the *resurrection* from the dead"
(Rom. 1:3,4). To Timothy, Paul wrote, "Remember Jesus
Christ, *risen* from the dead, descendant of *David*" (II Tim.
2:8). In Paul's mind the long-sought continuation of the promised Davidic kingdom was established by the resurrection
when the Son "inherited a more excellent name" (1:4; Rom.
1:4) and assumed the throne of the promised spiritual kingdom
of God. Paul's argument is that there are no angels who can
claim that kind of unique relationship with God, the Father.
The extension of Paul's thought is that Christians are the "temple of the living God" (II Cor. 6:16), and have a relationship in
Christ wherein God says, "I will be a Father to you, and you
will be sons and daughters to Me" (II Cor. 6:18), by the
indwelling presence of the resurrection life of the risen Lord
Jesus.

1:6　　Paul extends the documentation of his argument, writing, ***"And again, when He brings the first-born into the
world, He says, 'AND LET ALL THE ANGELS OF GOD
WORSHIP HIM.'"*** It is still the resurrection that Paul has in
mind, when "Christ was raised from the dead, the first fruits of
those who are asleep" (I Cor. 15:20). By the resurrection God
brought "the first-born from the dead" (Col. 1:18; Rev. 1:5)
into His eschatological economy, the salvific economy wherein
He would restore mankind by "bringing many sons to glory"
(Heb. 2:10) through the living Lord Jesus who was "the first-

born among many brethren" (Rom. 8:29). Let it be noted that if Jesus is the "first-born from the dead," then the Old Testament patriarchs and believers cannot be regarded as having passed from death to life spiritually in the same manner as new covenant Christians, for such regeneration is predicated on the prerequisite of Christ's resurrection (cf. I Peter 1:3). The word Paul employs concerning God's bringing "the first-born into the *world*" is not the Greek word *kosmos*, but the Greek word *oikoumene*, a derivative of the word from which we get the English word "economy," thus explaining the interpretation given above. As Paul will write in summation of this section of his epistle, "God did not subject to angels the economy to come" (2:5 - using the same Greek word, *oikoumene*), so his argument here is that the resurrected Son, the living Lord Jesus and His economy of grace, is superior to the actions of angels.

By the resurrection of "the first-born from the dead" (Col. 1:18; Rev. 1:5), Paul indicates that God's pronouncement is, *"LET ALL THE ANGELS OF GOD WORSHIP HIM,"* quoting from Deuteronomy 32:43. The quotation is from the Septuagint (*LXX*), the Greek translation of the Old Testament, rather than from the Hebrew text, where these words are not found. The verse in Deuteronomy is the conclusion of an extended "Song of Moses" before the assembly of Israel, and was regarded as Messianic prophecy in Jewish eschatological expectation. Paul, recognizing Jesus as the Messiah, utilizes the statement to assert that by His resurrection Jesus is worthy of angelic worship, and is therefore superior to the angels. Conversely the "worship of angels" is part of "self-made religion" (Col. 2:18,23), Paul advised the Colossians, and the apostle John in his vision was told not to worship the angel, but to worship God (Rev. 22:8,9). Paul puts the words of Moses into the mouth of God, with the admonition that the angels are to worship the superior Son. Worship of the Son implies that Jesus is God as Paul has previously explained.

Recognizing this, John Bunyan is reported to have stated, "If Jesus Christ be not God, then heaven is filled with idolaters," for the angels would be engaged in idolatrous worship of one who is not God. Paul's point to the Jewish Christians in Palestine is that Jesus Christ alone is worthy of worship, and they should not go back to inadequate forms of Jewish worship which placed an inordinate emphasis on or improper worship of angels, who are themselves subordinated in worship of the Son.

1:7   Revealing his own belief in angels, Paul cites Psalm 104:4, *"And of the angels He says, 'WHO MAKES HIS ANGELS WINDS, AND HIS MINISTERS A FLAME OF FIRE.'"* This was a typical Jewish interpretation of the verse from Psalms, identifying angels as the agents used by God within natural, physical phenomena such as wind and fire. It can certainly be questioned whether that was the original intent of the Psalmist, for in the context of explaining God's sovereign control and care of the created order the words can be, and perhaps are most legitimately translated with the meaning that "God makes the winds His messengers, flaming fire His ministers," indicating that God can use natural phenomena for His purposes. Keying off of the word *angelloi*, the Greek word for "messengers" in the Septuagint (*LXX*) version of the Old Testament, Paul applies these words to the actions of angels, and that for the purpose of contrasting such with the superior action of the Son, Jesus Christ.

1:8   *"But of the Son,"* God says through the Psalmist again, *"THY THRONE, O GOD, IS FOREVER AND EVER, AND THE RIGHTEOUS SCEPTER IS THE SCEPTER OF HIS KINGDOM."* Psalm 45:6, which Paul quotes here, is a Psalm celebrating the king's marriage, but Paul employs the words to indicate their Messianic fulfillment in Jesus Christ. Referring to the reign of Christ as Lord in the spiritual kingdom of God, Paul allows this verse to indicate the perpetuity and continuity of Christ's reign "forever and ever," i.e. the kingdom reign of Christ is eternal. Christ's reign as King in the spiritual kingdom of His people is the reign of the "Righteous One" (Acts 3:14; 7:52; 22:14; I Jn. 2:1). As Paul wrote to the Romans, "the *kingdom* of God is...righteousness and peace and joy in the Holy Spirit" (Rom. 14:17), for "the abundance of grace and the gift of *righteousness* will *reign* in life through the One, Jesus Christ" (Rom. 5:17). That is why Jesus, Himself, advised us to "seek first His *kingdom* and His *righteousness*." (Matt. 6:33). The very reality of Christ's reign is His inherent divine character of righteousness. It is the only manner in which He can reign or rule, for He *does* what He *does* only because He *is* who He *is*, the "Righteous One," the God who is righteous (I John 2:29; 3:7). All authority (cf. Matt. 28:18) of the reigning Christ as Lord is therefore a "righteous scepter," never abusive, seeking only the highest good of those united with Him in righteousness, allowing "grace to *reign* through *righteousness* to eternal life through Jesus Christ our Lord" (Rom. 5:21). The "O God" phrase may well have been interpreted by Paul to refer to the inherent deity of Christ, as he had explicitly affirmed such previously (1:2,3). Paul's intent in citing this verse was to express the superiority of the revelation of the Son over that of angels, but also perhaps to show the Jewish Christians of Jerusalem that the eternal kingdom of righteousness in Christ was greater and superior to any attempts to reestablish a Jewish kingdom in Palestine by revolt against the Romans.

1:9   In a continuation of the quote from Psalm 45, Paul quotes the next verse 45:7, *"THOU HAST LOVED RIGHT-EOUSNESS AND HATED LAWLESSNESS; THEREFORE GOD, THY GOD, HATH ANOINTED THEE WITH THE OIL OF GLADNESS ABOVE THY COMPANIONS."* Continuing to apply this to the resurrected and exalted Lord

Jesus, Paul recognized Jesus as "the Righteous One" (Acts 3:14; 7:52; 22:14; I John 2:1), the "Anointed One" Who was the Messiah (the Hebrew word for "Anointed One"). That He was "anointed with the oil of gladness" might well have brought the Messianic passage in Isaiah 61:1-3 to Paul's mind, "The Spirit of the Lord God is upon Me, because the Lord has anointed me to bring good news to the afflicted...to grant those who mourn...the *oil of gladness* instead of mourning" (cf. Lk. 4:18,19). As oil was long considered to be symbolic of the Holy Spirit (cf. I Sam. 16:13), there may be an allusion here to the "joy of the Holy Spirit" (I Thess. 1:6; Acts 13:52). The superior reign of the risen Lord Jesus, as the Spirit of joy Himself (cf. John 15:11; 16:22,24) is "above His companions" in the angelic realm, who were often associated in Jewish angelology with punishment and destruction, fostering fear rather than joy or gladness. As the Risen One, Jesus has become the "Spirit of Christ" (Rom. 8:9), and Christians have an "anointing from the Holy One" (I John 2:20,27) whereby He abides in them and manifests joy as the "fruit of the Spirit" (Gal. 5:22,23). This spiritual reality is far superior to anything available in the Jewish religion – this being the point that Paul wanted to emphasize to the Christians in Jerusalem.

1:10 Paul adds to his list of documentary quotations in an extended citation from Psalm 102:25-27, a paean of praise to God for His eternality and unchangeableness. ***"And, 'THOU, LORD, IN THE BEGINNING DIDST LAY THE FOUNDA-TION OF THE EARTH, AND THE HEAVENS ARE THE WORKS OF THY HANDS"*** (Psalm 102:25). These words are being applied to Jesus as Lord, noting once again (cf. 1:2) the preexistence of the Son and His involvement as the divine Creator. As the uncreated Creator, the Son of God is the originating source of the angels who are created beings, and thus Jesus is "better than the angels" (1:4).

1:11 *"THEY WILL PERISH, BUT THOU REMAINEST; AND THEY ALL WILL BECOME OLD AS A GARMENT"* (Psalm 102:26). The created order, including the angels, is a degenerating and disintegrating order which is not eternal. "Heaven and earth will pass away" (Matt. 24:35); "the sky will vanish like smoke, and the earth will wear out like a garment" (Isa. 51:6). The reality of the Son of God, divine reality, is alone eternal and unchangeable.

1:12 *"AND AS A MANTLE THOU WILT ROLL THEM UP; AS A GARMENT THEY WILL ALSO BE CHANGED. BUT THOU ART THE SAME, AND THY YEARS WILL NOT COME TO AN END"* (Psalm 102:26,27). The created order ages. It suffers from entropy, as the scientists have observed in the "Second Law of Thermodynamics." It will be rolled up like a tattered and worn-out garment, and cast aside as having no further use in God's economy. Even the angels will apparently perish, for God speaks through Isaiah saying, "All the host of heaven will rot, and the sky will be rolled up like a scroll; all their hosts will wither away as a leaf withers from the vine, or as one withers from the fig tree" (Isa. 34:4). But in the "new heavens and new earth" (Rev. 21:1) the unchangeableness of Jesus Christ "Who is the same yesterday and today and forever" (Heb. 13:8) will be experienced unto eternity, and Christians participate in the "eternal life" (I John 5:11,13) of that "eternal kingdom" (II Peter 1:11) even now. This is the superiority of the revelation of Christ's reign that Paul wanted the Jerusalem Christians to recognize.

1:13 In the last of seven Old Testament quotations used to verify that Jesus is "better than the angels" (1:4), Paul asks, *"But to which of the angels has He* (God) *ever said, 'SIT AT MY RIGHT HAND, UNTIL I MAKE THINE ENEMIES A FOOTSTOOL FOR THY FEET'?"* This text from Psalm 110:1 was alluded to previously when Paul stated that "when

He had made purification of sins, He sat down at the right hand of God" (1:3). Here, wording the question to elicit a negative response, Paul is arguing that no angels have ever been assigned the position of honor, exaltation and authority that is accorded to Jesus Christ alone by virtue of His victorious resurrection, ascension and enthronement as the reigning Lord of the universe who sits at God's right hand until the consummation of history. In the first sermon of the church Peter referred to Jesus "*raised up* by God,...exalted to the *right hand* of God," and quoted Psalm 110:1 (cf. Acts 2:32-36). Later in his first epistle Peter again alludes to Psalm 110:1 by referring to "the *resurrection* of Jesus Christ, who is at the *right hand* of God, having gone into heaven, after *angels* and authorities and powers had been subjected to Him" (I Pet. 3:22). Paul had also previously made mention of the ascendancy of the risen Lord Jesus and His "reign until He has put all enemies under His feet" (I Cor. 15:25). The "finished work" of Christ (cf. John 17:4; 19:30) involving the triumph of His resurrection, allows Jesus to be figuratively seated in the place of honor, reigning as Lord until the ultimate consummation of history when all enemies and anomalies become but a "footstool for His feet" in the metaphor of a triumphant King (cf. Josh. 10:24). No angel can ever assume the exalted position of the resurrected Jesus.

1:14 *"Are they not all ministering spirits, sent out to render service for the sake of those who will inherit salvation?"* The angels are worshipers, not the object of worship as is the Son, Jesus Christ. They worship the Son (cf. Lk. 2:13,14; Rev. 5:11,12). The angels are mere servants (cf. Psalm 103:20,21), whereas Jesus is the Son of God. Angels can serve, but only Jesus can save men from their sins. Angels exist for the sake of serving Christians, not as the object of the worship of Christians. Christians who are receptive to inheriting and experiencing the dynamic "saving life" (Rom. 5:10) of Christ are the recipients of angelic service, according to Paul. This is not a future inheritance of salvation that Paul is referring to, but the present process of being "made safe" (the meaning of the Greek word *sozo* meaning "to save") to function as God intended man to function by the indwelling function of the Triune God in the spirit of man. Salvation is not an achievement earned, nor is it a commodity possessed. Salvation must be understood only in the context of the resurrection reign of Jesus Christ in a Christian. Salvation is the Savior, Jesus Christ, at work in our lives, the dynamic saving activity of the Spirit of Christ "making us safe" from the misuse and abuse of Satan and sin, in order to manifest the character of Christ, the "fruit of the Spirit" (Gal. 5:22,23) in our behavior to the glory of God. The mission of the angels is to serve in facilitating that process of "being saved" (cf. II Cor. 2:15) in those identified with Christ as Christians. Angels are, therefore, not to be elevated in reverence or worship, for that is the sole right of Jesus Christ, the Son of God.

2:1 *"For this reason,"* Paul explains to the Jerusalem Christians, *"we"* (Paul identifies himself with his readers as Christians participating in salvation as the Savior lives within) *"ought to give much closer attention to what we have heard, lest we drift away."* That Jesus is the better revelation of God, "better than the prophets" (1:1-3) and "better than the angels" (1:4-14), has been Paul's argument, and now he concludes this section by arguing that Christians have a "better incentive" to continue to be involved in that better revelation of salvation in Jesus Christ. The superiority of Christ as the sole, divine Savior is sufficient reason for Christians to pay attention to the gospel revelation of the Son. Jesus is God's last Word – there is no additional revelation of God to man.

It has been suggested that the Greek word *prosechein*, meaning "to attend to," may have been used as a Greek nautical term meaning "to hold to port," which would serve as a contrast to the nautical figure of "drifting away." That seems to be Paul's primary objective in writing this epistle to the Jewish Christians of Jerusalem, to emphasize the "safe port" of salvation in Jesus Christ alone to those who were in danger of getting caught in the "drift" of Jewish nationalism and reversion to Judaism. Apparently Paul had received word at his residence of confinement in Rome that the Christians in Palestine were becoming listless and lax, and he wanted to encourage his "kinsmen according to the flesh" (Rom. 9:3) who were also "brothers in Christ" by telling them of the better incentive that we have in Christ to continue to live by His grace.

2:2 Paul, the little Jewish lawyer, sets up his argument using an "if...then" format. *"For if the word spoken through angels was validated, and every infringement and disobedience received a just recompense."* In this introductory lead-in Paul reveals his acceptance of the involvement of angels as intermediaries in the deliverance of the Law to Moses (Deut. 33:2; Gal. 3:19). He goes on to explain that "the word," the old covenant revelation of the Mosaic Law, was validated as a binding covenant of God as evidenced by the divine consequences meted out for its violation. The absolutely just and faithful God stood behind His word given through Moses, and if God demanded that He be "taken at His word" in the old covenant revelation, then we can be sure that He means what He says in the new covenant revelation of His Son, Jesus Christ. In the old covenant every violation and transgression received a just redress or punitive reward, Paul explains. The man who gathered sticks on the Sabbath did not escape the consequences (Num. 11:32-36). Moses, himself, in striking the rock twice, did not escape the consequences (Num. 20:11,12). Uzza reached out to steady the ark of God and did not escape the consequences (I Chron. 13:9,10). Time and again the nation of Israel disobeyed and did not escape the consequences (cf. I Cor. 10:5-12). If it was so in the old covenant, that very same God regards His revelation just as inviolable in the new covenant, "for he who does wrong will receive the consequences of the wrong which he has done, and that without partiality" (Col. 3:25). A sentimental emphasis on God's love and graciousness that does not take into account the corollary of His wrath against all that violates His character is not consistent with the new covenant gospel.

2:3   If that be the case, Paul argues, *"how shall we escape if we neglect so great a salvation?"* This is not an evangelistic ultimatum rhetorically asking, "How shall we escape God's condemnation if we reject so great a salvation?", though it has often been misused as such. Paul is writing to Christians to encourage them to "work out their salvation with fear and trembling; for it is God who is at work in you both to will and to work for His good pleasure" (Phil. 2:12,13), as he wrote to the Philippians. The Hebrew Christians in Judea were apparently becoming careless and unconcerned about the glorious, "so great" reality of Christ living in them. The rhetorical question that Paul poses again assumes a negative answer – there is no escape if we abandon the saving activity of the living Savior dwelling in us as Christians. The question implies that Christians are responsible to exercise the receptivity of faith that allows the "saving life" (Rom. 5:10) of Christ to "make us safe" from sin and to manifest His righteousness. This dynamic "so great" salvation in Christ is the better revelation, the complete revelation, the last revelation, the only viable revelation of God for the restoration of humanity. But because it is a dynamic union and action of God, there is the need for the Christian to "pay attention" (2:1), to continue to be receptive in faith to the grace of God in Christ, for as choosing creatures we remain accountable for our choices and the consequences thereof. Neglect and failure to allow the living Savior and Lord to live in us can have grave consequences, and the abandonment of relationship with Christ can put us into a place where there is no escape, as Paul will note later in this epistle to the Christians in Jerusalem (Heb. 6:4-6; 10:26-31).

Paul does not leave the discussion there, though. He proceeds to explain how the better revelation of God in Jesus Christ was proclaimed by Jesus, confirmed by the disciples, and signified by supernatural verification. *"After it was at the first spoken through the Lord, it was confirmed to us by those who heard."* The gospel of salvation in Christ was first proclaimed by the Savior-Son Himself as is recorded in the gospel narratives. It was not just a message delivered by angelic intermediaries, but the message was a Person, "the man Christ Jesus, the one Mediator between God and man" (I Tim. 2:5), the "mediator of a new covenant" (Heb. 12:24), delivered in Person, presenting Himself as the better revelation of God in the self-revelation of God by the Son, Who is the "Lord", Jehovah-God.

This better revelation of the gospel of salvation in Christ was then "confirmed to us" says Paul (including himself with the Jerusalem Christians who were the readers of this epistle), "by those who heard" – an apparent reference to those who heard Jesus teach first-hand. Paul was not one of the original twelve disciples who heard Jesus teach throughout His three years of physical, public ministry on earth. He had to obtain information about what Jesus "first spoke" through the twelve disciples "who heard" that teaching first-hand. That does not prevent Paul from asserting "that the gospel preached by me is not according to man, for I neither received it from man, nor was I taught it, but I received it through a revelation of Jesus Christ" (Gal. 1:11,12). Though not one of the twelve disciples who accompanied Jesus, Paul could still argue that he was a first-hand apostle (cf. Gal. 1:1), having been met by the living Lord Jesus on the road to Damascus, and there commissioned to share the gospel of Christ to the Gentiles (cf. Acts 9:3-8; 22:6-11; 26:12-18). Paul's direct, first-hand revelation of Christ by which he was commissioned as an apostle is in no way contradictory to his receiving the second-hand confirmatory reports of what Jesus "first spoke" through the twelve disciples who heard those teachings from Jesus' own mouth. The statements in this verse cannot legitimately be used to preclude Paul's authorship of this epistle, but are completely consistent with Pauline authorship. (cf. Introductory comments)

2:4   Having affirmed the proclamation of the better revelation by Jesus, and the confirmation of that gospel by the twelve disciples, Paul adds the authentification of the same by supernatural phenomena and the activity of the Holy Spirit. *"God also bearing witness with them, both by signs and wonders and by various miracles, and by distributions of the Holy Spirit according to His own will."* Supernatural phenomena do not establish God's revelation, but they do serve as an authenticating witness of divine activity. "Signs and wonders and miracles" authenticated Jesus' ministry (Acts 2:22), the ministry of the twelve disciples (Acts 8:13), and the ministry of Paul (Rom. 15:19; II Cor. 12:12). The divine expressions of the activity of the Holy Spirit also serve to testify of God's self-revelation in the Son. Though Paul does not here use the Greek words *charismata* or *pneumatikon* for the functions of the Holy Spirit as he does in Romans 12 and I Corinthians 12, he is still referring to the diverse distributions (*merismois*) of the active expression of the Holy Spirit in and through Christian people. It must always be remembered that the work of the Holy Spirit is the action of the risen and living Lord Jesus, the "Spirit of Christ" (Rom. 8:9). To unduly separate the Holy Spirit and the risen Jesus, or to over-emphasize the work of the Spirit to the neglect of recognizing the reality of the living Christ, is to engage in a deficient Trinitarian understanding of God's work that will inevitably diminish one's appreciation for "the better revelation of God" in the Son and by the Spirit, as Paul has sought to explain it in these verses.

Concluding Remarks

The pertinence of Paul's emphasis on the better revelation of God in Jesus Christ is quite apparent when we consider the contemporary religious emphases on "prophets" and "angels," rather than on the living Lord Jesus.

Angels, in particular, have had a renaissance of acceptability in recent years. The skeptical mind-set steeped in scientific method had regarded angels as empirically unverifiable religious superstition, to be tolerated only as cultural tradition in the depiction of angels in Christmas nativity scenes, the cupid-angel on Valentine cards, or as decoration in children's nurseries. But in typical cyclical emphasis, angels have been popularized as acceptable through such television programs as "Touched by an Angel," and by a plethora of books and art representations. The popularity of angelology in our society and in religious adoration today seems to re-create a situation similar to that confronted by Paul in the Judaism of first century Palestine – that of elevating angels to an object of adoration and worship, failing to recognize Jesus, the Son of God, as the better, complete and last revelation of God to man.

It is not that angels are to be denied, for Paul accepts their intermediary involvement in the delivery of the Mosaic Law on Mount Sinai (2:2), and regards angels to be involved in divine service to Christians (1:14). Angels are mentioned approximately 300 times in the Bible, and due consideration must be given to their existence and activity, but they must not be regarded as more important than the self-revelation of God in Jesus Christ.

The Mormon religion teaches that the angel Moroni brought additional revelation to the prophet, Joseph Smith, about Jesus being the first-created spirit-being. The Jehovah's Witnesses believe that the angel, Michael, is the Son of God, and that Jesus was Michael prior to becoming man, but is not to be equated with God. Paul's opening statements to the

Hebrew Christians in Jerusalem counter such teachings about "prophets" and "angels" by identifying Jesus as the self-revelation of God, the better revelation of God to man.

JESUS
The Better Man for Man

Hebrews 2:5-18

Being of Jewish heritage himself, and trained in the Jewish thought and expectations of his day, Paul could anticipate some of the difficulties and objections that the Jewish Christians in Jerusalem might have to his statements about Jesus being better than the angels (1:4-14). The angelic inter-mediaries between God and man might seem to be superior to a mediatorial man (cf. I Tim. 2:5), for every Jewish person familiar with the Psalms would know that man was "lower than the angels" (Ps. 8:5). To begin with, human beings have some space/time limitations that angelic beings do not have, such as corporeality and temporality. In addition to such limi-tations of humanity, mankind has fallen into sin, whereas the angelic beings seem to be fixed in their function of serving God (the demonic beings, likewise fixed in their function of serving the Evil One).

Despite the fact that Paul had already asserted that Jesus, as the Son of God, was the "express image of God's essence" (1:3), establishing His deity (cf. 1:8) as the God-man, Paul knew that the Jewish mind-set of the Jerusalem Christians would still struggle, not only with the deity of Jesus, but with the humanity of Jesus being superior to angels. The humanity of Jesus was also what allowed Him to die, to be put to death, something that angels were not subject to, and herein was the greatest "stumbling-block" (I Cor. 1:23) to Jewish thinking, that the expected Messiah could, or would be allowed to, suffer the ignominious death of crucifixion on a cross. Jewish Messianic expectations of the first century were completely triumphalistic. To suffer death at the hands of the Roman authorities was an inconceivable failure for any Messianic candidate, and to die as a common criminal on a cross was regarded as a "curse" (Gal. 3:13), inconsistent with one who would be Messiah. How could such a one be superior to the angels?

Paul addresses what he knew would be these underlying concerns of the Palestinian Christians by quoting the obvious and familiar passage in the eighth Psalm, contrasting man with angels, as it does in the Greek Septuagint version (*LXX*). Starting from the relative insignificance of man referent to God, the Psalm proceeds to explain the dignity and dominion of man. Using the same progression of thought, Paul explains that Jesus, in complete solidarity with man as a man, suffered the humiliation of death, taking such vicariously and substitutionally on behalf of all men, in order to facilitate the restoration of mankind to the dignity and dominion that God intended. Paul's objective was to demonstrate that it was the divine purpose of God to have His Son suffer humiliation and death in order to provide glorification of life for mankind.

As difficult as it might have been for the Jewish mind to understand, Paul was reiterating some of the basic foundations of Christian thought. The sin of mankind required death consequences as ordained by God (Gen. 2:17). If those death consequences were to be taken by Another, that One would have to be a man in order to die, for God cannot die (I Tim. 6:16). Thus, Jesus, the Son of God, became the God-man Savior in solidarity with humanity in order to take the remedial death consequences of sin and redeem humanity, and that for the purpose of restoring humanity with the divine presence of His life in man.

As paradoxical as it may have seemed to the original readers, the exaltation of mankind required the humiliation of a Man for man. The reinvestiture of God's life in man required the death of a Man for man. The only way for man to live as God intended was for a mediatorial Man (cf. I Tim. 2:5) to die for man. Jesus was that Man for man, who in solidarity with man, stood in our place, vicariously and substitutionally, to take the death that we deserved, the consequences of our sin (for He was without sin - cf. Heb. 4:15; 7:26), that we might partake of His life (cf. Heb. 3:14; 6:4), restored to the dominion that God intended for mankind. This life out of death, exaltation through humiliation (cf. Phil. 2:8-11) process is the divine will and way (cf. Isa. 55:8,9), which is always difficult for human thinking to understand. It is entirely consistent, though, with the *Christus Victor* theme that seems to underlay Paul's thinking as he emphasized the resurrection of Jesus (1:4-14) as the triumphant occasion and basis of life out of death.

The Jerusalem Christians needed to understand this was God's way, the divine purpose from the very beginning, even before the foundation of the world (cf. Eph. 1:4; I Pet. 1:20). There was no failure in the cross, rather the required means to God's victory in the restoration of mankind through the Son Who became Man for man. In this way Paul seeks to demonstrate Jesus is better than the intermediary angels who allegedly went back and forth to a distant, transcendent and unapproachable God on man's behalf, for Jesus was the better Man for man mediator (cf. I Tim. 2:5), who, though fully God, in solidarity with man took the death consequences that we deserved that man might receive God's life in an immanent union with God Himself, thus exalted to the dominion that God intended when He created man.

Since this is God's way – exaltation out of humiliation, triumph out of trial, salvation out of suffering, dominion out of apparent defeat, life out of death – Paul may also have been seeking to indirectly encourage the Jerusalem Christians by explaining that they, too, in identification with Christ Who lived in them, may for "a little while" (2:7,9) be tested, humiliated, and suffer defeat (especially with the volatile political situation that existed in Palestine at the time), but they could have the confident expectation of participating in Christ's victory and life. This is God's way!

2:5   Extending the thesis of Jesus being better than the angels (1:4-14), Paul turns the argument around to show that Jesus, as the Son of God, was not only superior to the angels, but His victory for man was won by His becoming lower than the angels, the representative Man for man who in solidarity with mankind could bring mankind into exaltation in identification with Himself. Continuing his prior argument (1:4-14), Paul declares, ***"For He*** (the sovereign God Who does all the subjecting, subordinating and prioritizing) ***did not subject to angels the world to come, concerning which we are speaking."***

So, what is it "concerning which we are speaking"? Paul has been referring to that "so great a salvation" (2:3) wherein the angels "render service to those inheriting salvation" (1:14) "in these last days" (1:2). The "world to come" is not a heavenly realm expected in the future. Paul uses a present participle, "coming." It is not a future "new heaven and new earth" (II Pet. 3:13; Rev. 21:1). The word Paul uses for "world" (as in 1:6) is not *kosmos*, but *oikoumene*, from which we get the English word "economy." The "coming economy" that God has ordained for man through His Son, Jesus Christ, is the Christian economy that has already come. It is the "day of salvation" (II Cor. 6:2) "in these last days" (Heb. 1:2) which has been inaugurated by the *Eschatos* Man, Jesus Christ (I Cor. 15:45). Christians, as partakers of the Spirit of Christ, already participate in this "age to come" (Heb. 6:5), the realized "heavenly places" (Eph. 1:3; 2:6), the "kingdom that cannot be shaken" (Heb. 12:28). In this new eschatological kingdom economy of living by Christ's "saving life" (Rom. 5:10), Christians are not subjected to angels (whether they be good or evil, God-serving or Satan-serving), but are subjected and subordinated only to Jesus Christ as Lord, reigning with "the righteous scepter of His kingdom" (1:8). The basis for this Lordship reign of the risen Lord Jesus in the lives of Christians, whereby we "reign in life" through Him (cf. Rom. 5:17), is that Jesus was identified in solidarity with man by becoming Man for man, and that in order that we might share in His victory, dominion and exaltation.

Why, then, Paul asks the Jerusalem Christians indirectly, would you even consider reverting to the secondary intermediaries of Jewish angelology, when Jesus Christ has secured intimate union with God Himself by becoming "the one mediator between God and man, the man Christ Jesus" (I Tim. 2:5), to Whom Christians are now subjected as He serves as the triumphant Lord? You already participate in the "coming economy" that God promised (cf. II Cor. 1:20), dwelling in "heavenly places" (Eph. 1:3; 2:6), and having full privileges in the new covenant realities of the Lord Jesus.

2:6   Paul introduces his extended quote of Psalm 8:4-6 by writing, ***"But one has testified somewhere, saying,"***. Steeped as he was in the Old Testament scriptures, Paul had not forgotten where this familiar passage was located or that David had written the Psalm. Rather, he makes an indirect rhetorical citation of the Psalm, recognizing that "one" of mankind, i.e., David, has questioned on behalf of all mankind concerning the purpose of mankind. The identity of the one posing the question is purposefully subdued or muted in order to emphasize the question posed of humanity in general.

"WHAT IS MAN, THAT THOU REMEMBEREST HIM?" This is a question that man has always asked concerning himself. Job asked, "What is man that Thou dost magnify him, and that Thou art concerned about him?" (Job 7:17). The Psalmist David twice asked the question (Ps. 8:4; 144:3), "What is man that Thou dost take knowledge of him?" When

53

man considers his creatureliness and limitations in reference to
God and all that God has created (including angels), he reason-
ably recognizes his apparent insignificance. Why would the
infinite Creator God be all that concerned about the finite creature, man?

**"OR THE SON OF MAN, THAT THOU ART CON-
CERNED ABOUT HIM?"** Who does "son of man" refer to?
Is this to be interpreted anthropologically or Christologically?
Is "son of man" a general reference to the offspring, descendants or progeny of mankind, the extended generations of
humanity? The absence of the definite article, "the," in this
citation seems to support such a general reference. When
Psalm 8:4 is interpreted within its context in the Old
Testament, the question of David almost certainly must be
understood anthropologically. But we must ask whether Paul is
taking an Old Testament text and applying it to Jesus Christ, as
he has done previously in this epistle (1:5-13). Such a
Christological interpretation would correspond with Jesus'
own self-designation as "the Son of Man" (Matt. 8:20; 9:6;
etc.) and with Stephen's statement of "the Son of Man standing at the right hand of God" (Acts 7:56), which are regarded
as Christological fulfillment of Daniel's vision of "a Son of
Man coming,... given dominion, glory and a kingdom" (Daniel
7:13). Some have avoided making a determination of whether
"son of man" refers to Jesus specifically or to mankind in general by suggesting that Paul meant it to be a purposefully
ambiguous double entendre which allows the Son and the sons
to merge as "brethren" (cf. 11,12) on the basis of the solidarity
of Jesus Christ with humanity. Such an avoidance of specific
interpretation seems to be an equivocation on the part of commentators unwilling to make difficult decisions. The preferred
interpretation is the retention of the anthropological understanding of the text's original meaning, and this has been the
predominant understanding of Christian commentators
throughout Christian history. When the quotation retains its

references to man and his descendants, Paul's argument of Jesus' solidarity with humanity is more clearly presented. In addition, the contrastual correspondence of the general pronouns "him," referring to humanity in verses 7 and 8, and the specific pronouns referring to "Him," Jesus, in verses 9 and 10, are made more contrastually apparent. We shall proceed, therefore, to interpret the remainder of the quotation from an anthropological perspective, noting the Christological interpretation as well.

2:7 *"THOU HAST MADE HIM FOR A LITTLE WHILE LOWER THAN THE ANGELS."* In what sense has God made humanity lower than the angels? Before we answer that question we must note the textual basis of the quotation. In the Hebrew original of Psalm 8:5, David declares that God has made man a little lower than *Elohim* (a plural Hebrew designation of God). Almost all English translations that seek to directly translate the Hebrew of Psalm 8:5 translate that man was made "a little less than God" (cf. NASB, RSV, etc.). The Greek translation of the Old Testament, the Septuagint (*LXX*), which Paul used among the Greek-speaking Gentiles, and from which he most often quotes in this epistle, translated the Hebrew word *Elohim* with the Greek word *angellous*, the plural for "messengers" or "angels," that despite the fact that the Hebrew word *malak* was the word for "messenger" or "angel." (Was this another example of Hebrew angelology being superimposed upon the Old Testament scriptures?) Some English translations, such as the Authorized Version (KJV) and the Living Bible (LB) have utilized the Greek translation (*LXX*) rather than the original Hebrew and have translated "angels" in Psalm 8:5. Still others have translated that man is a little less than "heavenly beings" (NIV), or "a god" (NEB), or "the gods" (Dahood).

Since Paul quoted from the Greek Septuagint (*LXX*), what did he understand David to mean by stating that "God made

man a little less than the angels"? Again, we must address
another textual issue. Is man "made a little less than angels" in
terms of extent or degree of functional capability? Or, is man
"made for a little while lower than angels" in terms of a temporal brevity of time that looks to a termination of such subordination? The Greek text allows for either translation, but
Paul's Christological reference to the same phrase in verse 9
seems to have a time reference, and it is therefore preferable to
employ a temporal translation and interpretation in this verse
also. How, then, is man made "for a little while lower than the
angels"? Is this a reference to the temporality of corporeal,
physical humanity as contrasted with angels who have a less
restrictive time/space context? Or is it, as some have suggested, a reference to the temporal period of man's humiliation and
suffering caused by the Fall into sin, the termination of which
has been effected and made available in the redemptive and
sanctifying activity of Jesus Christ? The former interpretation
of the temporality of man's corporeal humanity is to be preferred because the latter suggestion makes God culpable for
man's fall into sin.

The Christological interpretation of this phrase will be considered in verse 9 where Paul applies the words to Jesus
Christ.

The Psalmist David recognized that corporeal humanity
did not relegate man to insignificance. As the highest being in
God's creation, David could declare, *"THOU HAST*
CROWNED HIM WITH GLORY AND HONOR, AND
HAST APPOINTED HIM OVER THE WORKS OF THY
HANDS." From the initial creation of man, he was declared
by God to have the dignity of being able to bear the image of
God (Gen. 1:26,27), as his capability of spiritual function
allowed the presence of the Spirit of God within (cf. Gen. 2:7)
to manifest the invisible character of God visibly in the behavior of man. In so doing, man was to subdue the rest of creation
and have dominion over other created orders (ex. non-living,

56

plants, animals), ruling with an awareness of divine steward-
ship (cf. Gen. 1:28). Man was the "crown" of God's creation,
with the capacity to honor and glorify God (cf. Isa. 43:7) as no
other part of creation could because man alone had the spiritual functionality wherein he could receive God's Spirit (cf. Gen.
2:7) and be spiritually united with God Himself (cf. I Cor.
6:17). Functioning by the derived authority of God, man was
appointed to have dominion over the rest of God's creation.

This portion of the Psalmist's statement will be
Christologically applied in verse 9, when Paul will explain that
Jesus' death on the cross facilitated His being "crowned with
glory and honor" in order to restore mankind to their intended
dignity and dominion.

2:8 *"THOU HAST PUT ALL THINGS IN SUBJECTION
UNDER HIS FEET,"* the Psalmist continues. God's intent for
mankind was that he should function in the receptivity of
deriving all character and authority from God, manifesting the
"image of God" in visible behavior to the glory of God. As
man was subject to the indwelling dominion of God, man
would serve authoritatively with external dominion over the
created order.

When writing to the Corinthians Paul employed a
Christological application of these words, explaining that the
historical resurrection of Jesus assures the ultimate and eternal
dominion of Christ when "He has put all things in subjection
under His feet" (I Cor. 15:27).

Moving from quotation to personal comment, Paul writes,
*"For in subjecting all things to Him, He left nothing that is
not subject to Him."* It is the destiny of man to rule over
God's creation, as no other part of the created order is capable
of. This role of dominion is so comprehensive as to include
"all things" including the angels (cf. 1:14). The only exclusion
of subordination to man is, of course, God Himself, Who is
not part of the created order. Paul's argument is that man's dig-

nity and dominion is restored in Jesus Christ, for Jesus, functioning as the better Man for man, allows mankind in identification with Himself to once again rule over creation. "Do you
not know that the saints will judge the world?", Paul asked the
Corinthians (I Cor. 6:2).

   "But now we do not yet see all things subject to him,"
Paul admits to the Christians in Jerusalem. Their response may
well have been, "Amen, brother Paul, you can say that again!"
Subjected, as they were, to Roman occupation and oppression,
they did not see or perceive how all things were subject to
man in the way God intended. But Paul wanted them to recognize the victory that was theirs in Christ Jesus, whereby they
could now "reign in life through Christ Jesus" (Rom. 5:17)
while awaiting the eventual subjection of all things to those
"in Christ." As was true later for those to whom the Apostle
John wrote in the Apocalypse, it was (and is) difficult for
Christians, living in the "enigma of the interim" between the
"finished work" of Christ (cf. John 19:30) and the final consummation of His work in the future, to see the results of the
victory and triumph of Jesus Christ and how mankind will
exercise dominion over the created order "in Him." Paul's
objective was to assure the Jewish Christians of Jerusalem that
Jesus' solidarity with man as the better Man for man was sufficient to eventually restore the dignity and dominion of man.

2:9   It is here that the transition is made from general
anthropological interpretation of Psalm 8:4-6 to the particular
Christological interpretation that explains Jesus' identification
with humanity. "Now we do not see all things subject to him
(man), *But we do see Him, Jesus, who has been made for a
little while lower than the angels"* Conjoined in solidarity
with mankind, Jesus emptied Himself of divine prerogatives of
function and was made in the likeness of man as a man (cf.
Phil. 2:7,8). The Son of God accepted and assumed corporeal
humanity. The "Word was made flesh" (John 1:14) in the

incarnation. Had Paul been quoting from the Hebrew text of Psalm 8:5 it is doubtful that he would have made this Christological interpretation for he would not have said that Jesus was "made for a little while lower than God." But in indicating that Jesus "was made for a little while lower than the angels," Paul identifies Jesus (whose name means "Jehovah saves" - Matt. 1:21) with mankind in the temporary assumption of physical humanity whereby He would function in subordination to God the Father. "For a little while" – for 33 years in time during His redemptive mission to earth, Jesus was temporarily made a physical being "lower than the angels" and functioned as a man dependently contingent upon God. Such theological tenets as the "eternal humanity" of Jesus and the "subsumption of humanity into the Being of God" seem to be denied by this verse.

The temporary assumption of physicality, being "made for a little while lower than the angels," allowed for the death of the human Jesus. Building upon that physical basis of mortality, Paul continues to note that we observe Jesus *"because of the suffering of death crowned with glory and honor."* This was the primary "stumbling-block" (cf. I Cor. 1:23) for the Jewish people. Their triumphalist expectations could not accommodate a suffering Savior, a crucified Christ, a dying deliverer, a murdered Messiah. The Jewish Christians to whom Paul was writing seem to have accepted the fact that Jesus, the Messiah, had been historically crucified, but were apparently struggling with the question of how the tragedy of Christ's death could lead to the triumph of man's dignity and dominion. How could the ignominy and horror of the cross provide for the crowning of glory and honor for Jesus and those identified with Him? How could the pathos of a humiliating crucifixion be the basis of an honorable glorification and exaltation of Jesus and all mankind? This is the logical dilemma that Christian theology has faced from its inception – the explanation of how the vicarious crucifixion of Jesus facilitates the victor's crown for Jesus and for receptive humanity. Later in this epistle, Paul explains that "for the joy set before Him, Jesus endured the cross, despising the shame, and has sat down at the right hand of the throne of God" (Heb. 12:2). To the Philippians, Paul wrote that "as a man, Jesus humbled Himself by becoming obedient unto death, even death on a cross. Therefore God highly exalted Him and bestowed on Him the name which is above every name, that at the name of Jesus every knee should bow, ...and every tongue confess that Jesus Christ is Lord, to the glory of God the Father" (Phil. 2:8-11). The death of Jesus Christ was the necessary remedial action for "the triumph of the crucified"[1] wherein *"Christus Victor"*[2] assumes the *stephanos* crown of victory for Himself and for all mankind. It was only when Jesus was assured that the crucifixion and subsequent resurrection was set in motion, and that He "had accomplished the work that the Father had given Him to do," that He prayed, "Glorify Thou Me together with Thyself, ...with the glory I had with Thee before the world was" (John 17:4,5).

To further explain the redemptive death of Jesus as the necessary precursor to the restoration of life for all men, Paul states, ***"that by the grace of God He might taste death for everyone."*** Some have suggested that this phrase is *non sequitur* in relation to the previous phrase, and might better be placed prior to the phrase that mentions Christ's being "crowned with glory and honor," but Paul seems to be emphasizing that the sequence of dying in order to live, suffering in order to sanctify (cf. 10,11) is indeed the gracious intent and grace activity of God. It was God's "predetermined plan" (Acts 2:23; 4:28) to "demonstrate His love" (Rom. 5:8) and grace toward man by delivering His Son unto death as the "propitiation of our sins" (I John 4:10). Jesus was not a victim of the circumstances as enacted by the collusion of the Jewish and Roman leaders who conspired to put Him to death – rather, this was what God ordained from "before the foundation of the world" (I Pet. 1:20). Since the consequences of man's sin were death in its varied forms (cf. Gen. 2:17), the death consequences had to be taken by a man in order for the just consequences of the violation of God's character to be implemented. That Man Who came to take those consequences of death for man and as man was the God-man, Jesus Christ. He "came to give His life a ransom for many" (Matt. 20:28; I Tim. 2:6), i.e. "for everyone" as Paul states it in this verse, "for all" (Rom. 8:32; II Cor. 5:14), for the entire human race. His death was to be the vicarious and substitutional death of the sinless representative Man which would "pay the price" (I Cor. 6:20; 7:3) to redeem (Eph. 1:7; Titus 2:14) mankind. On our behalf, and in our place, Jesus, the better Man for man, "tasted death," meaning that He experienced the painful reality of death to its utmost extreme, even to the extent of experiencing the absence of God's presence, causing Him to cry out, "My God, My God, Why hast Thou forsaken Me?" (cf. Ps. 22:1; Matt. 27:46). This perhaps explains why there are some inferior Greek manuscripts that read that *"apart from* God Jesus tasted death for everyone." The sinless Jesus, undeserving of death, took the death consequences of sin which fallen mankind deserved, and that to elevate all mankind to the dignity and dominion that God intended for man by investing the life of God within man once again (cf. Gen. 2:7) through spiritual regeneration.

Paul wanted the Jerusalem Christians to be aware of the divine logic of the ways of God. Only then could they begin to understand how the crucified Christ was the better Man who was superior to all angels and elevated all men "in Him" to be higher than the angels. As an extension of his argument, Paul may have been advising the Christians in Jerusalem that those in whom Christ lives can expect the same divine logic of the ways of God in suffering that leads to sanctification (cf. 10,11), in humiliation that hopes for exaltation, in abasement that expects glorification, and in dying that is transformed into living, all in identification with Jesus. The political situation that existed in Palestine at the time of Paul's writing was such that his readers needed to be prepared for God's ways, and to be encouraged concerning Christ's victory.

2:10   Recognizing that the natural thought processes of man do not regard such divine logic to be "fitting" or appropriate to the accomplishment of objectives, Paul wrote, *"For it was fitting for Him, for Whom are all things, and through Whom are all things."* Despite how unnatural, absurd or abhorrent it might be to the ways of man, it was "fitting", suitable and appropriate to the ways of God to express His grace in such a way that death was the precursor of life. Acting out of His own Being, in complete congruity with His character, God knew it was necessary and appropriate to His intent to restore mankind, to allow His own Son to bear the death consequences of sin for all mankind. Even though the Jewish people could not conceive of a "crucified Christ," this was God's way.

God *does* what He *does* because He *is* Who He *is*. Consistent with His character of both justice and grace, it was "fitting" for God to send His Son and allow Him to die to assume the death consequences of sin for the whole human race. As God is the efficient and final cause of all things, He is the One Who determines and controls the end and the means of His activity. God determined the teleological end and objective of His actions to be His own glory ("for Whom are all things") through the restoration of human function by His Son. God effected the means or modality of His action by exercising the dynamic energizing of His grace ("through Whom are all things") in offering His Son to die in order that man might live. Paul refers to God similarly as he did to the Romans: "For *from* Him and *through* Him and *to* Him are all things. To Him be the glory forever" (Rom. 11:36).

The divine end and means are further explained in the next phrases. God's purposed end is stated: *"in bringing many sons to glory."* Since man was "created for His glory" (Isa. 43:7), God wanted to restore fallen mankind to their intended creative purpose. Who are these "many sons"? To the Galatians Paul wrote, "You are all sons of God through faith in Christ Jesus" (Gal. 3:26). Though he had just indicated that Jesus "tasted death for *everyone*" (2:9), implying the universality of His redemptive death and His restorative life available to all humanity, the individual application in the "many sons" comes by the volitional receptivity of faith for those willing to receive "Christ in them, the hope of glory" (Col. 1:27). This does not restrict the universality of Christ's work, but establishes the condition of receipt which safeguards man's freedom of choice by avoiding a universal imposition of God upon man. The singularity of God's Son (cf. 1:2,5,8), by His solidarity with humanity, "the Man for man," provides for a plurality of "many sons" in identification with Himself. The action of the One is effective for the many (cf. Rom. 5:17-21; 8:29).

The means to the end of "bringing many sons to glory" was by the action of God *"to perfect the author of their salvation through sufferings."* Why did Jesus need to be perfected? Was He not already perfect? Yes, Jesus was perfect in being and behavior, but He still needed to be made perfect (cf. Heb. 5:8,9) in benefit for all mankind. This was effected as Jesus became the sinless sacrifice in death on the cross, dying in the stead of all mankind. He thus perfected and achieved God's end objective by becoming the "author of salvation" for the "many sons" who would receive and identify with Him. The English word "author" may be a misleading translation here. The Greek word *archegon* can mean "founder, originator, initiator, leader, champion, implementer, empowerer, etc." (cf. 12:2). Whatever the meaning, Jesus made salvation available to mankind by means of His sufferings of death (cf. 2:9). The death of Jesus by crucifixion was sufficient for the just consequences of death for sin, setting man free and making him safe (Greek word *sozo* means "to make safe") from dysfunction in order to function as God intended by the presence and activity of God in the man. Salvation is not an entity or commodity detached or separated from the dynamic function of the Savior. Salvation is not a divine benefit or product dispensed apart from the function of the living Lord Jesus. All saving acts are the acts of the Being of the Savior, as receptive individuals are "saved by His life" (Rom. 5:10). "So great a salvation" (2:3) experienced by "those inheriting salvation" (1:14) was the objective of God accomplished by the "finished work" (cf. John 19:30) of Jesus through His sufferings unto death, "even death on a cross" (Phil. 2:8).

2:11 The singular Son of God and the "many sons" are brought together in a restored new humanity, based upon and as a result of the solidarity of the Son of God with mankind as "the Man for man." ***For both He who sanctifies and those who are sanctified are all out of one.*** Based on the divine logic of death leading to life and suffering facilitating sanctification, Jesus is "He Who sanctifies" by setting men apart to function as intended in the expression of God's holy character. Those "being sanctified" in the ever-present tense of salvation are those receptive to Christ in faith and identified as Christians, i.e., Christ-ones.

The Son and the sons, Christ and Christians, "are all out of one," Paul states. Does this mean that Christ and Christians are one because of the one event of crucifixion, resurrection and Pentecostal outpouring? Does this mean that the Son and the sons are united in the common experience of suffering? Does this mean that Jesus and believers are unified in one family or Body, or in the commonality of a new humanity? Does this mean that Christ and Christians are derived from one parent or father, and if so does this refer to Adam? ...Abraham? ...or God? The preferable interpretation seems to be that the singular Son and the plural sons both find their source of life and derivation of function out of the one Father, God, constituting them as one family *"for which reason He is not ashamed to call them brethren."*

The mutual derivation of spiritual life and function explains why Jesus is "not ashamed," i.e., He is proud to call Christians "brothers." Jesus, the Son, delights to identify Himself with the "many sons" who are Christ-ones finding their identity in Him. This was the intent of God, that Jesus would be "the first-born" from the dead "among many *brethren*" (Rom. 8:29); that His death on the cross would create a spiritual family, a new creation (cf. II Cor. 5:17; Gal. 6:16) humanity, all of whom would be "joint-heirs with Christ" (Rom. 8:17). Immediately after the resurrection Jesus said to Mary, "Go to My *brethren*, and say to them, 'I ascend to My Father and your Father, and My God and your God'" (John 20:17). The identification of Christ with mankind in the solidarity of His humanity with ours allows the spiritual identification of Christians in solidarity with Christ as *brethren* within the family of God, the Body of Christ, the Church.

It should be noted that the *brethren* who are united in one spiritual family with Christ will likely be called upon to identify also in the personal suffering that is often the avenue to sanctification. Paul explained to the Romans that being "fellow-heirs with Christ" implied "suffering with Him in order to be glorified with Him" (Rom. 8:17). The situation that confronted the Judean Christians when this letter was written was such that the *brethren* of Jesus would need to be encouraged to recognize the ways of divine logic, and to not be ashamed to be called *brethren* because Jesus was "not ashamed to call them *brethren*."

2:12 To provide scriptural documentation of the thesis of Christ and Christians as "brethren," Paul employs another Old Testament Psalm, the Messianic Psalm often called "the Psalm of the Cross," putting the words of the Psalm into the mouth of Jesus, having Him *"saying, 'I WILL PROCLAIM THY*

NAME TO MY BRETHREN, IN THE MIDST OF THE CONGREGATION I WILL SING THY PRAISE.'" Psalm 22 begins with the cry, "My God, My God, why hast Thou forsaken Me?", the cry of Jesus from the cross (Matt. 27:46; Mk. 15:34). It continues with a litany of suffering and affliction (which is often applied to the suffering of Jesus - cf. Matt. 27:35,43,46), followed by an exaltation of vindication which includes verse 22 which is quoted here. Placed in the mouth of Jesus, He is proud to proclaim the name and character of God to His "brethren," i.e., Christians identified with Him. Jesus will sing God's praise within "the congregation," the Church, the community of the "called out" which is the Body of Christ comprised of the "brethren." This " church of the first-born who are enrolled in heaven" (Heb. 12:23) are "brethren" who are mutually called to "continually offer up a sacrifice of praise to God" (Heb. 13:15). Perhaps indirectly Paul was encouraging the Jerusalem Christians to proclaim the name of Jesus and to sing His praise in the congregation of the church despite the religious and political turmoil that was going on around them.

2:13   Continuing to place Old Testament words into the mouth of Jesus, Paul writes, *"And again, 'I WILL PUT MY TRUST IN HIM.'"* Quoting from Isaiah 8:17 in the Septuagint (*LXX*), Paul indicates that Jesus, in solidarity with the "many sons," puts His confidence and dependence in God. How did Jesus live the life that He lived during His redemptive mission on earth? By faith – by repetitively chosen receptivity of God's activity for every moment in time for 33 years. Jesus said, "I do nothing of My own initiative; the Father abiding in Me does His works" (John 14:10). As the risen Lord in solidarity with Christians in the "brotherhood of faith," Jesus is "the author and perfecter of faith" (Heb. 12:2).

   "And again, 'BEHOLD, I AND THE CHILDREN WHOM GOD HAS GIVEN ME.'" Continuing the quote into

the following verse, Isaiah 8:18, Paul emphasizes again the solidarity of Christ and the Christian in the exercise of faith. The Son and the sons, the Savior and the saved, the Sanctifier and the sanctified, Christ and the brethren have a relational spiritual oneness in the family of God. Christians are the "children of God" (John 1:12,13; 11:52) whom God gave to the Son (cf. John 6:37,39; 17:2,6,9,24) in spiritual oneness with Himself (cf. I Cor. 6:17), as they eagerly await all that God will do. The practical inference is that the Christians in Jerusalem should recognize their oneness with the risen Lord Jesus, continue to trust God, and despite what circumstances might transpire eagerly await God's "signs and wonders in Israel" (cf. Isa. 8:18).

2:14   Keying off of the word "children" in the quotation from Isaiah 8:18, Paul returns to the theme of Jesus' participating in physical humanity in order to die and take the death consequences of sin on our behalf. ***"Since then the children share in flesh and blood, He Himself likewise also partook of the same."*** Since those who were to become "children of God" by faith in Jesus Christ had in common the corruptible characteristics of physical "flesh and blood," susceptible as it is to mortality, Jesus identified in solidarity with mankind by partaking of the same physical, human creatureliness, capable of dying. "The Word became flesh" (John 1:14), and "in the days of His flesh" (Heb. 5:7) in the "body prepared for Him" (Heb. 10:7), He took no more pleasure in dying than any other man. But "in the likeness of sinful flesh" (Rom. 8:3) with the fallen consequences of death and mortality, Jesus was willing to become the vicarious offering for sin, "bearing our sins in His body on the cross, that we might die to sin and live to righteousness" (I Pet. 2:24). The "flesh and blood" humanity of Jesus was not just a docetic "appearance" of physical humanness, but was a full participation in the human condition which included temptation (cf. Heb. 2:18; 4:15) and death (cf. Heb.

2:9,14,15). The incarnational enfleshment of "the man Christ Jesus" (I Tim. 2:5) was the necessary prerequisite for the atoning benefits of His death.

Jesus was fully man in order *"that through death He might render powerless the one having the power of death, that is the devil."* The very purpose of Jesus' becoming man "revealed in the flesh" (I Tim. 3:16) was that He might die and "offer His body once and for all" (Heb. 10:10) as the sufficient sacrifice in death for sin. As the sinless One dying in the substitutionary place of sinful mankind, He was "made to be sin" (II Cor. 5:21), being imputed with the sin of the entire human race. When the death consequence of sin is satisfied, then "death has lost its sting" (I Cor. 15:55-57). Jesus' vicarious death for the sin of all men sets in motion the "death of death," as His resurrection life, "the spirit of life in Christ Jesus" (Rom. 8:2), conquers death for all men willing to receive such. Though in the "enigma of the interim" between the historical death and resurrection of Jesus and the consummation of His work in the "new heaven and new earth" (Rev. 21:1), the residual consequences of physical mortality remain, Christians are confident that spiritual death has been overcome with spiritual life, Christ's life, and that they are liberated from the inevitable behavioral consequences of "the law of sin and of death" (Rom. 8:2) in "dead works" (Heb. 6:1; 9:14). Yes, the physical body is still mortal and susceptible to death, but as Jesus assured Martha, "he who believes in Me shall live even if he dies, and everyone who lives and believes in Me shall never die" (John 11:25,26) in the realm of their spiritual and eternal being, united as it is with the "eternal life" (John 3:16,36; I John 5:12,13) of Jesus Christ.

The devil is identified as "the one having the power of death." The verb is not a past tense, but a present participle. How is it that the devil, the accuser, the evil one has the "power of death"? This "power over death" is not an absolute power, for such would constitute a cosmic dualism between

Satan's power of death and God's power of life. Therefore, it must be regarded as a contingent power conferred upon the evil one to employ and enact as a consequence of the expression of his evil character in sinfulness. In the Jewish intertestamental literature, the writer of the *Wisdom of Solomon* explains the Jewish theological understanding of that time, writing, "God did not make death, and He does not delight in the death of the living" (Wisd. 1:13). Later he writes, "God created man for incorruption, and made him in the image of His eternity, but through the devil's envy death entered the world, and those who belong to his party experience it" (Wisd. 2:23,24). Jewish and Christian theodicy recognize that Satan has the derived "power of death" because of man's sin.

In taking the death consequences of sin upon Himself and extending life in Himself to mankind, Jesus renders Satan's "power of death" inconsequential, ineffectual and impotent. "The Son of God appeared for this purpose, that He might destroy the works of the devil" (I John 3:8). "By His appearing He abolished death and brought life and immortality to light through the gospel" (II Tim. 1:10). Jesus said that "the ruler of this world (Satan) would be cast out" (John 12:31) and "has been judged" (John 16:11), allowing us to be "delivered from the domain of darkness and transferred to the kingdom of the beloved Son" (Col. 1:13).

How is it that the devil is "rendered powerless" by Jesus death? Satan seems to be "alive and well on planet earth," continuing to empower death in its many forms. The evil one was not eliminated, annihilated or obliterated at the time of the crucifixion, but the victory has been won by Christ and the "finished work" is being worked out. Satan's "power of death" in man has been annulled and incapacitated by Jesus taking the death of mankind. The devil's derived legal right to enact death in man has been disenfranchised. The evil one has no right to empower spiritual death and behavioral death in those who have received Christ's life, made available by His death

69

that satisfied the just consequences of death for sin. Christians have been delivered "from the dominion of Satan unto God" (Acts 26:18), and the Spirit of Christ has been franchised to exercise His power (cf. Eph. 1:19; Col. 1:11) of life and right-eousness in our lives as Lord. Though our physical bodies are still mortal, that remnant of the devil's "power of death" will be removed when we receive a "spiritual body" (I Cor. 15:44), an "imperishable body" (I Cor. 15:42), and "the last enemy that will be abolished is death" (I Cor. 15:26) when Satan and his death power are thrown into the lake of fire (Rev. 20:14).

2:15 Let us not forget that the great "stumbling-block" (I Cor. 1:23) for those of Jewish heritage was the death of the Messiah. Paul is explaining how the death of Jesus was the necessary negation of the death consequences of sin, so that Christ's divine life could function in and through Christians. On a more experiential level, Paul proceeds to explain that by the death of Jesus which disenfranchised the devil's power of death, Jesus *"should have delivered those who through fear of death were subject to slavery all their lives."* The aware-ness of human mortality has long been a source of anxiety to mankind. Hopeless anticipation of physical death with no expectation of living beyond the grave can lead to a debilitat-ing phobia of diabolic enslavement. The gospel is the good news of our deliverance from the existential unknown of death.

In becoming "the better Man for man" Jesus fully identi-fied Himself in solidarity with humanity. His humanity includ-ed temptability and mortality, both of which He experienced as He prepared for and was crucified on the execution instrument of the cross. But His death was part of God's greater objective for mankind. Though Himself sinless, He took the death con-sequences of sin on our behalf, substitutionally and vicarious-ly. Jesus incurred all of the death consequences that had occurred in Adam, in order to restore us to God's intent.

70

Because He was without sin (cf. 4:15) "the one having the power of death" (14), the devil, could not hold Him in physical death. "He was not abandoned to Hades, nor did His flesh suffer decay" (Ps. 16:10; Acts 2:31). By resurrection He made His divine life available to mankind, that by the receipt of His Spirit individuals might also experience life out of death spiritually, being "raised to newness of life" (Rom. 6:4). Thereby Satan's "power of death" (2:14) was rendered ineffectual. Now having spiritual life in Christ and full provision for behavior expression that glorifies God, the Christian recognizes that the only remnant or residual of Satan's "power of death" is the physical death of the body. Since the life we have in Christ is eternal, we confidently expect the continuum of His life in perpetuity within the heavenly realm. Physical death of the body is just a transition necessitated for a new context of life, a "graduation to glory." We will not be "found naked" (II Cor. 5:3) or disembodied, but will shed the physical body and exchange it for a spiritual body, a heavenly body, a glorified body (cf. I Cor. 15:42-49). Christians are therefore "delivered from the fear of death," viewing physical death as part of the triumphant progress of life in Christ. As Paul expressed it to the Corinthians, "O death, where is your victory? O death, where is your sting? The sting of death is sin, and the power of sin is the law; but thanks be to God, Who gives us the victory through our Lord Jesus Christ" (I Cor. 15:55-57).

How, then, does the "fear of death subject men to slavery all their lives"? Apart from Christ and confidence in the continuum of His life, the fear of physical death enslaves men in mental and emotional uncertainty – the paranoid insecurity of asking, "Is there life after death? How about reincarnation? Am I just going to be devoured by worms?" The fear of death also enslaves men in the escapism of denial and avoidance – seeking to live for the moment (*carpe deim*) in self-indulgence, occupying their present physical lives to the fullest with material things and activities, saying, "Eat, drink, and be merry for tomorrow we die." The fear of death enslaves others in a preoccupation with attempting to please and appease God by their performance – the self-effort of religious striving within the confining and enslaving bondage of ethical rules and regulations and rituals of devotion.

Paul explains that Jesus' death and consequent life in Christians delivers us from the fear of death and its various forms of slavery. Yes, we will likely all die physically, for later he writes, "It is appointed unto man once to die, and then comes judgment" (Heb. 9:27). But judgment holds no fear for Christians. Fear of judgment is usually based on the psychologically enslaving fear of inadequate performance. Understanding the grace dynamic of the gospel, Christians do not rely on their own performance, but on Christ's performance on their behalf, both in dying for them and living through them. Divine judgment is but the glorious confirmation that Jesus took the judgment for our sin and the responsibility for our righteousness. Jesus said, "He who believes Him who sent Me, has eternal life, and does not come into judgment, but has passed out of death into life" (John 5:24). "For God did not send the Son into the world to judge the world; but that the world should be saved through Him. He who believes in Him is not judged; he who does not believe has been judged already, because he has not believed in the name of the only begotten Son of God" (John 3:17,18). By His death, resurrection and Pentecostal outpouring, Jesus has provided His life which delivers those receptive to Him from the enslaving consequences of the fear of physical death. Christians are set free to live life to the fullest with the confident hope of the perpetuity of life into the eternal future.

Perhaps Paul was aware that the Christians in Jerusalem were not very confident of the implications of life in Christ Jesus. They may have succumbed to some of the enslaving effects of the fear of physical death. The political situation in Palestine at that time could certainly have been a cause for anxiety. Rumors of the Roman army marshaling their forces to wage war on the insurrection of the Jewish Zealots would have been particularly frightening. Roman soldiers were notorious for committing every kind of atrocity against their defeated foes prior to slaughtering them in death. Paul wanted to assure the Christians of Palestine that the life effected by the death of the Man, Jesus, was sufficient to sustain them and deliver them from the "fear of death."

2:16 To assure them in their present situation and to affirm again that mankind, because of Christ's work as Man for man, is elevated to a divinely intended dignity and dominion above the angelic hosts, Paul confidently asserts, ***"For assuredly He does not give help to angels, but He gives help to the descendant of Abraham."*** The Christians in Jerusalem apparently needed the assurance that Jesus had identified with their humanity. Jesus did not act on behalf of the angels for there was no need to identify in solidarity with their angelic form, and there was no need to redeem them by death. Mankind, on the other hand, did need the divine help of Someone to act on their behalf, which could only be accomplished by the Son of God being incarnated in solidarity with humanity as the God-man. Only as man could Jesus then die and assume the death consequences of sin for mankind in order to redeem man. Only by the conquering of death in resurrection could the Savior restore divine life to the spirit of individuals, restoring their intended dignity and dominion. Only by the restoration of God's life in man, i.e., Christ's presence and function in the Christian, could man glorify God which is his purpose for existing. Jesus Christ has acted historically on man's behalf and continues to live and act on man's behalf in Christians today.

Who is "the descendant of Abraham" that Paul writes of? Some commentators have suggested that there is an allusion here to Isaiah 41:8-10 where the prophet refers to the "descen-

dant of Abraham" and goes on to say "surely I will help you."
It is possible that Paul had these verses in mind, but we must
still ask what he meant by "the descendant of Abraham" in this
verse. Physically, racially, or ethnically "the descendant of
Abraham" could refer to both the Hebrew and the Arabic people, descendants of Abraham through his sons Isaac and
Ishmael, respectively. The Jewish Christians to whom Paul
wrote were obviously physical descendants of Abraham. But
as Christians they were also spiritual descendants of Abraham.
Paul explained to the Roman Christians that Abraham was "the
father of all who believe" (Rom. 4:11), that the "descendants
of Abraham are...those who have the faith of Abraham" (Rom.
4:16), and that all Christians who are "children of the promise
are regarded as descendants" (Rom. 9:6-8) of Abraham.
Writing to the Galatians, Paul earlier indicated that "if you
belong to Christ, then you are Abraham's offspring, heirs
according to promise" (Gal. 3:29). Jesus acted objectively in
behalf of all men in the solidarity of His incarnation and in His
redemptive death, but the specific subjective efficacy of His
life and work is enacted in those persons who are receptive to
Jesus' activity in faith, and are thus "descendants of
Abraham." All Christians are thus "descendants of Abraham"
and "inherit the promises" (Heb. 6:12,13) of God to Abraham
(cf. Gen. 12-15), as those promises are affirmed and confirmed
as fulfilled in Jesus Christ and those who receive Him (cf. II
Cor. 1:20).

Paul was assuring the Palestinian Christians that Jesus
Christ had acted on their behalf in redemption and was continuing to act on their behalf in the present situation that they
were confronted with. He wanted them to know that the living
Lord Jesus was far more interested in them than He was in
assisting angels who needed no help. As the "better Man for
man" Jesus was superior to angels and made all those who are
"in Him" superior to angels.

2:17   In the concluding two verses of this section, Paul summarizes his argument of Jesus' identification with mankind and introduces a future theme of the priesthood of Jesus.
"Therefore, He had to be made like His brethren in all things." Because He came to deliver man, not angels, it was logically necessary that Jesus assume solidarity with the human race. The "brethren" with whom He identified are not just those of Jewish heritage, but are those human beings who became "brethren" (2:11,12) by their identification with Him through faith. Jesus partook of the full human experience "in all things," with the exception that He did not participate personally in sin. Though He was "in the likeness of sinful flesh" (Rom. 8:3), meaning that the death consequences of sin affected His body in terms of mortality, Jesus did not share in the depravity of spiritual death, and therefore did not develop the sinful patterning of the "desires of the flesh" (Gal. 5:24; Eph. 2:3). Such "flesh" patterning is not implicit in humanity, however, and therefore does not negate that Jesus was "made like His brethren in all things."

The purpose of this complete solidarity with mankind was ***"that He might become a merciful and faithful high priest in things pertaining to God."*** Here we have the first mention of Jesus as "the better high priest" which will occupy much of the rest of this epistle. Jesus became the fulfillment of the type of the high priesthood of Melchizedek (cf. 5:10; 6:20), as well as the Levitical priesthood. The high priest was a man who represented the people before God. Jesus, as "the Man for man," represented humanity as no religious high priest could ever do, for as the God-man He was fully aware of what was required to redeem, reconcile and restore man "in things pertaining to God" forever.

What was required was that as a priestly man Jesus should serve ***"to make propitiation for the sins of the people."*** The high priest in Judaism offered sacrifices for the sins of the Hebrew people on the Day of Atonement (cf. Lev. 16). Jesus not only served as the antetype of the high priest, but He Himself was the sacrificial satisfaction, offering His own life in death as the only sacrifice that could satisfy the just consequences of death that God had imposed for sin, the violation of His character. This was not an attempt to appease or placate an angry God offended in moral outrage (a concept prevalent in many religions), but this was what had to be accomplished for divine justice to be satisfied. God is a God of His word, and He had determined that death would be the consequence of sin (cf. Gen. 2:17). That penalty of death had to be paid for the expiatory and propitiatory satisfaction of God's justice. God was fully satisfied with the sacrificial death of Jesus for "the propitiation of the sins of the people" (cf. Rom. 3:25; I John 2:2; 4:10). Having died for the sins of all people, the stigma and penalty of sin that alienated God and man has been dealt with, allowing for reconciliation and atonement between God and man.

The Jewish high priests in the temple at Jerusalem were never able to effect redemption and propitiation for sin. Paul declares that they "can never by the same sacrifices year by year...make perfect those who draw near" (Heb. 10:1). Only Jesus, as the sinless God-man, could satisfy divine justice in the sacrifice of Himself in death. Why then, Paul might be asking the Jerusalem Christians, would you even consider reverting back to the inferior representation of religious priests in the temple at Jerusalem when Jesus was the only sacrifice sufficient?

2:18 Jesus can serve as "a merciful and faithful high priest" (2:17), *"since He Himself was tempted in that which He has suffered."* In the "suffering of death" (2:9) Jesus experienced the utmost of testing and temptation in full solidarity with mankind. As a man He was tempted to avoid death, saying, "Father, if it is possible, let this cup pass from Me" (Matt. 26:39; Mk. 14:36; Lk. 22:42). Those who advocate the divine impeccability of Jesus, and thus deny the possibility of Jesus' sinning in response to temptation, forget that the entire context of Paul's argument is Jesus' solidarity with humanity, and that it was in His function as a man that Jesus was "tempted in all things as we are, yet without sin" (Heb. 4:15).

Because of that solidarity of human temptability, *"He is able to come to the aid of those who are tempted."* Jesus knows how difficult the tests, trials and temptations of life can be, and now serves to intercede on behalf of Christians. "He holds His priesthood permanently, ...and always lives to make intercession...for those who draw near to God through Him" (Heb. 7:24,25). Jesus "intercedes for the saints" (Rom. 8:27), serving as the "Advocate" (I John 2:1) "at the right hand of God, who intercedes for us" (Rom. 8:34). As Christians continue in their humanity, susceptible to temptation, we can "draw near with confidence to the throne of grace, that we may receive mercy and may find grace to help in time of need" (Heb. 4:16). Never let anyone tell you that Christians should not be tempted, or that temptation is a result of unbelief or sin. To be human is to be tempted. It is intrinsic to our humanity, allowing for the continued exercise of our freedom of choice, that we might be receptive to His continued activity for us and in us and through us by faith.

Concluding Remarks

Paul has been encouraging the Jerusalem Christians to endure and not "drift away" (2:1) from all they have and are in Christ. They had "endured a great conflict of sufferings...by being made a public spectacle through reproaches and tribulation" (10:32,33). They were likely being tempted to revert back to the religious forms that predominated in the Jewish capital of Jerusalem. Paul wanted to encourage them that Jesus had identified with their humanity and temptation, and He remained compassionate and dependable as a permanent

priestly representative before God to intercede for them and
satisfy God's expectations for righteousness. The words that
Paul wrote to the Corinthians contain the basic theme that he
was attempting to convey to the Christians in Judea: "No
temptation/trial/testing has overtaken you but such as is common to man, and God is faithful, Who will not allow you to be
tempted/tested/tried beyond what you are able, but with the
temptation/trial/testing will provide the way of escape also,
that you may be able to endure it" (I Cor. 10:13). Peter's
reminder was that "the Lord knows how to rescue the godly
from temptation/testing/trial" (II Pet. 2:9).

In like manner as the death of Jesus was a "stumbling-
block" (I Cor. 1:23) for Jewish minds, many Gentiles today
cannot fathom or accept how a loving God could allow (or
purpose) His own Son to die by crucifixion. They fail to
understand the point that Paul is making in these verses, that
God's objective in sending His Son to become a man was that
He might die on behalf of all men in order to restore human
dignity and dominion as God first intended. Jesus is thus better
than any religious intermediary, angelic or otherwise, because
He became "the better Man for man," dying in our place on
our behalf to give us His life, and He continues to intercede
for us and provide all things for us by His grace. You cannot
get any better than that!

ENDNOTES

1   Sauer, Eric, *The Triumph of the Crucified.* Grand Rapids: Wm.
    B. Eerdmans. 1951.
2   Aulén, Gustaf, *Christus Victor: An Historical Study of the Three
    Main Types of the Idea of the Atonement.* London: SPCK. 1934.

JESUS

The Better
Ground of Faithfulness

Hebrews 3:1-19

Jesus is everything better! That is the message that Paul wanted to share with the Judean Christians, so they would avoid relapsing and reverting to their Judaic religion of old. Jesus is the better revelation of God (1:1–2:4). Jesus is better than the prophets (1:1-3). Jesus is better than the angels (1:4-14). Jesus is the better Man for man (2:5-18). But Paul was very aware that those of Jewish heritage had a high esteem that verged on veneration for Moses, who was the instrument for receiving the tablets of the Law on Mt. Sinai. Paul continues his thesis, then, to explain that Jesus is better than Moses.

Moses was one of the most elevated figures in Jewish history. Although the Hebrew peoples knew that Moses was a man, he was often not perceived as "lower than the angels" (Ps. 8:5) like other men, but as having a status higher than the angels because the angels served him in delivering the tablets of the Law (cf. Acts 7:38,53; Heb. 2:2) on Sinai. While the angels were intermediary messengers, Moses was regarded as the *mediatorial agent* of the Law. To the Galatians, Paul explained that "the Law...was...ordained through angels by the agency of a mediator," i.e., Moses (Gal. 2:19), preparatory to the fulfillment of God's promises to Abraham in Jesus Christ. Moses was the great *Deliverer* of the Jewish people as he "delivered the Israelites from the power of Egypt" (Exod.

3:8,10) in the Exodus. "The Law was given through Moses," John explained, but went on to write that "grace and truth were realized through Jesus Christ" (John 1:17). Moses was esteemed as a *prophet*, and Jewish Messianic expectations anticipated "a prophet like him" (cf. Exod. 18:15,18) who would dispossess the nations. Moses was regarded as a *priest* of God, along with Aaron (Ps. 99:6), having performed priestly functions (cf. Exod. 24:6). In fact, Moses was revered among the Jews as next to *God* Himself, and sometimes referred to "as God" (cf. Exod. 4:16; 7:1) or as "a god" in rabbinic literature.

The Jewish leaders of the first century considered themselves as "disciples of Moses," confident that "God had spoken to Moses" (cf. John 9:28,29), but were skeptical and antagonistic of Jesus and those who followed Him. So, for Paul to declare that Jesus was "better than Moses" was a bold declaration to make to Jewish people steeped in the Law. While the Jewish Christians of Jerusalem had accepted Jesus as Messiah, they still had high regard for Moses and the Law (cf. Gal. 1:6-10; 2:16-21).

Writing to the Corinthians, Paul had explained the glory of Moses' ministry, but noted that "the ministry of the Spirit (of Christ) would have even more glory" (II Cor. 3:8). Later in this Epistle to the Hebrews, Paul wrote that the ministry of Moses was but "a copy and shadow of heavenly things," whereas Jesus Christ "has obtained a more excellent ministry, as He is the mediator of a better covenant" (Heb. 8:5,6). Paul's assertion is that Jesus served as a better mediator of a better covenant, a better deliverer or Savior of God's people, a better prophet-spokesman, and a better priest-representative. That because Jesus was not only "as God" (Exod. 7:1), but was actually the God-man, the self-revelation of God Himself, functioning in His redemptive mission as a man faithfully receptive to God through temptation and death.

Though Moses was faithful in the roles that he played, in the ministry that he performed, in the service that he rendered in the old covenant preparatory period, there was not a sufficient ground of faithfulness for the Hebrew people. There was no grace-provision for the keeping of the Law, which led to the inevitable failure of self-effort and the faithlessness of sinful disobedience. The Israelite people who followed Moses were indeed responsible for their unbelief and faithlessness, repetitively refusing to be receptive to God's supernatural action on their behalf, and suffering the consequences of their "transgression and disobedience" (2:2). But Paul wanted to explain to the Jerusalem Christians that Jesus was "the merciful and faithful high priest in the things pertaining to God" (2:17), better than Moses, "counted worthy of more glory than Moses" (3:3), because "grace and truth are realized in Jesus Christ" (John 1:17), allowing for a "better ground of faithfulness," so that the new covenant "people of God" need not and should not repeat the pattern of unfaithfulness and disobedience exhibited by the old covenant "people of God." By the dynamic of Christ's life, Christians are able to "enter into the rest of God" (3:11,18,19), functioning by God's grace rather than self-effort. It was that faithful grace-rest that Paul wanted the Judean Christians to understand and function by in the midst of the difficult situation they were encountering.

3:1 *"Therefore,"* Paul writes – basing his forthcoming admonition on Jesus' ability to identify and intercede (2:18) for the faithfulness of Christians as He serves as "a merciful and faithful high priest" (2:17). He identifies the Jerusalem Christians as *"holy brethren."* Being "the sanctified" (Heb. 2:11; 10:14; I Cor. 1:2; 6:11), united with the Sanctifier (2:11), Jesus Christ, the "Holy One" (Mk. 1:24; Acts 3:14; 4:27) Who lives within them as Christians creating their identity as "holy ones" (Eph. 1:4; Col. 1:22; 3:12), "saints" (Rom. 1:7; 8:27; Eph. 1:18; 4:12), they are set apart to function by allowing the holy character of God to be manifested in their behavior, to the glory of God. Thus united with Christ, they are "brethren" (2:11,12,17) with Christ in the family of God.

They are also *"partakers of a heavenly calling."* All Christians are spiritually united (cf. I Cor. 6:17) with the living Lord Jesus, and are "partakers of Christ" (Heb. 3:14), "partakers of the Holy Spirit" (Heb. 6:4), and "partakers of the divine nature" (II Pet. 1:4). To be "partakers of a heavenly calling" does not mean that Christians are just "anticipators of a future calling to go to heaven," but implies that Christians participate presently in the heavenly realities that are "in Christ Jesus." Christians are "seated with Christ in the heavenlies" (Eph. 2;6), participating in the "heavenly things" (9:23), the "heavenly gift" (6:4) of Christ Himself in the realized "heavenly Jerusalem" (12:22) of the better "heavenly country" (11:16) of which they are "citizens" (Phil. 3:20). This "heavenly calling" gives Christians the privileged access (10:19) to enjoy God's presence, peace and rest presently, despite the turmoil of their surroundings. The Christians in Jerusalem were being pressured to align themselves with an "earthly calling," a *cause celebre* to join the Palestinian revolt against Rome, which was not destined to bring peace and rest, but destruction and death.

"Consider Jesus," Paul implores his Christian kinsmen. This admonition served as a primary motive for Paul's writing this epistle. It is an imperative exhortation to "pay close attention to" (2:1); to direct their thoughts attentively to the better spiritual realities that are in Jesus Christ. "Fix your eyes on Jesus" (12:2) and "consider Him" (12:3), Paul insists.

Jesus is *"the Apostle and High Priest of our confession,"* Paul explains. "God sent forth His Son" (Gal. 4:4; John 17:18), "that the world might be saved through Him" (John 3:17). The means of that salvation was Jesus serving as the High Priest representative (2:17; 4:14; 10:21) of man before God, a theme that will receive amplification throughout this epistle. Jesus was sent as the Apostle of God and serves as the

High Priest of God that we might agree and concur with God in confessing that Jesus is the Son of God (4:14), the only Lord and Savior of mankind, to Whom we should "hold fast in our confession, for He Who promised is faithful" (10:23).

3:2 *"He"* (Jesus the Son) *was faithful to Him* (God the Father) *who appointed Him."* Not only was Jesus faithful to His Father in His historical, physical, redemptive mission, but Jesus continues to be (present participle - "being") faithful in His divinely appointed and ordained function as mediator (I Tim. 2:5; Heb. 8:6; 12:24) of the new covenant and intercessor (Heb. 2:18; 7:25; 9:24) for those who are Christians.

The similitude of faithfulness between Jesus and Moses in their respective covenantal arrangements is made in the statement, *"as Moses also* (was faithful) *in all His house."* The faithfulness of Moses is not questioned, minimized or criticized, even though his double-striking of the rock at Kadesh could have been cited (cf. Numbers 20:1-13; Deut. 32:50-52). The point Paul wanted to make was that Moses was faithful in the implementation of God's provisional plan of the old covenant, as God pictorially prefigured His Christological intents through His household, the people of Israel, in the Old Testament. The faithfulness of Moses in God's House appears to be an allusion to Numbers 12:7 where God declares (after Aaron and Miriam had faulted Moses), "My servant Moses; he is faithful in all My household." Moses was faithful as the mediator (Gal. 3:19,20) of the covenant based on the Law, even though the Israelite people who followed him were unfaithful. Jesus, on the other hand, was faithful as the "one mediator between God and man" (I Tim. 2:5) to establish the new covenant of grace, and His faithfulness was exhibited in His being "obedient unto death, even death on a cross" (Phil. 2:8), allowing for a "better ground of faithfulness" for Christians living by the dynamic of His resurrection-life.

3:3   Despite the similarity of faithfulness between Moses and Christ, the redemptive and restorative efficacy of Christ's faithfulness is the reason that Paul encourages the Palestinian Christians to "consider Jesus" (3:1). *"For He (Jesus) has been counted worthy of more glory than Moses."* Moses had seen the glory of God on Mt. Sinai, and the Jewish people considered Moses worthy of much honor and glory. Some rabbinic literature indicated that Moses had more glory than the angels. Even Joshua explained that "no prophet has risen in Israel like Moses" (Exod. 34:10). But Paul had written earlier to the Corinthians explaining that the glory of Moses and the old covenant that he administered was a fading glory (II Cor. 3:7,11), whereas the glory of Jesus Christ and the new covenant has "even more glory" (II Cor. 3:8) for "the ministry of righteousness abounds in glory" (II Cor. 3:9). "For indeed what had glory (Moses and the old covenant), in this case has no glory on account of the glory (Jesus and His work) that surpasses it," (II Cor. 3:10). The superiority of the glory of Christ is based on the fact that while Moses' glory was merely reflective of the presence of God, Jesus is the essential reality of the presence of God, the self-revelation of the all-glorious character of God, and the self-generating source of God's glory. The glory of Jesus is that "which He had with the Father before the world was" (John 17:5), and was "beheld" in the incarnate Word (John 1:14). He is also "counted worthy of more glory than Moses" because He conveys and imparts His glory to those united with Himself as Christ-ones, those who have "Christ in them, the hope of glory" (Col. 1:27), and are thus being "crowned with glory and honor" (2:7).

Employing a truism or general principle of the construction trade, Paul wrote that Jesus is "worthy of more glory than Moses, *by just as much as the builder of the house has more honor than the house."* The analogy of a "house" merges the concepts of a material building structure and an interpersonal community of a "household," allowing for a double entendre of meaning. It is difficult to understand precisely what Paul meant by this analogy. Since the contrast has been made between the superior glory of Christ and the lesser glory of Moses, how is Jesus to be identified as "the builder of the house" and Moses with "the house"? The analogy necessitates an interpretation that transitions from the original material meaning to a figurative meaning of "house." If "the builder of the house" is the divine builder (looking ahead to the next verse), then God certainly has more honor than the physical universe that He created (otherwise we have monistic pantheism), and more honor than the community of His people identified with Him (who are what they are only because they are related to Him). Jesus, as "the builder of the house," is the divine builder, creatively active in constructing the universe as well as God's arrangements for the restoration of fallen mankind. Jesus was instrumental in the development of the provisional House of Israel which is connected with Moses, therefore has more honor as the divine builder than the Judaic "house."

3:4   To further explain the analogy he was using, Paul wrote (perhaps parenthetically), ***"For every house is built by someone, but the builder of all things is God."*** Again, we have the double entendre of a general truism: "For every house (whether a material structure or a figurative community of people) is built by someone." Houses do not just self-germinate, sprout and grow. They are the result and product of a personal builder. The personal builder that Paul is thinking of is God, who is "the builder of all things" through the creative agency of His Son, Jesus Christ (cf. 1:2). God in Christ (any reference to the deity of Christ here is implicit rather than explicit) has created and constructed "all things" (cf. John 1:3), including the physical construct of the universe as well as the figurative households of the "people of God" in both the old covenant and the new covenant. God, the divine builder,

was at work in the construction of both "households," the old
covenant "people of God" and the new covenant "people of
God," but the one in which Moses played a part was but the
prototypical blueprint, the preliminary prefiguring, the provisional preparation for the new covenant household enacted by
the saving work of Jesus Christ. Therefore, the faithfulness of
Jesus Christ in what He was appointed to do (3:2) is "counted
worthy of more glory" (3:3) than the faithfulness of Moses in
what he was appointed by God to do, for Christ's work serves
as a "better ground of faithfulness" by which Christian people
function as God intended, individually and collectively.

3:5 Continuing to explain the contrast, Paul writes, *"Now
Moses was faithful in all His house as a servant."* Moses is
not to be denigrated or depreciated. He was a faithful servant
(cf. Numbers 12:7) in the "house" that God built among the
Hebrew peoples. The "house of Israel," the household of the
"people of God" in old covenant Judaism, was purposed by
God, built by God, and is referred to as "His house" (3:2,5,6).
Though not a servile slave (*doulos*), Moses freely, willingly
and voluntarily rendered his service to the divine superior as
commanded (cf. Exod. 7:6; 16:16; 34:4) in order to build the
household of Israel; and he thus ministered with faithfulness,
honor and dignity.

But the old covenant "house of God" was preparatory *"for
a testimony of those things which were to be spoken later."*
Moses' ministry in Israel was a provisional witness of "those
things," the "last things" (1:2) of God's last Word for man in
the "last Adam" (I Cor. 15:45), Jesus Christ. Every detail of
the old covenant which is identified with Moses and the Law
was a figure, a type (cf. I Cor. 10:6,11; Heb. 8:5), a symbolic
representation of the "better things" that God would do to
redeem and restore mankind in Jesus Christ. The Jewish people of the old covenant household had great difficulty in
accepting that they were but the preliminary picture-people of

God's eternal plan. They considered themselves to be racially, religiously, and nationally "God's chosen people," an end in themselves. That is why Jesus had to explain to the Jewish leaders of the first century, "...if you believed Moses you would believe Me; for he wrote of Me" (cf. John 5:45,46). The Mosaic writings of the Torah dealt with the prototypical pre-figurings of the spiritual realities of Jesus Christ. The "testimony of those things which were to be spoken later" refers to the new covenant wherein "in these last days God has spoken in His Son" (1:2), in the full self-revelation of Himself and His intent for mankind.

3:6 *"But,"* in contrast to Moses who was faithful in God's old covenant household as a servant, *"Christ"* is faithful *"as a Son over His house whose house we are."* Jesus Christ, the Son, supersedes Moses, the servant, and is thus "better than Moses" – a similar argument to the Son (1:5,8) superseding the ministering service (1:7,14) of the angels. Whereas Moses was faithful "in" God's household of Israel as a servant, Jesus is faithful "over" God's household of the Church as the Son of God, implying His authoritative supremacy as divine Lord over Christian people. The Son has been "appointed heir of all things" (1:2), to sit on the eternal throne of God (1:8,13), whereas Moses simply performed his service in the temporary preparation period of the old covenant. But let it be noted that both covenantal arrangements were "His house," God's covenantal relation with His people. There is both a continuity and discontinuity of God's house. The continuity is in the recognition that both the people of the old and new covenants were God's people, and there was no intent or need for them to be antagonistic one with the other. The discontinuity is to be recognized in the provisional nature of the Mosaic covenant and the completed fulfillment of all God's promises (cf. II Cor. 1:20) in Jesus Christ, evidencing the superiority of the new covenant over the old covenant, and the necessary distinction between the nation of Israel and the Church of Jesus Christ.

Paul explained to the Jewish Christians of Jerusalem that they (along with all other Christians in every age) constituted the new covenant "house" over which the living Lord Jesus reigns – "Whose house we are." It is now made quite evident that "house" is being used figuratively as a community of people. The "house of God," "the temple of God," and "the people of God" can be used synonymously in the spiritual context of the new covenant. Christians are "being built up as a spiritual house" (I Pet. 2:5), the "household of God" (I Tim. 3:15; I Pet. 4:17), "which is the church of the living God" (I Tim. 3:15). The Gentiles along with the Jews are "fellow-citizens...of God's household" (Eph. 2:19). "We are the temple of the living God" (II Cor. 6:16; I Cor. 3:16), and "the people of God" (I Peter 2:9,10; Titus 2:14). In this case a house, a temple and people are all figures that represent receptacles of the personal presence and residence of God within them.

This was likely a difficult concept to assimilate for the Jewish Christians to whom Paul wrote. As ethnic Jews they were part of the household of Israel which regarded their physical race as Hebrews to be the primary criteria for being "the people of God," and considered the "house of God" and the "temple of God" to be primarily a physical structure in Jerusalem. As Christians who accepted Jesus as the Messiah, they were now of the "household of faith," the Church of Jesus Christ, and were the "people of God" based on a spiritual identification and relationship with Jesus Christ whereby they were "holy brethren" (3:1), "sons" (2:10) and "children" (2:13,14) of God. The "temple of God" and the "house of God" were now to be spiritually understood as the abiding presence of Christ within them. This required a radical transformation of perspective, and Paul wanted his kinsmen in the faith to understand that they were now in the "better household" of God's people which was more glorious than that associated with

Moses. These people were being sorely tempted to focus on the physical elements of Palestine, to fight for the physical preservation of the Jewish nation, and to fall back in reversion to the religious practices in the physical structure of the temple in Jerusalem where they lived. It would have been most difficult for the Jewish recipients of this letter to choose the unseen spiritual realities of Christ over the visible physical phenomena of Judaic religion.

With that in mind, Paul explains the conditional contingency of remaining a part of the household of faith: *"if we hold fast our confidence and the boast of hope until the end."* The Christian relationship with Christ is based on the dynamic function of His life. It is not a statically fixed connection enacted by a static mental assent. There was the possibility that the Jerusalem Christians might lapse and revert back to the Mosaic Law system and the Levitical priesthood still practiced in the temple there in Jerusalem. Paul was encouraging them to "hold fast," to persevere and endure, to accept "the better ground of faithfulness" in Jesus Christ and to live by the reality of the grace of God (cf. John 1:17), expressed in the faithful manifestation of the life of the indwelling Lord Jesus. This was not something that had to be generated out of their own resources and resolve, however. The grace-dynamic of Christ provides everything necessary for faithfulness, for as Paul explained to the Galatians, faithfulness is part of the "fruit of the Spirit" (Gal. 5:22,23). But, at the same time, these Christians were responsible to make the choice of faith whereby they would be receptive to God's activity of grace unto faithfulness. Only thus could they "hold fast their confidence," by "drawing near with confidence to the throne of grace, that they might receive mercy and find grace to help in time of need" (4:16). In a similar conditional statement that serves almost as a parallel to this phrase, Paul writes later in this section telling the Jerusalem Christians that they "have become partakers of Christ, if they hold fast the beginning of their

assurance (a synonym for confidence) firm until the end"
(3:14). "Do not throw away your confidence...for you have
need of endurance" (10:35), Paul adds later in the epistle.

Paul encourages the Christians of Judea to hold fast to
their confident assertions of faith in Christ and to their "boast
of hope." Both of these are verbal expressions of their faith in
Jesus Christ. "Let us hold fast to the confession of our hope"
(10:23), Paul writes later, for "we have laid hold of the hope
set before us, and this hope we have as an anchor of the soul"
(6:18,19). "Christ Jesus is our hope" (I Tim. 1:1), and
Christians should "always be ready to make a defense...to give
an account for the hope that is in them" (I Pet. 3:15).

Despite the difficulties and lack of visible assurance in the
"enigma of the interim" between Jesus' cry of victory (cf. John
19:30) and the final consummation of that victory, Christians
confidently expect that the sovereign faithfulness of God in
Christ will prevail. Such divine faithfulness is the basis for
consistent Christian faithfulness which remains "firm until the
end," whether that "end" be the end of our lives, the end of
time, the end of the world, or the end of the "last days" (1:2)
in Christ. The Jewish Christians to whom Paul wrote did not
know how it would "end" for them, but Paul encourages them
to persevere in the expression of faithfulness whatever might
happen.

This conditional clause serves as the transition in Paul's
argument from Christ's faithfulness to the necessary faithfulness of the Christian people to whom Paul wrote. The remaining verses of this section emphasize the need for the readers to
evidence a better faithfulness than that exhibited by the followers of Moses, having the "better ground of faithfulness" in
Christ Jesus.

3:7   *"Therefore,"* to relate the faithfulness of Moses and
Christ to the needed faithfulness of the readers, Paul leads into
an extended quotation of Psalm 95:7-11 by writing, *"just as*

the Holy Spirit says." Attributing scripture to the Holy Spirit (cf. 10:15), though the psalm was penned by David, Paul evidences his belief that the Old Testament scriptures were divinely inspired (cf. II Tim. 3:16; II Peter 1:20,21), divinely authoritative, and continuously contemporarily applicable.

This quotation of Psalm 95:7-11 is again from the Greek translation of the Septuagint (*LXX*). The importance of the words of this quotation for application in the lives of the Jerusalem saints is evident in Paul's repeated quoting of the text (3:13,15; 4:3,5,7) and the fact that it serves as the foundation of his argument all the way through the next section (4:1-13).

The psalmist, David, was encouraging his own generation to faithfulness by referring to a previous historical occasion when the Israelite people led by Moses in the wilderness failed to be receptive to God's direction and action. *"TODAY IF YOU HEAR HIS VOICE,"* David wrote, you should learn from the negative example (cf. I Cor. 10:6,11) of your forefathers. When God's people hear God's voice, however expressed, they should be receptive to what God wants to do. That was David's emphasis to his generation, and that was Paul's application of this text for the first-century Christians of Jerusalem.

3:8 *"DO NOT HARDEN YOUR HEARTS AS WHEN THEY PROVOKED ME, AS IN THE DAY OF TRIAL IN THE WILDERNESS."* David and Paul wanted their kinsmen to have open hearts that were receptive to God's action in their lives, individually and collectively. They were not to "turn a deaf ear," refuse to hear God's direction, and develop a fixed attitude of rebellious disobedience, "as when they (previous Israelites) provoked" God. Who are the "they" that David referred to in this psalm, and what is the particular occasion to which he referred? Was he referring to Moses and Aaron and the provocation when Moses struck the rock twice at Meribah toward the end of the forty year wilderness wandering and Moses and Aaron were disallowed from entering Canaan (Num. 20:1-13)? Or was David referring to "they," the Israelite people, and their rebellious quarrel with God about the need for water early in the wilderness journey prior to the giving of the ten commandments (Exod. 17:1-7)? Or does "they" refer to the people of Israel in the incident of their rebellion against God when ten of the twelve spies who surveyed Canaan gave a negative report of their likely success, and God responded by declaring that they would spend forty years wandering in the wilderness during which time the entire generation would die and only Caleb and Joshua would enter the land (Num. 13:1 – 14:45)?

The traditional rabbinic interpretation of the Hebrew text of Psalm 95:7-11 understood David's words to refer to the historical occasion in Exodus 17:1-7 when the people of Israel demanded water, and in obedience to God Moses struck the rock to produce water, but Moses named the place Meribah (Hebrew for "quarrel") and Massah (Hebrew for "test"). The Hebrew text of Psalm 95:8 is usually translated, "Do not harden your hearts, as at Meribah, as in the day of Massah in the wilderness." The Greek translation of the Old Testament (translated in the third century B.C. by 70 (*LXX*) Jewish elders in Alexandria, Egypt), however, translated these words with their generic meanings, rather than as place names, and it is the Septuagint that is quoted in this epistle to the Hebrews. Utilizing the Greek text of this epistle that has been preserved, it seems preferable to allow the words of this quotation to refer to the narrative recorded in Numbers 13 and 14. If this be the case, then we can observe the logical progression of Paul's thought from the allusion to Numbers 12:7 in 3:3,5 to Numbers 13 and 14 in the remainder of the chapter.

The Israelites who followed Moses in the exodus from Egypt "hardened their hearts," rebelling against the Lord (Num. 14:9) and blaming God for their plight (Num. 14:3,27).

They "provoked God" by their grumbling and complaining (Num. 14:27) and by their spurning of Him (Num. 14:11). They put Him to the test at least ten times (Num. 14:22), refusing to "listen to His voice" (3:8; Num. 14:22).

3:9 The Psalmist explains that it was there in the wilderness (Num. 14:2,32,33,35), *"WHERE YOUR FATHERS TRIED (ME) BY TESTING (ME)."* Their forefathers of a previous generation (1:1) repeatedly tried and tested God's patience (Num. 14:22), *"AND SAW MY WORKS FOR FORTY YEARS."* As a consequence of their testing God, they observed God's works for the next forty years in the wilderness (Num. 14:33,34). The Hebrew text, on the other hand, seems to connect the "forty years" with God's anger in the following phrase, as Paul does later in 3:17.

3:10 *"THEREFORE I WAS ANGRY WITH THIS GENERATION."* God, who is "slow to anger" (Numb. 14:18) was angry and provoked (Num. 14:12,28-35) with that "evil generation" (Num. 14:27,35) of Israelites, *"AND SAID, 'THEY ALWAYS GO ASTRAY IN THEIR HEART; AND THEY DID NOT KNOW MY WAYS'."* That particular generation of Hebrew people rebelled (Num. 14:9) against God in unfaithfulness (Num. 14:33), iniquity (Num. 14:19) and sin (Num. 14:40). They did not believe that God would be faithful to His promises (Num. 14:3,16), and they did not know His ways. Though "our ways are not His ways" (Isa. 55:8) and His ways are unfathomable (Rom. 11:33) to finite thinking, "His ways are always right" (Hosea 14:9) in accord with His Divine logic wherein suffering facilitates sanctification, humiliation leads to exaltation, and tragedy is often the way to triumph.

3:11 God's response to the sinful waywardness of the people of the exodus was *"AS I SWORE IN MY WRATH, THEY SHALL NOT ENTER MY REST."* God's character of lovingkindness and forgiveness (Num. 14:18) must, of necessity, be balanced by an intolerance for sin and iniquity (Num. 14:18,19,40) which is contrary to His character. The divine "Yes" must have its opposite divine "No!" The anger and wrath of God are not inconsistent with His character but are demanded by the absoluteness of His character, or else God becomes a sloppy sentimental sop. God was angry (Num. 14:12, 28-35) with the recalcitrant Hebrews who found Him faithful enough to get them out of Egypt, but would not trust Him to get them into Canaan. God determined that the consequences of their unbelief and unfaithfulness would be that they would not enter into the promised land (Num. 14:23) of "milk and honey" (Num. 13:27; 14:8), the land of Canaan, the place of rest (cf. Deut. 3:20; 12:9,10). The entire generation of Jewish people, those twenty years of age and older, would perish in the wilderness (Num. 14:29-35) during forty years of wandering (Num. 14:33,34), with the exception of Caleb and Joshua, the two spies who believed that God would keep His promises (Num. 14:24,38).

3:12   Paul now commences the application of these quoted verses to his readers in Jerusalem. *"Take care, brethren, lest there should be in any one of you an evil, unbelieving heart."* "Look out" and "see to it" that you, the "brethren" of Christ (2:7,9; 3:1), do not fall into the same pattern of unfaithful response that was exhibited by your forefathers of the exodus. A similar warning to avoid the unfaithfulness of the ancient Hebrews, and to allow their actions to serve as an example, was written by Paul to the Corinthians (cf. I Cor. 10:1-13). The possibility obviously existed that the Jerusalem Christians could develop "an evil, unbelieving heart," or there would have been no reason for Paul to warn against such. Given their adverse circumstances, there was always the temptation to revert to the religion of their past, to refuse to believe God's promises in Christ, to rebel against God's apparent inaction, to repudiate God's victory in Christ, and to reject Jesus as God's singular self-revelation of life and restoration. Their faith could turn to "no faith" (the Greek word for "unbelieving" is *apistias* meaning "no faith"), unreceptive to God's continuing grace actions, with a loss of hope that God would follow through on all that was promised in Christ. No one was immune from such temptation, as it was possible that this "could be in any one of you," or even "all" of them as was the case with the wilderness generation (3:16) in their unbelieving disobedience.

Such a "going astray in their heart" (cf. 3:10) by developing "an evil, unbelieving heart" is further explained as *"falling away from the living God."* The "drift away" (2:1) from a dynamic relationship of receptivity to the "living God" could result in apostasy (the Greek word for "falling away" is *apostenai*), a "standing away from" Jesus Christ in rejection. To thus desert, defect and depart from a vital relationship with Jesus Christ would have dire consequences, for "it is a terrible thing to fall into the hands of the living God" (10:31).

3:13   This need not happen if the Jerusalem Christians would *"But encourage one another day after day."* There was a mutual and collective responsibility among the Christians of the Jerusalem community to "encourage one another" in their faithful expectation of Christ's continuing work. The word for "encourage" (the Greek word *parakaleite*) means "to call alongside in order to comfort, help, counsel, assist, strengthen, encourage, etc." It is the same root word used of the Holy Spirit being the *Paraclete*, the Comforter, the Helper, the Counselor, etc. (John 14:16,26; 15:26; 16:7). As the Holy Spirit functions in Christians as the Encourager, we recognize that "we are one body, individually members of one another" (Rom. 12:5), and being "in Christ" together we have a responsibility to "encourage one another, and build one another up" (I Thess. 5:11). This mutual encouragement is one of the primary functions of the gathering together of Christian people, as Paul will explain later in this epistle: "Let us consider how to stimulate one another to love and good deeds, not forsaking our assembling together,...but encouraging one another" (Heb. 10:24,25).

Paul's encouragement to "encourage one another day after day" has prompted some to question whether the Jerusalem Christians were still meeting daily as they had in the earliest days of the church (cf. Acts 2:46; 5:42). On the other hand, the phrase may simply indicate the necessity of continuous and repetitive encouragement, *"as long as it is called 'Today'."* Apparently emphasizing the word "today" from the quotation made previously from Psalm 95:7 (cf. 3:7,15), Paul wanted the Christians of Jerusalem to recognize the present tense imperative of encouraging one another. "Now is the day of salvation," Paul wrote to the Corinthians (II Cor. 6:2). Christians need to encourage one another continuously throughout the Christian era from the first advent of Jesus Christ to the second advent of Jesus Christ, as long as the "day of salvation" remains "Today." The Jerusalem Christians needed to be reminded of this present perspective of Christ's saving life, for they were being tempted to seek a false utopia in the future through the zealotism of insurrection against Roman authority.

The necessity and purpose of present encouragement of Christians one to another was *"lest any one of you should be hardened by the deceitfulness of sin."* The possibility existed for "any one of them" to succumb to the forces that were being brought to bear against them – none were exempt. The passive voice, "should be hardened," indicated that the Christians were being acted upon by another who was attempting to solidify them in the deceitfulness of sin. Who would that be other than the diabolic deceiver who continually tempts Christians to behave contrary to who they have become in Christ Jesus? Similar to what he had written to the Corinthians, Paul is in essence saying to the Jewish Christians,

"I am afraid, lest as the serpent deceived Eve (cf. Gen. 3:13) by his craftiness, your minds should be led astray from the simplicity and purity of Christ" (II Cor. 11:3), and this often happens as religious agents "disguise themselves as instruments of righteousness" (II Cor. 11:15). There was surely a solicitory pressure being placed upon the Jerusalem Christians to join the religious cause of nationalistic sentiment in Palestine – to refuse to be receptive to God's promised victory in Christ. Such unbelief was sin, for "whatever is not of faith is sin" (Rom. 14:23). The sin of unbelief or unfaithfulness is inevitably evidenced in the self-concerns of self-aspiration and self-indulgence, and it might be (as some have suggested) that Paul had received word of the Christians in Jerusalem engaged in misrepresentative sinful behavior.

3:14   The only basis of avoiding such a fall into sin and away from God was by recognizing that *"we have become partakers of Christ."* Every Christian person has become a partaker, a participator, a partner of the living Lord Jesus – a "partaker of the divine nature" (II Pet. 1:4), a "partaker of the Holy Spirit" (Heb. 6:4), a "partaker of the heavenly calling" (Heb. 3:1). We are united with Christ (I Cor. 6:17), indwelt by the Spirit of Christ (Rom. 8:9,16), and are "joint-heirs with Christ" (Rom. 8:17). As "partakers of Christ" every Christian has so taken Christ into himself as to be identified by His name because He is the essence of that individual's life. "In Christ" every Christian has the sufficient grace-dynamic of divine strength and activity to overcome all temptation (Heb. 2:18; II Pet. 2:9) and all trials (I Cor. 10:13; James 1:2-4).

The conditional contingency of our responsibility (cf. 3:6) of continued faith-receptivity is expressed in Paul's words, *"...if we hold fast the beginning of our assurance firm until the end."* That which we have in Christ is not a static possession of a spiritual commodity, but a dynamic relationship with the living Lord Jesus. Such a dynamic relationship requires a

constancy and consistency of faith from "the beginning" of our
initial receptivity of Jesus Christ "until the end" of fully realized and unhindered receptivity of all things in Christ. That is
why Paul wrote to the Colossians, "As you received Christ
Jesus (by faith), so walk in Him (by faith)" (Col. 2:6). There is
the ever-continuing necessity of our receptivity of the dynamic
of His life. That is why Paul is encouraging the Jerusalem
Christians to continue and persevere in the faithful receptivity
of God's activity, "diligent to realize the full assurance of hope
until the end" (6:11). Continued faithfulness of receptivity
allows for a firmness of substantial assurance (cf. 11:1) that
we remain in the dynamic union with Christ "until the end" of
time, the end of the world, the end of the Messianic age, the
end of our lives, or the end objective of all that Christ desires
to be and do in us.

3:15   To reiterate the necessity of faithful receptivity, Paul
repeats a portion of the quotation from Psalm 95:7,8. The
then-present situation of the Palestinian Christians required a
renewed emphasis on the ever-present need of faithfulness,
"while it is said" (in the scriptural record of Psalm 95:7,8),
***"TODAY, IF YOU HEAR HIS VOICE, DO NOT HARDEN
YOUR HEARTS, AS WHEN THEY PROVOKED ME."***
Paul's point seems to be that, "Today," right now, is the time
to listen to God's voice as He reveals (cf. Phil. 3:15) His attitude and will, that "the eyes of your heart might be enlightened to know what is the hope of His calling" (Eph. 1:18), and
that you might respond in the "obedience of faith" (Rom. 1:5;
16:26), listening under God's instruction in order to be receptive to what He is doing. Jesus explained that those who follow Him are like sheep who know and hear the Shepherd's
voice (John 10:1-15). The Christians of Jerusalem needed to
keep listening to the revelatory voice of Jesus, being open and
receptive to His grace guidance and direction, rather than
being solidified, settled and fixed in an attitude of unbelieving

disobedience. Paul did not want the brethren in Jerusalem to respond like their Jewish forefathers in the nation of Israel who turned against God in unbelief, blamed God for their problems, and provoked God in their disobedience.

3:16 Paul commences a series of rhetorical questions directed to the Christians in Judea. The first question (16a) is answered by another question (16b). The second question (17a) is likewise answered by an interrogative response (17b). The third question (18a) contains the answer within an attached phrase (18b) that is part of the question.

Based on the text of Psalm 95:7-11 which was quoted earlier (3:7-11,15), and still seeking to apply these words to the Jerusalem Christians, Paul asked ***"For who provoked (Him) when they heard?"*** The identity of those who provoked God does not seem to be the issue in Paul's question. Although some have suggested that Psalm 95:7-11 referred to Moses and Aaron and the incident in Numbers 20:1-13, it is generally conceded that it has reference to the Israelite people in general, and Paul's interrogative answer certainly reveals that to be his understanding. But the real question has to do with the extent of the Hebrew peoples who provoked God. The subject of the sentence in the Greek text can have two different meanings depending on where the emphasis is placed in the word: *tínes* means "who," whereas *tinés* means "some," but there were no inflection marks in the original manuscripts. The predominant interpretation from the early church until the eighteenth century was to make the first question a statement indicating that "some" of the followers of Moses provoked God, but not all of them (cf. *KJV*). Biblical interpretation in the past three centuries has recognized the series of rhetorical questions being posed by Paul, with the first question asking, "Who provoked God?"

The answer in the form of a question is, ***"Indeed, did not all those who came out of Egypt through Moses?"*** The extent of those guilty of rebelling against God was inclusive of an entire generation (Num. 14:27,35) of the Jewish peoples. They rejected God *en masse*. There was an almost universal apostasy, with the exception of Caleb and Joshua, the two spies who believed God (Num. 14:26,30,38) and Moses and Aaron who provoked God in a later incident (Num. 20:1-13) and were disallowed to enter the promised land. These people of the exodus were a privileged people, delivered out of the slavery of Egypt, having observed the supernatural works of God on their behalf, and yet they "all" (Num. 14:1,2,10,22,35,36) acted together in unbelief to provoke God. Was Paul concerned that the entire community of Christians in Jerusalem would collectively reject the hope that was theirs in Jesus Christ? He had already implied that no one was exempt or immune from such temptation (3:12,13), and that they all needed to encourage one another.

3:17 The second rhetorical question is: ***"And with whom was He*** (God) ***angry for forty years?"*** Again, the question does not pertain so much to the identity of those with whom God was angry and provoked (cf. Num. 14:12, 28-35) as with the extent of the Hebrew population affected, and the duration of the consequences of having to wander in the wilderness for forty years (Num. 14:33,34) until every person over twenty years of age (Num. 14:29) had died.

Formulating the answer in the form of another question, Paul asks, ***"Was it not with those who sinned, whose corpses fell in the wilderness?"*** The overwhelming majority of the people of Israel, almost everyone (with but a few exceptions), had sinned (Num. 14:18,19,40) against God through unbelief (Num. 14:11) and unfaithfulness (Numb. 14:33). In accord with God's decree their corpses fell in the wilderness (Num. 14:23,29,32) as they were forced to wander for forty years. Jude confirms this when he writes, "The Lord, after saving a people out of the land of Egypt, subsequently destroyed those who did not believe" (Jude 5).

3:18 In Paul's third rhetorical question the answer is contained in the question. *"And to whom did He* (God) *swear that they should not enter His rest, but to those who were disobedient?"* Again, it was all of the people of Israel who were disobedient (Num. 14:22,43), failing to believe that God could or would do as He promised. God declared that the whole lot of them (except Caleb and Joshua and those under twenty years of age) would be excluded from "entering His rest," which for them meant the promised land (Num. 14:30,40) of Canaan or Palestine where they could rest from their imposed slavery in Egypt and cease from the exodus wanderings.

These questions were all asked of the readers, the Jerusalem Christians, to allow them to understand the analogical application that Paul was making from their forebears, and the incidents recorded in Psalm 95:7-11 and Numbers 13:1 – 14:45. Paul wanted the Jerusalem Christians to avoid unfaithfulness and the dire consequences incurred from such. He wanted them to learn from the Israelites' negative example (I Cor. 10:6,10), and to refrain from following the same course of action in disobedience. Paul wanted them to know that God's "rest" was not going to be found in a restoration of nationalist governance in the geographic location of Palestine, but could only be found as a spiritual reality in Jesus Christ (which he would further explain as the theme of the next section of the epistle in 4:1-11).

3:19 "Learn from their mistakes," Paul seems to be saying. *"And we see that they were not able to enter because of unbelief."* "We can observe the obvious," Paul explains. "They (all of them) were not able to enter into God's purposed intent for them because of unbelief." There are consequences for unfaithfulness, for as Paul had written earlier, "every transgression and disobedience received a just recompense" (2:2). The offending Israelites were excluded from the land of promise they sought, and that despite their best efforts to overcome God's decree and enter the land (Num. 14:39-45), which only resulted in the immediate destruction of many of them. They could not reverse their course after apostasy. Was Paul warning the Christians of Jerusalem that if they responded in unbelief, deserted Christ, and reverted to Judaism, that they, too, would find the consequences to be final, fatal and fixed (cf. Heb. 6:4-8; 10:26-31; 12:16,17), with no possibility of reversal?

Concluding Remarks

To fail to learn the lessons of history is often to unnecessarily repeat their failures. Paul's concern was that the brethren who were his Jewish kinsmen in Jerusalem would learn from the negative example of a previous generation of their own people. In his previous letter to the Corinthians Paul had written,

> For I do not want you to be unaware, brethren, that our fathers were all under the cloud, and all passed through the sea; and all were baptized into Moses in the cloud and in the sea; and all ate the same spiritual food; and all drank the same spiritual drink, for they were drinking from a spiritual rock which followed them; and the rock was Christ. Nevertheless, with most of them God was not well-pleased; for they were laid low in the wilderness. Now these things happened as examples for us, that we should not crave evil things, as they also craved. And do not be idolaters, as some of them were; as it is written, "THE PEOPLE SAT DOWN TO EAT AND DRINK, AND STOOD UP TO PLAY." Nor let us act immorally, as some of them did, and twenty-three thousand fell in one day. Nor let us try the Lord, as some of them did, and were destroyed by the serpents. Nor grumble, as some of them did, and were destroyed by the destroyer. Now these things happened to them as an example, and they were written for our instruction, upon whom the ends of the ages have come. Therefore let him who thinks he stands take heed lest he fall. (I Cor. 10:1-12)

The pilgrimage of living in faithful relationship with God is seldom easy. It was not easy for the Israelites as they wandered in the wilderness. It was not easy for the Judean Christians in the middle of the seventh decade of the first century. It is not easy for Christians in their varied circumstances in the twenty-first century. Engaged in the daily routine of living, it is often difficult to see what God is doing. All of the "appearances" around us may point to a reasonable human course of action, a logical alternative to faith. There is always the peril of losing sight of and disregarding the promises of God to act on our behalf. As Christians, living in the "enigma of the interim" between Christ's declared victory (cf. John 19:30) and the promised consummation of that victory, there is always the need to "hear His voice" (3:7,15) of revelation and "listen under" (the Greek word for obedience is *hupakouo*, meaning "to listen under") in the "obedience of faith" (Rom. 1:5; 16:26), persevering and enduring in continued receptivity of the promised activity of God in Christ.

Our dynamic relationship of deriving life from Christ is conditioned by the contingency of our continued faith and pattern of faithfulness. That is why Paul explains that we are part of the household of faith "*if* we hold fast our confidence and the boast of our hope firm until the end" (3:6). We are partakers of Christ "*if* we hold fast the beginning of our assurance firm until the end" (3:14). His warnings against doing otherwise are "*lest* there should be in any one of you an evil, unbelieving heart, in falling away from the living God" (3:12), and "*lest* any one of you be hardened by the deceitfulness of sin" (3:13). F. F. Bruce remarks on these conditional clauses:

> Nowhere in the New Testament more than here (Hebrews) do we find such repeated insistence that continuance in the Christian life is the test of reality. The doctrine of the final perseverance of the saints has as its corollary the salutary teaching that the saints are people who persevere to the end.[1]

The condition of persevering faith should not be viewed as "works" of performance that merit God's action or require God to act in certain ways. God's actions are not contingent on what man does. The only condition of responsibility that man has is to exercise the freedom of choice that God created us with, choosing and deciding to be receptive to God's activity in faith. God does not impose Himself upon us. A faith-love relationship with God cannot (by definition) be coerced. Christians, having initially been receptive in faith to Christ's performance on their behalf, and having experienced the blessing of Christ's presence and activity, still have freedom of choice and the responsibility to exercise such in receptivity to Christ's activity. "As you received Christ Jesus, so walk in Him" (Col. 2:6) – in faith and continued faithfulness. The failure and refusal to continue to be receptive to God's activity in faith puts us in jeopardy of final, fixed and fatal consequences of "standing against" God in apostasy.

The avoidance of such consequences, as were previewed in God's actions against the people of Israel in the wilderness, is what Paul was cautioning his readers about. The way to avoid such consequences is to avoid the Israelites' pattern of faithlessness. The means by which Christians can do so is to recognize and rely on the "better ground of faithfulness" in Jesus Christ. The faithfulness of Jesus (3:2,6) in accomplishing all that God wanted to do through Him in establishing the new covenant, being faithfully "obedient unto death, even death on a cross" (Phil. 2:8), allowed for a more glorious (cf. 3:3) reality than was ever available through Moses. By the resurrection of Jesus from the dead the grace-dynamic of God's divine activity is available to those who are receptive to Him. Christians, who are "partakers of Christ" (3:14) and "partakers of the heavenly calling" (3:1), have "all things pertaining to life and godliness" as "partakers of the divine nature" (II Pet. 1:3,4), and thus have the "better ground of faithfulness" in

God's dynamic provision of grace, as they remain receptive to such in faith.

ENDNOTE

1 Bruce, F.F., *The Epistle to the Hebrews*. Series: The New International Commentary on the New Testament. Grand Rapids: Wm. B. Eerdmans Pub. Co. 1964. pg. 59.

JESUS

The Better Rest of God

Hebrews 4:1-13

Paul continues to draw application from the Davidic text in Psalm 95:7-11 to the Christians residing in Jerusalem in the middle of the seventh decade of the first century (somewhere around A.D. 65). Hebrews 3:1 through 4:13 is a cohesive section of Paul's argument in this epistle, but we have divided our comments into two chapters to note the differing emphases in the two subdivisions of this section.

Having noted "the better ground of faithfulness" (3:1-19) in Jesus Christ, Paul now keys off of the idea of "rest" in Psalm 95:11 (cf. 3:11,18,19). The Hebrew participants of the exodus were anticipating a "rest" from the oppressive tyranny of the Egyptians and subsequently from the wearying wanderings in the wilderness. The "rest" they sought was in a geographic location, a "resting place" (Deut. 12:9) in a land beyond the Jordan river (cf. Deut. 3:20; 12:10), a "promised land" (cf. Num. 14:40; Deut. 9:28) which God had promised as an inheritance wherein they could "rest" from their enemies and live securely (Deut. 12:9,10). For the Exodus generation the concept of "rest" was to be achieved by entering into the land of Canaan or Palestine. "But they were not able to enter because of unbelief" (3:19). So after a delay of forty years due to the faithless disobedience of the generation that left Egypt, the next generation of the Jewish nation did enter into the Promised land under the leadership of Joshua (cf. Joshua 3).

The promise of God to the Jewish peoples for a physical form of "rest" was then fulfilled.

> The Lord gave Israel all the land He had sworn to give to their fathers, and they possessed it and lived in it. And the Lord God gave them rest on every side, according to all that He had sworn to their fathers, and no one of their enemies stood before them; the Lord gave all their enemies into their hand. Not one of the good promises which the Lord had made to the house of Israel failed; all came to pass. (Joshua 21:43-45)

Even though "the Lord had given rest to Israel" (cf. Josh. 23:1), there was still the continued conditional need for a faithfulness on the part of the Israelites (Josh. 22:4,5; 23:6) in order to enjoy and appreciate God's "rest" in the land of promise.

Long after the Jewish nation had entered into the promised land of rest under the leadership of Joshua, the psalmist David continued to refer to God's "rest" (Psalm 95:11). Paul infers (4:8) that such a reference indicated that there was still a divine "rest" beyond the possession of the Palestinian land. This was consistent with the Jewish Messianic expectations of an eschatological "rest" to be inaugurated by the Messianic deliverer, which usually retained the physical expectation of such "rest" in a self-governed nation of Israel in the land of Palestine.

The radical new understanding of Paul's conception of God's promised "rest" was that it was a spiritual fulfillment in the Person of Jesus Christ, rather than a particular physical and geographical land placement and ethnic nation. Paul regarded the "promised land rest" sought by the Hebrews in the Exodus to be but a pictorial prefiguring of the function of God's spiritual "rest" in Jesus Christ (4:3) in the new covenant. Since Jesus is "the heir of all things" (1:2), those who are "in Christ" are "joint-heirs with Christ" (Rom. 8:17) of all the promises of God (II Cor. 1:20), including the promise of entering God's "rest."

Once again, the connections that Paul makes in his argument are based upon his use of the Greek translation of the Old Testament, the Septuagint (*LXX*). Paul ties together the "rest" mentioned by David in Psalm 95:11 and the previous mention of God's "resting" on the seventh day of creation in Genesis 2:2. In the Hebrew text of the Old Testament, Genesis 2:2 uses the Hebrew word *shabbath*, meaning "to cease, desist, or rest." David's reference to "rest" in Psalm 95:11 uses the Hebrew word *menuhah*, meaning "resting place." These were such distinctly different Hebrew words and concepts that they would not likely be drawn together to support a common argument. But in the Greek translation (*LXX*) of the Old Testament, Genesis 2:2 uses the Greek word *katapause*, and Psalm 95:11 uses the Greek word *katapausin*, both words being from the same root word, meaning "to cease or refrain from" with the extended meaning of "rest." This allowed Paul to bring them together and merge the concepts of "rest" in order to explain that Jesus is the "better rest of God" for Christian people, the Sabbath rest (4:9) as well as the promised place of rest.

The historical context that precipitated Paul's epistle was such that Paul's emphasis on "rest" likely countered a contemporary prevailing emphasis on "rest" in the Judean region where the recipients of this letter resided. Consistent with the historical accounts of the Israelites in the wilderness seeking "rest" from the oppressive Egyptians and other enemy nations, the Zealots of Palestine in the first century were advocating that the Jewish peoples needed to seek "rest" from oppressive Roman rule by revolting against this occupying enemy of God's people. This was integrated, of course, with the long-held eschatological expectation of a Messianic "rest" wherein the Jewish people who regarded themselves as "God's chosen people" would occupy their "promised land" of "rest" as a self-governing nation once again.

The Jewish Christians in the church at Jerusalem had accepted Jesus as the promised Messiah, but they were repeatedly caused to question whether the expected Messianic "rest" was being realized in their experience. The physical forms of such "rest," as understood historically by their forefathers, were obviously not materializing. Their Jewish kinsmen were constantly pressuring them to expect the traditional understanding of "rest" rather than some ethereal concept of spiritual "rest" in Jesus Christ. Perhaps they were having reservations about whether the Messianic expectations were really fulfilled in Jesus, and were being tempted to revert back to tangible and physical Jewish expectations of national and religious "rest." What a tempting prospect that would have been, to join the insurrection against Roman rule in hopes of effecting a renewed Jewish kingdom in that geographic place of Palestine that had been promised to their forefathers of previous generations as a "land of rest," and to thereby also protect their Jewish religious worship practices on the Sabbath "day of rest," patterned as it was on God's resting on the seventh day of creation.

Understanding the Jewish mindset (being of Jewish heritage himself), Paul could sympathize with the struggle the Jerusalem Christians were confronted with. Perhaps he had also been appraised of their difficulties by someone who had recently visited the Jerusalem church. Paul writes to his "brethren" (both physical and spiritual), to explain that the risen and living Lord Jesus is the basis of "the better rest of God." The better rest of God is not to be sought in a restoration of a physical "place of rest" in Palestine, nor is it to be found in religious rituals on a particular Sabbath "day of rest." Paul's premise is that the spiritual reality of the presence and function of the Spirit of Christ in the Christian allows for the divine dynamic of God's grace to function in the Christian's life, and thus allows the Christian to "rest" from all performance efforts to seek God's approval, and thereby to enjoy God's creative, redemptive and restorative action.

The "better rest of God" in Jesus Christ is the fulfillment of the prototypical creation story, for now in the spiritual "new creation" (Gal. 6:15) of the Body of Christ, the new "Israel of God" (Gal. 6:16), God "rests" after having done everything necessary to create "new creatures in Christ" (cf. II Cor. 5:17) by the regenesis of spiritual regeneration. In the resultant new creation Sabbath rest (4:9) God's sustaining grace continues to function, allowing all of His new creation to enjoy all that He has done and is doing in His Son, Jesus Christ. Jesus also serves as the fulfillment of the new exodus, for Jesus has delivered people from the slavery of sin to the new place of rest "in Christ." This was God's spiritual intent for His people from "before the foundation of the world" (4:3), and the physical genesis of creation and historical exodus were typological prefigurings of what God determined to enact in Jesus Christ and those united with Him as Christians.

When the Spirit of Christ dwells and abides in Christians, the place of God's "rest" is within us. In his defense before the Jewish high priest, Stephen explained that "the Most High does not dwell in houses made with hands" (Acts 7:48), and quoted God's statement from Isaiah 66:1: "'Heaven is My throne, and earth is the footstool of My feet; What kind of house will you build for Me?' says the Lord; 'Or what place is there for My rest (Greek *katapauseos*)?'" (Acts 7:49). The place of God's "rest" is in His new creation people, in the "household" that Jesus Christ has built (3:6), in the church of the living God, in Christian people. Having "Christ in us, the hope of glory" (Col. 1:27), God "rests" in the temple house (I Cor. 3:16; 6:19; II Cor. 5:1; 6:16) of our individual bodies and the collective Body of the Church, expressing His own character in Christians' behavior by His grace, and enjoying the results of His new creation. Christians, who have experienced God's spiritual knife in the cutting off of sin in "the circumcision of the heart" (Rom. 2:28,29), continue to experience Christ's penetrating work as He exposes the subtle differences between religious performance and the inner "rest" of relying on God's grace. Paul's desire for the Jerusalem Christians was that they recognize "the better rest of God" and cease from their "works" as God has rested from His works (4:10), which would entail refraining from all nationalistic endeavors and avoiding all religious performance in order to enjoy the continuing grace-work of God in Jesus Christ.

4:1   In light of the failure and exclusion of the initial Exodus generation from the promised land of God's rest, Paul wrote, ***"Therefore, let us fear lest, while a promise remains to enter into His rest, any one of you should appear to have failed to obtain it."*** Writing with a sense of urgency, Paul explained to the Jerusalem Christians that God's promise remains open and available to enter His rest. God's "rest" was not revoked when the older Exodus generation rejected such in unbelief (3:19). The next generation (Num. 14:31) entered the land of rest with Joshua (Josh. 3). The promise of God's "rest" remained open in David's day (4:7), and continued in subsequent generations to be expected in the reign of the Messianic deliverer. Since the ultimate fulfillment of all of God's promises is in Jesus Christ (II Cor. 1:20), Paul explained to the Christians of Jerusalem that God's promised "rest" remained available only in Jesus. Since Jesus is the "heir of all God's promises" (1:2), those who are "in Him" as Christians are heirs of all God's promises (6:12; 9:15; 10:36; 11:39,40). The Christians in Jerusalem still had the opportunity to enter into the experiential efficacy of God's dynamic activity of grace, and "rest" in His sufficiency rather than trying to perform for God and make things happen for God. They were doubtless being encouraged by their Jewish relatives there in Judea to join the action of revolt against Rome in order to effect a utopian dream of restful self-rule in Palestine. Such striving performance that fought to acquire and orchestrate "rest" by their own endeavors was contrary to the spiritual "rest" that Paul was advising them was already available in Jesus Christ.

Identifying himself with his readers, Paul wrote, "Let us fear lest any one of you should appear to have failed to obtain it." Doesn't "perfect love cast out fear" (I John 4:18)? Yes, the action of the God Who is perfect love (I John 4:8,16) does overcome all human fears, but that does not negate a healthy fear-respect for God (II Cor. 7:1; Col. 3:22; I Pet. 2:17) and the divine consequences of unbelief (2:2,3; 3:12,13), nor genuine Christian fear-concern that our Christian brethren might miss the availability of the abundance of God's grace (cf. Eph. 3:20) and the opportunity to "rest" in His sufficiency (cf. II Cor. 3:5). The possibility of such failure obviously existed or there would not have been any cause for fearful concern about "coming short of the grace of God" (12:15). Paul was concerned that each individual Christian in the Jerusalem church ("any one of you" - cf. 3:12), should fail to enter God's grace-rest. The concern was not that these Christians might "seem" or "appear" to miss the opportunity of God's rest in some apparently delusionary misconception, but that it might be evidenced in the manifested appearances of their behavior that they were engaged in religious self-effort rather than relying on God's grace. Did it appear to Paul that the Jerusalem Christians were in danger of coming short of God's rest? In that the temptation of religious activism always opposes the availability of God's "rest," and the Christians in Jerusalem were tempted to engage in such activism to implement nationalistic and religious interests, then it is likely that Paul considered them in danger of failing to enter into God's "rest." Coming short of, or failing to obtain, God's "rest" is always a result of faithlessness, unbelief (3:12,19; 4:2), and unwillingness to be receptive to God's activity in accomplishing His objectives in His way.

4:2   To further explain the danger and peril of failing to be receptive in faith to God's "rest," Paul wrote, *"For indeed we are those having had good news presented to us, just as they also did."* Paul and the Jerusalem Christians to whom he wrote had the good news of God's promised grace-rest presented to them. The "good news" of the gospel is the Person of Jesus Christ, the living dynamic of His resurrection life which allows the grace-rest of God to be operative in Christian lives. The "good news" they received was not just historical data or doctrinal interpretations, but was the vital dynamic of the life of the risen Jesus who provides all the performance necessary for the Christian life, allowing them to "rest" in His grace-action.

There is a shared root of words in the Greek text that is not apparent in the English translation. The word "promise" in verse 1 is *epangelias*, and the word for "good news preached to us" in verse 2 is *euangelismenoi*, both employing the Greek word *angelia*, meaning "message." The message of God's promised "rest" was presented to the Exodus generation of Israelites as well as to Paul and his readers. This does not mean that the Hebrews who exited Egypt were evangelized with the gospel of Jesus as Paul and the Jerusalem Christians were. Paul's statement here is not equivalent to Paul's statement to the Galatians that "the gospel was preached beforehand to Abraham" (Gal. 3:8), so that Abraham could recognize that the promises made to him pertained to all that God was going to make available in Jesus Christ by faith. Paul's words in this verse simply mean that the initial Exodus generation was presented with the good news of a promised "rest" in the land of Canaan when Joshua and Caleb returned from their surveillance of the land (Num. 13:30; 14:7-9). Paul and his fellow Jewish Christians in Jerusalem were similarly presented with the good news of God's promised "rest," but the difference was that this spiritual "rest" was in Jesus Christ alone, wherein the "finished work" of Christ's redemptive performance allowed for the sanctifying performance of the indwelling Spirit of Christ in Christian behavior.

There was a similarity in the Exodus Israelites and the Jerusalem Christians in that both groups were presented with the good news of a promised "rest," but there was a dissimilarity in the content of that "rest" between a geographical land and the spiritual function of God's grace. Paul's concern was that there should not be a similarity in the way that these old covenant and new covenant "peoples of God" responded to the good news of promised "rest." Contrasting the Israelites' response with what he was advocating for the Jerusalem Christians, Paul wrote, ***"but the word they heard did not benefit them, because it was not connected with faith in those having heard."*** Those Hebrews who departed Egypt with Moses heard God's message of a promised "rest" in Canaan, but they never benefitted or realized the advantage of that promise because they were unwilling to connect or unite with God's promise in the receptivity of faith. It was a useless and futile promise to them because they cut themselves off from God's action through unreceptive disobedience. "Whatever is not of faith is sin" (Rom. 14:23). The conditional contingency for receiving all that God has available in His Son, Jesus Christ, is the receptivity of faith that is available to God's action. This theme of the responsibility of faith is repeated throughout this epistle as the Greek words for faith, *pistis* and its derivatives, are employed at least thirty-nine (39) times.

It should be noted that the final phrase of verse 2 has been translated by some, "because they did not share the faith of those who heard," indicating that the faithless wilderness generation did not share the faith of Joshua and Caleb, who listened to and were receptive to God's promised action of "rest." This interpretation is not the most accurate translation of the Greek text and not likely to have been Paul's intent when he wrote.

4:3   They, the rebellious Hebrews in the wilderness, did not connect with God's promised "rest" by faith (4:2) and did not enter because of unbelief (3:19), but in contrast, "we," Paul and the Jerusalem Christians, can enter God's new covenant "rest" by faith. *"For we, those having believed, can enter into rest."* "Those having believed" are Christians who "have been saved by grace through faith" (Eph. 2:8). Their initial receptivity of faith to Christ's redemptive work allows them to enter into the continued grace performance of Christ's life and to cease from repetitive religious performance. This "rest" is not an externalized objective place of "rest" outside of ourselves, but is the subjective experience of resting from self-effort by receiving God's activity. This is not a place of "rest" entered once and for all wherein we are statically confined, but is a dynamic "rest" to be constantly realized by "holding fast" (3:6,14) in the condition of faithful receptivity. This is not a place of "rest" in heaven in the future, but is the present process and experience of being receptive to God's grace. This present experience of "rest" is available to all Christians. "For we, those having believed, can enter into rest."

In contrast, *"just as He has said, 'AS I SWORE IN MY WRATH, THEY SHALL NOT ENTER MY REST'."* Whereas Christians have the opportunity to enter God's "rest" in Christ, God declared that the faithless grumblers of the wilderness could not, and would not be given the opportunity to, enter His "rest" in the land of Canaan. The way into God's grace-rest remains open to Christians, but the threat of exclusion based on unreceptiveness still remains, as illustrated in the faithlessness of the unbelieving Hebrews who serve as the example not to be followed (4:11; I Cor. 10:1-13).

Although God banned the initial generation of Exodus Hebrews from the land of "rest" in Canaan, Paul wanted to explain that God's "rest" was not to be statically historicized only as the entry of the Israelites into Canaan at the time of the Exodus. *"And yet,"* Paul breaks his train of thought with yet another contrast, *"the works"* (of God) *"had been brought into being from the foundation of the world."* The dynamic working of God that allows man to rest in God's working was effectively implemented from the founding and creation of the cosmos, and from the point of humanity being brought into being in the Genesis. God's works, His intent and willingness to do all the necessary energizing and performing within His creation, were established and available from the beginning of the created order. Man was created, not as a self-generative actuator, but as a receptive vessel, a contingent, dependent, and derivative creature, who would derive character and action from God. The divine generation and working of all things that would bring glory to Himself within His creation was actuated from the commencement of creation, thus allowing humanity to "rest" in God's activity by receptivity. In other words, God's "rest" for mankind is not a reality initiated at the time of the Exodus, but was brought into being in the Genesis of all created things.

Various misunderstandings result from mistranslating the verb in this phrase. The Greek word used here is *ginomai*, which is the root of the word *genesis*, meaning "to bring into being." When this verb is translated and interpreted as "finished" (KJV, RSV, NASB, NIV), as if it were the Greek word *teleo*, derived from *telos*, then interpreters often mistakenly indicate that the "finished work" of Christ (cf. John 19:30 - *tetelestai*) was completed from the inception of the cosmos, or even before the foundation of the world. Such interpreters often cite Revelation 13:8 as a parallel text, and if they are using the KJV translation mistakenly indicate that "the Lamb was slain before the foundation of the world" (Rev. 13:8 - KJV). Jesus' function as the sacrificial lamb "was foreknown before the foundation of the world" (I Pet. 1:20), and God's foreknowledge allowed the names of receptive believers to be written in the book of life before the foundation of the world (Rev. 13:8), but we must beware of mystical interpretations that project God's redemptive work outside of space and time, thus dehistoricizing God's work in Christ and making the historical passion of Christ into a redundant exercise.

4:4   The recognition that God's "rest" was available to man from the creation of the world when God's working in His creation was "brought into being," allows Paul to make a mental connection with God's "rest" from His creative work. ***"For He has said somewhere concerning the seventh day, thus..."*** Again, as in 2:6, it is not that Paul had forgotten the reference of the verse he was quoting from Genesis 2:2. This was a common indirect way of referring to a well-known text. "God has said somewhere (and we all know where)."

Continuing his documentation of the preexistence of God's "rest" prior to the Exodus, Paul quotes Genesis 2:2: ***"AND GOD RESTED ON THE SEVENTH DAY FROM ALL HIS WORKS."*** As usual throughout this epistle, Paul's quotation of the Old Testament text is from the Greek translation of the Septuagint (*LXX*). This allowed him to connect the idea of "rest" in Genesis 2:2 to the mention of "rest" in Psalm 95:11, for in the Septuagint the Greek word for "rest" in Genesis 2:2 is *katapause* and the Greek word for "rest" in Psalm 95:11 is *katapausin*, both derived from the same root word meaning "to cease or refrain from," often in the sense of "rest" from working. Had Paul been using the Hebrew text, the word *shabbath* in Genesis 2:2 (meaning "to cease or desist") and the word *menuhah* in Psalm 95:11 (meaning "resting place") would not have allowed for such a convenient connection, as they had very different connotations. Paul's objective in using the word connection of the Septuagint translation was to explain how God's "rest" pre-dates the pictorial land provision of the Exodus, and has been God's intent from the very beginning of man's existence.

Why did God cease from His creative work and "rest" on the seventh day of creation? It was not because He was exhausted or worn out, because God "does not become weary or tired" (Isa. 40:28). It was not because there was nothing else to do and God ceased working to become quiescent or inactive, for God "is working until now" (John 5:17) and His very Being requires active expression in sustenance, providence, grace, intercession, judgment, etc. within His creation. God's Being and action can never be separated or detached, for His Being is always expressed in consistent action, and His action is always expressive of His invested Being. This is why the deistic concept of God's creating all things and then passively detaching Himself from that creation to watch it function reduces God to an abstracted and impotent deity-figure. God rested from His creation work because He wanted to allow creation to function as intended by the dynamic of His working within it, and thus to allow the created order to "rest" in His expression of His Being within it. God looked down upon His creation after He created mankind, and said, "It is very good" (Gen. 1:31). Since God alone is good (Matt. 19:17; Mk. 10:18; Lk. 18:19), the creation can only be "very good" if God is functioning within His creation expressing His all-glorious character of goodness unto His own glory (Ps. 19:1). This is the *raison d'etre* of mankind; we were "created for His glory" (Isa. 43:7), and He can only be glorified as we "rest" in the receptivity of His active expression of His character. God "rested" on the seventh day of creation so He could enjoy the function of His creation and allow mankind to enjoy the creation with Him by "resting" in the divine dynamic and sufficiency of His continued working.

It was the *shabbath* "rest" of God mentioned in Genesis 2:2 that was the stated basis of the Jewish Sabbath celebration on the seventh day of each week, as explained when God gave the ten commandments on Sinai (Exod. 20:8-11). The seventh day Sabbath was intended to be a day when God's people would cease from their labors in order to enjoy God's working in celebration and praise. Unfortunately the Sabbath day observance in Judaic religion became loaded with legalistic limitations of what could and could not be performed on Saturday, and the intended function of the Sabbath was seldom realized. Paul will explain the spiritual fulfillment of the seventh day Sabbath when he refers to the new covenant "Sabbath rest" in verse 9.

4:5   Reiterating the connection he was making between Genesis 2:2 and Psalm 95:11 to explain that the "rest" of God was always God's intent for man, Paul repeats (cf. 3:11,18,19; 4:3) the quotation from Psalm 95:11: *"and again in this* (place, passage, text), *'THEY SHALL NOT ENTER MY REST'."* The failure of the followers of Moses to enter into the Canaan land of "rest" was due to their own unbelief (3:12,19; 4:2); they were culpable for their inexorable incredulity and inflexible iniquity. But God's promise of "rest" for His people would not be thwarted (cf. Job 42:2). God allowed the next generation of Israelites to enter the land, even though they seldom found the "rest" that could have been theirs in the land because of their continued faithlessness. David still believed in the promised "rest" many generations later when he wrote the Psalms (this will be Paul's subsequent argument in verse 7 and 8). God's promised "rest" could not be defeated! He continued to act on man's behalf to provide the "rest" that could only be fully realized in the dynamic grace function of His Son, Jesus Christ, when man was restored to function as God intended by His indwelling presence and activity in man. It has been noted that when God "rested" on the seventh day of creation there was no "evening" to the seventh day, as there was on all previous days of creation (Gen. 1:5,8,13,19,23,31), perhaps implying that the day of God's "rest" is eternal, without end, and never to be nullified. That eternal "rest" of God is available in Jesus Christ, who said, "Come to Me, all who are weary and heavy-laden, and I will give you rest. Take My yoke upon you, and learn

from Me, for I am gentle and humble in heart; and YOU
SHALL FIND REST FOR YOUR SOULS" (Matt. 11:28,29;
cf. Jere. 6:16).

4:6 *"Since"* God's rest was available and accessible prior
to and subsequent to the Exodus generation *"therefore it
remains for some to enter into it."* God's promised "rest" will
not lack for fulfillment. It remains open and available for
God's people (4:1). Paul's statement that it remains available
for "some" to enter into such rest does not constitute an arbitrary divine delimitation of the privilege of God's rest. Rather,
it takes into account that God's rest is conditioned and contingent upon a Christian's receptivity of faith to allow God to act,
and realistically recognizes that not all of God's people are
willing to receive His grace-provision in order to enjoy His
rest.

"*And*" a case in point of such refusal is that *"those previously having had good news presented to them did not enter
in* (to God's rest) *because of disobedience."* The faithless
generation at Kadesh had the good news (4: 2) of a promised
land of rest presented to them by Moses (Exod. 13:5) and by
Joshua and Caleb (Num. 13:30; 14:6-9), but they forfeited
their opportunity to enter into that provisional portrayal of
divine rest because of their defiant disobedience (3:18; 4:11;
cf. Num. 14:11,12, 21-23). In contrast to the "obedience of
faith" (Rom. 1:5; 16:26) that God desires, the initial generation
of Israelites that departed Egypt responded in "the disobedience of faithlessness," unreceptive to what God promised to do
for them, and not persuaded that God could or would provide
what He promised. It was their choice; they chose not to enter
into the land of promised rest, and God gave them the consequences of their choices. They had no one to blame but themselves!

4:7   As it is the ever-persistent desire of God to make His
rest available to man, *"He again delineates some day:*
'Today'," in which His rest can be realized. This is not a reference to a certain, specific or particular day, for Paul notes that
the word was used in David's "day," and Paul is employing the
Davidic text to apply to the Jerusalem Christians of the first
century. These "last days" (1:2) of the Christian era, the "day
of salvation" (II Cor. 6:2; cf. Isa. 49:8), constitute the continued period of opportunity to experience God's grace and rest
in Jesus Christ. But more specifically for the Jerusalem
Christians to whom he was writing, Paul wanted to emphasize
the ever-present "rest" of the ever-present I AM, for "right
now."

God was *"saying through David after so long a time, as*
has been said before, 'TODAY IF YOU HEAR HIS VOICE,
DO NOT HARDEN YOUR HEARTS'." The promised rest
was not terminated or withdrawn when the younger generation
of Israelites finally entered Canaan after forty years of wandering. "After so long a time," the interval between Moses and
David, between the account in Numbers 13 and 14 and the
statements of David in Psalm 95:7-11, a period of approximately 450 years, David could still encourage his generation to
be receptive to God's promise of rest by listening to God's
revelatory voice and refraining from hardening their hearts.
When David wrote these quoted words (which Paul admits
have been previously cited in his epistle - 3:7,13,15) the people of Israel were already in the land of Canaan, but they were
still being encouraged to enter into God's rest, evidencing that
such rest was not just the occupation of a particular geographic
land parcel, nor was it limited to a particular time period.
God's rest is still available, Paul is repeatedly explaining to his
readers.

4:8   Continuing to document his argument, as all good
lawyers do, Paul wrote, *"For if Joshua had provided them*

rest, He (God, through David) *would not have spoken of another day beyond that day."* The name *Iesous* is the Greek form of both Joshua and Jesus, both meaning "Jehovah saves or delivers." The context of Paul's argument concerning the historical usage and availability of God's "rest" dictates that the most likely reference here is to Joshua, just as the name is translated in Luke 3:29 and Acts 7:45. The Authorized Version (KJV) translated the name as Jesus, creating numerous unnecessary interpretive problems.

When Joshua led the next generation into the promised land of rest across the Jordan river, they remained a people of bickering unbelief. They had arrived in the promised physical location of rest (Neh. 21:43-45; Josh. 21:43-45; 22:4,5; 23:1), but they had not found the "rest" that faithfully derived from God's provision. God's "rest" was not encompassed merely in residence in a particular country. One need only consider the period of the Judges and Kings in Israel's history to observe the unrest that the Hebrew peoples experienced in Canaan. By the time David became king of Israel (approximately 400 years after Joshua), he was still speaking for God of an available "rest" that required the receptivity of "hearing His voice" and the availability that refrained from "hardening their hearts" in self-determined actions. That continued promise of "rest" evidenced that God's "rest" was not limited to a particular place/time context in Canaan in the fifteenth century B.C. The promised land where the Hebrews could cease from oppressive enslavement was but another shadow-picture of a physical representation that pointed to a spiritual reality that could only be fully realized in Jesus Christ.

Paul's argument in well-reasoned, as usual: If God's rest was to be in the land of Canaan, and Joshua led them into the land, but they continued to experience unrest, then there must be a rest of another kind that is beyond the located placement of the land and residence therein. Likewise, if the day of God's rest was in Joshua's day, and God (through David) still promised a rest in David's day, then the "Today" of God's promised rest is not limited to the yesterday of a particular historical period, but to "another day beyond that day" – to the ever-present "Today" of God's people.

4:9   The conclusion Paul draws is: *"There remains therefore a Sabbath rest for the people of God."* God's promised rest remains open, available and accessible to be experienced by His people "Today." Paul's emphasis is on the present availability of God's rest, for he wanted the Jerusalem Christians to focus on all that was available to them in Christ Jesus in the present, rather than on a future expectation of a nationalistic "rest" after the hoped-for defeat of the Romans – a false hope, indeed, as verified by subsequent history within a few short years. Paul was encouraging the Christians of Judea to live their present lives in receptivity to the divine dynamic of the indwelling Spirit of Christ within them, rather than thinking that the "rest" of God was only an historical phenom-enon of yesteryear or a utopian hope for the future. Those who have interpreted this verse to mean that "there remains in the future a Sabbath rest for the people of God" have missed Paul's point entirely, and fall prey to the same utopian hopes that Paul was warning his readers against. The "Sabbath rest" that Paul refers to is not a paradisiacal repose in a millennial period of time with governance located once again in the Palestinian land as some have speculated. This is not to deny, however, that the Sabbath rest already available to the Christian in the present does not also have a continuum of ful-fillment into the future and unto eternity.

Paul's reference to a "Sabbath rest" picks up on the previ-ous citation of Genesis 2:2 where the Hebrew word for "rest" was *shabbath*. As noted above (4:4), the seventh day Sabbath observance of the Jewish people was based on the seventh day "rest" of God in creation (Exod. 20:8-10), and was intended to be a celebration of God's provision and a time to enjoy God's creation. The people and the land did not "enjoy the Sabbaths" (cf. Lev. 26:34,35) in Judaic religion, but now in the spiritual fulfillment of the new covenant God's people can enjoy the Sabbath rest by being receptive to what God has done and is doing, by living in the abundance of God's grace-dynamic. Paul's use of the Greek word *sabbatismos*, "Sabbath rest," instead of *katapausis*, "rest" (3:11,18; 4:1,3,5,10,11), is apparently designed to emphasize to his Jewish readers in Jerusalem that the Jewish seventh day Sabbath observance was also a provisional figure of the grace-rest that is available every day in every place to enjoy God in every way as Christians.

Whereas the "people of God" in the old covenant were the Israelites who were divinely selected to provide the physical prefiguring of God's intent in His Son, the "people of God" in the new covenant are those who are identified with the Son as Christians. Later in the epistle Paul will quote from the prophecy of Jeremiah indicating that in the promised new covenant, when God puts His Spirit and laws into the hearts of those receptive to His Son, "I will be their God, and they shall be My people" (8:10; Jere. 31:33). The apostle Peter explained to the Christians to whom he wrote, 'You are a people for God's own possession...; you once were not a people, but now you are the people of God" (I Pet. 2:9,10; cf. Ezek. 37:23; Hosea 1:10). Christians are the new covenant "people of God," the spiritual fulfillment of Israel (Rom. 9:6,7; Gal. 6:16) and the people known as Jews (Rom. 2:28,29).

There remained available to the Christians of Jerusalem the opportunity to participate in the Sabbath rest of God, to cease from all their striving to please God by keeping the Law, to refrain from trying to bring into being what they might have perceived to be God's plan to reestablish the nation of Israel, and to restfully enjoy God's grace moment-by-moment of every day. Such a Sabbath rest remains available to the Christian "people of God" in every age.

4:10   Continuing to develop the theme of "Sabbath rest" available for all Christians, Paul more specifically connects Christian "rest" with God's creation "rest" in Genesis 2:2, noting that God's rest in both categories involves a resting from "works." *"For the one who has been entered into His rest has himself also rested from his works, just as God did from His own."* Who is "the one" who has entered into God's rest and rested from his works? Some have understood this in a Christological sense as referring to Jesus Christ and His having entered back into the Father's rest after having rested from His redemptive works, just as God the Father rested from His creative works. The problem with such an interpretation is (1) it bifurcates the work of the divine Father and Son, thus impinging upon the trinitarian oneness of the Godhead, and (2) there is nothing in the immediate context of Paul's argument that would justify the insertion of a reference to Christ's redemptive work at this point. It is preferable, therefore, to understand "the one" being referred to as any (and every) individual Christian who is part of "the people of God" (4:9). Every regenerated Christian person "has been entered into" God's rest in Jesus Christ. The verb (*eiselthon*) is passive, meaning that the subject has been (aorist tense) acted upon by another. As Joshua (4:8) had ushered the Hebrew nation into the promised land of rest in Canaan, Jesus has ushered every Christian into the opportunity and availability of God's rest in Himself. But, as previously noted in the case of those who went into the promised land with Joshua, to be led in entrance into the place of rest does not necessarily entail experiencing God's rest subjectively by faithful receptivity to His activity. Likewise, it is true for Christians that "having been entered into" God's place of rest in Jesus Christ, there remains the choice of faith to experience God's rest by ceasing from our "works" orientation of religious performance, in order to rest in the sufficiency of His grace. This Christian responsibility to choose to experience God's rest will be emphasized anew in the next verse in an exhortation to diligence.

When the Christian enters experientially into God's grace-rest, he/she ceases and refrains from trying to perform for God. The "works" theology of dedicated performance that motivates so much of religious endeavor must be exchanged for a "grace" theology that recognizes that the objective of the Christian life is what God *does* in and through us, not what we might try to *do* for God. We "work out our salvation" by recognizing that "God is at work in us both to will and to work for His good pleasure" (Phil. 2:12,13), and allowing for His outworking expression as we are receptive to His activity (cf. James 2:17-26).

Since Christians are to rest from their works "as God did from His own" (Gen. 2:2), this must mean that as we rest in His sufficiency we appreciate and enjoy His sustaining work. To participate in God's rest is not passivism, for God always functions in accord with His character, and by our receptivity of faith we continue to allow for the outworking of His character in our behavior.

4:11   Paul exhorts his Jewish readers again (cf. 3:12; 4:1), ***"We should be diligent, therefore, to enter that rest, lest anyone fall by the same example of disobedience."*** He is emphasizing that Christians are responsible for choosing to be receptive in faith to what God in Christ wants to do in their lives. They should be eager and zealous to enter in to that experiential "rest."

To make his point, Paul refers again to the "example of disobedience" (3:18; 4:6) of the initial exodus generation (Numbers 13 and 14), who had no confidence that God was trustworthy to provide what He had promised. As a consequence their bodies "fell in the wilderness" (3:17). Using the same word (Greek *pipto*) Paul expressed his concern that any one (cf. 3:12; 4:6) of the Jerusalem Christians should likewise "fall" and fail to participate in all that was available to them in Jesus Christ. Similar language was employed by Paul in his letter to the Corinthians, where he referred to the Hebrew fore-fathers of the Exodus who "fell" (I Cor. 10:8), and who should serve as an "example" (I Cor. 10:6,11 – Greek word *tupos* has essentially the same meaning as *hupodeigma* used here). The exhortation to the Corinthians is similar to that made here to the Hebrew Christians in Judea: "Let him who thinks he stands take heed lest he fall" (I Cor. 10:12).

4:12   Many commentators have struggled to explain the con-nection of verses 12 and 13 to the foregoing argument. Does the "word of God" relate to the previous mention of "hearing His voice" (Ps. 95:7; Heb. 3:7,15; 4:7)? Is Paul indicating that in order to enter into experiential Christian rest Christians must allow for a piercing and penetrating evaluation of their motivations to examine why they are doing what they are doing? The answer to both questions appears to be "Yes."

"For" (to facilitate entering into God's rest) *"the Word of God is living and energizing and sharper than any two-edged knife,..."* Prior to the Reformation in the sixteenth century, the "Word of God" was interpreted almost exclusively as reference to the personified Word of God (John 1:1) incarnated in the Person of Jesus Christ (John 1:14). Reformation reaction to the ecclesiastical authority and pronouncements of the Roman Church, emphasized *sola scriptura* and elevated the Bible as the ultimate authority of the "word of God." Protestant inter-pretation for almost five centuries has tended to interpret "word of God" in this verse to refer to the written revelation of scripture, or to a more generalized reference to the gospel mes-sage or teaching that accords with the biblical record. The con-text, however, seems to demand reference to the living Lord Jesus who indwells Christians by the Spirit (Rom. 8:9), Who as the living "Word of God" continues to speak to our hearts that we might "hear His voice" and enter in to the grace-rest

that God intends for Christians. The personal pronouns of the
following verse (13), *"His* sight" and "the eyes of *Him,"* serve
to verify that Paul wrote of the personified "Word of God,"
Jesus Christ.

A book is not a living and energizing entity, although
God's message can be effective and energizing (I Thess. 2:13).
Through Isaiah God said, "My word which goes forth from
My mouth; It shall not return to Me empty, without accomplishing what I desire, and without succeeding in the matter
for which I send it" (Isa. 55:11). As the living "Word of God,"
Jesus is alive. He is life (John 11:25; 14:6). The words that He
speaks "are spirit and life" (John 6:63). The power of his life
energizes within us (Eph. 3:20), providing an ongoing personal
revelation (cf. Eph. 1:17,18; Phil. 3:15) that penetrates into the
recesses of our hearts.

The analogy that Paul uses to illustrate the Spirit of
Christ's penetrating power is that of a "two-edged knife." The
metaphorical reference in Revelation 1:16 to a "two-edged
sword" proceeding from Jesus' mouth uses the Greek word
romphaia which refers to a larger sword, spear or lance. The
Greek word *machaira* used here usually referred to a smaller
instrument more like a knife or dagger. It is interesting that the
Greek Old Testament (*LXX*) uses this word *machaira* as the
instrument used when Joshua required all the males to be cir-
cumcised immediately upon entry into the promised land of
rest (Josh. 5:2-8). Is there an allusion here to Christ's "circumcision of the heart" (Rom. 2:29; Col. 2:11), and the continued
penetrating action of the Spirit of Christ as He seeks to expose
all considerations that would keep Christians from resting in
the grace of God?

Christ's action as the "Word of God" in the Christian is
analogous to a "two-edged knife," ***"piercing as far as the division of both soul and spirit, of both joints and marrow, and
able to discern the inner passions and insights of the heart."***
A physical knife can penetrate down to the bone, to the inmost

marrow of the bone and to where the bones fit together at the
joints. Metaphorically, Jesus Christ as the "Word of God"
functions like a two-edged knife that penetrates into the depth
of our innermost being of soul and spirit (cf. I Thess. 5:23).
The purpose of the penetration is not destructive, but a constructive division in order to expose differentiation. Christian
theologians, at least since the Reformation, have by and large
not wanted to admit any division or differentiation between
soul and spirit in man, choosing instead to perpetuate an
ambiguous merging of the psychological and spiritual functions of the human individual. In so doing they have obscured
the regenerative and sanctifying work of the Spirit of Christ,
and denied many Christians a clear understanding of Christ's
revealing work to lead us into God's grace-rest.

In His desire to protect us from a "hardened heart" (3:8,15;
4:7), and from "an evil, unbelieving heart" (3:12), the Spirit of
Christ penetrates "to discern the inner passions and insights of
the heart" of the Christian. The contrasted dichotomy of "soul
and spirit" is likely retained in the respective differentiations
of Christ's discernment between the inner functions of the
inner being of the Christian individual. The New Testament
usage of the word "heart" is inclusive of both psychological
function (cf. II Cor. 8:16; II Thess. 2:17; James 1:26; I John
3:19-21) and spiritual function (Rom. 5:5; II Cor. 1:22; Gal.
4:6; Heb. 8:10; 10:16). The indwelling Christ, the "Word of
God," is able to differentiate between the psychological patterns of impassioned commitment and dedication to please
God in the self-effort of performance and the spiritual impulse
to operate by "the mind of Christ" (I Cor. 2:16) allowing God
to function in and through us by the dynamic of His grace.
Many Christians have the spiritual intent and purpose (cf. I
Pet. 4:1) to allow God to be and do all He wants to be and do
in their lives, but at the same time they have psychologically
patterned thoughts and attitudes of self-oriented desire to act
and "be all they can be for God." The differentiation between

130

the spiritual motivations of God's intent and the psychological motivations of a fleshly desire to seek "a logical alternative to faith" can be very difficult to discern. Many Christians seldom take the time to evaluate their motivations of why they are doing what they are doing in their Christian lives. To that end the Spirit of Christ acts within us to make that discernment and to reveal such to us that we might choose to be receptive to God's grace and participate in His rest.

Paul wanted the Christians in Jerusalem to "hear the voice" of the indwelling Christ who could and would reveal to them that the psychologically-based, well-reasoned efforts to oust the Romans and establish their own nation would not accomplish the purposed spiritual rest of God. All of their impassioned efforts of the "flesh" would end in naught, and they would never experience God's grace-rest in Christ, if they would not open themselves up to Christ's penetrating evaluation of their real motives and let the "Word of God" reveal what was going on in their inner man.

4:13 Christ is able and willing to discern and reveal our hearts, *"and there is no creature hidden from His sight, but all things are exposed, having been opened to the eyes of Him, the Word, before Whom (we have to do)."* God is omniscient, i.e., all-seeing and all-knowing, and no created thing is obscured from His sight. Adam and Eve tried unsuccessfully to hide from God (Gen. 3:9). Ananias and Sapphira thought they could pull the wool over God's eyes, but the Spirit of the Lord revealed their charade to Peter (Acts 5:1-11). Christian people, in particular, are transparent before the Spirit of Christ, for He knows every thought, attitude and motivation. We are naked, bare, exposed and vulnerable before the living "Word of God." It is impossible to deceive Him with any masks, facades or pretenses.

The final phrase of this verse is difficult to translate, as it appears to lack adequate verb action. Literally translated in accord with original word-order it reads, "of Him before whom to us the word." Paul repeats his mention of "the Word" (Greek *ho logos*) with which he began the previous sentence (4:12). The objective was to explain to the Christians in Jerusalem that the personified "Word of God," the living Lord Jesus Who lived in them, knew what was motivating them and wanted to reveal how He could lead them into spiritual rest. Paul's intent was similar to his statement to the Romans: "He who searches our hearts knows what the mind of the Spirit is, because He intercedes for the saints according to the will of God" (Rom. 8:27). The theme of Christ's all-knowing discernment leads directly into the following explanation of Christ's intercessory work as high priest.

Concluding Remarks:

The first readers of this epistle found themselves in the turmoil of political unrest, as well as the unrest of religious and economic ostracism from their Jewish kinsmen for having accepted Jesus as the Messiah. A pseudo-rest was being promised by the Zealots of Palestine – a false-rest that corresponded with the land promise of rest made to another generation of their forebears approximately one and a half millennia earlier. The insurrectionists were promising that by revolt against Rome the Jewish people would again govern their own nation in the land that God promised them, and be able to "rest" from the oppression of Rome.

Paul explained to the Christians in Jerusalem that the risen Lord Jesus, the "Word of God" Who lived in them, knew the pressures that were being brought to bear upon them. Similar pressure was brought to bear upon Him to be a military and political deliverer when they wanted to make Him "King of the Jews." Paul seems to be saying, "Jesus knows your tendencies to put your faith in physical realities of land, race, nation and religion. Jesus knows your psychological inclinations to declare, "We can do it! We can pull it off!" by the fleshly self-effort of dedication and commitment to what is perceived to be 'God's cause.' But the "rest" of God is in Jesus Christ alone, for it is a spiritual rest that relies on God's grace within the dynamic of Christ's life, allowing you to cease from all your performance efforts to accomplish great things for God. Now is the time, 'Today,' to listen to His voice and remain receptive to God's supernatural divine activity. Jesus knows the external circumstances you are confronted with, as well as the internal motivations of your hearts, and that is why He can be a sympathetic high priest representing you before God as well as providing His rest within you."

The message remains pertinent to all Christians in subsequent times and in diverse places. The fallen world-order always presents us with a form of unrest, whether it be political, economic, religious, interpersonal, etc. Since the fall of man into sin we have been brainwashed with the humanistic premise that mankind has what it takes to solve the world's problems and create "rest." "The way to rest," the modern-day zealots declare, "is to get better educated, develop better skills, elect better government with better leaders, get better organized, and utilize better technology for increased productivity." On a more personal level "rest" is sought on the weekend, by taking a vacation at a resort or on a cruise liner, or by taking a new job or a new spouse. The false offers of "rest" are presented to us just as they were to the first recipients of this letter.

Jesus said, "Come unto Me, all who are weary and heavy-laden, and I will give you rest. You shall find rest for your souls" (Matt. 11:28,29). Augustine responded, "My heart, O Lord, does not rest until it rests in You." Rest is not found in increased religious dedication and commitment to performance and "works," but by living out of the divine dynamic of God's grace, by recognizing that "it is no longer I who lives, but Christ lives in me" (Gal. 2:20), by appreciating that our "good works" are only those which "God prepared beforehand that we should walk in them" (Eph. 2:10), and by enjoying "the power that works within us" (Eph. 3:20). This is not to imply that we replace the self-effort of performance with acquiescent passivism, but rather with the active power of God. Neither is there any implication that participation in God's rest in Christ will lead to avoidance of all the unrest of the world around us, for God's rest is not a rest *from* the circumstances and trials of life, but a rest *in the midst of* the problems of a life that may be busier than ever before. It is resting in His sufficiency, for "we are not adequate to consider anything as coming from ourselves, but our adequacy is of God" (II Cor. 3:5).

Christians continue to participate in God's rest as they continue to respond to God in faith (4:2). Christian faith is our receptivity to God's activity. Christians are not excluded from participating in the experience of God's rest because they have trials or are being tempted, nor even because they fail and misrepresent Jesus Christ in sinful behavior. Exclusion from God's rest comes only by a settled attitude of unbelief, a disposition of distrust in God that leads to disobedience day in and day out. In that case God will let such persons have their choice of unrest – without and within. But God continues to make available "the better rest of God" in Jesus Christ. "Let us be diligent, therefore, to enter that rest" (4:11).

JESUS

The Better
Divine-Human High Priest

Hebrews 4:14 – 5:10

Paul had previously given his readers a clue that he intended to address how Jesus Christ is the better High Priest of God. In the context of explaining that Jesus is the "better Man for man" (2:5-18), Paul noted that "He (Jesus) had to be made like His brethren in all things, that He might become a merciful and faithful high priest in things pertaining to God, to make propitiation for the sins of the people" (2:17). He continued by writing, "Therefore, holy brethren, partakers of a heavenly calling, consider Jesus, the Apostle and High Priest of our confession" (3:1). The topic of Jesus as "the better high priest" is a primary, if not the predominant, theme of this epistle, mentioned, as noted, in 2:17 and 3:1, considered preliminarily in 4:14–5:10 (the passage presently being exegeted), and dealt with at length in the four chapters 7:1–10:18. Taken together, these passages comprise over thirty-three percent (33%) of the epistle.

Reading these words almost two millennia after the termination of the high priesthood function in the Jewish religion, it is necessary that we recall the importance of this priestly office in the history of Judaism. The position of high priest or chief priest was implemented in the Levitical regulations that God revealed to the Israelites people through Moses (cf. Lev. 21:10; Num. 35:25). The first high priest was Aaron, the brother of Moses, and the succession of subsequent high priests was

135

transferred to a son (usually the eldest son) of the previous high priest (cf. Ezra 7:1-5). The lineage of the Jewish high priesthood was originally determined by heritage of birth, and the duration was for the lifetime of the high priest. One of the prominent high priests in the Aaronic succession was Zadok, who served during the transition of the royal throne from David to Solomon (cf. I Kings 1:32-48). Subsequent high priests often linked their hereditary right to the high priesthood through Zadok.

After the exile of the Hebrew people in Babylon and their return to Canaan, the absence of a king in the line of David allowed the high priest to assume a position of defining importance to the people of Israel, often effectively serving as both priest and king. In the second century B.C., when Antiochus IV Epiphanes (215-163 B.C.), king of Syria, invaded Palestine, there was a power struggle between Onias II, the last high priest in legitimate Aaronic succession, and Jason, who though from a priestly family, was appointed by Antiochus IV Epiphanes to serve as high priest (175-172 B.C.). Menelaus, from a non-priestly family, was subsequently appointed high priest by Antiochus, and served from 172-163 B.C. The atrocities of Antiochus IV Epiphanes in killing Jewish leaders, pillaging the temple, establishing pagan religion in the temple, and sacrificing a pig on the altar, led to the Maccabean Revolt (cf. I, II Macabbees). When Jonathan the Hasmonean assumed the robes of the high priesthood in 153 B.C., he was not from the Aaronic-Zadokian lineage, and the newly formed Pharisee movement protested the legitimacy of his high priesthood.

By the time of Herod the Great, Roman king of Judea (37-4 B.C.), the Jewish high priesthood was granted by appointment of the Roman king from among candidates in the Levitical priesthood, though not necessarily from the Aaronic-Zadokian family line. During the first century A.D., Herod Agrippa I, Herod of Chalcis, and Herod Agrippa II granted the high priestly office to a few wealthy priestly families with arbitrary depositions and appointments. The Jewish Talmud indicates that the high priest purchased the office from the Roman government in an annual auction to the highest bidder. The high priest continued to perform ceremonial duties in the temple at Jerusalem, especially on the occasion of the annual Day of Atonement, and served as a liaison between the Jewish people and the Roman government. This wealthy group of high priestly families was unscrupulous and took advantage of the common people by graft and assumption of others' property. "During the 106 years between 37 B.C. and A.D. 70, 28 high priests discharged the office, and 25 of them were of non-legitimate priestly families."[1]

Knowing that the high priests purchased their position from the Roman government, and being the victims of their avarice, the people of Palestine regarded them with suspicion and contempt. As the anti-Roman sentiment grew in the middle part of the first century, the high priests were increasingly suspected to be Roman collaborators and traitors. The Pharisees, always concerned with the Law, still wanted the high priesthood returned to the Aaronic and Zadokian descendants. The Zealots exploited that conservative desire to foment revolutionary aspirations of insurrection against Rome, promising that the success of such revolution would reestablish the legitimate high priest in the temple and reestablish the Jewish nation with a king in the Davidic line.

That was the situation when Paul wrote this epistle to the Jewish Christians in Jerusalem. The Judean Christians were being pressured to join the *cause celebre* to reestablish their ethnic rights in the land. It would have been very difficult to avoid getting drawn into the political, racial, and religious tidal wave of discontent. Paul wrote to explain to these Christians that what they had received in Jesus Christ was superior to all the utopian dreams being offered by the revolutionaries. Jesus is better than Moses in leading the people of God into faithfulness (3:1-19). Jesus is better than Joshua in ushering the people of God into divine Rest (4:1-13). Now Paul will explain that Jesus is better than Aaron, for He is the fulfillment of God's intent for a High Priest, serving as the universal and eternal High Priest in the order of Melchizedek. From Paul's perspective, to seek after the physical phenomena was but a backward reversion to the pictorial prefigurings that preliminarily pointed to Jesus Christ. Paul wanted the Christians of Jerusalem to understand that the intents and promises of God for His people were all fulfilled in the Person and work of Jesus Christ, Who now served as the more effective divine-human High Priest. Traditional Jewish thinking would have questioned how Jesus could serve as high priest since He did not have Aaronic and Zadokian heritage, and was from the tribe of Judah (cf. Matt. 1:3; Lk. 3:33) rather than the priestly tribe of Levi. Paul's explanation was that the previous high priesthood of Melchizedek took precedence, allowing Jesus to serve as the spiritual fulfillment of the ultimate High Priest of God, as well as the King of Kings in the fulfillment of David's royal rule.

From the perspective of historical hindsight we can look back to see the false promises being offered to the Christians of Jerusalem by the Zealot revolutionaries. Soon after this letter was written the Zealots took control of Jerusalem during the war that raged from A.D. 66-70. When they did so, they killed many from the wealthy high-priestly families. A new high priest was selected by random lot from among the priestly families. His name was Phinehas ben Samuel, a stonemason by trade. He was the last to serve as Jewish high priest, for the position was terminated in A.D. 70 when the Romans destroyed the temple in Jerusalem and decimated the Jewish people in Palestine, rendering the Jewish high priesthood as but an historical phenomenon.

Paul's assertion that Jesus is the universal, permanent High Priest of God was the only viable option that his Christians readers in Jerusalem had. Almost two millennia after Paul's

writing, Jesus continues to serve as the eternal divine-human
High Priest of God, verifying Paul's words to the Hebrews,
and allowing for "a kingdom of priests" (Exod. 19:6) as God
intended, a "royal priesthood" (I Peter 2:9) inclusive of all
Christians identified with Jesus Christ, functioning as the
"priesthood of all believers" in the Body of Christ, the Church.

4:14   *"Since then"* the Spirit of Christ lives in the Christian
as the living Word of God who penetrates to the core of our
being and knows our every thought and intent (4:12,13), *"We
have a great high priest who has passed through the heavens, Jesus the Son of God"*. Christians have a High Priest
Who is better and superior to the Judaic high priesthood,
which had been politically corrupted for centuries. The high
priesthood of Jesus, standing as the Man closest to God representing man before God, is of a different order that transcends
the physical priesthood that functioned in the temple at
Jerusalem. The high priests of the old covenant passed through
the outer courts and the Holy Place into the Holy of Holies of
the temple once a year on the Day of Atonement. Jesus, the
High Priest *par excellence*, has passed through the ultimate
Holy of Holies, the very presence of God, having come from
God (John 6:38,42; 8:42; 17:18) and returned to (John 14:3,4;
16:5,10; 17:5,13) the presence of God the Father, as He is in
Himself the Son of God (cf. 1:2,5,8; 3:6). The divine Son of
God (cf. John 10:30; 14:10) has become the human High
Priest on behalf of all mankind. This integration of the divine
Son and the human high priest (cf. 5:5,6,8,10) is central to
Paul's argument. The ontological Being of the divine Son is
expressed in the operational function of the human high priest
as could only be accomplished in the God-man, Jesus Christ.
As God, who alone can forgive sin, Jesus served as the human
high priest representative of man before God the Father,
becoming the only sufficient sacrifice that satisfied the death
consequences of man's sin before God. Having accomplished

what God the Father had sent Him, as the Son of God, to do (John 17:4; 19:30), He "passed through the heavens" and ascended again to take His rightful place seated at the right hand of the Majesty in the heavens (cf. 1:3; 8:1; 10:12; 12:2), thereby opening the way for all those "in Him" to enter into the Holy of Holies of God's heavenly presence also (cf. John 14:2-6; Heb. 10:19-23).

On the basis of this superior and supreme high priesthood function of Jesus, the Son of God, Paul encouraged the Jerusalem Christians, saying, *"We should hold fast our confession."* The precarious political situation in Jerusalem was such that prevailing winds of public opinion were clinging to the false hopes of revolutionary triumph over Rome. Paul wanted these embattled Christian brethren to cling to their confession of Jesus Christ instead of the false physical hopes. They had confessed Jesus as Lord (Rom. 10:9), agreeing and concurring with God that Jesus was the Messiah, the Son of God, the only basis of redemption from sin and the restoration of humanity to function as God intended. As Paul repeats later in the epistle, "Let us hold fast the confession of our hope without wavering, for He Who promised is faithful" (10:23).

4:15   The Jewish Christians in Palestine were vulnerable and susceptible to the temptation to revert to the physical aspirations of their kinsmen. No doubt they were sympathetic to their plight and their plea to join the effort to overthrow the oppression of the Romans. The frailty of human perseverance could easily have capitulated in volitional weakness.

Paul wanted to emphasize that even though Jesus was the supreme High Priest Who had passed through the heavens (14), He was not aloof, remote and transcendent to the extent that He was unable to understand what the Jerusalem Christians were being confronted with. *"For we do not have a high priest who cannot sympathize with our weaknesses."* The high priest was always human, and Jesus was "made like

His brethren in all things" (2:17), in complete solidarity with human experience, qualifying Him to serve as high priestly intercessor. The double negative of "do not...cannot" constitutes a positive expression of Jesus' ability to sympathize with the tough choice that the Jerusalem Christians were being asked to make in holding fast their confession. Such sympathy was not just an emotional feeling, but was the result of physical identification with humanity faced with life and death choices. The "weaknesses" with which Jesus could empathetically identify were not physical lack of strength, but the human vulnerability of volitional perseverance, the fallible and fickle weakness of the human will in continuing to choose God's way. The only way for the Christian to overcome such volitional lack of strength (the Greek word for "weakness" is *asthenos*, meaning "no strength") is to rely on "Him Who strengthens us" (Phil. 4:13).

Jesus, the supreme High Priest, could sympathize with the volitional vulnerabilities of the Palestinian Christians for He was *"one having been tempted in all things as we are, yet without sin."* The Greek word for "tempt" (*peirazo*) has a root meaning of "piercing in order to test or examine," but when used in reference to sin (as it is here), the English word that conveys a solicitation to sin is the word "tempt." The Christians in Judea were being sorely tempted to take the path of least resistance and to "give in" to the pressures being brought to bear upon them, and it would have been the easiest course of action to claim to lack the strength to resist and to hold fast to their confession of Jesus. Functioning as a man during His redemptive mission on earth, Jesus was likewise vulnerable to the temptation to choose to take the path of least resistance, to avoid the ostracism and the rejection of His own Jewish peoples, and that in the midst of life and death choices. But Jesus "held fast" to His confession of divine identity, and when faced with death declared, "Father, if You are willing, let this cup (of suffering and death) pass from Me; yet not My will, but Thine be done" (Matt. 26:39; Mk. 14:36; Lk. 22:42). Paul was asking the beleaguered Christians in Jerusalem to find their strength in Jesus Christ, and to "hold fast" as Jesus Himself had "held fast" when faced with temptation.

Some have questioned whether Jesus could actually be tempted to sin. They reason that since Jesus is God, and "God cannot be tempted by evil" (James 1:13), therefore Jesus experienced a trial of testing, but it was not a temptation to sin. The context of Paul's reference to Jesus' identification with the volitional vulnerabilities of humanity, and the statement that the solicitation to sin did not result in a choice to sin in Jesus' experience, serve as an exegetical dismissal of those who would deny Jesus' real temptation to sin. Theologically, this theory of impeccability that posits that it was not possible for Jesus to sin is based on a deficient Christology that fails to account for Jesus' functional humanity (the very emphasis that Paul is making in this passage concerning the human high priesthood of Jesus). Calvinistic theology, in general, tends to overemphasize the deity of Jesus to the neglect of His functional humanity and the human responsibility that Jesus faced in making choices of faith. The remarks of W. Ian Thomas are pertinent here:

> It is no explanation to suggest that though tempted the Lord Jesus Christ was not tempted with evil, but only in the sense that He was tested – for the statement "yet without sin," clearly indicates that the nature of the temptation was such that it would have led to sin had it not been resisted.
> ...inherent in His willingness to be made Man, was the willingness of the Lord Jesus Christ to be made subject to temptation, for strange as it may seem, inherent in man's capacity to be godly is man's very capacity to sin!
> ...it was not as God that Christ was tempted, but as Man...[2]

How can it be said that Jesus was "tempted in all things according to the likeness" of our temptations? Obviously there are external situations (trials) that Jesus never confronted, i.e., automobile traffic, marriage, parenting, technology, etc. But "made like His brethren (humanity) in all things" (2:17), He was "tempted in all things as we are" – tempted to make decisions to act and react contrary (outside of) the character and behavior derived out of God, which constitutes sin in its broadest sense. The "all things" of Jesus' temptation are not the same circumstances, but are the same manner of being solicited to choose selfish action and reaction. In the wilderness (Matt. 4:1-11; Lk. 4:1-13), Jesus was solicited to choose personal aspiration, personal gratification, and personal reputation (cf. I John 2:16) instead of being the available vessel of God's ministry of redemption. In the garden of Gethsemane, Jesus appears to have been tempted to react with fight and fright and flight, rather than choosing to give His life a ransom for all men (Matt. 20:28; I Tim. 2:6). It might even be argued that Jesus was tempted beyond the likeness of normal human temptations, being tempted to opt out of His functional subordination as man, and to act independently out of His inherent deity, in which case He would not have been totally identified with the experiences of mankind, and could not have fulfilled his redemptive and intercessory work on our behalf. Such is but hypothetical speculation, for the facts of the matter are that though "tempted in all things as we are," He was "yet without sin," choosing not to succumb to the solicitations to sin, but to functionally subordinate Himself in receptivity to God.

Some have argued that Jesus could not be "tempted as we are" because He did not share the fallen nature of fallen humanity. He was never a "natural man" (I Cor. 2:14), "by nature a child of wrath" (Eph. 2:3), spiritually constituted as a "sinner" (Rom. 5:19), as all the rest of humanity has been constituted by the Fall. Granted, Jesus did not partake of fallen humanity in the sense of being spiritually "dead in trespasses and sins" (Eph. 2:1,5), but He did come "in the likeness of sinful flesh" (Rom. 8:2) in the sense of being vulnerable to temptation and liable to mortality. The argument is specious, though, because the solicitation to sinful choices and actions does not require a fallen spiritual nature. Adam is the case in point, for he was tempted to sin prior to the Fall. Jesus, the "second man" (I Cor. 15:47) and the "last Adam" (I Cor. 15:45), in Whom Satan had no foothold (John 14:30), could be tempted to sin by the external solicitations of the Tempter, as was the first Adam. Others have argued that Jesus' temptations are not the same as those Christians confront because He did not share in the patterned propensities to selfishness and sinfulness in the desires of His soul – what Paul seems to identify as the "flesh" in a behavioral sense (cf. Rom. 7:18–8:13; Gal. 5:13-21). Granted, Jesus had no such patterning of sinfulness, but, again, the argument is not valid because Adam did not have such either when he was tempted to sin originally.

Jesus was fully human and fully vulnerable to the temptations to sin that "are common to man" (I Cor. 10:13). Functioning as a man, He chose not to succumb to such temptation, relying instead on God the Father in Him to manifest righteousness. Therefore, no one, and in particular, no Christian, can claim that "Jesus could live like He did, because He was God; but I am incapable of such avoidance of sin, because I am just human." This is an illegitimate cop-out. Jesus lived every moment in time for thirty-three years "without sin," not because He was God (though He was), but because He was a man who chose not to submit to Satan's solicitations to sin, but rather to submit Himself to God the Father (James 4:7) and the expression of divine character in the human behavior of the Son. These chosen actions, Paul argues, allowed Him to serve as the supreme High Priest of God for all mankind.

That Jesus was "without sin" does not mean, therefore, that Jesus was "without temptation to sin," or "without a sin-nature," or "without the patterning of sin in the 'flesh'," but refers to Jesus having been fully tempted to sin without succumbing to the solicitations of sin, and without manifesting sinful character and behavior. Later in the epistle Paul will note that Jesus was a "high priest, holy, innocent, undefiled, separated from sinners" (7:26), and thus capable of "offering Himself without blemish" (9:14). To the Corinthians, Paul explained that Jesus "knew no sin" (II Cor. 5:21). The Apostle John wrote that "in Him there is no sin" (I John 3:5), and the Apostle Peter, quoting from Isaiah 53:9, indicated that Christ "committed no sin, nor was any deceit found in His mouth" (I Peter 2:22). The sinlessness of Jesus was not merely passive avoidance of sin, but was the perfect expression of the divine character of perfection in the behavior of the man, Christ Jesus, as He was receptive to allow the Father to work in Him (John 14:10). Jesus could thus legitimately declare, "I always do those things which are pleasing to Him" (John 8:29).

4:16 Continuing his appeal to the Jerusalem Christians, Paul writes, *"Let us therefore"* (because we have such a sinless High Priest who can sympathize with our weaknesses) *"draw near with confidence to the throne of grace."* The redemptive and restorative work of Jesus Christ allows Christians to have free, unrestricted access to the presence of God. In the old covenant the Jewish high priest had access to the "mercy-seat" in the Holy of Holies of the tabernacle and temple just once a year on the Day of Atonement. In the new covenant arrangement, Jesus is the High Priest Who by the sacrifice of Himself has opened the way for all Christians to be priests (I Pet. 2:9; Rev. 1:6), the "priesthood of all believers," with immediate, always available, unending personal access to God's presence and provision. Throughout this epistle Paul implores the Christians in Jerusalem to "draw near to God" (7:19) "with a sincere heart in full assurance of faith" (10:22), for they "have confidence to enter the Holy Place" (10:19) of God's presence based on Christ's High Priesthood. Paul seeks to discourage these brethren from seeking to reinstall the Aaronic-Zadokian high priesthood of the Jewish temple with its annual mediated access to the mercy-seat. Instead, he desires that the Christians of Judea should prayerfully and worshipfully approach the "throne of grace," "the throne of the Majesty in the heavens" (8:1), the very presence of God, directly with a bold, freedom of speech in personal communion.

The God of the Christian is not a remote, impersonal god seated on a judgment-seat to be approached in cowering fear. Rather, He is a loving and personal God with Whom Christians are relationally united through Christ, and to Whom we can freely approach His "throne of grace," confident that He will "freely give us all things" (Rom. 8:32) in the free-flow of His sufficiency, *that we may receive mercy and may find grace to help in time of need."* Jesus, "the merciful and faithful High Priest" (2:17) "is able to come to the aid of those who are tempted" (2:18), and the Christian will continually discover the provision and empowering of God's grace-activity as he/she is receptive to such in faith. We are not left defenseless and helpless as orphans (John 14:18). "The Lord is our Helper" (13:6), providing everything necessary "in time of need." The Jerusalem Christians were certainly confronted with a "time of need" as the battle cries of revolution were sounding, and they were being pressured to declare their loyalties. They needed to "draw near with confidence to the throne of grace, in order to receive mercy and discover God's grace in their time of need."

5:1   As Paul did in his discussion of the superiority of Jesus Christ over Moses (3:1-6), he again notes first the similarities and then the dissimilarities with the old covenant prototype. Comparing the similarities of Christ's High Priesthood to the Judaic high priesthood in verses 1-5a, Paul then contrasts the uniqueness and superiority of Christ's High Priesthood, noting the dissimilarities in verses 5b-10. The contrasted dissimilarities will be further developed in chapters 7-10 of the epistle.

"For every high priest taken from among men is appointed on behalf of men in things pertaining to God." Every high priest was a human representative of mankind before God. Jesus was no exception to this rule. Jesus was fully human, a man "among men," fully identified with, sympathizing with, and representative of all mankind. Every human high priest was appointed, authorized and installed "on behalf of men in things pertaining to God." Despite the historical aberrations when Jewish high priests were appointed by Antiochus Epiphanes and the Roman kings, the intended appointment of high priests was to be divinely authorized selection and deployment. These high priests were representatives on behalf of their fellow men to "minister as priests to God" (cf. Exod. 28:1,3; 29:1).

The responsibility and duty of the high priests was *"to offer both gifts and sacrifices for sins"* before God. This sacrificial function of the high priests of Judaism was particularly employed on the Day of Atonement on behalf of the transgressions, impurities and sins of the Jewish peoples (cf. Lev. 16:16). Though some have emphasized the difference between "gifts" and "sacrifices," regarding them as cereal offerings versus animal sacrifices, or distinguishing between unbloody and bloody offerings, the differentiation of these words should not be unduly pressed, as they can be used synonymously. All of the "gifts and sacrifices" offered by the high priests of the old covenant were but pictorial prototypes of the singular offerings and sacrifice of Jesus Christ (cf. Heb. 9:11-28; 10:12) within His function as the ultimate High Priest in the new covenant. God wearied and was not pleased with the offerings and sacrifices of the old covenant priests (cf. Isa. 1:11,13; Jere. 6:20; Heb. 10:5-10), for He was fully aware that Christ's giving of Himself (cf. Matt. 20:28; Gal. 1:4; 2:20) and sacrifice of Himself (cf. I Cor. 5:7; Heb. 9:26) was the only offering that could effectively deal with man's sin.

Paul wanted the Jerusalem Christians to recognize that the High Priesthood of Jesus Christ had effected God's redemptive intents. There was no reason for them to place any expectation or hope in the reestablishment of the Jewish high priesthood and their sacrificial functions.

5:2   The similarity of the Jewish high priests and the High Priesthood of Jesus is further explained as Paul writes, *"he* ("every high priest" – 5:1) *can deal gently with the ignorant and misguided, since he himself also is beset with weakness;..."* All high priests (Jesus included), because they were human and thus encompassed by their own human weakness, susceptibility, vulnerability and fallibility can exercise a forbearing and moderated passion toward the ignorant and misguided masses of humanity in their sin. The Jewish high priests were surrounded (cf. 12:1) by their own weakness (Greek *asthenos*, meaning "lack of strength") and volitional vulnerability (cf. 7:28), which led inevitably to their own sinful actions (cf. 5:3). Jesus could "sympathize with such weakness" and volitional vulnerability of mankind, being "tempted in all ways as we are" as a man (4:15), but His temptation did not lead to sin, allowing Him to be "a Son, made perfect forever" (7:28). In both cases, however, the high priests of Judaism and Jesus the supreme High Priest of God, because they were identified with humanity in such volitional weakness, could fairly and gently respond to the masses of mankind who did not know the way or had wandered from the way of God, being ignorant and deceived. High priests, being human, ought to be able to recognize the limitations of human volition and its inability to self-generate either sinful or righteous character and behavior.

5:3   *"...and because of it* (his solidarity with the volitional weakness of humanity) *he* ("every high priest" – 5:1) *is obligated to offer* ("gifts and sacrifices" – 5:1) *for sins, as for the* *people, so also* (in the case of the Jewish high priests) *for himself."* Since the high priest is always human, "taken from among men" (5:1), and personally aware of the volitional vulnerabilities of human choices of receptivity, it is incumbent upon the high priest to offer sacrifices before God for the sins of the people whom he represents. In the case of the Jewish high priest, he also had to offer sacrifice for his own personal sins as well as those of the people (cf. Lev. 4:3; 9:8; 16:6,11; Heb. 7:27; 9:7). In the case of Jesus, Who was "without sin" (4:15), a "High Priest...separated from sinners" (7:26), He Himself could become the singularly sufficient sinless sacrifice that would suffice as the death consequences for the sins of all mankind forever. The dissimilarity of Jesus and the Jewish high priests is already evident in these initial verses (1-5a) which focus on the similarity of the Judaic and Christic high priesthoods.

5:4 *"And not one* (of the high priests) *takes the honor* (of the high priesthood) *unto himself, but is called under God, even as Aaron* (was)."* High priesthood is not a self-assumed, self-appointed position. Such self-assumption of such a position of honor and glory would evidence arrogant ambition and pride of position or power which would disallow compassionate identification with the people being served. Biblical examples of those who self-assumed a priestly position for themselves (ex. Korah – Num. 16:1-40; Saul – I Sam. 13:8-14; Uzziah – II Chron. 26:16-23) evidences the extreme displeasure and consequences of God for such self-assumption. The high priesthood is not a self-conferred and self-elected human institution, but was designed by God to be a divine vocation authorized by divine appointment, even as Aaron was originally appointed, anointed and ordained by God to serve as high priest (cf. Num. 3:3,10; 18:7,8; Ps. 105:26). To be thus "called under God" as high priest involves submitting oneself in dependency and humility to be the vessel that God uses to represent His people to Himself.

5:5 *"So also the Christ did not glorify Himself so as to become high priest."* The Christ, the Messiah, the Anointed One, by the very designation of His name, was elected, appointed and anointed by God to be the eternal High Priest of God for mankind. There was no self-elevation, but only a self-emptying (cf. Phil. 2:7) of independent divine prerogatives of function in order to serve as the ultimate divine-human High Priest. Jesus did not seek His own glory (cf. John 5:41; 8:50,54), but as the "Elect One" of God (cf. Lk. 23:35), He was "called under God" (5:4) to minister in the dependency and receptivity to God's activity, "doing nothing of His own initiative" (John 5:19,30; 8:28; 12:49; 14:10).

Ministering thus as the available High Priest representative of mankind, Jesus "did not glorify Himself...*but He* (God the Father) *Who said to Him, 'THOU ART MY SON, TODAY I HAVE BEGOTTEN THEE'."* Jesus glorified the Father by accomplishing the work He was given to do (cf. John 17:4), and in glorifying God the Father, He was Himself glorified in Him (John 13:31,32). The subsequent glorification of the Son came in the resurrection victory and Pentecostal outpouring of the Spirit of Christ (cf. John 7:39; 12:16; 13:31). This ties in, then, with the Father's declaration as quoted from Psalm 2:7, "Thou art My Son; Today I have begotten Thee." Paul previously employed this same quotation in arguing the superiority of Jesus over angels (1:5), but now he uses the statement to explain the superiority of Christ's High Priesthood over the Judaic high priesthood. This is not a statement about the commencement of the parentage of God the Father in begetting God the Son. Rather, as Paul noted in his message at Antioch of Pisidia (Acts 13:33) when he quoted this same verse, this is a declaration of the glorification of Jesus Christ when God raised Him from the dead (cf. Acts 2:24; Rom. 4:24; 6:4; Eph.

1:20; Col. 2:12) and brought Him out of death into life by resurrection. Jesus "was declared the Son of God with power by the resurrection from the dead" (Rom. 1:4), a declaration of the Son's empowerment to serve as the eternal divine-human High Priest for all mankind. The uniting of the "Son" and "high priest" (cf. 4:14, as well as the quotation from both Psalm 2 in this verse and Psalm 110 in the following verse) reveals the ontological and operation features of Christological essence and function.

5:6 Continuing to document the superiority of the High Priesthood of Jesus, Paul writes, *"just as He* (God the Father) *says in another* (place or passage), *'THOU ART A PRIEST FOREVER ACCORDING TO THE ORDER OF MELCHIZEDEK'."* This quotation from Psalm 110:4 will be a primary and recurring assertion of the superiority of Christ's High Priesthood throughout this epistle, mentioned again in 5:10 and 6:20, and quoted again in 7:17 and 21. The biblical narrative of Melchizedek's priesthood is located in Genesis 14:18-20:

> And Melchizedek, King of Salem, brought out bread and wine. Now he was a priest of God Most High. And he (Melchizedek) blessed him (Abram) and said, "Blessed be Abram of God Most High, Possessor of heaven and earth. And blessed be God Most High, Who has delivered your enemies into your hand." And he (Abram) gave him (Melchizedek) a tenth of all.

The Melchizedekan priesthood was a non-Jewish and universal priesthood which was archetypical of all priesthood; its priority of time and type making it superior to the Jewish Aaronic and Levitical priesthood. The Jewish high priesthood was provisional and temporary for a specific interim purpose preliminary to the coming of the Messiah in the provincial context of the Hebrew peoples. Soon, within approximately 5 years from the writing of this epistle, it would be historically terminated when the temple in Jerusalem was destroyed in A.D. 70. The Melchizedekan priesthood, on the other hand, is not based on generational succession, but is of a divine "order" wherein the divine Messiah assumes the divine priesthood forever, "unto the ages," never to be succeeded and having no successors. The anointed Messianic priesthood of Jesus in the high priestly "order of Melchizedek" is indisputably superior to all other priesthoods, Paul argues. The previous words of Psalm 110:4 are, "The Lord has sworn and will not change His mind." Paul wanted the Christians in Jerusalem to understand the unique superiority of Christ's priesthood as they faced the pressure to join the cause to fight for the reestablishment of an uncorrupted generational Jewish high priest in the Jerusalem temple.

5:7 To explain the development of Jesus' sympathizing (4:15) sensitivities with mankind, Paul indicated that *"In the days of His flesh, He offered up both prayers and supplications with loud crying and tears to the One able to save Him from death."* In His incarnate, earthly form, in the physicality of bodily human existence, Jesus participated in emotional identification with the anguish and agony of human experience. Contextual examples of such heart-felt emotional entreaties to God the Father might include the experiences in the garden of Gethsemane (cf. Matt. 26:36-46; Mk. 14:32-42; Lk. 22:39-46; John 12:27), as well as the anguish of Golgotha (cf. Matt. 27:33-50; Mk. 15:16-37; Lk. 23:33-46; John 19:17-30), though not to be limited to such.

Did Jesus pray that He might be delivered from death by crucifixion? He did pray, "My Father, if it is possible, let this cup (of suffering or death) pass from Me" (Matt. 26:39; Mk. 14:35.36). John records Jesus' words, "Now My soul has become troubled; and what shall I say, 'Father, save Me from this hour?' But for this purpose I came to this hour" (John 12:27). Jesus knew that He "came to give His life a ransom for many" (Matt. 20:28; cf. I Tim. 2:6). Were Jesus' supplicatory

x

prayers requests to be kept from physical death? Or were they requests to be preserved in the midst of "being made sin" (II Cor. 5:21), becoming the cursed (Gal. 3:13) recipient of the judgment of God against all sin, and experiencing the separation that caused Him to cry, "My God, My God, why hast Thou forsaken Me?" (Matt. 27:46; Ps. 2:1)? Or was Jesus praying, not only for Himself but in priestly concern for others, that He would be "made safe" by being raised out of death by resurrection in order to effect such for all men? Peter proclaimed that "God raised Him up again, putting an end to the agony of death, since it was impossible for Him to be held in its power" (Acts 2:24).

Paul goes on to record that *"He (Jesus) was heard because of His piety."* As the word "piety" has so many negative connotations in the English language, perhaps a better translation would be "reverence" (cf. Heb. 12:28) or "devotion" (cf. Acts 8:2). Does this mean that God the Father responded to Jesus' prayers because He was sinless (cf. 4:15) and could not be held in death's power (cf. Acts 2:24)? As the context refers to Jesus' human agony and anguish in the midst of death, is the reference to Jesus' "reverence" or "devotion" better understood to be His volitional dependence upon God which allowed Him to say, "Not My will, but Thine be done" (Matt. 26:39,42; Mk. 14:36), whereby He submitted to death by crucifixion and thereby in His priestly role made the sufficient and acceptable sacrifice for the sins of all mankind, and was raised out of death by resurrection to restore God's life to receptive humanity? We need not make this an either-or determination.

5:8 *"Although He was a Son,"* ontologically one with God the Father in the Triune Godhead, and inherently and intrinsically divine, He functioned as a man having emptied Himself of the independent function of divine prerogatives of operational action (cf. Phil. 2:7), and *"He learned obedience from* *the things which He suffered."* Divine function, operating as it does in the omniscience of knowing all things, has nothing to "learn." Neither does the absolute sovereignty of divine function "listen under" (Greek word *hupakouo*) another in "obedience." But having chosen to function as a man in identification with all mankind, Jesus the Son "kept increasing in wisdom and stature, and in favor with God and man" (Lk. 2:52) as a young man, and continued to "learn obedience" in all the experiences of earthly, human existence. In the context of the most intense pressures of temptation unto disobedience and sin (4:15), Jesus responded in the "obedience of faith" (cf. Rom. 1:5; 16:26), "obedient to the point of death, even death on a cross" (Phil. 2:8), allowing "the obedience of the One" (Rom. 5:19) to be the basis of righteousness for all men. For 33 years in time "the man, Christ Jesus" (I Tim. 2:5) "listened under" God in obedience and was receptive to all that God the Father wanted to do in Him by faith. The particularly difficult context for "learning obedience" was in the pathos of suffering that led to His crucifixion (cf. 2:9,10; 9:26; 13:12 for connection of suffering and death). The "suffering of death" (2:9) could only be experienced by One who had identified fully with humanity in mortality.

Paul wanted his readers in the church at Jerusalem to understand the full identification of Jesus with their sufferings. They were a suffering community continuing to "learn obedience from the things which they suffered," and continuing to need to apprehend that Christ's suffering unto death had effected a sinless sacrifice as part of His high priestly function, which effected "eternal salvation" (5:9). The divine logic of life out of death, exaltation out of humiliation, and glorification out of suffering (cf. comments on 2:9), could be realized in their own lives, though not with the same redemptive effects as in the life and work of the Savior.

5:9   The Son "learned obedience from the things which He suffered, ***and having been made perfect,*** He became to all those obeying Him the source of eternal salvation." Was Jesus not already perfect (cf. comments on 2:10)? Yes, He was "perfect in Being" as the God-man in whom the Spirit of God dwelt from His supernatural conception. He was also "perfect in behavior" as He exercised the "obedience of faith" in receptivity to God's activity in the man for every moment in time for 33 years, "without sin" (4:15). But it was by the "suffering of death" (2:9), when He was "obedient unto death, even death on a cross" (Phil. 2:8), that Jesus was made "perfect in benefit" by serving as the sinless sacrifice sufficient for the sins of mankind. By thus making the high priestly sacrifice for all human sin, the "Son, made perfect forever" (7:28) accomplished the perfect end objective of God for man, and cried out victoriously, "It is finished?" (John 19:30).

By His death wherein He took the death consequences of man's sin, Jesus set in motion the restoration of divine life to man by resurrection, and ***"He became to all those obeying Him the source of eternal salvation."*** As the Redeemer-Savior, Jesus is "the source of eternal salvation," for such salvation is derived only from Him. To indicate that Jesus is the "source" of salvation is not to imply that He is an objectified "dispenser" of a commodity called "salvation." No, He is the author (cf. 2:10) and originator of a dynamic salvation, the essence of which is integrally united with His ongoing functional presence and action as Savior. Salvation is not a static package of an entity called "eternal life," the benefits of which are alleged to be enjoyed in the future. Rather, salvation is the dynamic activity of the risen and living Lord Jesus as He "makes safe" the Christian from misused humanity in order that the Christian might function as God intends, by allowing the "eternal life" of Christ (cf. John 1:4; 5:26; 11:25; 14:6), the "saving life of Christ" (cf. Rom. 5:10) the Savior, to be operative in the Christian individual. This is "eternal" salvation because the eternality of God's character, both qualitative as well as quantitative, is dynamically operative in the Christian.

The conditional element of this living salvation is noted in the phrase, "to all those obeying Him". The dynamic saving activity of the Savior cannot be statically assented to or received. Nor is it universally applied apart from the freedom of human receptivity. The Christian must continue to "listen under" (Greek word *hupakouo*) the Lord Jesus in the dependence of submission in order to continue to be receptive to the dynamic activity of the Savior in faith. But let it be noted that Christ's obedience (5:8) allows for, and becomes the basis of, the Christian's obedience. The living, saving "Obedient One," Jesus Christ, lives in the Christian individual, providing everything necessary for the Christian to "listen under" and respond in the "obedience of faith" in order to allow the indwelling Christ to live out His life in sanctification (cf. 10:7-18).

The Christians in Palestine who received this letter from Paul were suffering in a physical situation that was not very "safe." Paul was assuring them that they were "made safe" in Jesus Christ, not only for a future deliverance and life beyond this life, but "made safe" to function by "listening under" the direction of the living Savior, in order to be faithfully receptive to the eternal character of God expressed in their obedient behavior, even in the midst of unsettling circumstances of ostracism and imminent war.

5:10 Paul returns to his theme of Jesus as divine-human High Priest, indicating that by His life and death Jesus *"has been designated under God as a high priest according to the order of Melchizedek."* This is an obvious reference to his previous citation of Psalm 110:4 (cf. 5:6) which he attributed to God the Father in reference to God the Son. The Melchizedekan high priesthood theme will be picked up again in 6:20, and more fully developed in 7:1-28. As noted in the comments of 5:6, the "order of Melchizedek" is a kind or arrangement of priesthood that is of a divine "order." The only known participants in that "order" of priesthood were Melchizedek and Jesus Christ. It is, therefore, not a group designation, as when one refers to the "Franciscan order," for example.

The statement of Jesus "being designated under God" as a high priest in the divine order of Melchizedek has precipitated much discussion of the timing of God the Father's designation or declaration, authorization or appointment, installation or investiture of Jesus as high priest representing mankind under God. Was Jesus functioning as high priest through His life on earth (cf. 5:7-9), or was He designated a high priest at His death (cf. 10:11,12), at His resurrection, or when He ascended into heaven (cf. 6:19,20; 8:1-4)? Or was Jesus "a priest forever" (5:6), "holy, innocent, undefiled, separated from sinners, and exalted above the heavens" (7:26)? Undue specification of the space/time context of Christ's high priesthood should be avoided, as it only produces man-made theological and eschatological limitations on the work of Christ.

Concluding Remarks:

The Jerusalem Christians who first received this letter were greatly tempted to revert back to their Judaic practices in accepting the false hopes of the Zealot revolutionaries. Paul, writing from Rome, understood their temptation, and wanted them to realize that Jesus had identified with mankind by becoming susceptible to the volitional vulnerabilities of temptation. The living Lord Jesus functioning as high priest in His intercessory work could sympathize with their weaknesses (4:15) and "lack of strength," having been "tempted in all things" as they were in their human temptations. Paul wanted to encourage those first century Christians that Jesus "deals gently" (5:2) with their weakness, which should make them comfortable to "draw near with confidence to the throne of

157

grace, in order to find mercy and grace to help in their time of need" (4:16). Only by God's grace activity could they expect to "keep on obeying" (5:9) by "listening under" God as they were "led by the Spirit" (Rom. 8:14) and responding in the receptivity of faithful obedience. Thus they would find the living Lord Jesus to be the "source of their eternal salvation" (5:9), as they were "made safe" by the eternality of Christ's character operative in their behavior, despite the external circumstances.

As Christians today, we continue to be tempted in the midst of our circumstances – tempted to react with violence, anxiety or desertion (fight, fright or flight). We must understand that it is not wrong to be tempted, for that is just part of the human experience, just as Jesus was tempted, "yet without sin" (4:15). We should not deny or decry our weakness of volitional vulnerability or that we have "times of need" (4:16), for if we cannot recognize our "times of need" we will not likely recognize God's grace sufficiency in the midst of such. Christ, as our living High Priest, sympathizes with our weaknesses (4:15), "suffering together with us" therein. He "deals gently" with us in a "moderated passion" that does not ignore us with a "silent treatment" or attack us with a "sledgehammer approach," but compassionately loves us with a gentle concern for our highest well-being. Such gracious provision should make us comfortable to "hold fast our confession" (4:14), and to "draw near with confidence to the throne of grace" (4:16), availing ourselves of the illimitable resources of God's grace as Christ continues to function intercessorily for us in His High Priestly work. As we "keep on obeying" (5:9) by relying on the Obedient One, Jesus Christ, we enjoy the "eternal salvation" that functions dynamically as the Eternal Savior lives in and through us.

ENDNOTES

1 Kittel, Gerhard (editor), *Theological Dictionary of the New Testament*. Article on αρχιερευς by Gottlob Schrenk. Grand Rapids: Wm. B. Eerdmans Pub. Co. 1972. pg. 268.
2 Thomas, W. Ian, *The Mystery of Godliness*. Grand Rapids: Zondervan Publishing House. 1972. pgs. 48,49.

JESUS

The Better Hope of Inheriting the Promises of God

Hebrews 5:11 – 6:20

The recipients of this letter were "the descendants of Abraham" (2:16). They were Jewish Christians residing in the Jewish capital of Jerusalem (or the nearby environs) in the middle of the seventh decade of the first century (approximately A.D. 65 as best we can reconstruct the setting of this letter from the external and internal evidence available). Their Jewish ethnic heritage constituted them as "descendants of Abraham" by physical heritage, and by becoming Christians they had become "descendants of Abraham" by participating in the "faith of Abraham" (Rom. 4:16), for the Christian "children of the promise are regarded as descendants" (Rom. 9:6-8) of Abraham. As Paul explained in his earliest correspondence with the Galatians, "If you belong to Christ, then you are Abraham's offspring, heirs according to promise" (Gal. 3:29).

It was not easy to be a Jewish Christian in the heartland of the Judaic religion in the middle of the first century. Because they had confessed Jesus as the promised Messiah, these Jewish Christians had "endured a great conflict of sufferings," had "been made a public spectacle through reproaches and tribulations," and had "accepted joyfully the seizure of their property, knowing that they had a better possession, and an abiding one" (10:32-34). These ostracisms, reproaches, tribulations and sufferings were inflicted upon them at the hand of their own Jewish peoples who regarded them as traitors for

161

confessing Jesus as the promised Messiah and becoming Christians.

The external circumstances surrounding these Jewish Christians did not seem to point to a "better possession" (10:39) or a "great reward" (10:35) in "receiving what was promised" (10:36) by God to Abraham. Having endured these sufferings without seeing any visible benefits of their Christian faith, they were in danger of losing their confidence (10:35), of "shrinking back" (10:38,39), and repudiating their Christian faith in order to join the prevailing socio-political movement of Jewish insurrection against Rome.

The rumblings of revolt were reverberating across the region of Judea. Zealot revolutionaries were promising that as a result of their planned rout of the Roman oppressors the Jewish peoples would obtain and inherit what was rightfully theirs – what God had promised to them through Abraham. The liberationists apparently claimed that God was on their side – that divine providence and angelic assistance would assure their victory. The Davidic kingdom would be restored and the Jewish people would rule themselves as they enjoyed "rest" in the promised land. The Aaronic high priesthood would be restored in the temple. These were their "divine rights" that must be fought for by ousting the Romans.

Throughout this epistle to the Jewish Christians, Paul has been countering the false premises and promises of the Jewish insurrectionists. "Promises, promises, promises!" Political promises are cheap, easy to make, and of little value, but people's hopes are often pinned on such promises in the myopic focus of the contemporary socio-political situation. The Jewish Christians of Judea were being pressured and seduced to place their hopes on the physical and material fulfillment of the promises of God to Abraham (cf. Gen. 12, 15, 17, 19). Paul seeks to remind them that Jesus Christ was the spiritual fulfillment of all the promises of God to Abraham, and that "through faith and patience they inherit the promises" (6:13). Whereas the Jewish peoples always sought a physical fulfillment to the promises of God to Abraham for a land, a nation, a posterity and a blessing, Paul's repeated explanation is that God has spiritually *blessed* His people in Jesus Christ (cf. Eph. 1:3; Gal. 3:8,9,14), brought them to a *place* in the presence of God (cf. Gal. 4:16; John 14:2,3; Heb. 4:1,9,13; 11:10-16; 12:22: II Pet. 3:13), and made them a holy *nation* (cf. I Pet. 2:9) with a plenitude of *posterity* (cf. Rom. 4:16; 9:8; Gal. 3:7,16,19,28). "Our hope," Paul seems to be saying to the Jewish Christians of Judea, "is not in political revolution and military war strategies. Our hope is in Jesus Christ" (cf. I Tim. 1:1). All of the promises of God to Abraham are fulfilled in Jesus Christ (cf. II Cor. 1:20; Rom. 15:8; Lk. 22:44-47). Christians are already inheriting those promises, even though in the "enigma of the interim" until the consummation of Christ's triumph becomes visible, it may not appear that the promises are fulfilled, but the continuity and perpetuity of the inheritance will be enjoyed through eternity.

Paul was aware that the Judean Christians were becoming "sluggish" (5:11; 6:12) in their resolve to live in the fullness of what they had in Jesus Christ. They were losing confidence (3:6; 4:16; 10:35) and "shrinking back" (10:38,39) to a Jewish perspective that focused on tangible and physical fulfillments. They were flirting with the option of jettisoning their Christian perspective of hope in Jesus Christ as the fulfillment of all God's promises. Paul is desirous that they "press on to maturity" (6:1), to the end-objective of all God has for Christians in Jesus Christ.

This historical context allows us to explain the textual context, for the content of this section (5:11– 6:20), when wrested from its historical and textual context, has often led to extracted and abstracted interpretations and applications that do not legitimately represent Paul's original intent. A text without its proper context often becomes a pretext for any fanciful formulation of thought or imagination. These verses are not just a parenthetical interlude or insertion of a *non sequitur* diversion or digression of thought, as some have charged. In the greater textual context of Paul's explanation of Christ's assumption of the high priestly function in the "order of Melchizedek" (4:14 – 10:39), Paul makes a direct and logical connection with Abraham who offered gifts to Melchizedek (cf. Gen. 14:18-20). That the Melchizedekan high priesthood is the context of Paul's reference to Abraham in this text (cf. 6:13) is obvious from the references to Melchizedek that bracket this section (cf. 5:10; 6:20).

Paul's perspective of the Melchizedekan high priesthood assumed by Jesus Christ was that it explained the entirety of the "finished work" (cf. Jn. 19:30) of Jesus Christ. This is evident in the statement which directly precedes this section: "Having been made perfect, He became to all those obeying Him the source of eternal salvation, being designated by God as a high priest according to the order of Melchizedek" (5:9,10). Christ's priestly sacrifice of Himself once and for all (cf. 7:27; 9:12,28; 10:10,12) was sufficient to satisfy the just consequences of sin. The "eternal salvation" (5:9) of the "saving life" (cf. Rom. 5:10) of the risen Lord Jesus continues to be sufficient to allow, and to cause, the Christian to be and do all that God wants to be and do in and through him. This "finished work" of God's grace by the dynamic of the "Spirit of Christ" (cf. Rom. 8:9) affords Christians the confidence that "He Who began a good work in them will perfect it" (Phil. 1:6).

The Christians in Jerusalem needed to recognize the broader expanded priesthood of Melchizedek that had been assumed by Jesus Christ and the implications thereof. The Aaronic and Levitical priesthoods were regional and provincial, relating to the Jewish peoples in a particular geographical location, as well as provisional and preliminary to the ultimate intentions of God in the fulfillment of Jesus Christ. The Melchizedekan priesthood, on the other hand, was universal for all people, and was an eternal (cf. Heb. 6:20; 7:17,21), permanent (cf. Heb. 7:24) priesthood that represented man before God. The restoration of the physical priesthood in the temple at Jerusalem and the restoration of an ethnic nation in the land parcel of Palestine were not God's objective, for God had already restored humanity spiritually through the universal priesthood and blessing of Jesus Christ, and had established a "holy nation" of people dwelling in God's presence. For the Christians in Jerusalem to consider jumping on the bandwagon of the Zealot liberationists was to engage in a retrogression to prior Jewish perspectives, a reversion back to expecting the promises of God to Abraham to be fulfilled by physical and material criteria rather than the spiritual fulfillment of all God's promises to Abraham in Jesus Christ.

When Paul refers to his readers as being "dull" (5:11) and "sluggish" (6:1), and needing to "press on to maturity" (6:1), it has often been assumed by commentators that the recipients were immature in their understanding of the Christian faith, having failed to grow and progress as they should have in their knowledge of Christian doctrine and behavior. It must be questioned, however, whether this was a pedagogical and didactic issue that Paul alludes to, or whether is was a practical and experiential issue. Was it an epistemological problem or an ontological negligence? Was this a *theorem* information deficiency, or was this a *practicum* faith deficiency? Many interpreters have indicated that Paul was referring to a learning problem – that the readers were slow learners, stagnated as ignorant "spiritual babies" who had not learned their ABCs and needed to go back to the elementary school of Christian learning. Several observations dictate against such an interpretation, however. All that Paul has written in this epistle, both prior to this section and subsequent to this section, presupposes and indicates an advanced understanding of the Christian faith on the part of the readers. The recipients appear to be regarded as well-taught and knowledgeable Christians. Paul does not seem to think that the readers needed to return to or review the initial and foundational tenets of Christian instruction (6:1,2), but in commonality with them writes, "let us press on to maturity." Maturation is not so much a matter of information as it is a matter of sanctification. Christianity is not essentially an epistemological belief-system, but is the ontological Being of Christ lived out in such a way that the end-objective (Greek word *telos*) of God is accomplished, and God is glorified as Christ's life and character are lived out despite how much information and knowledge one has, and despite the external circumstances. Those who are spiritually "mature" (Greek word *teleios* – 5:14; 6:1) are those who are spiritually discerning and are "listening under" God in obedience (cf. 5:8,9).

This kind of maturity was the need of the Jerusalem Christians. They were being pressured and "put in a bind" by the false hopes and expectations of the Zealot movement. There was an erosion in their boldness and confidence and hope in Jesus Christ. They were becoming "sluggish" (5:11; 6:12) and timid, and in danger of neglecting their salvation in Christ (2:3) and regressing to their prior Jewish perspectives of God's promises. Throughout this epistle Paul attempts to encourage these Christians in Judea to make the difficult decisions that are called for in their present situation – to "pay close attention to what they have heard" (2:1); to "hold fast their confidence" (3:6), and "confession" (4:14), and "assurance" (3:14), in order to "endure" (10:36; 12:1) and "persevere" (10:39). In this specific section (5:11 – 6:20) Paul exhorts them to "build on the foundation" (6:1) they have in Christ, to engage in the "things that accompany salvation" (6:9), "to be diligent to realize the full assurance of hope until the end" (6:11), to have "faith and patience to inherit the promises" (6:12), and this by "pressing on to maturity" (6:1), the end-objective of God in their lives.

Though the openings verses (5:11-14) of this section may appear to be a rebuke or reprimand of his readers, they are best understood as a corrective chiding or cajoling designed to stimulate and motivate the Jerusalem Christians to make the difficult decisions of Christian maturity. Rather than seeking to scold or shame the brethren in Jerusalem, Paul employs the sarcasm and irony of referring to them as needy pupils requiring elementary instruction or infants dependent on predigested milk if they are not able and willing to make the mature decision to persevere under pressure. Paul appeals to them to recognize that "Jesus is the better hope of inheriting the promises of God."

5:11   In direct connection with the preceding verses, Paul writes, *"Concerning this we have much to say, and* (it is) *difficult to explain."* The pronoun can be translated as a masculine, "him," or as a neuter, "this." If translated as a masculine pronoun, "him" can refer either to Melchizedek as the type of Christ, or to Christ as the antitype of Melchizedek, since both are mentioned in the preceding sentence. Translated as a neuter pronoun, "this" can refer to "this subject matter of Christ being high priest in the order of Melchizedek," which encompasses both of the interpretations of the masculine pronoun. Paul's use of the plural "we have much to say," has led some to speculate about plural authorship, but is best understood as an editorial "we" including himself with his ministerial colleagues and his readers. That there is indeed "much to say" about this subject is evidenced by the lengthy treatment of the theme in 7:1 – 10:18.

The subject of Christ's Melchizedekan high priesthood is without a doubt "difficult to explain," because it comprehends the entirety of Christ's "finished work." This is not an easy subject and requires careful spiritual understanding. The difficulty of the subject material, however, is often dependent on the maturity of the audience to understand and appreciate what

167

is being presented. In this case, the difficult subject matter was compounded by the apparent indolent and indifferent attitude of the readers in Jerusalem. It is doubly "difficult to explain" *"since you have become sluggish to the hearing,"* Paul writes. Theirs was not a limitation or inability to intellectually or spiritually grasp the subject matter. Neither was it a communication problem of finding adequate words. The problem with the Christians in Jerusalem was an unresponsive unwillingness to "listen under" God in obedience in the midst of their difficult socio-political situation. In the preceding sentence Paul had noted that "He (Jesus Christ) became to all those obeying ("listening under" – Greek *hupakouo*) the source of eternal salvation" (5:9). The Jerusalem Christians were "sluggish in their listening" (Greek word *akouo*). It is not that they were mentally dense or had a diminished capacity to understand. Rather, they were not being diligent (cf. 4:11; 6:11) to persevere (cf. 10:39) in a vital and legitimate (cf. 12:8 – Greek root word for "sluggish") expression of "the obedience of faith" (cf. Rom. 1:5; 16:26). There seems to have been a spiritual inertia precipitated by "listening" to the voices of the revolutionary instigators, rather than to the voice of God to ascertain how He wanted to live out His character in them.

5:12 *"For through this time you ought to be teachers,"* Paul implores. A teacher is not just an information processor who instructs others. A teacher is one who is responsible and takes the lead to speak out boldly, sharing out of what that teacher knows (cf. 8:11; I Cor. 2:12). A Christian teacher is one who has been taught by God (cf. I Thess. 4:9), "listening under" the divine instruction of the Spirit (cf. John 14:26; I John 2:27), and is willing to take the lead in obedience. "Through this time" of difficult turmoil in Palestine, the Jerusalem Christians were not leading boldly in faith, and Paul chides them saying, *"you have need again for someone to teach you the initial elements of the words of God."* These

Christians had apparently retrogressed into a pupil phase of spiritual progress. In their hesitancy to act in the obedience of faith, they were like students who were dependent on an instructor to receive second-hand knowledge concerning the basic rudiments of divine logic. The "initial elements of the words of God" are not just elementary biblical information, but the foundational (cf. 6:1) understanding of God's fulfilling all His promises in Jesus Christ (cf. II Cor. 1:20).

Changing the analogy, but continuing the irony, Paul adds, *"and you have come to need milk and not solid food."* Mature Christians should be able to accommodate both "the pure milk of the word that causes one to grow in respect to salvation" (I Pet. 2:2), as well as the "solid food" of spiritual discernment and digestion that understands the sufficiency of the "finished work" of Christ. Paul intimates that if the Judean Christians are not willing to persevere under pressure, they are like infants that can only tolerate the second-hand nourishment of predigested food.

5:13 The nourishment analogy is further explained: *"For every one partaking of milk alone is not experienced in the word of righteousness, for he is an infant."* Those unwilling to be spiritually discerning by partaking of the solid food of "listening under" God in obedience are being childish in their desire only for predigested milk provided by another. Paul's caricature of the Jerusalem Christians suggests that they might be immature in the discerning process of spiritual growth that partakes of the "word of righteousness" in order to yield "the fruit of righteousness" (12:11). The living Lord Jesus is the divine "Word of Righteousness," apart from Whom there can be no righteous behavior.

5:14 *"But solid food,"* Paul goes on to explain, *"is for the mature, those who through habituated experience have their perceptions exercised to discern both good and evil."* Mature

Christians, those recognizing the end-objective that God intends for their lives in the functional expression of the Christ-life lived out to the glory of God, can appreciate and accommodate the "solid food" of understanding and applying the reality of Christ's intercessory high priesthood in their lives. Christian maturity is the habituated experience or the practiced exercise of perceiving, appreciating and discerning (the English word "aesthetics" is derived from the same root as the word here translated "perceptions") the source and expression of the character of good and evil. This is not the same as an intellectual determination of true and false, nor an ethical discrimination of right and wrong, but is a spiritual discernment of the "good" character that is derived only from God (cf. III John 11) by the sufficiency of His grace, as distinguished from the "evil" character derived from the Evil One (cf. Matt. 12:35). In the case of the Christians in Jerusalem, Paul suggests they did not seem to have an appetite for the "good" character that "accompanied salvation" (cf. 6:9) and allowed them to minister to others in maturity (cf. 6:10) as they continued to be receptive to the "Word of Righteousness" (5:13), despite the difficulty of the then present circumstances. The "evil" character that they were tempted to partake of was the failure to appreciate the full significance of the risen Lord Jesus and the tendency to function in a manner that was not consistent with God's intent and character by desiring a physical and material fulfillment of God's promises rather than the spiritual fulfillment God had provided in Jesus Christ. Paul had such a deep-seated concern for his kinsmen, both physical and spiritual, that they should not lapse into the immaturity of seeking the second-best of the second-hand promises of the Jewish liberationists, but that the maturity of their sanctification would be manifested in the "diligence that would realize the full assurance of hope until the end" (6:11) as they remained receptive to God's "good" character effected only by the high priestly intercessory work of the living Lord Jesus.

6:1 *"Therefore,"* Paul continues, "since you are not in need of the preliminary and primary reasonings and study of Christ, and since you are not to be undiscerning and dependent on others, let us proceed and advance beyond the elementary principles and build upon the foundation that has been laid. You are not bottle-babies! You are not kindergarten pupils needing to learn your ABCs – despite the preceding sarcasm of hypothesized concern." This interpretation avoids any contradiction between 5:11-14 and 6:1-3. ***"Having left the initial word of Christ, let us be brought upon maturity."*** The "initial word of Christ," whether it is "the word *from* Christ" (subjective genitive) or "the word *about* Christ" (objective genitive), will necessarily include the six (6) foundational elements of Christian teaching that are delineated below (6:1,2). Including himself with his readers, Paul desires that they should be carried forward and enabled in the maturation process by the grace of God. Instead of the initial, starting elements of Christian instruction, they need to be brought unto the end-objective of Christian maturity, allowing the "finished work" of the living Lord to be operative in their lives.

Foundations are important, as is made clear by Jesus' parable of building on rock instead of sand (Matt. 7:24-27; Lk. 6:48,49), but foundations are not an end in themselves for they are designed for a structure to be build upon them. By referring to "having left the initial word of Christ," Paul is not advocating that the foundational factors should be abandoned, destroyed or denied, but is encouraging them to go on and build maturity on the foundation that has been laid, ***"not laying again a foundation of repentance from dead works and of faith upon God."*** Though some have interpreted these foundational elements to be the Jewish teachings that these Jewish Christians had built their Christian faith upon, the context of "the initial word of Christ" seems to dictate that they refer to initial Christian teaching. Initial Christian instruction involves an admonition to "repentance from dead works" (cf. Acts 2:38;

3:19; Heb. 9:14), a change of mind about one's sinful expressions that do not express the living character of God and are worthy of punitive death consequences. Initial Christian instruction also includes a call to "faith upon God" (cf. Acts 16:31), receptivity to the redemptive activity of God in His Son, Jesus Christ.

6:2   The list of foundational Christian teachings continues. *"Teaching about baptisms"* was part of the initial teaching of the Church (cf. Acts 2:38; 8:12). The use of the plural "baptisms" may refer to teaching that differentiated between Jewish proselyte baptism, the baptism of John the Baptist (cf. Acts 18:25; 19:3), and Christian baptism (cf. Acts 2:38; 19:5). Such teaching could also distinguish between baptism in the Spirit (cf. I Cor. 12:13) and the initial Christian rite of water baptism.

The *"laying on of hands"* was sometimes employed in healing (cf. Mk. 5:23; 6:5; 16:18; Acts 9:12,17), or in recognizing God's ordination to ministry (cf. Acts 6:6; 13:3; I Tim. 4:14; 5:22; II Tim. 1:6), but the more likely reference here is to the early Christian practice of "laying on of hands" as an outward sign to indicate receipt of the Holy Spirit (cf. Acts 8:17; 19:6). This accords well with the previous reference to "baptism" and the subsequent reference to the Holy Spirit in 6:4.

Teaching about *"the resurrection of the dead ones"* has always been a distinctive part of initial Christian instruction. Though Paul's teaching of "the resurrection of the dead ones" who died in Christ was not always well received (Acts 17:32) as it countered the popular Greek concept of the inherent immortality of the soul, he placed much emphasis on the Christian's resurrection from physical death, based on the resurrection of Jesus Christ from the dead (cf. I Cor. 15:1-58).

The foundational teaching of *"the judgment of the ages"* is closely associated with the eschatological teaching of "the resurrection of the dead ones." Such "judgment" is not invested with any negative or positive connotations, for the determinative judgment is based on an individual's spiritual union with either the Spirit of God or the "spirit of this world" (cf. I Cor. 2:12), and is but the consequence of one's freely chosen continuity and perpetuity of that spiritual union. Such talk of "the judgment to come" made Felix very uncomfortable (Acts 24:25), but Paul will reiterate later in this epistle that "it is appointed unto men to die once and after this comes judgment" (Heb. 9:27). The Christian who abides in Christ has no cause for fear of divine judgment (cf. 10:27), for Christ has taken the divine judgment upon sin (cf. Jn. 3:17-19) and the Christian "does not come into punitive judgment, but has passed out of death into life" (Jn. 5:24).

6:3   Having mentioned six (6) elements of initial and foundational Christian instruction (6:1,2), Paul returns to his primary emphasis of wanting his readers to "be brought to maturity" (6:1) by the grace of God. *"This we shall do, if God permits."* Paul tells his readers, "We shall proceed to discuss the difficult subject of the Melchizedekan high priest of Jesus Christ (cf. 7:1-10:39) in order to understand how the 'finished work' of Christ's intercessory high priesthood brings us into the maturity of living in faithful receptivity (cf. 4:2; 6:12; 10:22,39; 11:1-39; 12:2) to God's activity in our lives." We shall do so, "if God permits" (cf. I Cor. 16:7), Paul states. This is not an impious phrase of resignation like, "God willing and the creek don't rise." Paul subordinated everything to the will of God, and he was fully cognizant that such maturity in his own life and in those of the Jerusalem Christians was exactly what God wanted to effect, for "He Who began a good work in you will perfect (same Greek root word as "mature") it until the day of Christ Jesus" (Phil. 1:6). The grace of God was sufficient to effect such maturity, if they remained diligent (cf. 6:11) in their faith (cf. 6:12) to inherit the promises of God to Abraham (cf. 6:12,13). This delicate dialectic of grace and faith, of God's sovereign activity and the human responsibility of receptivity, provides the necessary setting for the interpretation of the next five (5) verses (6:4-8).

6:4   The chiding of the Christians in Jerusalem in 5:11-14, that their reticence to make the difficult choices to live in Christ could be construed as immaturity, is now expressed in the hypothetical possibility that they might choose to repudiate their Christian faith and apostasize (6:4-8). Paul does not believe that they will do so (6:9), but he pens these words to postulate the real possibility of apostasy, as he does throughout this epistle (cf. 2:1; 3:12; 4:1,11; 10:26-31; 12:15-17), and to warn the readers of the very real consequences to be incurred by such apostasy. As Paul returns to the hypothetical possibility of the Jerusalem Christians abandoning Christ, he changes from the inclusive first person plurals of "us" (6:1) and "we" (6:3), and employs the third person plurals of "those" (6:4), "them" (6:6) and "they" (6:6), to signify an anonymous speculation, and his unwillingness to identify himself with such.

"For," since Christian maturity is effected by God's grace activity responded to constantly by the faith receptivity of the believer (6:3), it is important to recognize the realities that a Christian has received in Christ, and the consequences of rejecting such. In the Greek text the word "impossible" (6:6) is placed prior to Paul's listing of the regenerative realities the Christian has received. This serves to evidence Paul's confidence in the preserving grace of God as well as the persevering faith of the Jerusalem Christians, rather than any pessimistic foretaste of a failure of faith. Without a doubt Paul wanted to encourage the Jerusalem Christians by listing these five (5) spiritual realities that had "once," without repetition, become theirs in spiritual regeneration. These are not a sequence of successive events in a theological *ordo salutis*, but are realities that every Christian receives in regeneration.

Paul first refers to Christians as *"those having been once enlightened."* This is not a psychological "enlightenment" whereby someone has "seen the light" by rationalistic understanding. Literally translated, Paul wrote of "those having been brought to the light," the passive voice indicating God's grace action, and the aorist tense indicating a definitive act. This spiritual "enlightenment" occurs at regeneration when an individual becomes a Christian by receiving the life of Jesus Christ. Jesus said, "I am the light of the world; he who follows Me...shall have the light of life" (John 8:12). John recorded that "In Him (Jesus) was life, and the life was the light of men" (John 1:4). Jesus is the "true light which came into the world, and enlightens every man" (John 1:9) who receives Him as their life. The "enlightenment" that Paul reminds the Jerusalem Christians of is the receipt of Christ's life. "The spirit of man is the lamp of the Lord" (Prov. 20:27), and when Christ's life is received within one's spirit a person is "turned from darkness to light, and from the dominion of Satan to God, in order that they may receive forgiveness of sins..." (Acts 26:18), for "by reason of His resurrection from the dead, Christ proclaimed light both to the Jewish people and to the Gentiles" (Acts 26:23). When he wrote to the Corinthians, Paul explained that "God Who said, 'Light shall shine out of darkness' (Gen. 1:3), is the One who has shone in our hearts to give the light of the knowledge of the glory of God in the face of Christ; ...we have this treasure in earthen vessels" (II Cor. 4:6,7).

Second, Paul writes of *"those having once tasted of the heavenly gift."* This, too, refers to the deliberate act of receiving God's gift into oneself at regeneration. The "tasting" is not a partial experience of "tasting with the tip of the lip" (cf. Calvin), but involves "taking into oneself for the full experience of..." For example, when Jesus "tasted death for everyone" (2:9), He experienced the full reality of death, not just a partial experience. How is the "heavenly gift" to be identified?

175

Some have called attention to "the gift of grace" (cf. Heb. 3:7; 4:7; Rom. 5:15,17; II Cor. 9:15), others to "the gift of redemption and salvation" (cf. Eph. 2:8,9; Rom. 6:23), and others to "the gift of the Holy Spirit" (cf. Acts 2:38; 10:45), but the "summing up of all things is in Christ" (Eph. 1:10), so the "heavenly gift" can be summed up in the Person of Jesus Christ. "God so loved the world that He gave His only begotten Son" (John 3:16), Who is "the gift of God" (John 4:10). "God has blessed us with every spiritual blessing in heavenly places in Christ Jesus" (Eph. 1:3). As the Psalmist said, "Taste and see that the Lord is good" (Ps. 34:8).

"Those having been once made partakers of the Holy Spirit" can only refer to those who have become partakers of the Spirit of Christ (Rom. 8:9) at regeneration. This spiritual reality cannot be separated from the foregoing mention of the "heavenly gift" of Christ, for otherwise one has a deficient Trinitarian understanding that fails to recognize the Holy Spirit as the Spirit of Christ. At regeneration the Christian becomes a "partaker of Christ" (3:14), a "partaker of the Holy Spirit" (6:4) and "a partaker of the divine nature" (II Pet. 1:4). "God sent forth the Spirit of His Son into our hearts" (Gal. 4:6). "The Spirit of Him who raised Jesus from the dead dwells in you; His spirit indwells you" (Rom. 8:11), Paul writes. "He abides in us, by the Spirit Whom He has given us" (I John 3:24), John adds. To be a "partaker of the Holy Spirit" necessarily involves partaking of the expressions of the Spirit in the *charismata* and *pneumatikon* of Romans 12 and I Corinthians 12, but the reference here is not to be limited to such, divorcing the spiritual manifestations from their source in the Holy Spirit.

6:5 Continuing his list of regenerative and salvific realities enjoyed by every Christian, Paul refers to *"those having once tasted the good word of God."* Again, as noted in 6:4, to "taste" is to take into oneself so completely that the experience of what one has taken in becomes part of the person receiving such. Paul's mention of the "word" of God here is a translation of the Greek word *rhema* (cf. 1:3; 11:3), rather than the Greek word *logos* (cf. 4:12; 5:13; 13:7), also translated "word." Some have made a sharp distinction between these words, explaining that *logos* means an objectively manifested revelation of God as in the historical incarnation of Christ (John 1:1,14), while *rhema* means a more subjectively experienced personal revelation of Christ. Jesus Christ is both the objective and subjective self-revelation of God, and can be referred to as *logos, angellos* or *rhema*. We must avoid, however, applying "the good word of God" only to the tangible book of the Bible or to an abstracted construct of the "gospel message," for the "good news" of the message of the gospel is Jesus Christ, and the purpose of the scriptures are to reveal the personified Word of God, Jesus Christ (cf. John 5:39,40).

Christians are also ***"those having once tasted the powers of the coming age."*** The "coming age" is the Christian age, during which time Christians experience the dynamics of divine power as never before. God "made the ages" (1:2) with the intent that "in the ages to come He might show the surpassing riches of His grace toward us in Christ Jesus" (Eph. 2:7). He has accomplished such, for "once at the consummation of the ages, He (Christ) has been manifested to put away sins by the sacrifice of Himself" (Heb. 9:26). This is "the mystery that has been hidden from the past ages and generations, but has now been manifested to His saints, ...which is Christ in you, the hope of glory" (Col. 1:26,27). The "coming age" is not just a future age, for Christians have already tasted and experienced the Christian age in "these last days" (Heb. 1:2; Acts 2:17; I Pet. 1:20) of the inaugurated and realized *eschatos* age, empowered as it is by "the *Eschatos* Man" Jesus Christ (I Cor. 15:45) – which is not to deny a completed consummation of that "age" and those "last days" in the future.

6:6 Despite the fact that the defection of the Jerusalem Christians was hypothetical and unexpected (6:9), Paul posits the real possibility of a Christian having experienced the regenerative spiritual realities he has listed, *"and* (then) *having fallen away."* This phrase follows the previous phrases with a single conjunction, "and," but the obvious contrast of the action of this phrase with the previous phrases often causes translators to add a contrastual word, such as "and *yet...*" (JBP), or a word of contrasted sequence such as "and *then...*" (NASB, NAB). The invalid translation is to add the word "if" (KJV, RSV, NIV) to indicate that such action and its consequences are but speculative and conjectural, rather than a real possibility. The aorist tense of this participial verb, like the four (4) previous participles, indicates a definite and deliberate willful action. The "once" that applied to the previous actions (6:4) can also apply to this phrase, "and then having once fallen away," indicating the singularity and non-repetition of the action.

To "fall away" does not mean simply to fall into an act of misrepresentative sin. The context demands that we understand that Paul is indicating the possibility of falling away from a relationship with Jesus Christ – falling away from the enlightenment of Christ's life; falling away from the heavenly gift of Christ; falling away from being partakers of the Holy Spirit in Christ; falling away from having received the word of God in Christ; and falling away from having experienced the power of the age to come in Christ. To "fall away" is to renounce and repudiate all that one has received in Christ. The Jerusalem Christians were in danger of doing just that – neglecting the saving life of Christ (2:1); falling away from the living God (3:12); falling into disobedience (4:11); trampling under foot the Son of God (10:29); and being defiled by a root of bitterness (12:15). They were being pressured by the Palestinian liberation movement to return to the Jewish hopes for the material fulfillment of the promises of God to Abraham, and thus to

abandon the hope they had in Jesus Christ as the spiritual fulfillment of God's promises. Such a definite decision to reject
Christ and revert to the Judaic religion; to "drift away" (2:1);
to develop an evil, unbelieving heart (3:12); to disobey (4:11);
and to "shrink back" (10:38,39) would constitute a deliberate
and willful apostasy of "standing against" Jesus Christ (cf.
3:12). It would have been a calculated capitulation to the coercive campaign of the Jewish religionists, a deliberate denial of
Christ and all of the spiritual realities inherent in Him – in
other words, a "reverse conversion." Such a decision would be
to blaspheme, to speak bad words of contempt and reviling of
God in Christ, and such blasphemous rejection of God is consistently stated throughout the scriptures to have irreversible
consequences of being "cut off" (Num. 15:30,31), of receiving
judgmental wrath (Ezek. 20:27-36), and being unforgivable
(cf. Matt. 12:32; Mk. 3:29; Lk. 12:10).

Paul connects the possibility of "falling away" with the
impossibility of returning to Jesus Christ. *"It is impossible to
renew them again unto repentance."* Paul is not saying "it is
very difficult" or "humanly impossible" to restore a Christian
who has rejected and denied Jesus Christ, but rather that it is
divinely impossible since it would be incongruous with the
character of God (cf. 6:18). Although "all things are possible
with God" (Mk. 10:27) and "nothing will be impossible" (Lk.
1:37), it is impossible for God to act contrary to Who He is,
for He only acts out of His Being, and cannot act contrary to
His character without ceasing to be God. Acting out of His
self-giving character, God has "given His only begotten Son"
(John 3:16). The singular sacrifice of Jesus Christ on the cross
"once and for all" (7:27; 9:12; 10:10) cannot be reenacted.
There is no other "sacrifice for sins" (10:26). If the salvation
of Christ has been once (6:4) experienced (6:4,5) and rejected
(6:6), then God has nothing more to give. The totality of His
grace and self-revelation are expressed in Jesus Christ. There
can be no more foundation of repentance (6:1), no second

basis of eternal life. As Peter stated, "Lord, to whom shall we go? You alone have the words of eternal life" (John 6:68). Later Peter declared, "There is salvation in no one else; for there is no other name under heaven...by which we must be saved" (Acts 4:12).

The impossibility (Greek word *adunaton*, meaning "no dynamic") of an individual receiving Christ, rejecting Christ, and then returning to be renewed or restored to Christ must be explained theologically as a divine impossibility. Paul Ellingworth writes that "the impossibility of a second repentance is not psychological...; it is in the strict sense theological, related to God's saving action in Christ."[1] The impossibility of a second conversion is not based on the psychological impossibility of a psychological hardness of heart whereby an individual has developed a fixed attitude of rejecting Jesus, calling good "evil" and evil "good," and having no concern for the things of God in Jesus Christ. It is not even a "judicial hardening" of the psychological function of mind, emotion and will. It is the theological impossibility of reenacting the necessary foundation of repentance and salvation in the death and resurrection of Jesus Christ. All of God's grace, love, and dynamic of restored life to mankind are extended in Jesus Christ. If the dynamic of Christ's life is experienced, and then rejected, then there is no theological foundation of repentance and salvation for that person. This is not just the logical impossibility of God going back on His word, having made a static declaration of "once apostasized, always apostasized," or "once revoked, always revoked." No, this is the theological impossibility of God's sending His Son again and reenacting redemption. William L. Lane notes that "to repudiate Christ is to embrace the impossible."[2] If the totality of divine dynamic is in Christ, and Christ has been rejected, then there is "no dynamic" to effect salvation again. It is a divine impossibility. Later in the epistle Paul will write, "Without faith (the receptivity of God's dynamic activity) it is impossible (there is no divine dynamic) to please God" (11:6).

Paul explains the rejection of Christ and the resultant impossibility of restoration to repentance by using a metaphorical figure: *"since they recrucify again to themselves the Son of God, and put Him to open shame."* Obviously, since it is not possible to crucify the Son of God again in an historical sense, Paul is employing a figure of speech. Those Christians who would reject Jesus recrucify Him again in the sense that they seek to eliminate and terminate their relationship with Jesus. They want to "put to death" and execute their identification with Christ, by "hanging Him up" in rejection. In so doing, they publicly disgrace the Lord Jesus Christ, exposing Him to public humiliation by inferring that the life of Jesus is of no value and does not work. To thus "despise and forsake" (cf. Isa. 53:3) Him, and "insult the Spirit of grace" (10:29), is to exhibit Him as contemptible before others, telling a shameful lie (cf. John 8:44) about the Lord, and making Him a mockery before men.

6:7   Paul utilizes an agricultural illustration, as was often employed by the prophets in the Old Testament (cf. Isa. 5:2-7) and by Jesus (cf. Matt. 3:10; 7:16-20; Mk. 4:1-20; Lk. 13:6-9; John 15:1-8) to relate to the agrarian societies of their day. Paul does so to present a picture of what he has referred to in verses 4-6. *"For earth that drinks the rain that often comes, and brings forth vegetation useful for those for whom it is cultivated, receives blessing from God."* The interpretation of these verses (7,8) must determine to what extent the agricultural analogy is to be understood as an allegory wherein the various details of the story are to be identified.

The "earth" or the "ground" seems to represent the readers, the Jerusalem Christians, with a similarity to the soils of men's hearts in Jesus' parable of the soils (cf. Matt. 13:3-23; Mk. 4:3-20; Lk. 8:5-15). Like the rain that repeatedly comes, the grace of God is continuously available. The Christians in Jerusalem "had drank" of the grace of God by their receptivity of faith, having "tasted" (4,5) and been made partakers (5:13; 6:4) of God's grace by receiving Him into themselves. By God's grace vegetation or spiritual "fruit" (cf. Matt. 7:20; John 15:4,5; Gal. 5:22,23; Heb. 13:15) had been brought forth in the behavior of the Judean Christians. Such fruit is "useful" as it brings glory to God (cf. I Cor. 10:31; II Cor. 3:18; Heb. 13:21) and serves to cause the Christian community, the Body of Christ, to function as intended in unity and unto God's glory. As God's grace continues to be received by faith, Christians continue to receive the "blessing" of God's dynamic function of grace, and the "good word" (the Greek word for "blessing" is *eulogias*, meaning "good word") of God's approval, culminating in the words, "Well done, good and faithful servant" (cf. Matt. 25:21).

6:8   In contrast to the foregoing scenario which represented the Jerusalem Christians as Paul knew them, he makes the hypothetical contrast of what he perceived the readers to be in danger of doing, and the real consequences of such action. ***"But bringing forth thorns and thistles,*** it (the "ground" or "earth") is **not approved** (of God) **and near a curse; the end of which is unto burning."** Should the Christians in Jerusalem reject Christ and not continue to manifest the fruitful productivity of God's grace in their lives, but instead bring forth "thorns and thistles," the fruit of disobedience (cf. Gen. 3:17,18; Hosea 10:8; Matt. 7:16-20), they would not be approved of God, but disqualified and rejected (cf. I Cor. 9:27; II Cor. 13:5) for not serving God's functional purpose of bringing glory to Himself. As a consequence of such a choice there existed the real possibility that the Jerusalem Christians were subject to and "near" a "curse" of God rather than the "blessing" referred to previously (6:7). "Blessing" and "cursing" have always been consequences of man's responsibility of obedience and disobedience (cf. Deut. 11:26-28). "The end," the terminal result, of such rejection of God's grace and the bringing forth of the fruit of disobedience is "burning." In the agricultural situation the farmer sets the undesired vegetation on fire to destroy it, so the field, ground or earth, can be used for the constructive purpose of growing productive crops again. The "burning" is a procedure employed to purify the land for new sowing of crops. It is here that the metaphor becomes murky. Is it just the "thorns and thistles" of the fruit of disobedience that are to be burned, or is it the ground (representing the people to whom this epistle is written) that is to be burned? Is the "burning" indicative of a destructive eschatological judgment, or is it a burning of purification? It seems preferable to understand that Paul is portraying some kind of judgment of God upon disobedient people, rather than the works of man being burned up like "wood, hay and stubble" (I Cor. 3:12-15). Jesus referred to "every tree (person) that does not bear good fruit is cut down and thrown into the fire" (Matt. 7:19, and to people being cast into the "furnace of fire" (Matt. 13:42,50). Likewise, in the analogy of the vine and the branch, Jesus said, "If anyone does not abide in Me, he is thrown away as a branch, and dries up, and they gather them, and cast them into the fire and they are burned" (John 15:6). In the passage that is parallel to this passage (6:4-8) in 10:27-39, it is obvious that Paul is referring to a judgment of God upon apostate Christians, for he writes of God "judging His people" (10:30) in a destructive (10:39) punishment (10:29) that involves the "terrifying expectation of judgment, ...the fury of a fire that consumes" (10:27). Let it be noted that "God is a consuming fire" (12:29) with the prerogative of divine judgment. It is not man's prerogative or the church's prerogative to burn Christians as recalcitrants or heretics in pogroms or inquisitions, as unfortunate incidents of church history record.

Paul was warning the Jerusalem Christians that the rejection of Jesus in apostasy would lead to divine judgment, and at the same time appealing to them to refrain from such action by building upon the foundation (6:1) they had in their personal experience of receiving Christ (6:4,5). He was confident, however, that they would not deny Christ and depart from the faith, but would bring forth the "fruit" that accompanies salvation (6:9).

6:9 *"But,"* in contrast to the foregoing allusions to immaturity (5:11-14) and apostasy (6:4-8), *"beloved, we have been persuaded of better things concerning you."* Despite the chiding (5:11-14) and the warning (6:1:4-8), there is no animosity or antagonism between Paul and the readers; only a pastoral concern of Christian love wherein he refers to them as "beloved" (cf. Rom. 12:19; II Cor. 7:1). The possibility of apostasy is not, and should not be, used as a club of incentive to chastise, to create fear and doubts, or to manipulate and motivate by guilt. Paul is convinced by the evidence he has observed or heard that the Jerusalem Christians are in a better condition of Christian progress than that of immaturity (5:11-14) and apostasy (6:4-8). Of the two illustrative options previously mentioned (6:7,8), the Christians of Jerusalem are still operating in the better scenario of verse 7, manifesting the "better things...*that* (pertain to and) *accompany salvation."* These Christians were being "made safe" from misused humanity in order to function as God intended (that is "salvation"), allowing the "fruit of the Spirit" (Gal. 5:22,23), the character of God, to be expressed in their behavior by God's grace. Paul was convinced of such better progress *"even if we so speak"* of sluggishness (5:11) and the danger of "falling away" (6:6). Notice that he has returned to the editorial "we" of personally inclusive plural pronouns, rather than the hypothetical distancing of "those," "them," and "they" (6:4-6).

6:10 Emphasizing the positive progression of which he is persuaded, Paul writes, *"For God is not unjust to have forgot-*

ten your work." The statement, "God is not unjust," is a double negative that states the positive reality that "God is just." God is righteous (cf. Ps. 11:7; 119:137; I John 2:29; 3:77), and does not forget or fail to recognize the grace outworking in the lives of the Christians in Jerusalem. These were "good works which God prepared beforehand that they should walk in them" (Eph. 2:10), and He "equipped them in every good thing" (Heb. 13:21) in order to "work in them for His good pleasure" (Phil. 2:13). This "work" is explained later as "sharing with those who were mistreated, showing sympathy for the prisoners, and accepting joyfully the seizure of their property" (10:33,34).

As "love and good works" go together (10:24), Paul continues to explain that God will not forget or overlook *"the love which you have shown unto His name, having ministered and continuing to minister to the saints."* Divine love "has been poured out in our hearts by the Holy Spirit" (Rom. 5:5) and is always the "fruit of the Spirit" (Gal. 5:22). The Judean Christians had been receptive to God's expressing His character of love unto the glory of His own name. Their "love of the brethren" (13:1) was evidenced in "ministry to the saints," which is always the overflow of Christ's life of love and service for others through the Christian. These were, no doubt, the grace-expressions of the *charismata* (Rom. 12; I Cor. 12). Jesus said, "To the extent that you did it to one of these brothers of Mine, you did it unto Me" (Matt. 25:40), and "whoever gives to one of these even a cup of water to drink, …shall not lose his reward" (Matt. 10:42). God does not neglect to see, nor does He forget when Christians are available to His active expression of His character.

6:11 Changing from positive reinforcement to challenge, Paul writes, *"But we desire each one of you to show the same diligence towards the full assurance of hope until the end."* Paul's desire (cf. Rom. 10:1) for the Jerusalem Christians is that they individually, and thus collectively, understand their responsibility to exhibit an eager and zealous diligence of faith in the midst of their present difficult situation. This is the "same diligence" as they have previously manifested in their ministry of love and good deeds (10), as well as the "same diligence" evidenced in "those, like Abraham, who through faith inherit the promises" (12), thus relating to both the prior and subsequent context. Earlier in the epistle Paul had encouraged them to "be diligent to enter God's rest" (4:11). Now he advocates a diligence that is directed toward a "full assurance" and confidence of understanding (cf. Col. 2:2), faith (cf. 10:22), and expectant hope in inheriting the promises of God. Later Paul will make a corollary challenge: "You have need of endurance, so that when you have done the will of God, you may receive what was promised" (10:36). This is similar to Peter's admonition to "apply all diligence" (II Pet. 1:5) "to make certain about His calling and choosing you" (II Pet. 1:10). Paul is concerned that the Christians in Palestine should fully bear the present difficulties and "hold fast their confidence" (3:6) that God would be faithful to His promises (10:23) "until the end," whether that be the "end" of the Judaic religion in A.D. 70, the "end" of their lives, the "end" of time, or the "end-objective" of rest (4:9-11) and maturity (6:1).

6:12 The opposite of "diligence" is "sluggishness," so Paul expresses his desire negatively, *"that you should not be sluggish."* He had already intimated that they seemed to be "sluggish in hearing" (5:11), hesitant and reticent to boldly move forward in the instructional maturity of faith. Paul did not want the readers to be "dragging their feet" in unreceptive indolence, *"but imitators of those who through faith and patience are inheriting the promises."* Though the word "imitators" translates a word, the root of which is *mimos*, the etymological basis of the English word "mimic," the linguistic meaning of the word is not mere mimicking of external actions, such as "parroting," aping," or "monkey see, monkey do." The word refers to patterning oneself after an exemplary model, and following by functioning in like manner as the behavioral pattern of another. Paul commended the Thessalonian Christians saying, "You became imitators of us and of the Lord" (I Thess. 1:6), as he had "offered himself as a model for them, to follow his example" (II Thess. 3:9). Later in this epistle to the Hebrew Christians in Jerusalem, Paul will encourage them to "imitate the faith" of those who led them and taught them (13:7). A pattern of functional faith-receptivity of God's activity is worthy of following after in like manner. The Christian life, however, is not merely imitation of another's external actions (even those of Jesus), but the manifestation (cf. II Cor. 4:10,11) of the character and activity of the living Lord Jesus by faithful receptivity thereof.

Who is it that Paul is encouraging the Jerusalem Christians to pattern their faith after? "Those who through faith and patience are inheriting the promises" could be taken to refer to other Christians, whether in Jerusalem or elsewhere, who were evidencing exemplary faith and patience. The present tense of the verb "inheriting" lends itself to such an interpretation. But the following context (vss. 13-15) indicates that Paul was probably thinking of "those, like Abraham, who through faith and patience are inheriting the promises." It is a distinctive Pauline theme to set forth the "faith of Abraham" as a model for Christian faith (cf. Rom. 4:1-22; Gal. 3:6-29), and he seems to be elevating Abraham as a pattern for faith and patience (vss. 12,15) here again, but with an even stronger emphasis on the faithfulness of God (vss. 13-18).

All Christians, along with Abraham, "are inheriting the promises" of God – the promises of God to Abraham (Gen. 12-17) and all of the divine historical promises that are confirmed and fulfilled in Jesus Christ (II Cor. 1:20). "The promise which God has made is eternal life" (I John 2:25), and this divine life of the Son (John 14:6; I John 5:12) is presently

187

realized by all Christians. Christians are "heirs of the promise" (6:17; Gal. 3:29), presently "inheriting" all that God has promised in His Son, Jesus Christ. The inheriting of God's promises must not be projected just to the future (as in Jewish eschatology), but must be recognized as being presently inaugurated and realized, even though there is a "not yet" completion and consummation of such hoped for and expected in the future.

In the meantime, Paul is encouraging the Jerusalem Christians to have similar "faith and patience" as Abraham exhibited. Such receptivity to God's activity requires patient long-suffering when such divine activity is deferred or is being masked by adversity and testing, as was the case for both Abraham and the Christians of Judea.

6:13 *"For,"* to explain the patterning of Abraham in inheriting the promises, *"God, having promised to Abraham, since He had no one greater by which to swear, He swore by Himself."* Abraham is certainly on Paul's mind throughout this epistle (cf. 3:16; 6:13-15; 7:4,5; 11:8-19). Paul, like every Jewish person, made much of the promises of God to Abraham (cf. Gen. 12:1-7; 13:14-17; 15:1-7,13-18; 17:1-8,19). Paul's reference here, though, goes beyond the initial promises of God to Abraham, to refer to the confirmation of God's promises to Abraham after Abraham had faithfully been willing to sacrifice his promised son, Isaac, on the mountain in the land of Moriah (Gen. 22:1-14). God spoke to Abraham, "By Myself I have sworn, declares the Lord, because you have done this thing, and have not withheld your son, your only son, indeed I will greatly bless you, and I will greatly multiply your seed... And in your seed all the nations of the earth shall be blessed, because you have obeyed My voice" (Gen. 22:16-18). In like manner as men (vs. 16) swear an oath to validate a promise, God confirms His previous promises to Abraham by a sworn oath to guarantee His word. Whereas men always swear by something or someone greater than themselves (vs. 16), such as the temple, the book, heaven, or God Himself, God could swear by no one greater than Himself (cf. Isa. 45:23; Jere. 22:5; 49:13). God *does* what He *does* because He *is* who He *is*. His act expresses His Being, and His Being is always expressed in consistent act. This integral oneness of character and conduct is consistently expressed by any and every word He speaks.

In traditional Jewish interpretation of Genesis it was understood that God had confirmed His promise to Abraham with an oath. Philo, a Jewish commentator and philosopher, who lived from approximately 20 B.C. to A.D. 50, and was thus a contemporary of Paul, comments on Genesis 22:16-18:

> God confirmed His promises solemnly by an oath, and by an oath, too, such as could alone become God. For you see that God does not swear by any other being than Himself, for there is nothing more powerful that He is; but He swears by Himself because He is the greatest of all things. [3]

Commenting on Abraham, Philo wrote,

> God, admired this man for his faith in Him, giving him a pledge in return, namely, a confirmation by an oath which He had promised him; no longer conversing with him as God might with a man, but as one friend with another. [4]

These quotations serve to document the traditional Jewish interpretation of the two-fold promise and oath of God to Abraham, which Paul refers to in these verses.

6:14   Citing Genesis 22:17, Paul quotes God as *"saying, BLESSING I WILL BLESS YOU, AND MULTIPLYING I WILL MULTIPLY YOU."* The Hebrew infinitive absolutes emphasize by repetition, as in Genesis 2:17, when God declares, "DYING, YOU SHALL DIE." Though the Hebrew text has God declaring that He will "multiply your seed," Paul shortens this to "you," for his emphasis is on God's faithfulness and Abraham's response of faith, rather than on the universality of the promises for all nations.

6:15 *"And so,"* to explain God's sworn oath to Abraham in Genesis 22:17, *"having patiently waited, he* (Abraham) *obtained the promise."* With patient long-suffering (vs. 12) Abraham held fast in faith and hope, expecting God to fulfill His promises. Despite the delay in the birth of the promised son, and despite the test to sacrifice Isaac (11:17,18), Abraham faithfully endured and "inherited" (vs. 12) or "obtained" (vs. 15) the promise of God. Since the event being cited (Gen. 22:16-18) was subsequent to the birth of Isaac, the "obtaining of the promise" does not refer to Isaac's birth, but to the blessing of multiplied posterity thereafter. Abraham obtained the results of the sworn promise of God in the fulfillment and blessing of multiplied physical progeny, and the Hebrew peoples received all that God had promised (Joshua 23:14), but Paul will explain later that there was another sense in which he, and they, "did not receive what was promised" (10:13,39). The direct spiritual fulfillment of the promises to Abraham would occur later in history in Jesus Christ, though Abraham "saw by faith" (John 8:56) that the Messiah would fulfill the promises (Gal. 3:16), and all the nations of mankind would be blessed spiritually because of him (Gal. 3:8). So, by anticipated prospect Abraham inherited (vs. 12) and obtained (vs. 15) the promises of God in the "blessing" of Christ (cf. Eph. 1:3) and the universality of gospel availability to the multiplied peoples of all nations of the world (cf. John 3:16; Matt. 28:19; Rom. 16:26).

It was important that the Jewish Christians in Jerusalem understand that the "blessing" and the "multiplied posterity" were fulfilled in Christ, and that all Christians were spiritual "heirs of the promise" (vs. 17). Why? Because the Jewish revolutionaries were promising that they were going to effect the fulfillment of God's promises to Abraham in a physical, mate-

rial, racial, national and geographical way when they liberated
Palestine from the occupying Romans. Paul did not want the
Christians in Jerusalem to jettison the greater spiritual fulfillment of the Abrahamic promises for a lesser and inferior false
promise of physical nationalism and religion.

6:16   Paul goes back to explain the confirmatory oath that
was often employed in human interactions and transactions.
***"For indeed men swear according to the greater, and all the
oath is to them is a confirmation for the end of a dispute."***
To create binding agreements men often made fiduciary oaths
to guarantee their trustworthiness. Such oaths were often taken
by appealing to one greater than themselves who might ensure
or vouch for their fidelity. The Israelites were encouraged "to
swear by the name of God" (cf. Deut. 6:13; 10:10), and
Abraham, himself, did so on several occasions (cf. Gen. 14:22-
24; 21:22-24; 24:2-4). These human oaths served as a form of
binding validation of fidelity, and the violation of the terms of
the agreement would constitute perjury. The oath was intended
to avoid and resolve any dispute of contradictory claims concerning the agreement, under the threat of dishonesty and a
loss of integrity. To "swear falsely by God's name" (cf. Lev.
19:12; Num. 30:2; Deut. 23:21; Zech. 5:4) was to incur grave
consequences in Hebrew society. But by the first century,
Jesus was quite critical of the chicanery of unreliable oaths,
full of loopholes and tricky verbiage, made with no intent to
keep them (Matt. 7:33-37). He cautioned against making such
farcical oaths and admonished that one should speak honestly
and straight-forwardly with a simple "Yes" or "No."

6:17   ***"In this way,"*** employing the acceptable ways of men
at that time, and ***"resolving even more to demonstrate to the
heirs of the promise the unchangeableness of His purpose,
God interposed with an oath."*** An oath was not required from
God. God does not need to vouch for or guarantee His faithful-

ness to His promises. Integrity, the integral oneness between what one says and what one does, is inherent in the character of God. He can only act out of His absolute Being and character of faithfulness and truth. Though men try to confirm their words of promise with an oath, enforced by the threat of perjury, God cannot and will not perjure Himself. He cannot lie (18) or speak falsely or fail to keep His word and promise. Therefore, God's utilization of an oath (Gen. 22:17) was but a determined desire to demonstrate (cf. Acts 8:28) more abundantly beyond any human agreement that His immutable purpose and will was expressed in His promise. What God promises to be His purpose is unalterable, irrevocable, and cannot be annulled. He "will not change His mind" (Ps. 110:4) in a fickle withdrawal and cancellation of His stated purpose. The Jewish writer, Philo, understood this:

> God is not able to speak falsely, as if He were a man, nor does He change His purpose like the son of man. When He has spoken, does He not abide by His word? For He will say nothing at all which shall not be completely brought to pass, since His word is also His deed. [5]

"The counsel of the Lord stands forever" (Ps. 33:11; Prov. 19:21; Isa. 40:8). On another occasion of self-swearing, God said, "I have sworn by Myself; the word has gone forth from My mouth in righteousness and will not turn back" (Isa. 45:23).

God's ratifying of His promise with an oath, swearing by the absoluteness of His own character, was "even more" a desire to affirm and prove that His immutable and irrevocable purpose could and would be achieved only in His Son, Jesus Christ. The "heirs of the promise" are Christians. "If you belong to Christ, then you are Abraham's offspring (descendants, seed), heirs according to promise" (Gal. 3:29); "children of promise" (Gal. 4:28). "Those who are of faith are sons of Abraham" (Gal. 3:7) and "blessed with Abraham" (Gal. 3:9) with the "blessing of Christ" (Eph. 1:3). The "heirs of the promise" are not just the patriarchs of the past in the old covenant, nor are they just the projected participants of the future. The "heirs of the promise" are those Christians who by faith in Jesus Christ are part of the multiplied posterity of the "descendants of Abraham" (Rom. 4:16; Gal. 3:29), having received the "blessing" of Christ (Eph. 1:3), and looking forward to the completed and unhindered blessing of Christ's life in the heavenly realm.

Paul was desirous that the Christians in Jerusalem understand that "even more" than a sworn guarantee of His promise of blessing and multiplied posterity to Abraham and his physical descendants, this was an oath to prove His unchangeable purpose to spiritually bless men abundantly and universally in all the nations of the world through Jesus Christ. In the midst of their trials, the Jerusalem Christians needed to recognize that God was not going to let them down. "The plans of His heart stand from generation to generation" (Ps. 33:11), and God's unalterable purpose in Jesus Christ will not fail. So the oath to confirm the promise was for the purpose of encouraging (18) Christians, like those in Jerusalem, that their faith and hope in Jesus Christ is as sure as the Being and character of God.

6:18 God confirmed His promise with an oath (Gen. 22:17) ***"in order that by two unchangeable things,"*** His promise and His oath, both expressions of His unchangeable character and purpose (17), He might demonstrate ***"in this way that it is impossible for God to lie."*** To provide a double certainty of His unchangeable and reliable character, God made promises to Abraham (Gen. 12-17) and confirmed such with an oath (Gen. 22:16-18). This is not an example of the "two-fold witness" (Deut. 17:16; 19:15; Matt. 18:16; II Cor. 13:1), as some have suggested, but just a double assertion, with the oath validating the promise, that the divine character of truth can be trusted. The connection of an "oath" made to Abraham with the greater context of the priesthood of Melchizedek is obvious from Psalm 110:4: "The Lord has sworn and will not change His mind; Thou art a priest forever according to the order of Melchizedek." This verse was quoted in 5:6, alluded to in 5:10, and will be again mentioned in 6:20, but the concept of an "oath" will be specifically emphasized in 7:20-28.

The double attestation serves to verify "it is impossible for God to lie." As in 6:6 the "impossibility" is based on the absolute character of God. The dynamic activity of God can only be expressive of His Being. God *does* what He *does* because He *is* who He *is*. "It is impossible," i.e., there is "no dynamic," to express that which is contrary to His character of absolute Truth. God can only act consistent with His character. The Hebrew forefathers understood this: "God is not a man, that He should lie... Has he said, and will He not do it? Or has He spoken, and will He not make it good?" (Num. 23:19). "The Glory of Israel will not lie or change His mind, for He is not a man that He should change His mind" (I Sam. 15:29). Man may be fickle, but God is not! "He does not retract His words" (Isa. 31:2). God, Himself, says, "I have spoken and truly I will bring it to pass" (Isa. 46:11), for His action always expresses His Being. Jesus declared such in His prayer, saying, "Thy word is truth" (John 17:17). "He Who promised" through Abraham and many prophets, that "the hope of eternal life, which God who cannot lie, promised long ages ago..." (Titus 1:2) was to be fulfilled in Jesus Christ – "He Who promised is faithful" (10:23).

The purpose of the double promise and oath of God to Abraham was that *"we should have strong encouragement, those having fled to lay hold of the hope set before us."* Paul explains to the Jerusalem Christians that God's duplicated verification of the promise of divine blessing and multiplied posterity (Gen. 12:2,3,7; 13:15,16; 17:7,8; 18:18; 22:17; Heb. 6:14) should provide Christians with a strong encouragement and assurance that He is faithful to fulfill such in Jesus Christ

– despite the discouragement of the present circumstances. Paul does not indicate what the Christians have "fled" *from*, but only what they have "fled" *to*. Those who have received Jesus Christ to become Christians may be said to have "fled" *from* the slavery of Satan and the spiritual misuse of humanity, *from* the consequences of sin, *from* the frustration of meaning-lessness and finding no hope in anything or anyone else, *from* religion, *from* persecution, etc. In a sense, Christians are, therefore, refugees who have sought asylum in God. They are "citizens of heaven" (Phil. 3:20); "in the world, but not of the world" (John 17:11,14,16,18). It is questionable, however, whether Paul had the "cities of refuge" (Num. 35:6-8; Deut. 19:1-13) in mind as he wrote, or whether there was to be an underlying and indirect reference in these words that the Christians to whom he was writing should flee Jerusalem (cf. Acts 14:6). Paul's emphasis is that the Christians have "fled" *to* "lay hold" and "hold fast" to "the hope set before them." The "hope set before" the Christian is only in Jesus Christ. "Christ Jesus is our hope" (I Tim. 1:1); our "living hope" (I Peter 1:3). Christians have "fled" *to* Christ. Jesus is the *objective* content of our hope, "set before us" as the historical self-revelation of God and the theological explanation of God's redemptive and restorative action for man. In spiritual union with Him, Jesus is also the *subjective* basis for the confident expectation of Christians, "set before us" as the encouraging assurance of hopefulness for the ultimate realization of all that He provides in Himself. This is why "hope" is not "wishful thinking," but the objective and subjective foundation of stability and security in Christ.

6:19 *"We have this hope as an anchor of the soul, both secure and firm."* Jesus is the hope of the Christian, for He is the realized promise of God. Paul employs the metaphor of Jesus as "the anchor of the soul." Such a nautical figure was familiar to those surrounding the Mediterranean Sea, and may have been on Paul's mind due to his recent shipwreck (Acts 27:29,30,40) on his voyage to Rome. An anchor (the English word "anchor" is etymologically derived from the Greek word *angkura* used here) provides a firm (cf. 3:6,14) security (cf. Acts 16:23,24) by holding the ship secure in a position as the anchor is firmly lodged in the seabed. Paul wanted the Christians in Jerusalem to know that God's promises would not fail (cf. Rom. 4:16), for His character precludes falsehood and perjury. Christian security and assurance is based on the unchangeable character of God, Who is faithful to His promises. Christian security is not based on proof-texts of "eternal security" or on logical circumlocutions of "once saved, always saved." Jesus Christ, as the very Being of God and the living expression of the character of God, is the dynamic basis of Christian security. As the "anchor of our soul," Jesus anchors the Christian to the immutable character of the God Who keeps His promises in Jesus Christ, allowing us to have the confident expectation that we can endure and persevere in the midst of any turmoil as we anticipate the completed fulfillment of our heavenly gift (6:4) in Jesus. This was the verse that prompted Priscilla J. Owens to write the chorus of the hymn:

> We have an anchor that keeps the soul,
> Steadfast and sure while the billows roll,
> Fastened to the Rock which cannot move,
> Grounded firm and deep in the Saviour's love. [6]

It is also interesting that Clement of Alexandria (c. A.D. 200 – cf. Introduction) was apparently the first to use the representation of the anchor as a Christian symbol of Christ.

Mixing his metaphors of Christ as an anchor and Christ as the curtain-opener, perhaps because the Jewish peoples were far more temple-oriented than maritime-oriented, Paul morphs the security of Christ in the image of an anchor to the security that the Christian has because Christ is the ***one entering into the inside of the veil.*** Paul is obviously referring to the veil or curtain in the tabernacle and temple that concealed the Holy of Holies (cf. Exod. 26:31-35), also called the "Holy Place," where the presence and Shekinah glory of God dwelt in the Judaic covenant arrangement. Whereas the Aaronic high priest entered into the Holy of Holies once a year on the Day of Atonement (Lev. 16:2-22), Jesus, as High Priest, "has entered into the Holy Place once and for all" (9:12), and the veil was torn in two (Matt. 27:51; Mk. 15:38) to represent that Jesus had opened access to the presence of God for all God's people who were spiritually united to Him. This "hope through which we draw near to God" (7:19) allows the Christian to have direct communion with God in the intimacy of personal relationship.

6:20   It is "within the veil" in the Holy of Holies of God's presence *"where Jesus has entered as a forerunner on our behalf."* Jesus promised His disciples, "I go to prepare a place for you, ...that where I am you may be also" (John 14:2,3). Where was that "place"? It was the place of God's presence "where," because Jesus "has entered once and for all" (9:12) by His death, resurrection and ascension (cf. 4:14), Christians now have direct access to "draw near to God" (4:16; 7:19,25; 10:22) in intimate relationship. Jesus went through death to prepare a place for us "near to the heart of God," as Cleland McAfee's hymn states. [7]

The Aaronic high priests of the old covenant entered the Holy of Holies of the physical temple once a year as a representative of the Hebrew people of God, but the people could not follow them into that chamber of God's presence and glory. Jesus, however, *"having become a high priest forever according to the order of Melchizedek,"* entered into God's heavenly presence as a "forerunner," the point-man and precursor, that facilitates all those "in Him" to enter into continuous communion with God. When Jesus "entered once and for all" (9:12) into the Holy of Holies of God's presence, it was a *fait accompli*, setting in motion the "finished work" (cf. John 19:30) of Christ whereby He continues to function as "a high priest forever according to the universal and eternal order of Melchizedek." He opened the curtain for every Christian to be a priest unto God (cf. Exod. 19:6; I Pet. 2:9; Rev. 1:6), to have direct access to God's presence and intimate communion with Him, and to live by the continuing intercessory work of Christ, functioning as High Priest.

Concluding Remarks:

Though written in a particular historical context to the Judean Christians of the first century, these words continue to address needs of Christians in every age. They remain "profitable" (II Tim. 3:16) for our instruction and application.

There may be times when every Christian is "sluggish" (5:11; 6:12) and less than "diligent" (6:11) in their willingness to "listen under" God in obedience. When chided about such immaturity, even when it is suggested that we may be like elementary pupils or suckling infants in our spiritual progress (5:11-14), we must not take offense, particularly when one like Paul is goading us to maturity, seeking our highest good, and believing that we have everything necessary in Jesus Christ.

There may be times when Christians need to be warned of the real possibility of apostasy, and the dire consequences of repudiating and "standing against" Jesus Christ (6:4-8). Such warning should not, however, be used as a threat to create fear and doubts of one's standing with Christ, or to manipulate others into increased performance of "works."

Paul's desire was that Christians should "be brought unto maturity" (6:1) by the grace of God. Spiritual growth unto maturity is always for the end-objective of glorifying God, as "the things that accompany salvation" (6:9) are manifested in the "fruit of the Spirit" (Gal. 5:22,23).

There is always a tension in the Christian life between God's grace-action and what "we shall do" (6:3). Christians have a personal responsibility to exercise a "diligence" (6:11) of faith "until the end." This can be facilitated by observing the pattern of faithful responses made by others (6:12), not in the sense of simulated imitation, but in the emulation of how others have been receptive in faith to allow for the manifestation of Christ's life and character.

We must always trust that God is absolutely faithful and trustworthy (6:13-18). God's actions are always consistent with His character. Every promise of God will be fulfilled in accordance with His word in Jesus Christ (II Cor. 1:20).

In the midst of competing voices and the pressures of difficult circumstances, Christians can have the confident expectation of hope (6:11,12,18,19) that God will bring to pass (cf. I Thess 5:24) what He has promised in Jesus Christ. This may require patient long-suffering (6:12,15) in the midst of trials, but this, too, is empowered by the Spirit of Christ (Gal. 5:23). Even in the discouragements of apparent delays and defeats, Christians are to remain receptive to God's activity in faith (6:12).

As "the anchor of our soul" (6:19), Christ provides stability and security in our lives. In a world of insecurity, Christians have the divine dynamic of security in Christ.

Because of Christ's function as High Priest, Christians have direct access into the intimacy of God's presence (6:19,20). We can "draw near" (4:16; 7:25) to the calm security of God's presence and power, participating in the "finished work" of the continuing intercessory function of Christ's High Priesthood according to the order of Melchizedek (5:10; 6:20).

ENDNOTES

1   Ellingworth, Paul, *The Epistle to the Hebrews: A Commentary on the Greek Text*. Series: The New International Greek Testament Commentary. Grand Rapids: Wm. B. Eerdmans Pub. Co. 1993. pg. 323.

2   Lane, William L., *Hebrews 1-8*. Series: Word Biblical Commentary. Vol. 47A. Dallas: Word Books, Publishers. 1991. pg. 142.

3   Philo, *The Works of Philo: Complete and Unabridged.* "Allegorical Interpretations, III, 203." Hendrickson Publishers. 1997. pg. 73.

4   Philo, *The Works of Philo: Complete and Unabridged.* "On Abraham, 273". Hendrickson Publishers. 1997. pg. 434.

5   Philo, *The Works of Philo: Complete and Unabridged.* "On the Life of Moses, I, 283. Hendrickson Publishers. 1997. pgs. 485,486.

6   Owens, Priscilla J., "We Have an Anchor." As published in *Favorite Hymns of Praise*. Chicago: Tabernacle Publishing Co. 1970. Hymn 287.

7   McAfee, Cleland B., "Near to the Heart of God." As published in *Favorite Hymns of Praise*. Chicago: Tabernacle Publishing Co. 1970. Hymn 464.

JESUS

The Better Permanent
and Perpetual Priest of God

Hebrews 7:1-28

Whenever a movement of social activism wants to fire up
the populace to support its cause, it seeks a "hot-button issue"
to ignite the flames of popular passion into a fervor that will
promote the objective. The Jewish revolutionaries who were
seeking the liberation of Palestine from Roman occupation in
the seventh decade of the first century had apparently selected
the restoration of the legitimate Aaronic high priesthood and
the propriety of the Levitical priesthood in the temple as issues
of sufficient concern to compel the Jewish populace to support
their cause of insurrection and revolt against Rome.

Paul, under house arrest in Rome (Acts 28:30), was
advised of this ploy and felt compelled to advise the Christians
of Judea that they should avoid getting involved in this politically inspired power-play that was playing on their religious
sentiment. His argument was that the old covenant priesthood
was already obsolete. He wanted his "kinsmen after the flesh"
and "brethren in the spirit" to recognize that Jesus, their
Messiah and Savior, was the High Priest according to the order
of Melchizedek, and the priesthood of Jesus had superseded
the entire Aaronic and Levitical priesthoods, which had now
been invalidated by the annulment of the entire old covenant
with its Mosaic Law. Paul's thesis is that the living Lord Jesus
is the "better permanent and perpetual priest of God" in the
context of a "better covenant" (7:22), providing a "better

201

hope" (7:19) of relational intimacy with God. There was no reason for the Jerusalem Christians to revert back to the cultic Judaic premises and practices of priesthood, and no reason to support the promotion of such in revolt against Rome.

The little Pharisaic Jewish lawyer was meticulous in crafting his case. This entire section of the epistle to the Hebrew Christians in Jerusalem (chapters 6-10) reads like a "legal brief" wherein Paul carefully documents his argument that the royal priesthood of Jesus Christ is superior to the entire Judaic priesthood. Trained in the rabbinic legal and scriptural interpretive techniques of his time, Paul employs them masterfully, even though contemporary hermeneutic scholars might question Paul's exegetical rationale. Paul, for example, uses "the argument of silence" (cf. 7:3,8), arguing from the absence of any stated lineage of Melchizedek to establish the permanent and perpetual priesthood of Jesus. Paul also argues that priority in time establishes superiority, claiming that Melchizedek's priority to Levi serves as a precedent (cf. 7:9,10) to establish the superiority of Christ's priesthood over the Levitical priesthood. Though we might have reservations about Paul's legal and logical reasoning, it was consistent with the arguments of the accepted rabbinic hermeneutics of his day. This does not make it easy for the modern reader to follow Paul's argument, however. "Legal briefs" are never easy reading for the general public, and we can appreciate that Paul had forewarned his readers that he had "much to say" about Melchizedek and his relation to Jesus Christ, and that it was "hard to explain" (5:11).

7:1   Getting to the point that he has been aiming at, Paul writes, *"For this Melchizedek,"* previously mentioned in the foregoing verse (6:20) and earlier in the epistle in 5:6,10, and first mentioned biblically in the historical narrative of Genesis 14:17-20, was the *"king of Salem, priest of the Most High God."* Paul wanted to emphasize the king-priest combination of Melchizedek in order to apply such as a prefiguring of Jesus Christ as both King and Priest. Other than the information from Genesis 14, we have little or no information about Melchizedek. His identification as "king of Salem" probably indicates that he was the king of one of the city-states of Canaan, and particularly the one where Mt. Zion was located. The city-state of Salem eventually became the location of Jerusalem. Psalm 76:2 seems to equate the location of Salem and Zion, when Asaph writes that God's "tabernacle is in Salem, His dwelling place also is in Zion."

The very first mention of priesthood in the Bible, Genesis 14:18, identified Melchizedek as "priest of the Most High God." The designation of "the Most High God" is a translation of the Hebrew *El Elyon*, meaning not just the highest god in a pantheon of polytheism, but the singular, ultimate and absolute God above all, the transcendent deity who is Creator of heaven and earth, Jehovah God (cf. Gen. 14:22), the universal God who is unlimited and cannot be claimed as a proprietary deity by any group of people. This was the point that Paul wanted to make to the Jerusalem Christians who were being pressured to espouse the cause of Jewish nationalism and religionism that claimed Jehovah God as the proprietary God of the Jews, instead of recognizing Jesus Christ as the priest of the universal and absolute God of the universe. When Stephen made his defense, he explained that "the Most High does not dwell in houses made by human hands" (Acts 7:48), and by implication indicated that the priesthood of God's action could not be contained in tangible tabernacles and temples, as were the hallmark of Judaic religion.

Continuing the recitation of the brief appearance of Melchizedek on the horizon of biblical history, Paul notes that Melchizedek *"met Abraham as he was returning from the slaughter of the kings and blessed him."* Four kings and their armies from the north had invaded, attacked and defeated five kings and their armies from the city-state kingdoms of Canaan.

Abraham's nephew, Lot, and his family lived in Sodom (Gen. 13:12) which was one of the cities defeated, and he and his family were taken captive. Abraham and his people pursued these intruders and defeated them "north of Damascus" (Gen. 14:15), and Abraham was bringing back Lot, his family and possessions, and the spoils of war when he met Melchizedek. Melchizedek, priest of the Most High God, "blessed" Abraham with "good words" of encouragement and assurance that he was indeed acting in accord with God's design, desire, and activity. Later (vss. 6,7), Paul will use this occasion of "blessing" as an argument for the lesser (Abraham) being "blessed" by the greater (Melchizedek).

7:2   Accurately relating the details of Genesis 14, Paul notes that it was Melchizedek *"to whom also Abraham divided a tenth part of all"* the spoils of war. Paul will parlay this fact into an argument that the one-tenth tithe collected by the Levitical priests is superseded by the one-tenth presentation of the spoils of war to Melchizedek by Abraham (cf. vss. 4-10).

Paul explains that Melchizedek *"was first of all, by interpretation"* of his name, *"king of righteousness."* Noting the etymology of the name Melchizedek, which is derived from the Hebrew words *melek*, meaning "king," and *sedeq*, meaning "righteousness," Paul is indirectly intimating that Melchizedek prefigured Jesus Christ as the "King of Righteousness." Previously in this epistle, Paul had applied Psalm 45:6 to Jesus and His possession of "the righteous scepter of His kingdom" (Heb. 1:8). Stephen (Acts 7:52) and Paul (Acts 22:14) had both announced Jesus as the promised "Righteous One" in fulfillment of the prophetic declarations of a Messianic "King of Righteousness" (cf. Ps. 22:31; 72:7; Isa. 32:17; 51:5,8; Jere. 23:6; 33:15,16).

Paul adds that Melchizedek was *"also king of Salem, which is king of peace."* The place name, "Salem," is derived from the Hebrew word *shalom*, which means "peace." Paul is already thinking of how Melchizedek prefigured Jesus as the "King of Peace," the "king who speaks peace to the nations" (Zech. 9:9,10), the One in Whom "the work of righteousness will be peace" (Isa. 32:17) for "righteousness and peace will kiss each other" (Ps. 85:10) in the work of the Messiah. Jesus was the Messianic "Prince of Peace" Who would have "no end to His kingdom" (Isa. 9:6,7). Indeed, "Jesus, Himself, is our peace" (Eph. 2:14), as well as our righteousness (I Cor. 1:30).

7:3   Employing the "argument of silence," Paul argues that since there is no record of his genealogy with date of birth and death in Genesis 14, Melchizedek is *"without father, without mother, without genealogy, having neither beginning of days nor end of life."* Obviously, this is not literally true, for as an historical character Melchizedek did have birth and death, paternity and maternity, and genealogical family connections. But the absence of a record of these allows Paul to figuratively apply these details to similitude with the priesthood of Jesus Christ, and perhaps to the apparent ambiguity of His birth and death. It is the contrast with Judaic priesthood that Paul is primarily emphasizing by this "argument of silence," however. In the Aaronic and Levitical priesthoods the lineage of descendancy was extremely important. The credentials of genealogy were essential for the succession of the Jewish priesthoods, and this point was being emphasized by the Zealots who were mobilizing the Palestinians against Rome. Paul, on the other hand, was arguing that Melchizedek was *"made like the Son of God,"* i.e., that the Melchizedekan priesthood, like the priesthood of Christ, was established by God without temporal and physiological restrictions. The absence of the external limitations and requirements of physical succession allows the Melchizedekan/ Christic priesthood to be one that is eternal and forever (Ps. 110:4). Melchizedek, as a forerunner/ type of Christ, *"remains a priest unto perpetuity,"* in a priesthood that is not limited by time or physical succession, but carries through in continuity and perpetuity. It is this ongoing and eternal character of Christ's priesthood that Paul is attempting to contrast with the physical succession characteristic of the Judaic priesthoods.

7:4 Verses 4-10 constitute a corollary argument in Paul's reasoning to emphasize the superiority of the Melchizedekan priesthood (and thus the priesthood of Christ) over the Levitical priesthood, based on Abraham's payment of one-tenth of the spoils of war to Melchizedek. Paul does not seem to be concerned about the difference in Abraham's giving a tenth of the spoils of war and the God-ordained practice of the peoples of Israel giving a tithe of one-tenth for the Levitical priesthood, because the Greek word *dekate* means both "tenth" and "tithe." Instead, he focuses on the one-tenth similarity to argue for the superiority of the priesthood of Melchizedek and Christ.

"Now observe how great this man was," Paul appeals to His Christian readers in Jerusalem. His objective is to establish the greatness of Melchizedek in order to demonstrate the greatness of Jesus Christ. Despite later attempts by commentators to cast Melchizedek as an apparitional theophany or a pre-incarnate Christophany, Paul seems to regard Melchizedek as an historical human king and priest *"to whom Abraham, the patriarch, gave a tenth of the spoils of war."* Abraham was regarded by the Jewish people as "the patriarch," the ancestral founder, the "father" (cf. John 8:33-40), the progenitor of the Hebrew people and the nation of Israel. Paul's argument is that "the patriarch," Abraham, who represented the entire genealogy and ethnicity of the Hebrew people-group, felt obliged to give "a tenth of the spoils of war" to Melchizedek, the priest, thus establishing the superiority of Melchizedek over Abraham. Melchizedek's priesthood was not based on ethnic ancestry, for he was a Gentile unrelated to the Hebraic bloodline, but his priesthood was established by "the Most High

God" to be a timeless and universal priesthood culminating in Jesus Christ.

7:5   Paul begins his comparison of the Melchizedekan priesthood and the Levitical priesthood, basing his argument on the authority of the two orders of priesthood to collect a tenth from their constituents, and arguing that the lesser always pays the greater, while the greater "blesses" the lesser.

"And, indeed, those of the sons of Levi receiving the priesthood have a commandment to collect a tithe from the people according to the Law, that is, from their brethren, although these are descended from Abraham." The use of present tense verbs in this statement likely indicates that the Levitical priesthood and the collection of tithes were still functioning at the time when this epistle was written, prior to A.D. 70. Paul was noting that the Mosaic Law of the old covenant did indeed establish the commandment that the Hebrew people pay a tenth of their income to the priestly tribe of Levi (Num. 18:21-24), and a tenth of that tithe was then to be distributed to the high priest (Num. 18:26-28), and was to be used in the maintenance of the temple (Neh. 10:37). By the time this epistle was written in the first century A.D., the collection of tithes was severely corrupted, and the Jewish historian, Josephus, records that the high priests were extorting the tithes directly from the people to such an extent that some of the Levitical priests were starving to death.[1] It is not difficult to see why the reform of the priesthood was being used as a rallying point for the revolutionaries, and why Paul was attempting to counter such among the Judean Christians by appealing to the priesthood of Christ.

7:6   Returning to Melchizedek, Paul writes, *"But the one not tracing his genealogy from them received a tenth from Abraham."* Melchizedek, the priest, whose genealogy is not recorded (cf. vs. 3), was not related by ethnic descendancy from Abraham nor from the priestly tribe of Levi. He was apparently a Gentile whose priesthood was established by the Most High God, and Abraham spontaneously recognized the rightful claim of Melchizedek to receive one tenth of the spoils of war. This payment of one tenth was not mandated by the legal necessity of a commandment of law, but by the patriarch's spiritual discernment and awareness of one who was a priestly representative of God. The functional basis of Melchizedek's priesthood was not that of legal mandate, ethnic succession, or authoritative position, but the function of God in the person of the priest.

Melchizedek, in turn, *"blessed the one having the promises."* This does not indicate that Melchizedek conferred a "blessing" of particular privilege upon Abraham, but refers simply to Melchizedek's expressing God's "good words" of assurance and encouragement that Abraham was indeed being used of God. Abraham, the one being "blessed," was the one who had received the promises of God (cf. Genesis 12,13) concerning God's intent in Jesus Christ (cf. II Cor. 1:20).

7:7   Paul's conclusion is that *"without any contradiction the lesser is blessed by the greater."* Unquestionably and without dispute, Paul argues, it is an axiomatically accepted certainty that the greater or superior (in this case, Melchizedek) blesses the lesser or inferior (in this case, Abraham). Paul does not entertain the fact that a lesser might encourage or assure a superior, and seems to consider the action of "blessing" as a certain criteria of superiority.

7:8   Now contrasting the duration of the two priesthoods, Paul writes that in the case of the Levitical priesthood, *"here, dying men receive tithes."* The priests of the tribe of Levi were mortal; they were subject to death, whereupon they would be succeeded by others, who would in turn serve God for a few years and die also. But in the case of the

Melchizedekan priesthood, the priest received tithes, and *"there it is witnessed that he lives."* Is Paul basing the validity of this "witness" on the "argument of silence" and the absence of any record of the death of Melchizedek in Genesis 14 (cf. vs. 3)? Or is Paul arguing that the "witness" of the perpetuity of the priesthood of Melchizedek is based on Psalm 110:4 and the divine oath that the Messiah would be "a priest forever according to the order of Melchizedek" (an argument that will be amplified in 21-28)? Or is Paul arguing backwards from Christ's assumption of the Melchizedekan priesthood, that he and his readers, as Christians, have "witnessed" that the living Lord Jesus lives in the immortality of an eternal and perpetual function of the Melchizedekan priesthood? Perhaps, "all of the above."

7:9,10   Drawing the conclusion for his argument of the superiority of the Melchizedekan priesthood over the Levitical priesthood, Paul employs the Hebrew logic of solidarity through representative descendancy, explaining that *"it might be said that through Abraham even Levi, having received tithes, paid tithes, for he was still in the loins of the father when Melchizedek met him."* This concept of solidarity was an important theme in Hebrew thought. Levi was "in Abraham" seminally and genetically, and therefore Abraham's actions were representative of Levi's actions. So when Abraham offered a tenth of the spoils of war to Melchizedek, Levi, who was "in Abraham", in essence paid tithes to Melchizedek. Since the one who pays the tithe is inferior to the one who receives the tithe, therefore, Levi (and the priesthood he represents) is inferior to Melchizedek (and the priesthood he represents, which includes that of Jesus Christ). This is the gist of Paul's argument.

Abraham was actually the great-grandfather of Levi, but previous generations were regarded as "fathers" or "forefathers," and thus Levi can be said to be "in the loins of his father," Abraham. Technically, if this were but an argument of physical solidarity, it could be noted that Jesus was genealogically a descendant of Abraham (cf. Matt. 1:1-17), and Jesus, being "in Abraham" by physical representation, paid a tithe to Melchizedek. Since it was not pertinent to his argument, Paul does not address this fact, for it was his intent to establish the solidarity of Levi and Abraham in order to assert the superiority of Melchizedek and his priesthood, and thus of Christ's priesthood. A similar concept of spiritual solidarity and representation is to be found when Paul refers to mankind as either being "in Adam" (cf. Rom. 5:12; I Cor. 15:22) or "in Christ" (cf. Rom. 8:1; II Cor. 5:17), implying that Adam's actions represented all those spiritually identified with him, and the actions of Christ were representative of all those spiritually identified with Him.

7:11   Whereas the argument in 7:1-10 was based on Genesis 14:17-20 and was concerned with the superiority of the Melchizedekan priesthood over the Levitical priesthood, the emphasis changes in 7:11-28 to the superiority of Jesus Christ and His priesthood "according to the order of Melchizedek" over the Aaronic and Levitical priesthoods in accord with the prophetic text of Psalm 110:4 (quoted in verses 17 and 21).

Paul begins by denying that the Aaronic and Levitical priesthoods, integrally connected, as they were, with the old covenant Mosaic Law, could achieve God's ultimate and eternal intent to mankind to be redeemed and restored to function as intended. *"If indeed perfection was through the Levitical priesthood (for the people have been given it on the basis of Law), why was there yet a need for another priest to arise according to the order of Melchizedek, and not designated according to the order of Aaron?"* Paul is not questioning whether the system of the Levitical priesthood was a perfect system, or whether it achieved the purpose that God intended for it. Instead, Paul is noting that "if (as is not the case) the

perfection of humanity could have been achieved so that
mankind could have been restored to their created end-objective via the Levitical priesthood and the old covenant Mosaic
Law to which it was integrally connected, there would have
been no need for the eschatological expectation (in accord
with Psalm 110:4) of an effectual and eternal priest 'according
to the order of Melchizedek'." The Judaic priesthood and the
old covenant Mosaic Law (cf. 19) could not make mankind
function in the perfection of the end-objective that God intended. They were but an imperfect, preliminary and provisional
measure – a stop-gap system that foreshadowed the "Son,
made perfect forever" (cf. 28), the perfect sacrifice and the
perfect dynamic by which mankind can be restored to their
perfect purpose. The Levitical priesthood and the Mosaic Law
are integrally connected and mutually dependent. The old
covenant priesthood was established by the Law, and the Law
governed the regulations of the Levitical priesthood. On the
other hand, it can be stated that the inevitable violation of the
Law necessitated the Levitical priesthood for temporary expiation and reconciliation, and the Law was established to expose
the need of the priesthood of Jesus Christ which was to operate through divine grace rather than through legal performance. The Mosaic Law and the Judaic priesthood are insepara-
ble. The failure of one to achieve God's purpose implies the
failure of the other (cf. 12). When one is invalidated and cancelled (cf. 18), the other is likewise nullified and abrogated.

The Mosaic Law and the Judaic priesthood were insufficient and inadequate to achieve God's objective of the restoration of human function to the glory of God, for such required
the sacrifice of the God-man in order to allow for the grace-
provision of deity within humanity. If the Law and priesthood
had been adequate there would have been no reason for the
eschatological expectation of a Messianic priest "according to
the order of Melchizedek" (cf. Ps. 110:4), rather than in the
existent traditional and legal order of Aaron.

7:12   The integral oneness and inseparability of priesthood and Law are explained in the statement, *"For the priesthood being changed, out of necessity becomes a change of Law also."* The priesthood and the Law each necessitate the other, and are dependent on the other. Since the priesthood is being altered and exchanged from the Aaronic and Levitical priesthood to the Melchizedekan priesthood of Jesus Christ, Paul argues that the entire Judaic and Mosaic Law is also exchanged from a system of legal performance to the grace-dynamic of God's Law "written on the hearts and minds" of Christian people (cf. 8:10; 10:16) in the new covenant.

7:13   To explain the exchange of priesthood that Paul was referring to, he writes, *"For the One concerning Whom these things are expressed has partaken of another tribe from which no one has served at the altar."* "The One concerning Whom these things are expressed," both in Psalm 110:4 and in Paul's argument here in the epistle to the Hebrew Christians in Jerusalem, is obviously Jesus Christ. In His incarnation Jesus partook (cf. 2:14) genetically and genealogically from the tribe of Judah, from which tribe the Messiah was expected as a king in the line of David, and no one from the tribe of Judah had officiated as a priest in the Jewish tabernacle or temple, for that was reserved for the priestly tribe of Levi (cf. Deut. 21:5).

7:14   *"For it is clear that our Lord has arisen out of Judah, a tribe unto which Moses spoke nothing concerning priest-hood."* Paul drives home his argument. It is logically, theologically and genealogically (cf. Matt. 1:2,3; 2:6) evident and obvious that our Lord Jesus Christ descended from the tribe of Judah, a tribe that Moses never connected with priesthood. The reference to Jesus as "Lord" conveys a definite connotation of Jesus' essential deity, as in 2:3 and 13:20 (cf. I Tim. 1:14; II Tim. 1:8), implying that Jesus was essentially one with Yahweh, the "Lord God" of Israel. The Messiah was expected to be a king from the same tribe of Judah, as was King David (cf. Rom. 1:3; II Tim. 2:8; Rev. 5:5). In order to be a combined King-Priest, Jesus' priesthood would have to be of a different order than the Levitical priesthood which was dependent on the legalities of physical descent from Levi.

7:15 *"And this"* change of law and priesthood *"is more abundantly clear, if another priest arises according to the likeness of Melchizedek."* The clarification of how Jesus could be both king and priest simultaneously is obviated by the fact that the priesthood of Christ is in accord with the prior and superior priesthood of Melchizedek. As the eschatological fulfillment of the prefiguring of David, as king, and Melchizedek, as priest, Jesus became the King-Priest sufficient to perfect mankind to the purpose God intended, and to establish the "royal priesthood" of "a people for God's own possession" (I Pet. 2:9).

7:16 As the fulfillment of the Melchizedekan priesthood, Jesus *"has become such, not according to the law of a fleshly commandment, but according to the power of an indestructible life."* Jesus' priesthood is not based on the legal requirement of physical heredity from the tribe of Levi or the family of Aaron. The priesthood of Jesus is based on "the power of an indestructible life." That "indestructible life" emerged out of the grave in the resurrection. In the resurrection the divine life of Jesus Christ was raised indestructible, incorruptible, and imperishable (cf. I Cor. 15:42-45). The permanent, eternal and immortal life of God in Christ was displayed by Jesus' resurrection from a vicarious death that could not and did not dissolve the eternality of His divine life. In the first sermon of the church, Peter explained that "God had sworn to David to send one of his descendants upon his throne, and He looked ahead and spoke of the resurrection of the Christ... Therefore, let all the house of Israel know for certain that God has made Him

(Jesus) both Lord and Christ" (Acts 2:30-36). Paul begins his epistle to the Romans by indicating that the "Son was born a descendant of David according to the flesh, and was declared the Son of God with power by the resurrection from the dead..." (Rom. 1:3,4). The dynamic power of the resurrection-life of the risen Lord Jesus is the "power of an indestructible life" that confirms the priesthood of Jesus and the kingship of Jesus, as well as the unconquerable eternal and immortal life of Jesus available to restore all mankind to God's perfect purpose. The Christians in Jerusalem needed only to rely on the "indestructible life" of the risen Lord Jesus, rather than on joining a social and political campaign to destroy Rome in order to establish a physical kingdom with a religious priesthood.

7:17 Paul connects the "indestructible life" of Jesus back to the prophetic words of the Psalmist in Psalm 110:4. *"For it is witnessed that 'THOU ART A PRIEST FOREVER ACCORDING TO THE ORDER OF MELCHIZEDEK'."* A priesthood that is "forever" must, of necessity, be indestructible, indissoluble, and unconquerable; i.e. permanent, immortal and eternal. It is an intercessory life that is not quantifiable, but only qualitatively defined as the very life of God.

7:18 Returning to the idea of the integral unity of priesthood and Law (cf. 12), and the fact that a change in one involves a change in the other, Paul explains that *"a putting away of the former commandment is effected, because of its weakness and uselessness."* The "former commandment" could conceivably refer specifically to the commandment in the Law concerning the Aaronic and Levitical priesthoods, but more likely it is to be inclusively identified as the entirety of the old covenant Mosaic Law, for the clarification in the following parenthesis (vs. 19) refers inclusively to "the Law." "Commandment" and "Law" are sometimes used synonymously in the scriptures (cf. Exod. 16:28; Rom. 7:8-13). This "former commandment" of the Law was not only prior in terms of time, but preliminary and provisional in terms of preparation, to the grace-dynamic of Christ's "indestructible life" in the new covenant with its effectual power to restore man to God's perfect functional intent. The Law was impotent to do so. It provided no strength, power, or vitality to the people of God in order to implement God's objectives. Its commands for conformity by external performance without any divine dynamic to effect the demands, made it "useless," unhelpful, and ineffectual – of no profit, benefit or advantage. The Law did not need to be adjusted, altered or "tweaked." The only solution was that it be "put away" (cf. 9:26), set aside, nullified, annulled, invalidated, cancelled, abrogated, and rejected.

7:19 Parenthetically Paul explains, *"(for the Law perfected nothing)."* As he had stated earlier (vs. 11), the Jewish priesthood could not bring perfection, so now Paul explains that the Law could make nothing perfect (cf. 10:1). This is not to say that the Law did not serve its God-ordained preliminary and provisional purpose preparatory to Jesus Christ, but the Law could not bring mankind to the perfect functional end-objective of God for humanity. The Law made man aware of his frustrating inability to perform in accord with God's expectations and character, but only the "Son, made perfect forever" (vs. 28) could provide the eschatological fulfillment of the grace-dynamic of His own divine resurrection-life in order to perfect receptive mankind unto the functional end that God intends by His Being in action in and through man.

Only in Jesus Christ is there *"a bringing in of a better hope, through which we draw near to God."* The "indestructible life" of the risen Lord Jesus, acting in His perpetual intercessory priesthood, and serving as the dynamic of all divine demands by "the law written in our hearts" (8:16; 16:10) brings into and upon Christian people the internal provision of God's efficacious and effectual grace. Whereas the only hope of the Judaic Law and priesthood was in the future hope of a Messianic deliverer, Jesus now personally serves as the "better hope," the eschatological fulfillment of the Jewish expectations, and the dynamic living hope for all Christians. "Christ Jesus is our hope" (I Tim. 1:1), Paul explained to Timothy. And to the Christians in Colossae, Paul wrote that "Christ in you is the hope of glory" (Col. 1:27).

The revolutionary insurrectionists of Palestine were offering the Judean Christians a false hope in a promised restoration of Jewish nationalism and religion. Paul assures them that the "better hope" that all Christians have in Jesus Christ is the confident expectation of being restored to God's perfect objective for man by the indwelling dynamic of Christ's resurrection-life. That is not just a future expectation in heaven, but is the present expectation of functioning as fulfilled humanity as Christ lives in and through us to the glory of God. It is the present confident expectation "through which we draw near to God" in relational intimacy, based on a spiritual oneness with the Spirit of Christ (cf. I Cor. 6:17). Our "drawing near to God" (cf. 4:16; 7:25; 10:1,22; James 4:8) will include the communion of prayer, but should not be limited only to the Christian's prayer life, for the phrase is inclusive of the entirety of the intercommunion of God and man in Christ.

7:20　Continuing to document the exchange (cf. 12) of priesthoods from the Aaronic and Levitical to the Melchizedekan priesthood of Christ, Paul returns to the phrases of Psalm 110:4, addressing the topic of the "divine oath" in verses 20-22, and the idea of the "eternal priesthood" in verses 23-25.

Earlier in the epistle Paul had emphasized that God's promise to Abraham concerning Jesus Christ and the new covenant community of Christians was confirmed by an oath in Genesis 22:17 (cf. 6:12-18). Paul now takes the theme of the "divine oath" from Psalm 110:4, which he quotes in the next verse (21), and uses it as verification for the superior priesthood of Jesus Christ. *"Inasmuch as"* (the priesthood of Christ was) *"not without oath-swearing,"* Jesus has become the surety of a better arrangement between God and man (cf. 22). The priesthood of Christ has been established and validated by a divine oath-taking. God's word is based on His unchangeable character, so His sworn oath assures absolute veracity and the reliability to achieve by His own dynamic what has been sworn.

7:21   Again, apparently parenthetically, Paul inserts that *"(for they indeed are those having become priests without oath-swearing."* The Levitical priests were successively installed and invested as priests in accord with the legal order of the Mosaic Law. They followed the requirements of the legal system and took their turn in the progression of priests. There was no divine oath assuring that their actions were expressive of the Being and character of God.

   "But" in contrast to the Levitical priests, *"He,"* Jesus, was declared a priest *"with oath-swearing, through the One"* (God the Father) *"saying before Him* (Jesus), *'THE LORD HAS SWORN AND WILL NOT CHANGE HIS MIND, THOU ART A PRIEST FOREVER')."* By the binding oath of God, who must always act consistent with his faithful and inviolable character, and Whose word is dependable and expressive of His Being, Jesus was sworn in as a priest by God Himself, and vested as the Son-priest with the very Being of God in action. God the Father declared, beforehand in time, and before the Son personally, "Thou art a priest forever."

7:22   *"According to such a great"* declaration of God's sworn placement as priest, *"Jesus has become the guarantor of a better covenant."* Jesus is not just the legal guarantee and surety of a better and more effectual arrangement between God

and man, but He is the personal "guarantor" of a new order
wherein He will personally bring into being the perfect objective that God has for man. Jesus is not just the "security
deposit" of a new contract with mankind, but He is the personal substance and reality of the "better covenant" that God has
unilaterally put in place by His grace. The covenant of Law
that established the Levitical priesthood has been annulled and
invalidated (cf. 18) as obsolete (cf. 8:13). The covenant of
grace has been established by God's sworn decree whereby
Jesus is "a priest forever" – the permanent and eternal priest of
God. The efficacy of this intercessory priesthood of Jesus
Christ is assured by the essential activity of the divine Being.
"He Who promised is faithful" (Heb. 10:23). "He will bring it
to pass" (I Thess. 5:24). The "eternal security" of one's personal relationship with God in this new "eternal covenant"
(13:20) is not based on man's actions or performance, nor even
necessarily on a legally sworn statement, but on the reality of
Christ's personal function as the "guarantor" that "He Who
began a good work in you will perfect it..." (Phil. 1:6).

7:23   Employing the same contrast of "they indeed...but He"
as he did in verse 21, Paul now contrasts the permanency and
perpetuity of the Judaic priesthoods and the priesthood of
Christ. ***"And they indeed are many, having become priests
because they were prevented by death from continuing."*** The
Levitical priests were plenteous and multiple. This multiplicity
was necessitated by the temporality and mortality of the
priests. They died, and were succeeded by others. The legal
system of Levitical priesthood continued, but the priests kept
dying. The continuity of the Levitical priesthood was constantly interrupted and disrupted. The inevitability of death in the
mortal priests of the Jewish priesthoods necessitated the legal
regulations of priestly succession. The continuity and perpetuation of the old covenant priesthoods came only by repetitive
succession, which implies a segmented and temporal effective-

ness. Though the Aaronic priesthood was referred to as a "per-petual priesthood" (cf. Exod. 29:9; 40:15; Num. 25:13), the perpetuation was only by sequenced succession of sons from generation to generation.

7:24 *"But He,"* Jesus Christ, *"through His abiding forever, has the priesthood that is not passed on."* Whereas the Jewish priesthoods involved the multiplicity of the "many" (23), the priesthood of Jesus Christ is singular. "There is one mediator between God and man, the man Christ Jesus" (I Tim. 2:5). Whereas the old covenant priesthoods were discontinuous because of the death of the priests, Jesus abides forever, "a priest forever" (Ps. 110:4), by "the power of an indestructible life" (vs. 16) displayed in resurrection. Whereas the priest-hoods of Judaism were perpetuated by legal and familial suc-cession, the priesthood of Jesus is perpetuated by the eternality of His own divine Being. The priesthood of Christ is "not passed on" to any successor, even though some ecclesiastical institutions in Christendom practice "priestly succession." Jesus is the better, supreme priest of God, whose priesthood is permanent and perpetual by reason of His own divine Being.

7:25 By logical deduction we may infer that *"From this, indeed, He is able to save to the very end those drawing near to God through Him."* Jesus is able, by the dynamic inherent in His own Being, to save those who through Him, as Christians, are drawing near in personal and spiritual intimacy to God. The need of fallen humanity is not for a religious paci-fier or a reformation of behavioral performances. The need of mankind is, rather, to be "made safe" from the misuse and abuse of dysfunctional humanity, and to be restored to func-tional humanity by the indwelling presence of God in Christ. To "be saved" is, therefore, not just a personal event or a trans-actional experience of conversion, nor anticipated benefits in the future. To "be saved" is the dynamic process whereby

God's perfect (cf. 11,19) objective is enacted in the restoration of a functional humanity in those receptive to God's presence and activity in Jesus Christ. Jesus Christ, functioning as priest, is able to do that, without any additional supplementation, to the very end of time and to the fullest extent of salvation. The "finished work" (cf. John 19:30) of Christ, functioning by His own "saving life" (Rom. 5:10), is able to "save" us completely, all the way through, unto God's ultimate end. "He Who began a good work in you will perfect it until the day of Christ Jesus" (Phil. 1:6). This happens as we are "drawing near" (cf. 4:16; 7:19; 10:1,22) by receptivity and availability to an ever-deeper relational intimacy with God. And this is only "through Him", Jesus Christ, for "no man comes to the Father, but through Him" (John 14:6).

This continuous relational intimacy of salvation is effected in Christians by Jesus, the eternal priest, who is *"living always to intercede on our behalf."* "Christ Jesus is He Who died, Who was raised, Who is at the right hand of God, Who also intercedes for us" (Rom. 8:34). The "power of an indestructible life" (16), which was victoriously displayed in the power of His resurrection from the dead (cf. Rom. 1:4), is dynamically expressed as the One who is a "priest forever" (Ps. 110:4) lives always to intercede, to intervene, and to attain God's perfect (cf. 11,19) end in our lives. The priestly function of the risen and living Lord Jesus makes Him far more than just a figure of history or a premise of theology, for He "lives always" as our intercessor and advocate (I John 2:1). He lives always to encourage, sustain, protect, minister, and to make Himself real to us and through us.

7:26 Paul begins to summarize his argument (vss. 26-28) of the superiority of the priesthood of Christ over the Judaic priesthoods. *"For this was fitting for us."* The priesthood of Jesus is just what we needed! It corresponds with the necessity, meets the demands, and fits the circumstances required to remedy man's fallen sinful condition, and to restore man to functional humanity. It is perfectly appropriate that God should provide such *"a high priest, holy, blameless, undefiled, having become separated from sinners and exalted above the heavens."*

Paul returns in verses 26-28 to referring to Jesus as "high priest." Since Paul is contrasting the old covenant Judaic priesthoods, both Aaronic and Levitical, to the priesthood of Jesus, there is no essential difference in the argument whether he speaks of Levitical priests or a high priest. As priest, Jesus is "holy," devout and consecrated (the Greek word is *hosios* rather than *hagios*). He is "blameless," being pure and having no evil. Such purity of character allows Him to be "undefiled" and uncontaminated by sin or anything contrary to the character of God. The phrase that Paul uses to describe Jesus' "having become separated from sinners" has been interpreted in various ways. Does Paul mean that by His sinlessness, despite being tempted (cf. 4:15), Jesus is distinct from all other men? Does Paul mean that Jesus as priest is distinguished from all other priests who are all sinners (cf. 27)? Or is the phrase to be integrally connected with the following phrase to indicate that Jesus was separated from all priests and other sinners by the historic occurrence of His ascension, whereby He, on the basis of His purity and perfection (sinlessness), could enter into the divine presence of the Father, and be exalted above the heavens in the triumph of transcendent glory, thus to intercede for mankind as priest with unhindered access to God? The latter interpretation seems best to correspond with Paul's earlier reference to our having "a great high priest who has passed through the heavens, Jesus the Son of God" (4:14).

7:27 Jesus, as High Priest, *"does not have any need to day by day offer up sacrifices, as do the* (Jewish) *high priests, first for their own sins, then for those of the people."* Paul's merging of the function of priests and high priests has caused consternation for some commentators. The primary responsibility of the high priest was to make the yearly sin-offering on the Day of Atonement (cf. Lev. 16:6-10; Heb. 9:7,25; 10:1,3), whereas the Levitical priests conducted the daily Jewish sacrifices at the temple. Yet, Paul seems to be referring to high priests offering daily sacrifices. His combining of the old covenant Jewish priesthoods was for the purpose of emphasizing the contrast between the plurality of the Jewish priests and the singularity of Christ; the sinfulness of the Judaic priests and the perfection of Christ; and the repetitiveness of the priestly sacrifices in the temple (whether annual or daily) as contrasted with the singularity and finality of Christ's sacrifice. Paul had previously mentioned the need of the Jewish priests to first offer sacrifices for their own sins prior to doing so for others in 5:3 (cf. 9:7; Lev. 4:3; 9:8; 16:6,11). Here his emphasis is on the final, all-sufficient completeness of Christ's sacrifice, *"because this He did once and for all, having offered up Himself."* While Melchizedek only offered "bread and wine" to Abraham, perhaps symbolic of the communion meal of the Lord's Supper, there is no record of his offering sacrifices relating to sin. Paul uses the Judaic priests as the prototype of priestly sacrifices for sin. The complexity of the argument is also amplified by the fact that Jesus Christ serves both as the sacrificing priest as well as the sacrifice (cf. 9:11-14, 23-28; 10:5-14, 19,20). As priest "He offered up Himself" as the singularly sufficient sacrifice for the sins of mankind, taking upon Himself the death consequences for all sin. He chose volitionally to thus "offer up Himself" as the vicarious sacrifice which alone would be sufficient to substitutionally take death for all men. But such death did not interrupt His priesthood (cf. 23), for death could not hold Him in its power (cf. Acts 2:24), and He was "raised from the dead, never to die again" (Rom. 6:9), but to function eternally as intercessory priest for all those "in Him." The death sacrifice of Christ in "offering up Himself once and for all" was the singularly sufficient sacrifice which

finally and completely put an end to the old covenant system
of sacrifices in the Jewish priesthoods.

7:28   Paul summarizes his foregoing argument, *"For the
Law appoints men as high priests who are weak."* The
Mosaic Law of the old covenant regulated the appointments of
many men unto the position of high priesthood. The Jewish
priests were "beset by weakness" (5:2), being volitionally vulnerable to temptation, and succumbing to sinfulness as obviated by the need to make sacrifices for their own sins (5:3;
7:27). Their functional priesthood was also "weak," as the
Jewish priesthood and its integral corollary, the Mosaic Law,
had "no strength" to perfect (11,19) and restore humanity to
the functional end-objective of God.

   "But," in contrast, *"the word of oath-swearing,* (which
came) *after the Law,* (appoints) *a Son having been perfected
forever."* "The word of oath-swearing" is God's declaration in
Psalm 110:4, "Thou art a priest forever according to the order
of Melchizedek," declaring and appointing the Son of God to
be the eternal priest. Chronologically, the declaration of Psalm
110:4 came almost 1000 years after the establishment of the
Mosaic Law as recorded in Exodus. Paul's argument in this
case is that the divine declaration of priesthood in Psalm 110:4
is subsequent to and superior to the Law-based priesthoods
which preceded, though previously he had argued that
antecedence was the basis for superiority (cf. 9,10). The point
Paul is making, however, is that the singularity of the Son of
God is superior to the multiplicity of mere men as priests in
Judaism, and this Christic superiority is because the Son was
"made perfect forever." In contrast to the personal and functional "weakness" of the Judaic priests, Jesus was essentially
perfect in Being, functionally perfect in behavior (sinless), and
was "made perfect" (cf. 2:10; 5:8,9) in benefit for all mankind
by His sinless substitutional sacrifice on their behalf. By the
resurrection display of "the power of an indestructible life"

(16), Jesus could function in a priesthood whereby His intercessory "finished work" can perfect (cf. 10:14; 11:40; 12:23) receptive humanity to God's functional end-objective, to bring glory to Himself by exhibiting His all-glorious character in created mankind. This perfect priesthood of Jesus is permanent and perpetual. He had been "made perfect forever," and is "a priest forever" (Ps. 110:4). The Greek text for "forever" is "unto the age." Jesus' finished work as priest in sacrificing Himself and in interceding for His own is operative in the eschatological age of these "last days" in which we now participate, and extends in perpetuity unto eternity.

Concluding Remarks:

When the Palestinian Christians, the original recipients of this letter, read Paul's arguments for the superiority of the priesthood of Jesus Christ, they were being pressured by their ethnic countrymen to "jump on the bandwagon" of revolt against Roman oppression. The false promises of the Zealot insurrectionists was that the Jewish priesthoods would be restored to their original forms when the Jewish people controlled their own nation, religion, and destiny.

Paul wanted to forestall any participation by the Jerusalem Christians in the Jewish cause and its false premises. In order to do so he argues for the superiority of the priesthood of Jesus, "according to the order of Melchizedek," over all Judaic priesthoods, both Aaronic and Levitical. In Paul's mind, the priesthoods of Judaism were designed with planned obsolescence. They were only intended to be a pictorial prefiguring of the sacrificial nature of Christ's priesthood and Self-sacrifice. The incarnation of Jesus and His redemptive and restorative work fulfills the eschatological expectations pictured in the legal order of the Jewish priesthoods. The Aaronic and Levitical priesthoods, and the Mosaic Law which was foundation to such in the old covenant, have all been annulled, abro-

gated, and completely set aside (cf. vss. 11,12,18,19). There
was no reason for the Judean Christians to expect or desire the
restoration of the Jewish priesthood that was impotent and had
been rendered obsolete.

Paul wanted to draw the Palestinian Christians away from
proprietary views of priesthood that gave exclusive right to the
Jewish peoples. He wanted to broaden their horizons from a
provincial priesthood that functioned geographically in
Palestine, and more specifically at the location of the temple in
Jerusalem, to the universal priesthood of Christ for all men in
every place. Whereas the Jewish priesthood was a priesthood
pro tempore, for the temporary time that God intended to use it
to illustrate what He was going to do in Jesus Christ, Paul
wanted to emphasize that the priesthood of Jesus is eternal,
final, permanent and perpetual.

The priesthood of Jesus Christ involved the sacrifice of
Himself on the cross of Calvary to effect redemption from sin
for all men, but His priesthood continues perpetually in His
continuing intercessory work, as the "saving life" (Rom. 5:10)
of Christ facilitates Christians "drawing near" to God in ever-
deeper relational union and intimacy. The Jerusalem
Christians, in the midst of their persecution and ostracism,
may have been wondering whether the risen Lord Jesus was
indeed interceding on their behalf. On the verge of impending
war against the Romans, they needed to be assured that Jesus,
"the priest forever," was continuing His priestly work to perfect them in His eternal life, despite what external circumstances might transpire.

Paul's meticulous arguments for the superiority of the
priesthood of Jesus can often appear to the modern reader to
be arduous and even redundant. But we trust that this "legal
brief" was sufficiently understandable to the Christians in
Palestine to cause them to trust in Jesus as their only hope,
recognizing Jesus as "the better permanent and perpetual priest
of God."

ENDNOTE

1   Josephus, Flavius, *The Works of Josephus: Complete and Unabridged.* "The Antiquities of the Jews." Book 20, Sect. 181,206,207. Peabody: Hendrickson Publishers. 1996. pgs. 536,538.

JESUS

The Better Minister
of the New Covenant

Hebrews 8:1-13

The radical change from the Judaic religion to the vital dynamic of Jesus' life required a change of priesthood (7:12), and change of law (7:12), and a change of covenant (7:22). In this section of the epistle (chapter 8) the perpetual priestly ministry of Jesus, the "priest forever" (7:21,24), is emphasized (cf. 8:1,2,6), and this is the context of a "better covenant" (8:6), a "new covenant" (8:8,13), wherein the law of God is no longer externally codified, but is internally personified in Jesus Christ.

As the concept of "covenant" is so prominent in this chapter, it will be instructive to consider some background for this subject.

The Hebrew word for "covenant" is *berith*, and it is used 285 times in the Old Testament. It is used of bilateral agreements between persons, such as Jacob and Laban (Gen. 31:44-55) and David and Jonathon (I Sam. 20:5-23). Marriage between husband and wife is also regarded as a covenant relationship (Malachi 2:14). Often in both the Hebrew culture and other ancient cultures, such bilateral covenants included terms of agreement, an oath by both parties to keep the agreement, and the slaying of an animal to seal the agreement. This latter feature of the ancient "blood covenant"[1] was the basis for the common references to "cutting a covenant."

The primary usage of the Hebrew word *berith* in the Old Testament is in reference to the unilateral covenants that God established with man. God established a covenant with Noah (Gen. 9:8-17), promising with the sign of a rainbow never to send another flood to destroy all flesh on the earth. God also made a covenant of promise with Abraham (Gen. 17:1-14) to multiply his descendants and make Abraham the father of a multitude of nations. A covenant arrangement was also made with the people of Israel when Moses went before God on Mt. Sinai (Exod. 24:4-8). These unilateral covenants, where God was the superior and authoritative party, could still require a responsibility of the lesser party to respond and participate. The Abrahamic covenant of promise and the Mosaic covenant of law together formed the basis on which the Israelite people considered themselves "the covenant people of God."

The Israelites could not fulfill their commitment (Exod. 19:8; 24:3,7) to keep the requirements of the Mosaic Law. The prophets foretold that God would establish a "new covenant" (Jere. 31:31), an everlasting covenant of peace (cf. Isa. 55:3; Ezek. 37:26-28), that would be a personified "covenant to the people" (Isa. 42:6). The expectation of the Messianic deliverer and the "new covenant" arrangement were merged in Judaic eschatological anticipation.

The Jewish Christians of Judea, to whom this epistle was written, were thoroughly steeped in the Hebrew tradition of God's covenants and the identification of the Jewish peoples as "the covenant people of God." At the same time, the Greek language had become the language of the land of Palestine and the Roman Empire. The concepts of "covenant" in the Greek culture, as expressed in the Greek language, were not the same as the Hebraic concepts. Prior to, and continuing into, the first century A.D. there was an integrative merge of attempting to express Hebraic concepts of God's covenants with man in the Greek language.

The Greek language had two words for "covenant." Bilateral covenant agreements between human parties were referred to with the Greek word *suntheke*, meaning "to place or put together with" another. Conditions were mutually determined by the parties involved in the arrangement, and a covenant compact or contract (verbal or written) was agreed to by both parties, whether in the context of business, politics, marriage, etc. But this word, *suntheke*, is never used in the Greek New Testament. Instead, all New Testament references to "covenant" employ the Greek word *diatheke*, meaning "to put or place through" by a party that holds an authoritative and superior decisive position, whereupon the other parties can either accept or reject any stated conditions or stipulations. All references to such a unilateral *diatheke* covenant in the Greek culture were in reference to "the last will and testament" of an individual, the conditions of which were to be enforced upon the occasion of the person's death.

Given the Hebraic emphasis on the unilateral covenants that God established with man, it is not difficult to see why the Greek word *diatheke* was chosen to translate the Hebrew *berith* throughout the Septuagint (*LXX*), the Greek translation of the Hebrew Old Testament. The Greek word *diatheke* was being invested with a Hebraic meaning that it had never previously conveyed in the Greek language and culture. On only one occasion in the Greek New Testament (Heb. 9:15-22; possibly alluded to in Gal. 3:15) is the Greek concept of *diatheke* as a "last will and testament" applied to the necessary death of the testator, referring to the death of Jesus Christ (and even this is debatable).

Within the Greek New Testament the covenant of God with Abraham (cf. Lk. 1:72; Acts 3:25) is regarded as a covenant of promise (cf. Gal. 3:16-19), having permanence and continuity through its fulfillment of the promises in Jesus Christ (II Cor. 1:20). On the other hand, the covenant of God with Israel enacted through Moses at Mt. Sinai is regarded as a temporary covenant of law that was divinely designed with planned obsolescence. It is this Sinaitic covenant that is identified as the "first" or "old covenant" (cf. II Cor. 3:6-14; Gal. 4:24; Heb. 8:7,9,13; 9:15), intended only as a provisional or preliminary agreement to prepare God's people for what God was going to do through His Son, Jesus Christ. The legal context of the Law covenant, with its external codification of performance requirements (cf. II Cor. 3:6), is contrasted with the "new covenant" (cf. II Cor. 3:6; Heb. 9:15; 12:24) of grace in Jesus Christ. There is a radical discontinuity between the old Mosaic covenant of law and the "better covenant" (Heb. 7:22; 8:6) personified in Jesus Christ, Who by the Spirit brings life and righteousness (II Cor. 3:6) and an internal provision of the divine character that Law required (Heb. 8:10; 10:16).

The Christians of Palestine in the first century were caught in this integrative transition of Greek and Hebrew concepts of "covenant." The Pharisaic forms of Judaism, prevalent at the time, had corrupted the Hebraic concepts of "covenant" by casting them in reciprocal contractual categories. The unilateral covenant of promises to Abraham was regarded as conferring unconditional physical rights and privileges to the Jewish peoples, allowing them to leverage God for their fulfillment. The Mosaic covenant of Law was regarded as a contract of bilateral reciprocal conditionalism. "If we do this, God is obliged to do this for us. If God does this, we will worship Him." The legalistic rules and regulations of human performance were regarded as human contingencies of God's activity.

In this context the Palestinian liberationists of the seventh decade of the first century A.D. were attempting to garner support for their revolt against Roman rule, and they wanted the Jewish Christians to join their cause. They might have been saying: "This land is our land. We have exclusive rights, as God's special covenant people, to rule ourselves in our own land, and to reestablish the Jewish religion, as it ought to be. Then, we will do what is right before God, and God will continue to bless us as He promised." These insurrectionists wanted to be assured of everyone's participation in this revolutionary endeavor, and were probably pressuring all the ethnic population of Palestine, including the Jewish Christians, to make a commitment to "sign on" to their "social contract" of liberation that would assuredly result in the renewal of the privileges of God's covenant with the Hebrew people.

Such an historical context allows us to understand why Paul was explaining to the Judean Christians that there was no reason for them to revert back to the Judaic religion, or to engage in the political aspirations of the Zealot revolutionaries to restore Judaic rights and regulations. Paul emphasized to his Christian brethren that as Christians, united with the Spirit of the living Lord Jesus, they were already participating in the "new covenant" of God's unilateral action of grace. As Christians, they had an entirely new orientation to God's law, for the law was now a personified provision indwelling them as the Spirit of Christ was available to manifest God's character in their behavior. The Judaic priesthood in the temple in Jerusalem had been superseded by the continuing and eternal priesthood of Christ's heavenly intercession for Christians, whereby He provides and enables everything necessary for the Christian life and Christian worship. Paul wanted the Christians of Palestine to recognize that Jesus is "the better minister of the new covenant."

8:1   The little Jewish lawyer knew how to emphasize his point by using legal and rhetorical methods to bring people's attention back to the central issue. *"Now the main point concerning the things being stated"* in the foregoing arguments of chapter 7 concerning the permanent and perpetual priesthood of Jesus is that the intercessory priesthood of Jesus continues as the vital dynamic of the Christian life. The headline (the Greek word is derived from *kephale*, meaning "head"), the primary issue, the principal thing, the "main point" to be emphasized is the ongoing priesthood of the living Lord Jesus. Paul is not summarizing. He is emphasizing.

"We have such a high priest, who has sat down at the right of the throne of the Majesty in the heavens." Previously Paul had written, "For it was fitting for us that we should have such a high priest...exalted above the heavens" (7:26). "Such a high priest" was just what we needed, and since we have "such a high priest" we do not need another. There was no need to attempt to restore the high priesthood of Judaism, as the revolutionaries were promoting. There was no need to seek a high priest in speculation about the reinstitution of the priesthood in the future. We presently "have such a High Priest" in the Person of the risen Lord Jesus Who is sufficiently encouraging, sympathizing, sustaining, protecting and empowering the Christians in whom He lives. He is serving, ministering and working as High Priest to perform all that God wants to do in Christian lives.

Jesus "has sat down at the right hand" of God. Paul referred to this fact in the introduction of this epistle (1:3), and will do so again on two more occasions (10:12; 12:2) in this letter. These all seem to draw from the imagery of Psalm 110:1 where "the Lord says to my Lord, 'Sit at My right hand'." This is the very context of the text that Paul has been emphasizing from Psalm 110:4 concerning the priesthood of Jesus (cf. 5:6,10; 6:20; 7:11-28). The Judaic priests of the Aaronic and Levitical priesthoods never "sat down." There was no place to sit in the Holy Place or the Holy of Holies of the Jerusalem temple. The "mercy-seat" (Exod. 25:17-22; Heb. 9:5) was not a place for the high priest to be seated. The old covenant priests were always standing. Their work was never done, as they engaged in their repetitive priestly performances. The figurative language of Jesus "taking His seat at the right hand of God" indicates that He had completed His sacrificial work as priest, and could be seated to continue to function within His "finished work" (cf. John 19:30), continuing His priestly ministry as intercessory advocate (cf. I John 2:1) and empowering agent (cf. Matt. 26:64). That He is seated at God's 'right hand" indicates an operational empowering, for the one who was the "right hand man" of an authority figure had the power to implement His dictates. "All authority is given to Me on heaven and on earth" (Matt. 28:18), Jesus declared prior to His ascension. The triumphant *Christus Victor*[2] had received His crowning affirmation to assume His royal priesthood. "We have a great High Priest who has passed through the heavens," Paul wrote earlier (4:14), and we can "therefore draw near with confidence to the throne of grace" (4:16), where Christ functions as priest in conjunction with the great and eminent Majesty of God the Father.

This continuing transcendent priesthood of Jesus "in the heavens" is the "main point" that Paul is driving home to his readers. In the midst of their ostracism and persecution at the hands of their Jewish kinsmen, they were being tempted by the liberationists to seek an earthly king to rule them in Palestine, and a rejuvenation of the physical high priesthood for the repetitive sacrifices in the temple. To forestall this reversionism, Paul reminds the Palestinian Christians that "we presently have a High Priest, the living Lord Jesus, Who has finished His sacrificial work, and now functions as the divine King-Priest in the heavens." There is a purposed contrast between the earthly priests functioning in the physical and tangible temple in Jerusalem and the transcendent priest, Jesus Christ, functioning "in the heavens." Such a quasi-spatial differentiation is not to be dismissed as an antiquated concept of a "two-story universe," but is to be understood as the comparative superiority of the divine, eternal priesthood of Christ, beyond all space-time cosmological, geographical, and historical limitations of human priesthoods.

8:2 The risen and living Lord Jesus Who now serves as transcendent high priest in the heavens is *"a minister in the* *sanctuary."* The word for "minister" is not the same Greek word, *diakoneo,* used in 1:14 of the angels as "ministering spirits" and in 6:10 of the Hebrew Christians "having ministered and still ministering to the saints." Here Paul uses the Greek word *leitourgos,* from which the English word "liturgy" is derived. This word refers to the continuing functional activity of Jesus Christ as a priestly ministrant or a temple liturgist attending to His intercessory work. He is doing so "in the sanctuary," in the "holy places" of God's presence where He is "seated at the right hand of God." When Ezekiel made his prophecy of a new, everlasting "covenant of peace," God spoke through him, saying, "I will set My sanctuary in their midst forever. My dwelling place will be with them... The nations will know that I am the God Who sanctifies Israel, when My sanctuary is in their midst forever" (Ezek. 37:26-28). Jesus ministers as the priestly liturgist in the "sanctuary" of God's presence, which is not located in some far away cosmological location or in an elevated place far above where we now live, but in the heavenly place (cf. Jn. 14:2) and presence of God where all Christians have access "to enter the holy place by the blood of Jesus" (10:19).

In synonymous parallelism, Paul indicates that Jesus serves as priest "in the sanctuary, *and in the true tabernacle, which the Lord erected, not man."* The physical tabernacle in the old covenant was a temporary tent set up or pitched in various locations as the Israelites moved from place to place. It was a portable worship place where the Aaronic and Levitical priests served in representing the people before God. In contrast, Paul explains that Jesus is the temple priest in the holy place and Holy of Holies of "the true tabernacle." By referring to the "true" or "real" tabernacle, Paul is not implying that the tabernacle of the old covenant was a "false" tabernacle, but only contrasting the superiority of Christ's priestly work in the reality of God's eternal, spiritual, and heavenly presence with the temporary, transient, preliminary, and imperfect function of the priests in the earthly tabernacle-tent. The heavenly and eternal tabernacle is divinely set up by the very presence of God, and not a temporary tent erected by man, thinking that the God of the universe could be enclosed in the parameters of a partitioned place. "The Lord of heaven and earth does not dwell in temples made with hands," Paul declared in Athens (Acts 17:24). Later he will write in this epistle, "Christ appeared as High Priest" to function in "the greater and more perfect tabernacle, not made with hands, ...not of this creation" (9:14). "For He did not enter a holy place made with hands, ...but into heaven itself, to appear in the presence of God for us" (9:24). Several commentators have attempted to explain Christ's ministry in the tabernacle as [1] the historical incarnational tabernacling of Jesus in a physical body (cf. John 1:14; II Pet. 1:13,14), or [2] the Spirit of Christ dwelling spiritually within Christian believers (cf. Rom. 8:9; Eph. 3:17; Col. 3:16; Rev. 21:3), or [3] Christ's dwelling in the Body of Christ, the Church (cf. I Cor. 3:16; II Cor. 6:16; Eph. 2:21,22), but all of these interpretive options seem to import ideas not present in this text or its context. The living Lord Jesus continues to function as intercessory priest in the "sanctuary" and "true tabernacle" of God's heavenly presence which cannot be circumscribed by any place or location. This will be developed more fully in 9:11-28.

8:3 The contrast of Christ's priesthood with the Judaic priesthoods is continued. *"For every high priest is appointed to offer both gifts and sacrifices."* This is essentially the same statement made in 5:1 (cf. comments), and the same idea will be referred to in 9:9 and 10:11. The Jewish high priests (which might be generically inclusive of all Judaic priests) repetitively and continuously offered a plurality of gifts and sacrifices (the differentiation of which should not be unduly pressed).

Correlatively, *"hence the necessity to have something which this One* (Christ as High Priest) *should offer."* Since priests are known to make sacrifices for sins, there is a logical necessity that Jesus as priest should have something to offer. This "he did once and for all when He offered up Himself" (7:27; cf. 9:14,25,26,28; 10:12). The multiple "gifts and sacrifices" are replaced by a single sacrifice in the death of Jesus Christ. The repetitive sacrifices of the Jewish priests become a single, "once and for all" (cf. 7:27; 9:12, 27, 28) sacrifice in the crucifixion of Jesus that completed and "finished" (cf. Jn. 19:30) all sacrificial necessity, taking the death consequences for the sins of all men for all time, and allowing Christ to function forever in His priestly ministry of intercession for the restoration of humanity.

8:4 Reiteratively (cf. 7:13), Paul states, *"For if He were on earth, He would not be a priest, since those priests are offering the gifts according to the Law."* Obviously this does not mean that Jesus was not "on earth," for He did come to earth incarnated as a man (cf. Phil. 2:6-8). The statement means that "if (as is not the case) Jesus was meant to function as an earthly and physical Judaic priest, He would be ineligible and disqualified, since those Judaic priests offering gifts according to the Mosaic Law were required to be from the family of Aaron or the tribe of Levi, and Jesus was descended from Judah (7:14)."

8:5 The Jewish priests are those *"who serve as an example and a shadow of the heavenly things."* In their temple ministry the old covenant priests served as examples (cf. 4:11) or copies (cf. 9:23); the pictorial pre-figuring that provided a sample and a sketch of what God had predetermined to do in the redemptive and restorative work of His Son, Jesus Christ. The Judaic priesthood and the Law (10:1) were but a "shadow" that foreshadowed the reality that was to be effected in Christ. Paul used the same word when writing to the Colossians, explaining that the old covenant festivals and

Sabbath days were "a shadow of what was to come, but the substance belongs to Christ" (Col. 2:17). The substance of God's intent was the reality of Christ's eternal priestly ministry of "heavenly things" while "seated at God's right hand in the heavenlies" (cf. Eph. 1:20; 2:6). The imperfect procedures of the old covenant priesthood served only as "copies of the things in the heavens" (9:23). Again (cf. 8:2), it should be noted that these "heavenly things in the heavens" do not necessarily refer to cosmological location or placement, but rather to the effectual priestly work of Christ in drawing all Christians into the presence of God (cf. 3:1; 12:22).

The present tenses of the verbs describing the Jewish priests "serving" and "offering" (vs. 4) in their priestly duties, seems to indicate that the priesthood was still functioning in the temple at Jerusalem when this epistle was written, prior to A.D. 70 Paul wanted the Jerusalem Christians to know that the religious procedures taking place within the temple walls were only a preliminary sampling of the eternal and heavenly spiritual realities of the priestly ministry of Christ in their lives. There was no reason for them to even consider reverting back to the shadow-pictures of Judaism as the socio-political activists were encouraging them to do. They already had the superior provision of eternal spiritual realities in Jesus Christ.

To illustrate that the function of the priests in the tabernacle and temple were but preliminary prototype models, Paul refers to the occasion when *"Moses had been warned when he was about to erect the tabernacle."* Although Bezalel (cf. Exod. 31:2; 35:30; 36:1,2; 38:22) was actually the construction supervisor for the tabernacle, he constructed it under the authority of Moses. God had warned Moses, *"saying, 'SEE THAT YOU MAKE ALL THINGS ACCORDING TO THE PATTERN HAVING BEEN SHOWN TO YOU ON THE MOUNTAIN'."* This quotation from Exodus 25:40 was utilized by Paul to document that the old covenant priesthood in the tabernacle was but a "pattern" or a "type" (the Greek word is *tupos*, from which we derive the English word "type," which is the translation in Romans 5:14) of the heavenly priesthood of Jesus. Some have speculated that God showed Moses a model or a "blueprint" of the prescribed tabernacle, either in tangible form or as a mental image, while on Mt. Sinai. This would add another prior "copy" to the sequence of tabernacles. More likely, Paul is keying off of the words "type" and "copy" (or "example") to emphasize the well-known Jewish interpretation that the tangible tabernacle and temple of Judaism were but representative of the heavenly presence and dwelling of God. In the apocryphal *Wisdom of Solomon*, Solomon says, "You commanded me to build a temple on Your holy mountain, ...a copy of the sacred tabernacle which You prepared from the very first" (9:8). Philo, the Jewish commentator and philosopher from Alexandria (c. 20 B.C. – A.D. 50), wrote, "We ought to look upon the universal world as the highest and truest temple of God, having for its most holy place that most sacred part of the essence of all existing things, namely, the heaven..."[3] Still, Paul's documentary quotation seems somewhat convoluted. In fact, Exodus 25:40 seems to refer to the *superiority* of the Mosaic tabernacle, based on revealed heavenly realities, whereas Paul seems to be using it to refer to the *inferiority* of the Mosaic tabernacle, based on revealed heavenly realities in Christ. But the point Paul is making is quite evident: the tabernacle and the temple of the Old Testament were used by God as a preliminary pictorial pattern, a preparatory pre-figuring paradigm, of the perfect, permanent and perpetual priesthood of Jesus Christ in the heavenly presence of God. Why would the Judean Christians want to revert back to pictures and patterns of religious priesthood when the reality of Christ's functional priesthood was operative in them by the Spirit?

8:6 *"But now,"* logically and chronologically, *"He"* (Jesus) *"has obtained a more excellent ministry."* By the sacrificial "offering of Himself" (7:27), setting in motion His "finished work" (cf. John 19:30), Jesus has obtained (cf. 11:25) a superior and eternally effectual priestly ministry of expressing the grace of God intercessorily in Christian lives. Everything that is legitimately called "Christian" is made operative by the high priestly intercession of the Spirit of Christ, whether it be prayer, worship, fellowship, service, the expression of divine character in the behavior of Christians, etc. The "more excellent" priestly ministry of the risen Lord is the eternally effectual dynamic of Christianity.

This is integrally related, *"inasmuch as He* (Christ) *is also mediator of a better covenant."* The eternal priesthood of Jesus takes place in the context of a superior unilateral covenant arrangement between God and man, "put through" by God's grace initiative in His Son, Jesus Christ. A "mediator" is one who "stands in the middle," in this case between God and man, to negotiate or effect the terms of a covenant. Writing to Timothy, Paul referred to "the one mediator between God and man, the man Christ Jesus" (I Tim. 2:5). As the God-man mediator, Jesus could represent both parties in order to reconcile man with God. But "having been reconciled, we shall be saved by His life" (Rom. 5:10). Jesus is not just the historic redemptive mediator between God and man, but He is presently the dynamic "mediator of the new covenant" (9:15; 12:24). The eternal Christ continues to mediate the new covenant in the sense of being the effecter, the enactor, the energizer, the facilitator, the implementer, the actuator, the guarantor (7:22) of this new and final covenant between God and man, the integral reality and activity of which is inherent in His own Being, and does not function without Him. This is a "better covenant" because it has superseded the old Mosaic covenant with its legally mandated priesthoods, replacing it with a covenant arrangement wherein God's grace is operative in the redemptive and restorative activity of Jesus Christ.

This better covenant is one *"which has been enacted on better promises."* The new covenant has been rightfully and properly established in accord with God's character. What, then, are the "better promises" which underlie and are intrinsic within the new covenant? If these are "better promises," what are they better than? Are they "better promises" than those offered in the Abrahamic covenant of promise? No, for Paul explained that what we have in Christ is the fulfillment of the promises of God to Abraham (cf. Rom. 4:1-25; Gal. 3:15-29). Are these "better promises" than were available in the old Mosaic covenant of Law (cf. Exod. 29:45,46; 34:6,7)? Yes, in the sense that the spiritual provision for the fulfillment of the promises made to Moses was not inherent in the performance-oriented stipulations of the Law, and only the dynamic provision of God's grace in Jesus Christ allows for the fulfillment of God's promises to restore mankind. The "better promises" are certainly to be interpretatively aligned with those made through Jeremiah concerning forgiveness, the internal reality of the law, and the personal relationship with God in the new covenant (Jere. 31:31-34; quoted in the following verses of 8:8-12). And within the historical context of this epistle, the "better promises" of this final and ultimate "better covenant" in Jesus Christ were certainly better than the false promises of the Zealot nationalists who were promising the restoration of the benefits of the old covenant Law and priesthoods – nothing but vacuous promises concerning a covenant that could not produce what it promised. Since "all the promises of God are fulfilled in Jesus Christ" (II Cor. 1:20), and the Judean Christians had, by receiving Christ in faith, become "heirs according to promise" (Gal. 3:29), to "receive the promise of the eternal inheritance" (Heb. 9:15), there was nothing "better" to receive that the fulfillment of the promises of Christ's "more excellent priestly ministry" in their lives.

8:7 Returning to the inadequacy of the old Mosaic covenant compared to the complete sufficiency of the new covenant, Paul argues, *"For if that first* (covenant) *was fault-less, no place for a second would have been sought."* This is essentially the same logic that Paul had expressed concerning the imperfection of the priesthood in 7:11. Paul is logically defending and documenting his assertion of a "better covenant" (vs. 6) in Jesus Christ. "If (as was not the case) that first covenant (cf. 9:15), that old Mosaic covenant of Law (cf. Ps. 78:10), had not been faulty, flawed and defective in its functional provision... If the covenant of Sinai had not been inadequate, ineffective and impotent to provide what man required for restoration to God's intended objective for mankind... If the covenant of Law could have led man to God's perfect end (which it could not; cf. 7:19), then there would have been no need or occasion to look for and seek a second (10:9) or subsequent covenant." But the Mosaic covenant was preliminary, provisional, and preparatory, intend-ed to be *pro tempore* (for a temporary period of time) with planned obsolescence, because there was no functional provi-sion whereby man could perform behaviorally in accord with God's character.

8:8   The inadequacy of the old covenant to provide the functional ability to behave as God intended is evident, *"For finding fault, He* (God) *says to them* (the Hebrew people), *'BEHOLD, DAYS ARE COMING, SAYS THE LORD, AND I WILL EFFECT A NEW COVENANT WITH THE HOUSE OF ISRAEL AND WITH THE HOUSE OF JUDAH'."* Did God "find fault" in the Hebrew people, or in the basic nature of the old covenant itself that He had unilaterally established? Primarily, the "fault" (same Greek root word as in previous verse 7), the inadequacy, was in the impotent inability of the Law to make men perfect (7:19). Only secondarily was there responsible fault and culpability in the Israelite people in repetitively acting unfaithfully in their covenant relationship with God (vs. 9; cf. 4:11; I Cor. 10:1-12).

Paul then proceeds to quote the prolonged passage of
Jeremiah 31:31-34 from the Septuagint (*LXX*). This, by the
way, is the longest quotation from the Old Testament within
the New Testament. It is also important to consider the greater
context of these words, for the prophecy of Jeremiah is decid-
edly Messianic. The "coming days" that God spoke of through
the prophet Jeremiah had already come when Paul wrote this
letter. Paul began the epistle by writing, "God, after He spoke
in the prophets in many portions and in many ways, in these
last days has spoken to us in His Son" (Heb. 1:1,2). These
were also the "last days" spoken of by the prophet Joel (cf.
Joel 2:28; Acts 2:16,17). The "coming days" had come in
Christ! The "new covenant" had been brought into being,
accomplished in the very Being of Jesus Christ, with the full
provision of grace to bring God's perfect end to mankind. The
"new covenant" is not the "old covenant" renewed, reconstituted, refurbished, or reformed. There is a radical replacement of
the old covenant by the new covenant, a definite discontinuity
between law and grace. But the "new covenant" brings all
God's people, the divided houses of Israel and Judah within
Hebrew history, and the ethnic division of mankind as Jew and
Gentile (cf. Gal. 3:7-20; Eph. 2:11-22), into a unified covenant
family, operating by the sufficient dynamic of the life and
priestly ministry of Jesus Christ.

8:9   The "new covenant" that God declares He will establish is ***"NOT LIKE THE COVENANT I MADE WITH
THEIR FATHERS ON THE DAY WHEN I TOOK THEM
BY THE HAND TO LEAD THEM OUT OF THE LAND OF
EGYPT."*** It is obvious that the covenant being referred to is
the Mosaic covenant, for that was the covenant inaugurated at
the exodus of the Israelite people from bondage in Egypt.
Though both were unilateral covenants of God, the old
covenant of law was "not like" the new covenant of grace in
terms of their functional provision. The old covenant was pur-

posefully temporary, comprised of externally codified rules and regulations inculcating human performance of the "works" of the Law, in order to expose the inability of the Israelite people to generate the character of God in their behavior, unto the glory of God. The new covenant, on the other hand, is eternal, comprised of the internal presence and function of the life of the risen Lord Jesus, the very Being of God in action, expressing His grace ability to manifest the character of God in Christian people, unto the glory of God. The two covenants are "not like" one another. They are opposite of each other in a polarized dichotomy of functional provision.

"FOR THEY DID NOT CONTINUE IN MY COVENANT, AND I DISREGARDED THEM, SAYS THE LORD." The Israelite people did not continue, remain, or "abide in" the conditions of the covenant that they so confidently committed themselves to perform (cf. Exod. 19:8; 24:3,7). Though they were responsible and culpable for their faithless disobedience (I Cor. 10:1-13), it simply revealed the weakness and inadequacy of the covenant of law to provide any functional dynamic for keeping the law. This entire phrase in the Septuagint takes wide latitude of liberty from, if it is not a gross perversion of, the original Hebrew text, which reads, "They broke My covenant, even though I was a husband to them, says Jehovah." But if we take the Greek words as Paul quoted them from the Septuagint, we must carefully note that the word that describes God's response to the disobedience of the Hebrew people is capable of a wide variety of meanings. Etymologically it means "to have no care about," but it can be translated "to disregard," "to pay no attention to" (cf. Matt. 22:5), "to neglect" (cf. Heb. 2:3), "to be disinterested or disgusted," or even "to reject, abandon, or give up on." Since Paul, in his letter to the Romans, asked the question, "God has not rejected His people, has He?", and then responded, "May it never be!" (Romans 11:1), it is not likely that Paul considered God's response to Israel to be that of rejection. Rather, it is

more likely that Paul thought that God had "disregarded" the Hebrew people, that by regarding them as having served His prefiguring purpose. Now, in conjunction with all the rest of mankind, for "God is not one to show partiality" (Acts 10:34), the Jewish people have the same opportunity to receive Jesus Christ and participate in the new covenant as anyone else.

8:10 *"FOR THIS IS THE COVENANT THAT I WILL MAKE WITH THE HOUSE OF ISRAEL AFTER THOSE DAYS, SAYS THE LORD."* In the Hebrew text the word for "making" a covenant is the Hebrew word for "cutting" a covenant, hearkening back to the ancient practice of the sacrificial "cutting" of a "blood covenant."[4] In the case of the "new covenant" the sacrifice of Jesus Christ in "offering Himself" (7:27) serves as the defining unilateral establishment of God's final, eternal covenant with mankind. The "house of Israel" was used as an inclusive reference to the "people of God." In the "new covenant" the "people of God" are all Christians who have received Jesus Christ as their life. To the Romans, Paul explained, "They are not all Israel who are descended from Israel..." (Rom. 9:6), for all who are in Christ are God's people (Rom. 9:25). The "Israel of God" (Gal. 6:16) is now the community of Christians in whom "God rules" (*yisra-el*, the Hebrew word for Israel, seems to have an etymological meaning of "God rules") through the Lordship of Jesus Christ. During the very time that Paul wrote this epistle to the Hebrew Christians in Palestine, he explained to the Christian brethren in Rome, "I am wearing this chain for the sake of the hope of Israel" (Acts 28:20). In other words, Paul regarded Jesus Christ, and his own participation "in Christ," to be the fulfillment of "the hope of Israel" – everything that Israel was promised and expected. The "new covenant" would be effected "after those days," after the preparatory and pre-figuring days of the old covenant (B.C.), when "in the fullness of time, God

244

sent forth His Son, ...to redeem them under the Law" (Gal. 4:4,5).

The positive content of the new covenant was promised by God through Jeremiah, *"I WILL PUT MY LAWS INTO THEIR MINDS, AND I WILL WRITE THEM UPON THEIR HEARTS."* Here is the promise of a "change of law" that Paul indicated was necessary in 7:12, for the externally codified Law of behavioral rules and regulations "made nothing perfect" (7:19). The old covenant Law could not restore mankind to the perfect end-objective for which God had created them. But in the "new covenant," the law, which expresses the character of God, is no longer externally codified but is internally personified, as the dynamic of Christ's life becomes the functional provision to express God's character of godliness. "We have been granted everything pertaining to life and godliness" (II Pet. 1:3). The new covenant is "not of the letter, but of the Spirit; for the letter kills, but the Spirit gives life" (II Cor. 3:6). The law is no longer letters engraved on stone tablets, but now in the new covenant the dynamic of deity has engraved God's presence and character upon our minds and hearts. Christians no longer have hearts that are "desperately wicked" (Jere. 17:9), but have been "given a new heart" because God has put His Spirit, the Spirit of Christ (Rom. 8:9), into our hearts in order to cause us "to walk in His statutes and observe His commandments" (Ezek. 11:19,20; 36:26,27), i.e., to function in the expression of His character. It is important to note that this implantation of God's law in Christians is not an objectified legal imputation of Christ's law-keeping put on our account in the heavenly bookkeeping department (as has been such a prominent thought in Protestant theology). Neither is this engravature of God's law in the "inner man" (cf. Eph. 3:16) an event that is yet future for the Christian in an alleged physical millennial kingdom. The internally personified law of Jesus Christ is presently experientially operative in every Christian, allowing for the expression of godly character as

Christ continues His intercessory priestly ministry in the Christian life.

Continuing to explain what would transpire in the "new covenant," God says through Jeremiah, *"AND I WILL BE THEIR GOD, AND THEY SHALL BE MY PEOPLE."* God's intent from the beginning was to have a covenant relationship with humanity wherein they would function by His dynamic to express His character unto His glory. "They will be My people, and I will be their God" (cf. Exod. 6:7; 29:45,46; Lev. 26:12; Deut. 26:18; Jere. 24:7; 31:33; Ezek. 11:20; 37:23). The unfaithfulness of the people of Israel, in even failing to desire such a relationship, was graphically illustrated by the prophet Hosea marrying a prostitute (representing Israel), and naming his first son, Lo-ammi, meaning "you are not My people, and I am not your God" (Hosea 1:9,10). This illustrates the "disregard" (cf. vs. 9) that God had for old covenant Israel. In the new covenant, Christians are "the people of God, ...a people for God's own possession" (I Pet. 2:9,10) in a covenant that is not legal and contractual, but personal and relational – the continuum of which will be eternal (cf. Rev. 21:3).

8:11   In this new covenant that Jeremiah prophesied of, *"THEY SHALL NOT TEACH EVERY ONE HIS NEIGHBOR, AND EVERY ONE HIS BROTHER, SAYING, 'KNOW THE LORD,' FOR ALL SHALL KNOW ME, FROM THE LEAST TO THE GREATEST OF THEM."* The essence of all human religion is an attempt on man's part to "know God," and then to tell others (their neighbors and brothers) how they might "know God." The old covenant of Judaism was a law-based religion that exhorted each generation to instruct future generations to "know God" (cf. Deut 4:9,10; 6:20-25; 11:19), by reviewing their history, and explaining their theology, and admonishing moral conformity to the Law. The new covenant of Christianity is not essentially a belief-system or a moral code that can be instructively taught, cognitively known, and behaviorally applied. It is the dynamic presence and activity of the living Lord Jesus, Who said, "I am the way, the truth, and the life" (John 14:6). Christianity is not a collection of propositions, precepts and principles, but the living Person of Jesus Christ.

Christians, within the new covenant, are those who "know God." "You have come to know God, or rather to be known by God," Paul told the Galatians (Gal. 4:9). Jesus told His disciples, "If you know Me, you know the Father" (John 14:7). "This is eternal life, that they know the only true God, and Jesus Christ whom Thou hast sent" (John 17:3). It is interesting to note that the Greek words for "know" are different in the first and second parts of this sentence (*ginosko* and *eideo*). Some have differentiated between a Gnostic knowing of God and a relational knowing of God, but we must not make too much of these different Greek words, since they are often used synonymously, and the two words are the same in the Hebrew text. The point of Jeremiah's prophecy seems to be that the new covenant will not be a religion based on instructional education of epistemological ideology, but will instead by an intimate relational knowing of spiritual union (cf. I Cor. 6:17) between God and man, wherein Christians are "taught of the Lord" (cf. Isa. 54:13; I Thess. 4:9) by the Spirit. Jesus told the disciples, "The Holy Spirit will teach you all things" (John 14:26). "The Spirit of Truth will guide you into all truth" (Jn. 16:13). Later, the apostle John would write, "The anointing (of the Spirit) abides in you, and you have no need for anyone to teach you, but His anointing teaches you about all things" (I John 2:27). This does not mean that Christians do not need teaching from those spiritually gifted as "teachers" (cf. Rom. 12:7; Eph. 4:11), as previously noted in the need of the recipients of this epistle "for some one to teach them" (5:12). But Christians do "know God" (cf. Gal. 4:9; I John 2:3), "from the least to the greatest of them," whatever their natural abilities, social strata, or spiritual maturity, and can "listen under" God

(Greek word *hupakouo*) in obedience to be receptive to God's activity in causing them to be and to do all that He wants to be and do in them.

8:12 *"FOR I WILL BE MERCIFUL TO THEIR INIQUI-TIES, AND I WILL REMEMBER THEIR SIN NO MORE."* The unrighteousness of sin, which is contrary to and violates the character of God, has alienated (cf. Col. 1:21) man from God. The sacrifices offered by the old covenant priests could "not take away sins" (10:4), could not bring forgiveness (10:18), could not make men perfect (7:11; 10:1), and could not make men righteous (Gal. 2:21). Conversely, in the new covenant the alienation from God because of sin has been resolved in reconciliation, for "although you were formerly alienated, ...He has now reconciled you in His fleshly body through death, in order to present you before Him holy and blameless and beyond reproach..." (Col. 1:20-22). The mercy of God in Jesus Christ extends forgiveness to mankind, no longer necessitating any more offering for sin (10:18), and "perfecting for all time those who are sanctified" (10:14) in Christ.

That God "remembers our sins no more" does not indicate that the recollection of such is erased from God's memory, for this would impinge on the omniscience of God. Nor does it mean that God is henceforth indifferent to sin, for sin is always contrary to the character of God and He hates (cf. Prov. 6:16) unrighteousness and all that is not derived from His own Being. Rather, it means that God no longer holds our sins against us, for the price and penalty of death for sin has been paid once and for all by the death of Jesus Christ, allowing for His continued "finished work" (cf. John 19:30) via the ongoing priestly ministry of Jesus.

8:13 Paul adds a concluding commentary to the extended quotation just cited from Jeremiah, explaining, *"When He*

(God) *said, 'a new* (covenant),*' He has made the first*
(covenant) *antiquated."* When God declared through Jeremiah
that there would be a "new covenant" (Jere. 31:31), this logically indicates that the first covenant, the old covenant, the
Mosaic covenant of Law, is displaced and replaced when the
new covenant is inaugurated. The new covenant (*He Kaine
Diatheke*, the Greek title of "The New Testament") supersedes
the old preparatory arrangement of the old covenant which
was designed with planned obsolescence. Paul was advising
the Jewish Christians in Jerusalem that the old covenant was a
thing of the past – out-dated, antiquated, and obsolete. The old
covenant had served its provisional purpose and was now
untenable, invalidated and nullified. It had been "set aside"
(7:18) – annulled, abrogated, and abolished. There was no reason for the Palestinian Christians to seek to restore the old
covenant procedures, as the Zealots were promising to do as a
consequence of their revolt against Rome. But, if the old
covenant was cancelled by the redemptive and restorative
work of Jesus Christ, the Hebrew Christians in Judea might
have asked, "Why is the religion of Judaism still functioning
in Palestine, and why are the Jewish priests still performing
their procedures in the temple at Jerusalem?"

Paul explains that as a consequence of the already accomplished antiquation of the old covenant, *"the thing being antiquated and growing old is near to disappearing."* The old
covenant was dying of old age. Its temporal and temporary
purpose had been expended. It was no longer viable. The
Greek word translated "growing old" is the word from which
we derive the English word "geriatrics." The old covenant was
in its "dying days." It had been superseded, and was, at the
time this letter was written, being "fazed out" and eliminated.
It was "near to disappearing," Paul wrote. How near? The time
for the disappearance of all the religious activities of the old
covenant was imminent when Paul wrote this letter. In just a
few years (perhaps five or less), the whole of Palestine was

destroyed, and the people who remained to fight against the Roman armies were decimated and annihilated in the Jewish wars of A.D. 66-70. The temple was demolished and laid desolate. The Jewish priesthoods vanished (cf. Lk. 24:31; James 4:14), and all Judaic practices were terminated.

Did Paul have an intuitive suspicion that the Jewish revolt against Rome was going to fail? ...that the entire Jewish enterprise was going to be eliminated? ...that a catastrophic judgment was going to come upon the Jewish rebels of Judea (as Jesus seems to have foretold; cf. Matt. 24, 25)? We do not know the answers to those questions, but he certainly seems to indicate that the old covenant was "on its last legs," antiquated and geriatric, and would soon meet its terminal demise and disappear.

Concluding Remarks:

As we study the details of this chapter, we must not lose perspective of the "big picture," the over-all theme of the eternal priesthood of Jesus. The "main point," Paul explains, is the present, on-going, continuous, and eternal priestly ministry of the living Lord Jesus Christ. And this priestly ministry transpires within the context of a relational and dynamic "new covenant" arrangement with mankind that has been unilaterally determined by God, and yet is interactive.

Paul wanted the Palestinian Christians to take their focus off of the physical practices of the Jewish priests in the physical location of the temple in Jerusalem. He wanted them to "think outside the box," so to speak, and focus on the priesthood of Jesus that is outside of time and space. God cannot be contained in a tabernacle "pitched by man" (8:2) or a "temple made with hands" (9:11). The present function of the risen Lord as intercessory priest is in the heavenlies (8:1,5), in the presence of God (9:24), where Christians are presently seated in Christ (Eph. 2:6). This is not a cosmological location or a geographical place. It is a spiritual reality, in contrast to the physical realities of the old covenant.

Christ functions on the basis of His "finished work" (cf. John 19:30), having made the sufficient sinless sacrifice for the sins of all mankind (to be developed further in chapters 9 and 10), and now continuing His priestly work of intercession (7:25) as the permanent and perpetual priest of God. Jesus in us, as us, and through us is intercessorily praying our prayers (cf. Rom. 8:26,27); intercessorily worshipping the Father in our worship (cf. John 4:23,24); intercessorily making the sacrifice of praise (cf. Heb. 13:15); intercessorily proclaiming Himself as the Self-revelation of God in our witness and evangelism (cf. Acts 1:8); intercessorily fellowshipping with other Christians in whom He lives (cf. I John 1:3); intercessorily living out His life through us (cf. Gal. 2:20); intercessorily laying down His life for others (cf. I John 3:16). The priestly ministry of Jesus, the "Son made perfect forever" (7:28), provides the divine dynamic for the "perfecting" of humanity (cf. 7:11,19; 9:9), the process of perfection that the Hebrew Christians were encouraged to pursue (6:1). The continuing priestly ministry of Jesus allows mankind to function in accord with the end-objective of God, to allow the all-glorious character of God to be expressed in His people unto His glory. And this can only happen when deity is functioning within humanity, when Christ is living out His life in Christians. "He Who began a good work in you will perfect it..." (Phil. 1:6). The continuous and eternal priestly ministry of Jesus is the dynamic of all Christian reality and activity!

Within the new covenant priesthood of Jesus the concept of "law" has been radically changed (7:12). The law is no longer an externally codified inculcation for performance "works" of conformity to the prescribed rules and regulations. Rather, the "law is put into our minds and written on our hearts" (8:10; 10:16) in an internally personified (Jesus) provision of the grace expression of God's character. These concepts of "law" and "covenant" are antithetically juxtaposed one to the other.

In a law-based, legal and contractual concept of covenant there is the bilateral "bargaining power" of an "If...then..." conditionalism. "If you do this, then God will love you, or bless you." "If God does this, then I will serve Him." Such conditional terms of performance and meritorious action provide the basis for "legalism." The imperatives become a contingency for the indicatives. The "performance imperatives" (what some might call "categorical imperatives") indicate the willingness to engage in reciprocated action. Based on the performance of such imperatives one has "rights" of expectation, or even of leverage for the performance of the other party. Obedience is regarded as the obligatory performance conformity to the prescribed rules and regulations, the principles and precepts of the Law.

In a grace-based, relational and ontological perspective of covenant the unilateral covenant concept is retained, while still allowing for interactive responsibility. The contractual "If...then..." stipulations are displaced by the "I AM...I will..." of God's declaration and active sufficiency. "I AM God, and I will act out of My own Being, consistent with My own Being." The ontological dynamic of divine grace still allows for human receptivity of God's activity in faith. The indicative of God's presence and function provides the context for the imperatives. "God is the God of grace." "Jesus Christ is Lord." God acts indicative of His own Being. He *does* what He *does*, because He *is* who He *is*. Out of His own Being He acts in expression of His own character in consistent Self-revelation. Because He has given Himself to man through His son, Jesus Christ, He can consistently issue "grace imperatives" with the expectation of consistency with His character. He is the dynamic of His own demands. He is the expression of His own expectations. There should be no self-orientation of "What's in it for me?", nor any regard for personal "rights" by which one establishes contingencies or leverage. The other-orientation of God's love (I John 4:8,16) is the basis for the love obligation of consistency with God's character. Obedience is not performance conformity to the external codes of conduct, but is an internal and relational "listening under" (Greek *hupakouo*) to understand the next opportunity to allow for receptivity to His activity in the "obedience of faith" (Rom. 1:5; 16:26). Our response-ability allows for the freedom and joy of recognizing, "I can't; but He can!"

This part of the epistle was very timely for the Jerusalem Christians. The time was very near when the old covenant law and priesthood would vanish in 70 A.D. But these words are just as pertinent to Christians in every age, who are naturally prone to turn God's grace covenant into a legal contract of behavioral performance. Even the prevailing streams of contemporary theology (Dispensation theology and Covenant theology) have a tendency to drift into fallacious concepts of covenant, law and priesthoods. The need of the hour is to recognize that the vital dynamic of all Christian life, activity and ministry is the continuing and eternal intercessory priesthood of the living Christ.

ENDNOTES

1   Trumbull, H. Clay, *The Blood Covenant: A Primitive Rite and Its Bearing on Scripture.* Minneapolis: James Family Christian Publishers. n.d.

2   Aulén, Gustaf, *Christus Victor: An Historical Study of the Three Main Types of the Idea of the Atonement.* London: Society for Promoting Christian Knowledge. 1934.

3   Philo, *The Works of Philo: Complete and Unabridged.* "The Special Laws I," Section 66. Trans. C. D. Yonge. Hendrickson Publishers. 1993. pg. 540.

4   Trumbull, *op. cit.*

JESUS

The Better Sacrifice
Sufficient for Forgiveness

Hebrews 9:1 – 10:18

This portion of Paul's epistle to the Hebrews is integrally related to the previous argument of the superiority of Jesus Christ over the Judaic priesthoods. Having established the continuity of the eternal and heavenly priesthood of Melchizedek in the person of Jesus, Paul then proceeded to document how Jesus fulfilled all that the Aaronic high priesthood prefigured in the annual Day of Atonement sacrifice.

Jesus was a unique priest. He was both a priest and the sacrifice that the priest offered. His priesthood is from the order of Melchizedek, but His sacrifice is patterned after the annual sacrifice of the Aaronic priesthood on the Day of Atonement. In this section (9:1–10:18), Paul returns to that crucial event of Christ's "offering up himself" (7:27) on the cross in sacrificial death for mankind.

Some might think that this section of the epistle is *non-sequitur*, or that there is a regression as Paul moves from the eternal priesthood of Jesus back to the historic sacrifice of Christ on the cross. Paul's logic follows the chronologic sequence of the old covenant narratives – the historic progression from Melchizedek to the Mosaic guidelines of the Aaronic and Levitical priests and their practices in the tabernacle and temple. As Melchizedek predates Moses, so the progression of Paul's thought moves from the eternal Melchizedekian priesthood to Christ's historic sacrifice of

255

Himself as the singularly sufficient sinless sacrifice for the sins of mankind.

By establishing and reiterating the superiority of Christ's priesthood and sacrifice, Paul continues to encourage the beleaguered Christians of the Jerusalem church in the middle of the seventh decade of the first century not to succumb to the inferior and antiquated practice of the Jewish religion, as advocated by those who wanted to restore such by ousting the Romans from Palestine. Paul knew it was so important for the Judean Christians, who were socially under siege by their religious kinsmen and nationalistic countrymen to join the insurrection against Rome, to "think outside of the box" – to realize that the objects and practices in the "temple-box" that was still standing in Jerusalem were intended by God to be merely illustrative of the permanent access to God that was effected only in the work of Jesus Christ. Within the context of the "new covenant" (8:8,13; 9:15; 12:24) all of the practices of the old system of Judaic religion became antiquated and obsolete (8:13), displaced and replaced. Perhaps the Christians of Jerusalem were questioning: Why, then, is the temple still standing? Why is the Jewish priesthood still functioning? Why are sacrifices still being offered by the priests in the temple? Paul explained that the Jewish practices were outmoded and in decline, and the entire religious system was "near to disappearing" (8:13) – a rather prophetic anticipation of what would transpire in only a few years when the Romans destroyed Jerusalem and the "temple-box" in A.D. 70.

Paul's objective in this section is to walk his readers through the details of the tabernacle/temple system of sacrificial worship in the old covenant, and to point out the superiority and supersession of such in the redemptive work of Jesus Christ. Any thought of returning and reinvolving themselves in the sacrificial practices of the temple and its priesthood would be an unthinkable, abominable reversion to the imperfect and inadequate practices of the old covenant, which were only intended to be provisional and temporary, preliminary to the perfection of forgiveness and access to God afforded by the Son, Jesus Christ. To return to the Judaic worship practices – to consider the temple sacrifices to be of any value – would be to deny all that Jesus accomplished in His priesthood and sacrifice. To engage again in the restricted access of the "temple-box" after Jesus had opened unrestricted access to the Holy of Holies of God's presence (cf. 10:19) to all Christians would be to try to "put God in the box" again. May it never be! The "place" (cf. John 14:2) that has been prepared for Christians, "near to the heart of God," has been opened forever in the "new and living way" (10:20) of Jesus Christ in the "new covenant."

By extension we might add that any attempt by Christians in any age to rebuild and reconstruct the Jewish temple, and to restore and reinstitute the cultic activities of Jewish priesthood and sacrifices, would also be an abominable affront to God's redemptive work in Jesus Christ. Paul tells the Judean Christians of the first century and Christians in every subsequent century that they must never go back to the insufficient objects and practices of the old covenant, having accepted Jesus as "the better sacrifice, sufficient for forgiveness," allowing for unrestricted eternal access to God.

9:1   Paul lays the groundwork (9:1-10) for emphasizing the all-sufficient sacrifice of Jesus by reviewing the historic and physical details of the tabernacle in the old covenant. The progression of his thought begins with the context of the two chambers of the tabernacle (9:2-5), and moves to the regulated religious activities within those two chambers (9:6,7). First the places, then the practices. First the setting, then the sacrifices. First the logistics, then the liturgy. First the furniture, then the functions.

Making a transitional connection, Paul resumes his argument for the superiority of the "new covenant" (8:8,13) by writing, *"Indeed, even the first* (covenant) *had regulations of worship and the holy place of this world."* Though "the first" has no qualifier, the immediate preceding context (8:13) dictates that Paul is referring to the proto-covenant, the first covenant, the old covenant, the Mosaic covenant of Law, and not to "the first tabernacle" as some interpreters have suggested, even though "first covenant" and "first tabernacle" are connected (cf. 9:6) in this paragraph.

The paragraph begins and ends with the concept of "regulations" (9:1,10). The old covenant certainly had rules and regulations for the proper administration of all activities in the tabernacle and temple. God had carefully directed (cf. Exod. 25-31; 35-39) the legal guidelines for the "right way" of doing things in the Jewish worship center. There was a proper way to place the furniture and a proper way to engage in every worship practice. The word Paul uses for "worship" conveys the idea of "serving God in subservience."

By referring to the tabernacle as "the holy place of this world," Paul is indicating that the Jewish worship center was tangible, terrestrial and temporary. It was material and manmade, in contrast to "the perfect tabernacle of God, not made with hands" (8:2; 9:11). The physical tabernacle was earthly and this-worldly in contrast to the heavenly tabernacle (8:1; 9:23,24) which is "not of this creation" (9:11), and served as the pattern from which the earthly was but a picture (8:5). Paul is already alluding to the inferiority and insufficiency of the Jewish "holy place" or worship center, in order to explain its limited significance.

9:2 Beginning his review of the old covenant worship place, Paul wrote, *"For there was a tabernacle prepared...".* The precise regulations for the construction of the original worship tent are recorded in Exodus 26. Though Paul uses the word "tent" which indicates a temporary enclosure, his references to the tabernacle as "the holy place of this world" (9:1) is surely inclusive of the more permanent extension of the Jewish worship center in the subsequent constructs of the Jewish temple. Paul refers to the tent of the tabernacle to connect the Jewish worship center to the original establishment of the old covenant and Moses' instruction for the construction of the portable tabernacle (Exod. 25:40; Heb. 8:5). Solomon's temple (I Kings 6), the second temple which was rebuilt after the exile (Ezra 3:8–6:15), and Herod's reconstruction of the temple (John 2:20), though constructed of more permanent materials, were just as temporary as the tabernacle tent when compared to the eternal and heavenly dwelling place of God (8:1,5; 9:11,23,24). Paul wanted the Jewish Christians in Jerusalem to realize that the Jewish worship center of the tabernacle (and its later extension in the temple which still stood in Jerusalem) was temporary and transient, but the heavenly dwelling place of God was eternally opened up for direct access to God in Jesus Christ. In just a few years, in A.D. 70, the temporarily of the Jerusalem temple would be made evident when it was totally destroyed by the Roman army.

Both the tabernacle and the temple were constructed in a bipartite design with two compartments or chambers. There was *"the first one, in which* (were) *the lampstand and the table and the setting forth of the loaves."* The first room or chamber in the tabernacle/temple housed the lampstand on the south side of the enclosure (cf. Exod. 25:31-39; 26:35; 37:17-24). The *menorah* (the Hebrew word for the lampstand) was a candelabrum with seven candles, three on each side of a single upright post. Though there was only one *menorah* in the original tabernacle (Exod. 25:31), there were ten such lampstands in the temple of Solomon (I Kings 7:49), but Josephus mentions only one in the first-century temple (5.216).

On the north side of the first chamber of the tabernacle and temple was the table of showbread on which the loaves were displayed (cf. Exod. 25:23-30; 26:35; 37:10-16). The loaves were replaced either daily (cf. II Chron. 13:11) or weekly on the Sabbath (Lev. 24:8). Jesus, the Bread of Life (John 6:35,48), indicated His superiority and divine privilege over the Sabbatarian rules concerning the temple showbread (Matt. 12:4; Mk. 2:26; Lk. 6:4).

"This (first chamber) *is called the holy place,"* Paul explained in his recapitulation of the architecture of the tabernacle (cf. Exod. 26:33).

9:3 *"And after the second curtain there was a tent which is called the Holy of Holies."* At the entrance to the first compartment there was a curtain or veil or screen (cf. Exod 26:36; 36:37) through which the priests passed into the "holy place" (9:6). Between the "holy place" and the second compartment there was a much heavier curtain or veil (cf. Exod 26:31-33; 36:35; 40:3,21) through which only the high priest entered once a year (9:7).

Behind the second curtain "there was a tent," i.e., a temporary enclosure which was the rear chamber of the larger tabernacle-tent. This back-room was called "the Holy of Holies" (cf. Exod 26:33) or "the Most Holy Place" (cf. I Kings 8:6). This was the place where the holy presence of God was thought to be contained in the old covenant worship center of the tabernacle and temple.

9:4 Paul's list of the objects that were in the Holy of Holies chamber is problematic. He begins by indicating that the Holy of Holies *"had a golden altar of incense."* In the Old Testament narratives the altar of incense seems to have been located in the front chamber of the "holy place" in front of the second curtain (cf. Exod 30:1-10; 40:26). When Solomon constructed the temple the altar of incense may have been placed in the inner chamber of the Holy of Holies (cf. I Kings 6:21,22). Since the physical tabernacle was patterned (8:5) after the heavenly sanctuary, it might be noted that John saw "the golden altar before the throne" (Rev. 8:3) in the heavenly dwelling place of God.

The centerpiece of the furniture in the Holy of Holies was *"the ark of the covenant covered on all sides with gold..."* This was the most important object in the inner chamber. It was a sacred chest made of acacia wood and covered with gold, having rings of gold on each corner so staves could be placed through the rings for transportation (cf. Exod. 25:10-26; 37:1-5). The "ark of the covenant" chest was designed primarily to contain *"the tablets of the covenant,"* i.e. the "testimony" (Exod 25:16,21) of God, the replaced tablets given to Moses on which were inscribed the Ten Commandments (Exod. 34:28; Deut. 10:1-5).

In another variance from the Old Testament accounts, Paul seems to indicate that *"a golden jar containing the manna, and Aaron's rod which budded"* were also placed within the sacred box of the "ark of the covenant." The Mosaic account indicates that a sampling of "the bread from heaven" (Exod. 16:4), the manna provided to Israel in the wilderness, was placed within a jar that was to be placed within the Holy of Holies, but in front of the ark (Exod. 16:31-34) rather than inside of the ark. Likewise, Aaron's rod which had budded and bore almonds was to have been placed within the Holy of Holies in front of the ark (Num. 17:1-11), but not within it.

Are these variances in the placement of the temple objects to be considered as contradictions in the scriptures? Not necessarily, for in the long history of the Hebrew people and their worship centers there were no doubt different placements of sacred objects and movements of the furniture. It was noted earlier (9:2), for example, that Solomon had ten lampstands in the "holy place" when he tripled the size of the temple structure.

9:5 Paul continues his brief explanation of the furniture and objects within the Holy of Holies. *"And above it* (the ark of the covenant) *were the cherubim of glory overshadowing the mercy seat."* The top or lid that covered the ark of the covenant was a golden slab that was called "the mercy seat" (Exod. 25:17-22). It was on this lid covering the chest that the high priest sprinkled the blood of the bull and the goat on the annual Day of Atonement (Lev. 16:14-16), as a "covering" for his own sins and the sins of the Hebrew people. Paul's argument was that the merciful, propitiatory satisfaction of God had been made once and for all in the sacrificial death of Jesus Christ (cf. Rom. 3:25), allowing for an atonement reconciliation between God and man that provided genuine cleansing and eternal forgiveness for sins, rather than just a temporary covering of such.

At each end of the mercy seat were "the cherubim of glory." These were sphinx-like figures, both facing inward with their wings arching over the mercy seat (Exod. 25:18-22). These angelic figures represented God's heavenly *shekinah* glory residing above the mercy seat (cf. I Sam. 4:4; II Sam. 6:2; II Kings 19:15; I Chron. 13:6; Ps. 80:1; 99:1) in the Holy of Holies.

Cutting short his description of tabernacle/temple details in order to proceed to the argument at hand, Paul writes, *"but of these things we cannot now speak concerning each piece."* The tabernacle objects and furniture, and their particular placements, were of relative importance to what Paul had to say. They were just the stage setting. And if Paul did not deem it necessary to explain all the details of the usage of each object, and the possible figurative or typological meanings of each piece, neither should we! The two chambers or compartments of the Jewish worship center, and the practices that took place with them, provide the framework for the point that Paul seeks to make.

9:6 *"Now these things* (the objects of 9:2-5) *having been arranged, the priests keep going into the first tent, perform-*

ing the worship." The Levitical priests continually entered
into the first chamber of the tabernacle and temple to perform
and accomplish their subservient service of worship unto God.
They trimmed the lamps of the *menorah* (Exod. 27:20,21),
burned incense on the altar (Exod. 30:7,8), and replaced the
loaves of bread on the table (Lev. 24:8,9). The present tense
verb that the priests "keep going" into the chamber of the
"holy place," likely indicates that this activity was still taking
place at the time when this epistle was written.

9:7 *"...but into the second* (chamber) *only the high priest*
(enters)*, once a year."* Contrasting the worship practices in the
two compartments of the tabernacle and temple, Paul notes
that only the high priest of the Aaronic high priesthood (cf.
discussion in the introductory comments to 4:14–5:10) was
supposed to enter the Holy of Holies, and that on only one day
of the year, the Day of Atonement (Lev. 16:3-24). There was
an exclusive limitation of entrance into and access unto the
presence of God in the Jewish worship practices. Paul will use
the singularity of the high priest's entry on the Day of
Atonement to point to the singularity of Christ's self-sacrifice
(7:27; 9:12,26,28; 10:10), providing open access to all who are
in Christ into the Holy of Holies of God's presence (10:19-22).
    The high priest entered the Holy of Holies annually, but
*"not without blood, which he offers for himself and for the
ignorances of the people."* The purpose of the high priest
going into the Holy of Holies on the Day of Atonement was to
sprinkle blood on the mercy seat lid of the ark of the covenant.
He actually entered the second chamber twice on that day, first
to apply the blood of a bull on and before the mercy seat, to
cover the sins of himself and his household (Lev. 16:11-14),
and second, to sprinkle the blood of a goat on and before the
mercy seat to cover and make atonement for the sins of the
people of Israel (Lev. 16:15,16). Although the atonement sacrifice was for "all the sins" of Israel (Lev. 16:34), rabbinic inter-

pretation had restricted its application to only unintentional or unknown sins committed in ignorance, allowing no remedy for intentional sins. It is apparently this popular and traditional interpretation that Paul refers to. The sacrifice of an animal in death, and the application of the blood before God, was regarded as having a cleansing and purging effect for the impurities of the people (Lev. 16:16). Paul adroitly refers to the high priest as "offering" the blood, even though the Old Testament refers to "sprinkling" or "applying" the blood, as this corresponds to Christ's "offering" of Himself (9:14, 25-28; 10:10,12,14) as the sacrifice sufficient for spiritual cleansing and forgiveness. The necessity of blood (cf. 9:18,22) is explained by the need for a counteraction of the death consequences of sin.

Can you imagine what the mercy seat, the cover-lid of the ark of the covenant, must have looked like, caked with layer-after-layer of blood year-after-year? Can you imagine how it must have smelled? Can you imagine how the flies and the maggots must have been present in the heat of the desert? Perhaps the burning of incense served another purpose other than just representing reverence and honor unto God, i.e., providing a fragrance to offset the stench.

9:8   Paul now begins to draw his conclusions in this paragraph. Based on the personal revelation of God's Spirit to Paul, he explains that *"The Holy Spirit* (is) *signifying this"* by the difference between the two chambers of the tabernacle/temple and the worship practices that transpired within them. Paul sees a parallel between the "first chamber" (9:2,6,8) of the tabernacle and the "first covenant" (8:7,13; 9:1,15,18), the "old covenant" (cf. II Cor. 3:14); and between the "second chamber" (9:7) of the tabernacle and the "second covenant" (8:7), or "new covenant" (8:8,13; 9:15; 12:24). The first compartment of the "holy place" was a figure of the temporal, old covenant Jewish religion. The second compartment of the

Holy of Holies prefigured the sacrifice of Jesus Christ and the new covenant access into the eternal and heavenly presence of God's glory. Only when the physical, old covenant, Jewish worship center of the temple was destroyed and eliminated would the eternal significance of open access into the Holy of Holies of God's heavenly presence be fully realized by the Judean Christians who were the recipients of this letter.

The spiritual significance, Paul writes, is *"that the way into the Holies has not yet appeared while the first tent has standing, which is a parable unto the present time."* Jesus Christ alone is the only "way" into the holy presence of God (John 14:6). But this had not become manifestly apparent to the Christians of Judea. The physical temple was still standing in Jerusalem, claiming to offer an indirect access to God once a year through the high priest's actions on the Day of Atonement. The Christians in Jerusalem were still tempted to give credence to the Jewish worship practices – to regard them as having status, value and worth. The tabernacle/temple system of the old covenant still had "standing" and respect in the eyes of many of the Jewish Christians. Not until that "first tent," the physical temple (both the first chamber and the second chamber), was destroyed (as it was in A.D. 70) would the insufficiency of Jewish worship become apparent, and the full significance of access into the eternal Holy of Holies be disclosed and revealed to the Christians to whom Paul was writing.

So the temple that still stood in Jerusalem, with its two worship chambers, served as a parabolic illustration, a symbolic analogy, for those Christians who were at that "present time," in the middle of the seventh decade of the first century, the mid 60s, struggling to give full allegiance to Jesus Christ. Paul wanted them to move into the full experience of the "second chamber" within the "second covenant", i.e., the "new covenant" of Jesus Christ. While the old temple still stood and had "standing" in the minds of the people, the way to God was still pictorially blocked and barricaded by the veil that separated the Holy Place from the Holy of Holies. The sacrifice of Jesus Christ on the cross had caused the veil in the temple to be "torn in two from top to bottom" (Matt. 27:51; Mk. 15:38; Lk. 23:45), signifying that the separation of God and man had ended. Those who accepted Christ's offer of life could "enter within the veil" (6:19), "having confidence to enter the holy place by the blood of Jesus, by a new and living way which He inaugurated through the veil, that is, His flesh" (10:19,20). This is what Paul wanted the Christians in Jerusalem to understand and to live by.

9:9   Paul continues by explaining that, *"In accord"* (with the imperfect symbol of the still-standing temple that still claimed to be the only proper place to worship God), *"both gifts and sacrifices are offered which are not able to perfect the conscience of the one worshipping."* In accord with the old covenant worship practices, gifts and sacrifices were still offered in the temple at Jerusalem, but there was no divine dynamic of God grace provision in those "works" activities to bring about the intended objective and purpose of God. "The Law made nothing perfect" (7:19). The legal requirements of Judaic worship were unable to cleanse from sin (9:13,14; 10:2), to effect forgiveness (10:4,11), to make one perfect (10:1), or to provide direct access to God. Those who participated in such religious actions knew in their inner conscience that there was still evil (10:22) and a "consciousness of sins" (10:2) that had not been cleansed (9:14). There was still a haunting emptiness of loneliness and alienation that hindered their "drawing near to God with a sincere heart in full assurance of faith" (10:22). F.F. Bruce remarks,

> The really effective barrier to a man's free access to God is an inward and not a material one; it exists in his conscience. It is only when the conscience is purified that a man is set free to approach God without reservation and offer His acceptable service and worship.[1]

266

Paul wanted his Christian kinsmen in Judea to see through and beyond the Jewish worship practices, and to "serve the living God" (9:14) with a clear conscience that allowed them to enter in and worship God directly and intimately in the fullness of His holy presence.

9:10 The gifts and the sacrifices of the old temple worship, and all of the old covenant regulations of Jewish life, ***"because they are only upon food and drink and various washings,*** (are but) ***regulations of the flesh being imposed until a time of setting things straight."*** The peripheral externalities of the right and proper way to do everything that were imposed by the Jewish Law (cf. Lev. 11 for food laws) were but "a shadow of things to come" (Col. 2:17). They were not beneficial to spiritual development (Heb. 13:9), and were "of no value against fleshly indulgence" (Col. 2:23). Jesus had confronted the Jewish leaders about such "food and drink and washings," referring to their religious regulations as "precepts" and "traditions of men" (Mk. 7:1-15). Paul calls them "regulations of the flesh," meaning that they pertain to physical matters, but cannot provide any cleansing of the conscience (9:14). Such earthly and human rules and regulations certainly do not effect the heavenly realities that Paul is pointing his readers towards. The Palestinian revolutionaries, who were using religious issues as a rallying cry, were tempting the Judean Christians to put stock in such religious regulations, and this is what Paul wanted to forestall.

The temporality, transience, and impermanence of such bodily regulations is evidenced by Paul's statement that they are only "being imposed until a time of setting things straight." The old covenant religion was out-dated, antiquated, and obsolete (8:13). Paul anticipated that time when the misunderstanding of worship and behavior in Judaism would be rectified and corrected. He is not referring to a time of "reformation" when

Judaism would be "re-formed," reconstituted, or restored. That was the stated objective of the insurrectionists fomenting war against the Romans. Paul was adamant that Christianity was not a "re-formed" Judaism, but was a radically new reality of the living Lord Jesus in mankind. "The time when things would be set straight" would come in A.D. 70 when the Christians to whom Paul was writing would realize that all the worship practices and all the behavioral regulations of Judaism were totally defunct, and that Jesus Christ was indeed "the only way into the Holy of Holies" (9:8) of God's presence for all worship and life.

9:11 This verse commences the second major section (9:11-28) of Paul's argument concerning Jesus as the better sacrifice (9:1–10:18). The first section (9:1-10) provided the stage-setting of his theme, by considering the two compartments of the Jewish worship center, with their distinct fixtures (9:2-5) and differing functions (9:6,7), followed by an explanation of their significance (9:8-10). This second section (9:11-28) considers both parallels and contrasts between the sacrifices of the Jewish old covenant and the superior Self-sacrifice of Jesus Christ. It seems to be divided into three subsections or paragraphs: [1] sacrificial blood and cleansing (9:11-14), [2] sacrificial death and covenant (9:15-22), [3] sacrificial singularity and salvation (9:23-28).

In the old covenant worship, the high priest arrived at the temple on the Day of Atonement to apply the blood of the representative animal sacrifices in order to cover the sins of himself and the people of Israel (9:7) until the promised fulfillment of all that was yet to come by the action of the Messiah deliverer. Contrasted with this, Paul writes, ***"But Christ having arrived as High Priest of the good things having come."*** Christ, the promised Messiah, arrived at His heavenly destination (cf. 7:26; 8:2; 9:12,24) as the eternal High Priest after the order of Melchizedek (6:20; 7:1-17). But in likeness with the

Aaronic high priests, He entered the Holy of Holies to make a representative sacrificial offering for the sins of the people. As an absolutely unique High Priest, He served as both the priest and the sacrifice. Whereas the Jewish high priests offered sacrifices on the cover of the mercy-seat which were but a temporary covering for impurity, anticipating more permanent "good things to come" in the future, the Messiah-Priest brought those "good things" of God into being in fulfillment of all the promises (cf. II Cor. 1:20). The anticipated "good things to come" are now the completed "good things having come." This is the difference between Jewish eschatology and Christian eschatology. All that was anticipated and expected in the old covenant has now been made available for viable spiritual experience in the living Lord Jesus. All of the "good things" – all of the "better things" that this epistle points to – have historically (ex. crucifixion, resurrection, ascension) and theologically (ex. redemption, salvation, sanctification) and personally or experientially (ex. forgiveness, cleansing, perfection, access to God) been brought into being in Jesus Christ.

Christ entered *"through"* the veil (10:20) and into *"the greater and more perfect tent not made with hands, that is, not of this creation."* Jesus Christ serves as the High Priest in the heavenly chamber (9:3,6) of God's presence (cf. 4:14; 8:2; 9:24) – the superior dwelling place of God that achieves the real end-objective of God's intent for man, i.e., allowing man into His presence, and His presence into man. This worship place is obviously not man-made (cf. Isa. 66:1) of physical materials (cf. Mk. 14:58; Acts 7:48; 17:24; Heb. 9:24), but is "the tabernacle of God" (Rev. 21:3) "pitched by the Lord" (8:2). This dwelling place of God "in heaven itself" (9:24) is "not of this creation," thus it cannot be identified with any physical temple in Jerusalem, nor can it be identified as the physical body of Jesus (cf. John 1:14). The heaven-chamber is not subject to shaking (12:26-28) or perishing (1:11), for it is not part of the natural creation, and Paul wanted the Jerusalem

Christians who were reading this epistle to take their eyes off of the physical temple and its practices which would indeed be shaken and perish in the very near future.

9:12 Jesus Christ, the Messiah-Priest, entered the heaven-chamber of the divine presence *"not through the blood of goats and calves, but through His own blood."* The medium of access for the Christic High Priest was not the blood of animals, as it was for the Aaronic high priests (9:7) who offered animal sacrifices annually on the Day of Atonement in the tabernacle in the temple in Jerusalem. Jesus accessed heaven by a unique and superior representative sacrifice, i.e., "through His own blood," which served as the instrumental means allowing all who accept His representation to enter God's presence "in Him." Reference to "the blood of Jesus" (9:12,14) does not necessarily refer to the material substance of plasma, corpuscles or platelets of the human blood of Jesus, but rather to the action of Jesus' sacrificial death,[2] for by His death He counteracted the death that had come upon mankind (2:14), and effected the death of death.[3]

Reiterating Christ's access into heaven, Paul writes, *"He entered the holy place once for all, having secured the redemption of the ages."* Unlike the Judaic priests who entered the Holy of Holies repetitively once every year (9:7,25), Jesus' entrance into the heavenly divine presence was singular and final. He had secured the liberation of mankind from the clutch of sin and death, finally and forever by the ransom payment (Matt. 20:28; Mk. 10:45; I Tim. 2:6) of His own death, the perfect price paid (cf. I Cor. 6:20; 7:13; I Pet. 1:18,19; II Pet. 2:1) to free mankind from the slavery of sin. His sacrifice in death is validated as satisfactory and sufficient by the securing of the eschatological redemption and "eternal salvation" (5:9) for mankind, confirming divine acceptance and the fulfillment of all God intended for mankind.

9:13   In antithetical contrast to the finality of Christ's sacrifice, and to emphasize the insufficiency of the ceremonial cleansings of the old covenant, Paul argues, *"For if the blood of goats and bulls, and the ashes of a heifer sprinkling those having been defiled, sanctified for the cleansing of the flesh,...".* Paul is not doubting or questioning the effects of the old covenant sacrifices, but is affirming the limited efficacy of such when compared to the sacrifice of Christ (14). The blood sacrifice of goats and bulls occurred on the Day of Atonement, but Paul seems to generalize in order to include all old covenant sacrifices (cf. Num. 7:15,16), particularly inclusive of the sin-offering of the red heifer (cf. Num. 19:1-22). The application of animal blood by sprinkling was regarded as a setting apart of the objects or persons that had been defiled, polluted, or made impure, in order to cleanse them of their physical defilement and make them available for God's holy purposes. These religious rituals of ceremonial cleansing had limited efficacy, for they were only a temporary and external "cleansing of the flesh," i.e., of the outward and physical defilement and corruptions, and could not deal with the internal conscience and its consciousness of sin.

9:14   The superior and surpassing efficacy of Christ's sacrifice is exclaimed, *"...how much more will the blood of Christ, who through the Spirit of the ages has offered Himself without defect to God, cleanse your conscience from dead works unto worship of the living God."* The new covenant is not established on the blood of animals, nor even on the blood of a martyr, but on the representative sacrifice of the Messianic Son of God. The "blood of Christ" once again (12) refers not to some mystical efficacy of the material substance of Jesus' blood, but to the representative death of Jesus. Divinely empowered by the Holy Spirit (cf. Lk. 4:18), "the Spirit of the ages," Jesus actively, willingly (10:5-10) and obediently (cf. 5:8,9; Phil. 2:8) offered Himself (7:27), serving as both the priest and the sacrifice. His was a voluntary sacrifice (cf. John 19:30), whereas the animals of the old covenant were sacrificed involuntarily and passively. But like the animal sacrifices which were to be without spot, blemish or defect (Lev. 1:3,10; 22:18-25; Num. 19:2; Deut. 17:1), Jesus was "without sin" (4:15; II Cor. 5:21), "holy, innocent, and undefiled" (7:26), the sinless sacrifice sufficient to deal with the internal and spiritual separation of mankind from God.

Whereas the animal sacrifices could only assuage the external defilement in a ceremonial "cleansing of the flesh" (13), the representative death of Jesus can "cleanse your conscience from dead works." The Jewish rituals could not deal with the internal cleansing or perfecting of the conscience (9:9; 10:2). Sin, and its consequence of death, is much deeper than external defilement and behavioral transgression. Only Jesus' death can "cleanse the conscience" from the guilt of sin and the condemnation of thinking one has to pay or offer something to appease and please God. Religion, on the other hand, capitalizes on this nagging need of performance "works" to "measure up" and "get right" with God, advocating that their adherents go through the motions of endless rituals and confessional cleansings to feel connected to God. To the Romans, Paul wrote, "There is now no condemnation for those who are in Christ Jesus" (Rom. 8:1). On the basis of Jesus' death, Christians are reconciled (Rom. 5:10) and have peace with God (Rom. 5:1). The positive side of "cleansing from dead works" is the provision of being "made righteous" (Rom. 5:17,19; II Cor. 5:21) in order to participate in the "good works" that God prepares (Eph. 2:10), equips (Heb. 13:21), and supplies sufficiency for by His grace (II Cor. 9:8).

Paul did not want the Hebrew Christians in Jerusalem to be conscientiously bound to their past worship practices, or to revert back to the ineffectual temple rituals of Judaism, which were but the "dead works" of religion. He wanted them to operate out of a cleansed conscience, a "good conscience"

(13:18; I Pet. 3:21) that did not wallow in the "consciousness of sins" (10:2). He wanted them to recognize their freedom "to worship the living God" in spiritual worship (cf. John 4:24; Rom. 12:1), accessing the Holy of Holies of God's presence transcendently and immanently.

9:15   In this second subsection (9:15-22) the sacrificial death of Jesus is connected to the concept of "covenant." In the previous study of "JESUS: the Better Minister of the New Covenant" (8:1-13), background material was presented concerning the ancient practices of "blood covenants," and the Hebrew concept (*berith*) of God's establishment of unilateral covenants with mankind. Paul took the prophecy of Jeremiah 31 concerning a "new covenant" and explained that this involved an internalization of God's Law upon the hearts and minds of His people (8:10; 10:16). Consistently, Paul continues his present argument, *"Through this,"* the death of Jesus that allows for the internal cleansing of the conscience and the positive ramifications of reconciliation, justification and spiritual union, along with experiential peace and assurance, *"He is the mediator of a new covenant."* The old Jewish covenant explained in the Old Testament was obsolete and antiquated (8:13), nullified and abrogated (7:18; 10:9). The new covenant promised through Jeremiah (Jere. 31:31-34) was inaugurated by the death of Jesus, and that is why Jesus explained that the Eucharist observance represented "the new covenant in My blood" (Matt. 26:28; Mk. 14:24; Lk. 22:20; I Cor. 11:25). The new covenant (7:22; 8:6,8; 10:16; 12:24; 13:20) was the new arrangement, agreement, and settlement that God had "put through" in His Son, Jesus Christ, who was the mediator (8:6; 12:24), the one who "stood in the middle" between God and man as the God-man, "the one mediator between God and man" (I Tim. 2:5), to effect and enact what was God's intent for man from the beginning.

The means of Jesus' mediatorial enactment of a new covenant is explained, *"so that a death has occurred for the redemption of the transgressions at the time of the first covenant."* The inadequate animal sacrifices of the old covenant have been superseded by the historical representative death of Jesus Christ, the Son of God, who effected the purchased losing and liberation of redemption (9:12; Eph. 1:7), the buying back of mankind by the price of His own death (I Cor. 6:20; 7:23), even from the consequence of the transgressions that occurred at the time of and under the regulations of the first covenant (cf. Rom. 3:25).

The result of Jesus' mediatorial enactment of a new covenant is explained, so that *"those having been called might receive the promised fulfillment of the inheritance of the ages."* The "calling of God" (Rom. 11:29; Eph. 1:18) to Himself is in the Person and work of Jesus Christ, who as "the Elect One" (Lk. 23:35) is the basis and dynamic of the divine effectual calling. "Those having been called" are all those who have responded to God's calling in Jesus Christ and received Jesus Christ (cf. John 1:12,13), and in so doing may/should receive (not a future tense) the fulfillment of the promises of the eschatological inheritance of all the blessings of the new covenant "in Christ" (cf. Eph. 1:3). This inheriting (1:4) of the "eternal salvation" (5:9) involves becoming heirs that inherit the fulfillment of all God's prophetic promises in the old covenant (6:12,17), an inheritance that is "imperishable and undefiled and will not fade away" (I Pet. 1:4). This inheritance is not just a future expectation, but is the fullness of Christ experience "already" in the present, with a "not yet" consummation in the future.

It is here that we must address the most problematic issue in this passage. Paul's reference to "covenant" (15,16,17,18,20) has been interpreted in several ways due to the divergent Hebrew and Greek concepts of "covenant" that existed in the first century. The Hebrew word *berith* was used for both bilateral agreements between persons, and for the uni-lateral arrangements that God established with man. The Greek language had two separate words: *suntheke* ("to put together with") for bilateral agreements, and *diatheke* ("to put through") for the unilateral arrangements of a "last will and testament." Since the Greeks had no theological understanding of divine unilateral arrangements, the word *diatheke* was never used for such. But when the Jewish people of the Middle East began using the Greek language as their medium of expression, the only viable word for a unilateral arrangement was *diatheke*, and they employed the word in reference to God's unilateral covenants. When Jesus, and the subsequent Christian community, began to refer to the "new covenant" in Christ, they also employed the available Greek word *diatheke*. So, the Jewish and Christians communities were using the word *diatheke* in a way that it was never used in the Hellenistic community.

The question before us is: How did Paul (who grew up as a Jew in the Hellenistic community of Tarsus, and then became a Christian) use the word *diatheke* in this particular passage of his epistle to the Hebrews? Some have concluded that all references to *diatheke* in this paragraph refer to the original Greek concept of a "last will and testament." Others have concluded that all references to *diatheke* in this paragraph refer to the Jewish concept of a divine unilateral "covenant" of God with man. Still others have concluded that Paul jumps back and forth, switching his meaning from "covenant" (15), to "last will and testament" (16,17), and then back to "covenant" (18,20); or even more ambiguously, integrating the concepts in a merged double *entendre*. Though the mention of "inheri-tance" (15) could create a legal connection to the Greek idea of "testament" in the following verses (16,17), it will be our contention in the following comments that Paul, a Hebrew Christian, writing to his fellow Hebrew Christians in Jerusalem, retains a Hebrew concept of *berith* in his use of the

Greek word *diatheke*, and that the concept of a unilateral "covenant" of God predominates throughout this passage.

9:16 Continuing to explain Jesus as "the mediator of a new covenant" (15) – and let it be noted that mediators were not necessary for a "last will and testament" – Paul writes, *"For where there is a covenant a death is necessary to be represented by the one covenanting."* As the ancient covenants were almost exclusively "blood covenants," usually requiring the death of a sacrificial animal to ratify the agreement, so God's covenants utilized the confirmation validation of sacrificial death (18). The Hebrew word *berith* was derived from the word *bara*, meaning "to cut," and the one covenanting was regarded as "cutting a covenant," which involved the cutting and death of a representative sacrifice. A "covenant," in the Hebrew sense of the word, required a representative death performed by the one cutting the covenant in order to seal the covenant. The Greek concept of "testament" does not make sense here, for the testator's death was not necessary in order to make a "last will and testament."

9:17 Explaining a general principle of covenants, Paul continues, *"For a covenant is ratified upon corpses, since it is not even binding as long as the one covenanting* (allows the sacrifice) *to live."* God speaks through the Psalmist, of "those who have made covenant with Me by sacrifice" (Ps. 50:5), thus stating the same covenant principle of sacrifice and representative death. Covenants were ratified and confirmed "upon corpses." Usage of the Greek term *nekrois*, "corpses," had no known usage in reference to "last will and testaments" in Greek literature. Its usage here refers to dead bodies, whether animals or men, but there is nothing in the word itself that requires it to refer to humans. Covenants (bilateral or unilateral) were not regarded by the Hebrews to have any strength for binding enforcement as long as "the one cutting the covenant" allowed the representative sacrifice to live without the cutting that led to blood and death.

It must be admitted that in the Greek text the verb "lives" appears to connect with the subject of "the one covenanting," rather than to the one being sacrificed, which leaves the door open for an interpretation of "testator death" instead of the representative death of a sacrifice. But all the other words and grammar in this paragraph seem to point to the idea of "covenant" rather than "testament."

9:18 Moving from the general principle (16,17) to the particular of the inauguration of the old covenant, Paul wrote, *"This is why the first* (covenant) *was not initiated without blood."* The first covenant, the "old covenant," the Mosaic covenant of Law, was not inaugurated, confirmed, validated or ratified, so as to become legally binding, without representative blood sacrifice. The sacrificial blood of a representative death established, confirmed, sealed, and made the covenant agreement effectual.

9:19 The historical occasion of the establishment of the old covenant by sacrificial blood is recorded in Exodus 24:3-8. Paul reviews this, *"For when every commandment according to the Law had been spoken by Moses to all the people, taking the blood of calves, with water and scarlet wool and hyssop, he sprinkled both the scroll itself and all the people."* The Old Testament text does not mention the blood of goats, only of bulls, and the oldest manuscripts of the Greek text of this epistle (dating to approximately A.D. 200) do not contain the word "goats" either. The primary variance, then, is Paul's addition of applying the blood "with water and scarlet wool and hyssop." This is not recorded in Exodus 24, but these items were sometimes used for the application of blood sacrifices on other occasions (cf. Lev. 14:4-7, 51,52; Num. 19:6). Though Exodus does not specifically indicate that the blood of the bulls or calves was applied to the "scroll of the covenant," this may have been part of Jewish tradition that Paul remembered.

9:20 Upon applying the blood for the initiation of the covenant, Moses *"said, 'This is the blood of the covenant which God commanded towards you.'"* Paul is quoting this statement of Moses from Exodus 24:8, made after the Hebrew people had accepted the covenant and promised to abide by it. There does not appear to be any veiled allusion in these words to the word of Jesus when taking the last supper with His disciples.

9:21 Paul's reiteration of the inauguration of the old covenant with blood sacrifices has additional details not recorded in Exodus 24. *"And likewise, he* (Moses) *had sprinkled both the tent and all the vessels of the tabernacle worship with the blood."* When the tabernacle was later erected there was an anointing of the tent and all its utensils with oil (Exod. 40:9,10), but there is no record of such action when the old covenant was established. These utensils and vessels included the shovels and snuffers, and all of the pots, jars, plates, bowls, basins, spoons, etc., which were utilized in the Jewish worship center (cf. Num. 4:7-12).

9:22 In summary of his argument of God's Mosaic covenant inaugurated with blood sacrifices, Paul concludes this subsection paragraph, *"And according to Law, almost all things are being cleansed by blood, and without the application of blood nothing is pardoned."* In the limited context of the Law covenant, almost all things (but not all), underwent the ceremonial and ritualistic cleansing by blood to remove contamination and defilement. There were situations, though, where the poor could bring a sin-offering of flour (Lev. 5:11), and when defilement could be cleansed with water (Lev. 15:10-12; Num. 31:23) or with fire (Numb. 31:23).

In contradistinction to "almost all things" being cleansed with blood, Paul notes that "nothing" is pardoned without the application of blood. This part of the summary statement is still qualified by "according to the Law," and refers to old covenant understanding of the expiatory and propitiatory value of blood sacrifices. It is not the release of blood from the animal in blood-letting or blood-shedding that is being referred to, but the blood-pouring ritual application of the sacrificial blood that was regarded as being efficacious for the discharge, pardon or forgiveness of transgressions (15) or sins. The Hebrew word for this atoning action, *kaphar*, meant "to cover," and by figurative theological extension, "to place" or "to appease" God in order that He might be satisfied in order to condone, pardon, or cancel the effects of the sin-offense. In the old Mosaic covenant of Law the application of the blood sacrifice of animals was regarded as efficacious for the release of culpability and liability for transgressions of the Law. Paul's objective in this reiteration of the old covenant application of blood sacrifices was to set up his argument that "it is impossible for the blood of bulls and goats to take away sins" (10:4), and thus to discourage the Hebrew Christians in Judea from reverting back to their inferior and inadequate worship practices, as were still practiced in the temple in Jerusalem.

9:23   In this third subsection (23-28), Paul returns (cf. 11-14) to the contrasts and parallels between the old covenant sacrifices and the singularly sufficient and final sacrifice of Jesus Christ. ***"Then, it was necessary for the models of the things in the heavens to be cleansed by these means, but*** (now) ***the heavenlies themselves*** (are accessed) ***by better sacrifices than these."*** Utilizing a "then – but now" contrast, Paul explains that "it was necessary" (cf. 7:12; 9:16), logically, theologically, and particularly legally (22), for the old covenant worship center models or examples (4:11; 8:5) to be cleansed in ceremonial purification from external defilement and contamination, by the means of representative blood sacrifices. The Jewish worship places and practices were but "a copy and show of the heavenly things," Paul explained previously (8:5), and God told Moses to erect the tabernacle "according to the pattern" (8:5) of the heavenly worship place. For this reason Paul refers to the old covenant worship rooms as "models," examples, or facsimiles which were both, patterned after the heavenly reality, and prefiguring of the access to heavenly worship in Jesus Christ. The tangible tabernacle and temples were but the temporary, inadequate and imperfect subdemonstration of the heavenly presence and worship of God. The Greek word for "model" or "example" means "to show under," and could be transliterated as "hypodigmatic."

The "heavenlies," on the other hand, in contrast to the earthly "models," are accessed not by ceremonial animal sacrifices, but by the singularly sufficient sacrifice of the representative death of Jesus Christ. The verb action of "cleansing" in the first phrase cannot be inserted as the non-specified verb action of the second phrase in this verse. There is nothing in the heavenlies of God's presence that requires cleansing, but access to the dwelling place of God did require the cancellation and abolishment of sin by the sacrifice of the Son of God (26). So, the verb action of "entering" access from the following contextual phrase must be supplied as the absent verb in this second phrase. The "better sacrifice" of the death of Christ is the only sacrifice that can "cleanse the conscience" (14) internally, and allow Christians to participate in the "living sacrifice" (12:1) of themselves, and the offering of "the sacrifice of praise" (13:15) for all that was accomplished on our behalf by the Savior.

9:24 Returning to a contrast of the activities of the old covenant Aaronic high priests on the Day of Atonement, Paul explains, *"For Christ has not entered the holy places made with hands, an antitype of the real things."* Again, Paul indicates that the physical tabernacle and temple that were manmade (9:11), temporary and inferior, were but a copy, representation, reproduction, or "antitype" (Greek word *antitypa*) of the heavenly realities.

The divine-human Jesus never physically entered the Holy Place or the Holy of Holies of the temple in Jerusalem, for He was from the tribe of Judah, not Levi; but that is not the point Paul is making. The contrastual point is, *"but* (Christ has entered) *into the heaven itself, to appear in the presence of God on our behalf."* "Heaven itself" is not a cosmological consideration of a spatial locality, but refers to the presence of God where God can be worshipped face-to-face. The Greek word for "presence," *prosōpon*, means "before the face." Jesus Christ, crucified, resurrected and ascended, has entered (the verb is supplied from the previous phrase), and now, in the eschatological period of Christian fulfillment, has been manifested and made apparent in the heavenly and glorified presence of God. Not only does His returning entrance into the presence of God allow Him to intercede "on our behalf" (2:18; 4:15,16; 7:25; Rom. 8:34; I John 2:1) as a mediating High Priest, but is also opens immediate access for all Christians who are "in Christ" to "draw near" to the presence of God (4:16; 6:20; 7:19; 10:19,20) in direct face-to-face worship. F. F. Bruce writes,

> His entrance into the presence of God is not a day of soul-affliction and fasting, like the Day of Atonement under the old legislation, but a day of gladness and song, the day when Christians celebrate the ascension of their Priest-King. [4]

9:25 When Christ entered the Holy of Holies of God's presence, it was *"not in order that He should offer Himself often, even as the high priest enters into the holy place annually with the blood of others."* In contrast to the Aaronic high priests, Jesus does not have to offer Himself as a representative sacrifice over-and-over again in the multiplicity of repetition. Using a present tense verb that may indicate the present continuation of the activity of the high priests in the temple at Jerusalem, Paul notes that the high priest enters the holy place, the Holy of Holies, year-after-year in annual repetition, to sprinkle the blood of slain animals (not his own) serving as representative sacrifice to "cover" the sins of the people.

9:26 Jesus is not like the Aaronic high priests, *"Otherwise, it would have been necessary* (for Him) *to suffer often from the foundation of the world."* If, as is not the case, Jesus had to make repetitive sacrificial offerings of death, as the Jewish high priests had to do, this would have required Jesus to suffer and die repetitively "from the foundation of the world," i.e., throughout human history. Underlying this statement of Paul may be a presupposition of Jesus' preexistence (1:2; John 1:1) "from the foundation of the world," but nowhere does scripture indicate that Jesus died before the foundation of the world (despite the mistranslation of Revelation 13:8 in the KJV), or that He died repetitively since the foundation of the world. This is patently impossible, for Jesus, the eternal High Priest, made the historic representative sacrifice of death as a man (2:9-16), and Paul would soon note that a man only dies once (27).

The counterbalance to the absurd hypothesis of Jesus' repetitive dying is, *"...but now, once, upon the climax of the ages, for the abolition of sin through the sacrifice of Himself, He* (Jesus) *has been manifested."* In contrast to any hypothesis of a multiple repetitive dying, Jesus as High Priest offered Himself "once and for all" as the singularly unique and sufficient representative sacrifice for mankind. This served as the completing climax and consummation of the ages, the eschatological fulfillment of "the last days" (1:2; Acts 2:17), the "end of the ages" (Matt. 13:39,40; 24:3; 28:20; I Cor.

282

10:11), serving in the "fullness of time" (Gal. 4:4) to establish the Christian age, the last age, the new age, and fulfill God's intent for mankind. The High Priest, the Son of God, voluntarily allowing for the sacrifice of Himself, the Sinless One (4:15; 7:26), in a representative death for all mankind, could do far more than cover up sin, as the Jewish high priests did in their ceremonial sacrifices. Jesus could set aside (7:18) sin, put it away (I John 3:5), cancel it, remove it, abolish it, and absolve it by His own death. The God-man, Priest and sacrifice, did just that when He was historically manifested as a man in the incarnation (John 1:14; Gal. 4:4; I Pet. 1:20), and that for the purpose of dying as a man (Matt. 20:28; Mk. 10:45; John 12:27), a representative death to take upon Himself the death consequences of mankind.

9:27   To show the logical relationship and personal application of these themes, Paul writes, *"And accordingly, it is laid upon man to die once, and after this judgment."* Because of the fall of man into sin (Gen. 3:1-7), the death consequences (Gen. 2:17; Rom. 6:23) that came into being through "the one having the power of death, that is, the devil" (Heb. 2:14) have been the common plight of mankind. It is not the particular divinely appointed time of death (cf. Eccl. 3:1,2) that Paul is referring to, but the general inevitability of human death. The mortality of man is universal, and the singularity and finality of physical death necessarily (though not necessarily immediately) leads to a final determination, evaluation and assessment of the life that was lived (Lk. 16:22,23; John 5:28,29; Rom. 2:5-11; II Cor. 5:10). Judgment does not necessarily have a negative connotation of condemnation or damnation. The word "judgment" (Greek word *krisis*, from which we get the English word "crisis") does not have positive or negative connotations, but recognizes man's accountability for the consequences of freedom of choice. "God will bring every act to judgment, everything which is hidden, whether it be good or evil" (Eccl.

12:14). It is sin that links death with negative consequences of judgment, but Christ's removal, abolition and absolution of sin (26) by His own death, allows death for the Christian to be linked to salvation (28) and the confident expectation of hope (3:6; 6:11,18; 7:19). Paul connects the death of Christ to the death of mankind in general, and this is what the Christians in Judea needed to hear as they faced the ominous situation of the possibility of their own deaths in confrontation with the overpowering Roman army.

9:28   Connecting the singularity of human death to the singularity of Christ's death, Paul continues the sentence, *"so Christ having been offered once to have born the sins of many…"*. Christ, in conjunction with all humanity, dies once (not repetitively), but His is a representative death whereby He is offered by God (Isa. 53:6,13; Acts 2:23) in the Priestly Self-sacrificing of Himself (7:27; 9:14,26; Gal. 2:20; Eph. 5:2) to vicariously bear the sin consequences for "many." The "many" for whom Christ has borne the sin-consequences of death, refers to all mankind, not just a few arbitrarily predetermined "elect" as some would have us to believe. Isaiah prophesied that the Suffering Servant would "bear the sins of *many*" (Isa. 53:12). To the Romans, Paul explained, "the gift of the grace of the one Man, Jesus Christ, abounded to the *many*" (Rom. 5:15), and "through the obedience of the One the *many* will be made righteous" (Rom. 5:19). The apostle John wrote, "He Himself is the propitiation for the sins…of the *whole world*" (I John 2:2). Earlier Paul wrote, "By the grace of God, Jesus tasted death for *everyone*" (Heb. 2:9). This universality of the efficacy of Christ's death for the sins of all mankind is inclusive of all men other than Himself (7:26,27; 9:7), for He was "without sin" (4:15; II Cor. 5:21), and could thus serve as the sinless representative sacrifice sufficient to remove sin from all the remainder of the human race.

This is what Christ accomplished in His first appearance when as the incarnate God-man He put away sin and its death consequences (26), but *"He shall be made visible a second time without* (reference to) *sin, to those eagerly awaiting Him unto salvation."* Jesus was manifested on earth in the incarnation (26), appeared in heaven on our behalf (24), and will be made visible on earth in a second advent. Some would interpret this second appearance of Christ as the coming of divine judgment that was soon to occur in A.D. 70 (cf. 10:37), but the context of the eternal High Priesthood of Christ seems to indicate a reference to the impending (though not imminent) second physically visible appearance of Jesus Christ on earth, which Christians have expected from the beginning. Since sin and its consequences were removed (26) in the first incarnational coming of Jesus, the second coming of Christ will not pertain to sacrificial atonement for sin and the redemptive efficacy of representative death. The man, Jesus, could only die once (27), and that representative death was totally sufficient to take the death consequences of sin (26). His second coming will serve as the consummation of the salvation made available in the "saving life" of Christ (Rom. 5:10). Christians are already "made safe" from the misused humanity that was enslaved (II Tim. 2:26) by the one having the power of death (2:14), and liberated to function by Christ's life (Gal. 2:20; Col. 3:4) unto God's glory, but the removal of all hindrances (Rev. 21:4) to such salvation-living will transpire after Christ's second advent on earth in the experience of "eternal salvation" (5:9).

The eager expectation of Christ's return can be linked to the return of the high priest on the Day of Atonement. The people of God waited eagerly for the high priest to return from the Holy of Holies, whereupon they were assured that God had accepted the representative sacrifice to cover their sins for another year. Jewish literature records the return of Simon the high priest,

How glorious he was when the people gathered round him as he came out of the inner sanctuary! Like the morning star among the clouds, like the moon when it is full; like the sun shining upon the temple of the Most High, and like the rainbow gleaming in glorious clouds. ...Then the sons of Aaron shouted; they sounded the trumpets; they made a great noise to be heard for remembrance before the Most High. Then all the people made haste and fell to the ground upon their faces to worship their Lord, the Almighty, God Most High. (Sirach 50:5-7, 16,17)

In similar manner Christians eagerly await (Rom. 8:25; I Cor. 1:7; Phil. 3:20) the earthly return of the eternal High Priest, Jesus Christ, in glory, already assured of the singular sufficiency of Christ's representative sacrifice, but desiring to see the completed consummation of salvation unto the ages. By faith they eagerly anticipate "a salvation ready to be revealed in the last time" (I Pet. 1:5), and the privilege of an eternity of worshipping God (Rev. 22:9). Jesus' final words were, "Yes, I am coming quickly" (Rev. 22:20).

10:1 The third major section (10:1-18) of Paul's assertion that Jesus is the better sacrifice, sufficient for forgiveness (9:1–10:18), exposes the inadequacy of the Mosaic covenant of Law to do away with a constant reminder of the consciousness of sins (1-4), explains that Jesus' physical death in accord with the will of God does away with the old covenant sacrifices (5-10), asserts that Jesus' priestly sacrifice singularly and finally brought mankind to their intended purpose of holiness (11-14), and concludes that the internal provision of the new covenant does away with sin-consciousness and animal sacrifices (15-18). In these four subsections Paul makes the point that the death of Jesus Christ is the termination of all old covenant sacrifices.

Paul reiterates what he wrote earlier (8:3-5; 9:23-26), but makes different points of emphasis. *"For the Law, having a shadow of the good things coming, not itself the image of those things..."* It is not to denigrate the Law, but to show its deficiency, that prompts Paul to characterize the Law as but "a shadow of the good things to come." Previously Paul had written that the priests "offering gifts according to the Law, serve as a copy and show of the heavenly things" (8:5). To the Colossians, he explained that the old covenant food laws and festivals were "a shadow of what is to come; but the substance belongs to Christ" (Col. 2:17). Everything in the old covenant arrangement was insubstantial and temporal (space/time) – an unreal profile or outline that prefigured and foreshadowed the good things yet to come in Jesus Christ. The "good things" expected in Jewish eschatology are the "good things having come" (9:11) in Christian eschatology. Jesus Christ is the essential eschatological fulfillment of all the promises of God (II Cor. 1:20), and the essence of all new covenant realities. The "image" or visible manifestation, the form and reality, the substantive embodiment of all that the old covenant Law foreshadowed is realized in Jesus Christ. Jesus is the new covenant substance that cast the old covenant shadow. Christ is the "image" (II Cor. 4:4; Col. 1:15), the visible manifestation of God. All the pragmatic (Greek word *pragmatōn*) good things (cf. James 1:17) that God intends for man are summed up in Christ (Eph. 1:10), "every spiritual blessing in heavenly places" (Eph. 1:3). Paul is attempting to dissuade the Jewish Christians in Jerusalem from settling for the insubstantial shadows of the old covenant Judaic system. Instead, he wants them to be "conformed to the image of the Son" (Rom. 8:29).

The Law *"by the same sacrifices year-after-year, which they offer repetitively, is never able to make perfect those drawing near."* The old covenant Law and the sacrificial rites mandated by that Law, particularly the repetitive annual sacrifices of the high priest on the Day of Atonement, are ineffectual religious formalities, futile mechanical motions that cannot develop any real personal relationship with God. Those who would "draw near" to the Jewish worship center, sincerely desiring to worship God, can never be "made perfect" by the Jewish sacrifices. They can never be brought to God's intended objective or end-purpose of bearing His image (Gen. 1:26,27) and glorifying Him (Isa. 43:7) by manifesting His character, apart from Jesus Christ (14).

10:2 *"Otherwise"* (as is contrary to fact, i.e., the assumption that the old covenant sacrifices were efficacious for perfection), *"would not they* (the sacrifices) *have ceased being offered, because those worshipping would not still have a consciousness of sins, having once been cleansed?"* In typical lawyer fashion, Paul asks a rhetorical question which implies and necessitates an affirmative answer, "Yes, of course!" Would not the animal sacrifices have been discontinued as superfluous, their repetition terminated, if they were indeed efficacious to bring mankind into right relationship with God? If you have to do this over and over again, is it really working? The ceremonial sacrifices of the Jewish worship could only cleanse the externalities of flesh (9:13), and could not perfect the internal conscience (9:9). That is why Jewish worshippers continued to have an "evil conscience" (10:22), an on-going consciousness of guilt and shame and condemnation. They continued to have a burdened heart haunted by sin-consciousness.

Paul wanted his brethren in Jerusalem to know that their hearts had been cleansed by faith in Jesus Christ (Acts 15:9); their "consciences cleansed from dead works to serve the living God" (9:14). "There is now no condemnation for those who are in Christ Jesus" (Rom. 8:1). The sin-consciousness of repetitive confessionalism is indicative of Jewish theology and practice, but Christian theology and worship focuses on Jesus (12:2). Jesus said, "This is the new covenant in My blood. Do this in remembrance of Me" (Lk. 22:20; I Cor. 11:25), not in reminder of your sins! "Why would you even consider returning to the Jewish temple practices and their guilt-producing rituals?" Paul is asking the Judean Christians.

10:3 *"In fact,* (there is) *in those* (old covenant sacrifices) *a reminder of sins year-after-year."* The Day of Atonement included confession of sins (Lev. 16:21) and humbling (Lev. 23:26-32). Other ritual offerings were a "reminder of iniquity" (Num. 5:15). The repetition of the sacrifices, whether annually (1,3) or daily (11), kept a continual remembrance of sin in the consciousness of the Jewish worshippers. There was no remission in the old covenant system, just reminder that their sins separated them from God.

10:4 *"For it is impossible for the blood of bulls and goats to take away sins."* This is a concise and succinct denial of the effectiveness of old covenant worship practices. The ritual sacrifices of Judaism offered an external cleansing from contamination, pollution and defilement, but not the internal cleansing and spiritual transformation required to forgives sins and take away sin (10:11). The sacrifices may have provided a temporary and psychological cathartic relief and a religious sense of piety, but only the death of Christ inaugurating the new covenant could "take away sins" (9:26; Rom. 11:27).

10:5 Drawing a conclusion based on the ineffectiveness of the old covenant sacrifices and the sufficiency of the singular sacrifice of Jesus Christ, Paul employs Old Testament scripture as evidence to support his argument. *"Therefore, the One coming into the world says..."* Jesus' "coming into the world" may include a presupposition of His preexistence (1:2; John 1:1), but it is certainly a reference to His incarnational birth (John 1:14), and is a common Johannine expression for such (John 1:9; 6:14; 16:28; 18:37). When writing to Timothy, Paul stated, "Christ Jesus came into the world to save sinners" (I Tim. 1:5).

Using a technique he had utilized earlier (2:12,13), Paul puts Old Testament words into the mouth of Jesus. Since Jesus was instrumental in all Old Testament history and the focal point of all its prefiguring, Paul felt free to project Christ as the implied speaker of the words in Psalm 40:6-8 (quoted again from the Greek translation of the Old Testament [*LXX*], the Septuagint). His objective is to document and demonstrate that even the Old Testament literature critiques the efficacy of the animal sacrifices.

Projecting these words of David into statements of Christ, ***"He says, 'SACRIFICE AND OFFERING YOU HAVE NOT WILLED."*** Didn't God command the sacrifices and offerings of the old covenant? Yes, but as with the entirety of the old covenant, it was provisional to prefigure and foreshadow the sacrificial death of Jesus Christ. Through the prophet Jeremiah, God says, "I did not command your fathers…concerning burnt offerings and sacrifices. But this is what I commanded them, 'Obey My voice, and I will be your God, and you will be My people'"(Jere. 7:21-23). The primary intent of God was for a people who would obey Him and humble themselves before Him. "Does the Lord take delight in thousands of rams? …What does the Lord require of you, but to do justice, to love kindness, and to walk humbly with your God" (Micah 6:,7,8). "Has the Lord as much delight in burnt offerings and sacrifices as in obeying the voice of the Lord? Behold, to obey is better than sacrifice" (I Sam. 15:22; cf. Mk. 12:33,34).

God knew what he was going to do to remedy man's sin problem. ***"BUT A BODY YOU HAVE PREPARED FOR ME…"*** In solidarity with humanity (2:14), Jesus was "made in the likeness of men" (Phil. 2:7), incarnated in a human body. It was only in a human body that He could be "obedient unto death, even death on a cross" (Phil. 2:8). A textual problem is evident as the Hebrew text of Psalm 40:6 reads, "You have pierced My ears," while the Greek translation reads, "You have prepared a body for Me." How, and why, the text was altered is an open question. What we do know is that Paul quotes from the Greek Septuagint (*LXX*).

10:6   The quotation of Psalm 40:6 continues, *"IN WHOLE BURNT OFFERINGS AND SIN-OFFERINGS YOU HAVE NO PLEASURE."* God is not a "God of gore" who takes delight and pleasure in bloody animal sacrifices. Through Jeremiah, God declares, "Your burnt offerings are not acceptable, and your sacrifices are not pleasing to Me" (Jere. 6:20). Through Isaiah, "I have had enough of burnt offerings... I take no pleasure in the blood of bulls, lambs, or goats. ...Bring your worthless offerings no longer" (Isa. 1:11,13). "Even though you offer Me burnt offerings, I will not accept them" (Amos 5:22). What does God delight and take pleasure in? "I delight in loyalty rather than sacrifice, and in the knowledge of God rather than burnt offerings" (Hosea 6:6; cf. Matt. 9:13; 12:7). The psalmist, David, writes elsewhere, "The sacrifices of God are a broken spirit; a broken and contrite heart, O God, Thou wilt not despise" (Ps. 51:17). God's deepest interest is in the spiritual condition of man, and not in the carcasses and corpses (9:17) of animal sacrifices.

10:7   The quotation from Psalm 40:7,8 is continued as the statement of Jesus, *"THEN I SAID, 'BEHOLD I COME (IN THE SCROLL OF THE BOOK IT HAS BEEN WRITTEN OF ME) TO DO YOUR WILL, O GOD.'"* Paul uses these verses to show Jesus became incarnate in accord with the prophecies of the Old Testament. The primary emphasis is on the projected statement of Jesus from Psalm 40:8, "Behold I come to do Your will, O God." This is always what God wanted from man (I Sam. 15:22; Jere. 7:21-23; Hosea 6:6). God's will is always that His invisible character might be made visible in the behavior of His human creatures, imaged (Gen. 1:26,27) unto His glory (Isa. 43:7). This was accomplished perfectly in the body of Jesus (John 1:18; II Cor. 4:4; Col.

1:15) without sin (4:15; II Cor. 5:21). More specifically, in the God-man, Jesus Christ, God's will was that the Son should be "obedient unto death" (Phil. 2:8) to be the representative sinless sacrifice, sufficient to remove the sins of all mankind. This was the "will of God" that Jesus came to do. As He approached death, He said, "Not my will, but Thine be done" (Lk. 22:42).

10:8   Paul now dissects the statement from Psalm 40:6-8 into two parts. The first part is the negative comments about the old covenant sacrifices. *"After saying above, 'SACRIFICES AND OFFERINGS AND WHOLE BURNT OFFERINGS AND SIN-OFFERINGS YOU HAVE NOT WILLED, NOR HAVE YOU TAKEN PLEASURE,' (which are offered according to the Law)."* Paul loosely summarizes Psalm 40:6,7 and lumps together all the various kinds of sacrificial offerings in the old covenant: (1) peace offerings, (2) meal offerings, (3) burnt offerings, and (4) sin offerings, to indicate God's disdain and rejection of the entire sacrificial system of worship practices, advocated "according to the Law" (9:22; 10:1). Reference to "a body having been prepared" is omitted in this recap, since it will be referred to later (10).

10:9   The second part of the quotation, from Psalm 40:8, is the positive portion that Paul has cast into the Christological context of Christ's willingness to become the representative sacrifice for mankind. *"Then He said, 'BEHOLD, I COME TO DO YOUR WILL.'"* The old covenant animal sacrifices are not in accord with God's will, but the new covenant sacrifice of Jesus Christ for all mankind is the accomplishment of God's will.

The first and second portions that Paul has divided from the quotation of Psalm 40:6-8 are then expanded to apply to the first (8:7,13; 9:1,15,18) and second (8:7) covenants, as a whole. *"He takes away the first in order to establish the sec-*

ond." Paul, the lawyer, chooses his words carefully and deliberately, using juridical language to explain how the first covenant is *retracted* in order that the second covenant might be *enacted*. The first is *invalidated* in order that the second might be *validated*. The first covenant, the old covenant (8:13), the Law covenant (7:12; 8:4; 9:19,22; 10:1), with all its rules and regulations of external performance "works," and all its rituals of sacrifices and offerings in the tabernacle/temple worship center, is annulled, abrogated, and abolished. It is taken back, retracted, and done away with, because it served its purpose in planned obsolescence (8:13). The entire Jewish system of religion is *displaced*, in order to be *replaced* by the establishment, enactment, and confirmation of the new covenant (8:8,13; 9:15; 12:24) in the representative death of Jesus Christ. In contrast to the first covenant, the second covenant operates by the internal dynamic of God's grace instead of external Law regulations. The obedience of faith (cf. Rom. 1:5; 16:26) replaces the performance obedience of the works of the Law (Gal. 2:16; 3:5,10). The new worship center allows direct and immediate access to God's heavenly presence (10:19,20), with the worth-ship of God's character manifested in human behavior by the grace of God (4:16; 12:15; 13:9,25) to the glory of God (13:21).

This is a radical statement that Paul makes. He has jettisoned the entire Jewish religion and replaced it with the eschatological fulfillment of God's objective in Jesus Christ. What is Paul telling the Christians in Jerusalem? He is categorically asserting that the old covenant and the new covenant are mutually exclusive – antithetical and irreconcilable. There should be no consideration given to returning to the vacuous and worthless practices of Judaism.

10:10 Still emphasizing the second part of the quotation from Psalm 40:8, Paul writes, ***"By this will we have been sanctified through the once for all offering of the body of Jesus Christ."*** Christ's willingness to be "obedient unto death" (Phil.

2:8) as the representative sacrifice for the sins of mankind
allowed for the establishment of the second covenant. The
Self-offering (7:27; 9:14) of the physical body (5) of Jesus
Christ in sacrificial death was the singular and final (7:27;
9:12) remedial act that removed the sin-consequences from
man and ratified the new covenant. Through the death of Jesus
atonement for sin has been made, allowing for a reconciled at-
one-ment and spiritual union with the Holy God. Christians
who have accepted the efficacy of Christ's death on the cross
are "sanctified by faith in Christ" (Acts 26:18). As sanctified
"holy ones" or saints (Rom. 8:27; Eph. 1:18; 4:12), they are
set apart to function as God intended in the manifestation of
His holiness. This sanctification is both an initially received
spiritual condition of the Christian (Acts 20:32; I Cor. 6:11), as
well as a behavior process of growth in the expression of His
Holy character (14; John 17:19; I Thess. 4:3).

10:11 Paul returns to the repetitive and ineffectual sacrifices
of the Jewish priest to make a renewed argument for the singularity and finality of Christ's sacrifice, and its efficacy for the
restoration of mankind. ***"And many a priest indeed has stood
day-after-day ministering, and offering the same sacrifices
over-and-over again, which are never able to take away
sins."*** This initially appears to be a summarizing restatement
of 10:1-4, but Paul wanted to emphasize the finished work of
the One Who was High Priest as well as sacrifice. The Jewish
priests stood day-by-day and year-by-year (9:25; 10:3) ministering or liturgizing (Greek word *leitourgōn*), by offering the
same kinds of sacrifices time-after-time. The type of priests
(Aaronic or Levitical), and the frequency of their sacrifices
(yearly or daily) is not the real issue Paul is addressing; rather,
he emphasizes the plurality and repetitiveness of the monotonous sacrifices. The fact that the old covenant priests were
standing to do their priestly work will be contrasted with
Christ being seated (12). There was no place to sit in the

Jewish worship center of tabernacle or temple. Their work was never done, never completed; that because their sacrifices were impotent and ineffective, never able or adequate to take away or cancel sins. Theirs was an exercise in futility, as they calculatingly put the sins of the people in the debit column of last year's ledger.

10:12 Again, contrasting Jesus to the Jewish priests, Paul writes, ***"But having offered one sacrifice for sins unto perpetuity, He has sat down at the right hand of God."*** As the High Priest in the order of Melchizedek (5:6; 6:20), Jesus offered the sacrifice of Himself (7:27; 9:14). This sinless sacrifice was singularly efficacious as an acceptable expiation and propitiation to remove the sin-consequences of mankind, as well as to perfect and sanctify (14) those receptive to such in order to make them safe from the power of sin. Jesus' sacrifice in death was singularly efficacious, in contrast to the plurality and repetition of the Jewish sacrifices. Jesus' sacrifice was efficacious unto perpetuity, in ultimate extension forever, in contrast to the temporality and ineffectiveness of the Jewish sacrifices. The finality and finished work of Jesus' sacrifice is evidenced by the fact that "He sat down at the right hand of God." As High Priest, Jesus had finished His work (John 19:30) and sat down in the Holy of Holies of God's presence. This was almost inconceivable to Jewish thinking for they viewed God as an antagonist Who was against them because of their sins. They would even tie a rope around the high priest's leg to pull him out of the Holy of Holies of the tabernacle/temple in case he should die in there while performing his duties on the Day of Atonement. The ever-enduring finished work of Jesus Christ allowed Him to be exalted to the highest place of glory (Phil. 2:9-11) at the "right hand of God" the Father, and to share His authority. Christ is enthroned as the King-Priest in the heavenly sanctuary, an image that Paul uses several times (1:3; 8:1; 12:2; Eph. 1:20; cf. Mk. 16:19).

Christians who are "in Christ" are "seated in the heaven-lies" (Eph. 1:3; 2:6) with Him, and can likewise "cease from their labors" in order to appreciate God's "rest" of grace (4:10,11). They can sit down and rest. That is what Paul wanted his readers to understand, appreciate and experience; rather than reengaging in the repetitious, never-ending Jewish practices and causes.

10:13 Thus seated at the right hand of God, our triumphant Lord is *"in the meantime waiting, "UNTIL HIS ENEMIES ARE PUT AS A FOOTSTOOL FOR HIS FEET."* Drawing again (1:3,13; 8:1; 12:2) from Psalm 110:1, Paul emphasized the completion of Christ's finished work (John 19:30) by noting that it transcends history and awaits ultimate consummation. The triumph of *Christus Victor*5 is already complete, yet there is the anticipation of the subjugation of all contrary powers and persons under the authority of the triumphant Christ. Writing to the Ephesian Christians, Paul explained that God "raised Him from the dead, and seated Him at His right hand in the heavenly places, far above all rule and authority and power and dominion, and every name that is named, not only in this age, but in the one to come. And He put all things in subjection under His feet, and gave Him as head over all things..." (Eph. 1:20-22; cf. Col. 2:15). To the Corinthians, Paul noted the yet awaited "end, when He delivers up the kingdom to the God and Father, when He has abolished all rule and all authority and power. For He must reign until He has put all His enemies under His feet. The last enemy that will be abolished is death. "FOR HE HAS PUT ALL THINGS IN SUBJECTION UNDER HIS FEET" (Ps. 8:6). "And when all things are subjected to Him, then the Son Himself will also be subjected to the One Who subjected all things to Him, that God may be all in all" (I Cor. 15:24-28). The "already" and the "not yet" of Christ's triumph must be kept in scriptural balance.

The embattled recipients of this epistle were caught in the enigma of the interim of the victory of Christ. They were being bombarded by the principalities and powers of religious and political dominion and authority. Paul was warning them not to join the "enemies" who would be ultimately defeated at the feet of Jesus Christ, and encouraging them to participate in the peace and rest of the eternally triumphant Lord.

10:14 The finality of Christ's finished work objectively in history (and beyond) is now applied subjectively in its effects for Christians. *"For by one offering He has perfected unto perpetuity those being sanctified."* Whereas Christ "abides as a priest perpetually" (7:3), and "offered one sacrifice for sins unto perpetuity" (12), now the Christian's perfection in Christ is declared to be "unto perpetuity;" a permanent result that carries through forever. There was no perfection of man under the law (7:11,19; 10:1), and the old covenant worship could bring no perfection of the conscience (9:9). Mankind can only be brought to God's intended objective in their lives by the perfect sacrifice of Christ and the indwelling presence of the Perfect One (2:10; 5:9), Jesus Christ. Thus perfected (Phil. 3:15) in spiritual condition, as "the spirits of righteous men made perfect" (12:23), Christians can "press on towards perfection" (6:1) in behavioral expression. Just as there is an "already" and "not yet" in Christ's triumph, there is an "already" of Christian perfection in spiritual condition, and a "not yet" of perfect in behavioral expression. Likewise, Christians have "already" been sanctified (10) and set apart to function as God intended in holiness, and "yet" are "being sanctified" in the process of the progression of Christian growth (II Pet. 3:18), pursuing sanctification (12:14) in the consistent expression of God's holy character in their behavior. **10:15** In this final subsection of the paragraph, Paul quotes again (8:7-12) from Jeremiah 31 to connect the internalizing provision of the new covenant with the absence of sin-consciousness (2) and the abolishment of all Jewish sin offerings (18). Adding to his Old Testament citations to document his case for the superiority of the sacrifice of Jesus, Paul writes, *"And the Holy Spirit also witnesses to us."* Believing "all scripture to be inspired by God and profitable for teaching, for reproof, for correction, and for training in righteousness" (II Tim. 3:16), Paul also understood the Holy Spirit to be the active divine agent who utilized the Scriptures as an instrumental means to provide an evidentiary witness to Christians (3:7; cf. I Thess. 1:5,6). This witness of the written revelation is not the same as the personal revelation of "the Spirit bearing witness with our spirit that we are children of God" (Rom. 8:16), but is the witness of the Spirit through scripture.

10:16 The witness of the Spirit in scripture is this: *"...for after having previously said, 'THIS IS THE COVENANT I WILL COVENANT TOWARDS THEM AFTER THOSE DAYS SAYS THE LORD: GIVING MY LAWS UPON THEIR HEARTS, I WILL ALSO WRITE THEM UPON THEIR MINDS'."* Paul again (cf. 16,17) dissects a text into two parts to make his point. The first part is the quotation of Jeremiah 31:33 which explains that the new covenant that will be made with God's people after the old covenant period, will not be an external codification of regulations on "tablets of stone" (II Cor. 3:3), and contained in external phylacteries (Matt. 23:5) on Jewish foreheads, but God's law which expresses His character will be subjectively internalized in "human hearts" (II Cor. 3:3). The divine dynamic of God's grace for manifesting the character expression of law is received by Christians in Christ. What God desires and wills (5) is inscribed in the minds of Christians, for they have "the mind of Christ" (I Cor. 2:16).

10:17 The second part of the sequence, from Jeremiah 31:34, reads, *"AND THEIR SINS AND THEIR LAWLESSNESSES I SHALL NOT AT ALL HAVE REMEMBERED."* In contrast

298

to the constant reminder of sins (3) in the Jewish sacrifices, the new covenant does not foster sin-consciousness (2) and con-demnation (Rom. 8:1). The new covenant emphasizes forgive-ness and freedom, in a positive focus (12:2) on the Savior, Jesus Christ, rather than on sin. Religious and psychological techniques of introspection to become more conscious of sins and sinfulness have no place in the new covenant experience of Jesus Christ. Yes, there is a proper place for "confession of sin" (I John 1:9) that is brought to our attention by the Holy Spirit, but not for a guilt-producing preoccupation with sins and sinfulness that results in a depressive confessionalism, rather than a vibrant and intimate communion with Christ. How tragic that even in so-called "Christian religion" many revert to wallowing in sin-consciousness, and even accuse those who point to the "finished work" of Christ in the new covenant of a "triumphalism" that is not realistic.

10:18 *"Now where there is forgiveness of these things,* (there is) *no longer* (any) *offering for sin."* In the inaugurated new covenant there is pardon and release from sins and law-lessnesses (17). The consequences of these are discharged and cancelled, allowing the Christian to operate in freedom and liberty, with bold (Eph. 3:12) and confident (3:6; 4:16; 10:35) access to the presence of God (10:19,20). "There is no longer any offering for sin," for the offering was made finally and forever in the death of Christ (12).

Paul wanted the Hebrew Christians in Jerusalem to know that the repetitive offering of animal sacrifices that were still taking place in the temple there in Jerusalem were monotonous meaninglessness. Even the offering of repetitive confessions for the absolution of sin were of no value. It was extremely important that the Jerusalem Christians repudiate all old covenant practices, for to fail to do so was to deny the efficacy of Christ, and for such apostasy "there no longer remains a

sacrifice for sins, but a terrifying expectation of judgment"
(26).

Concluding Remarks

In this extended passage (9:1 – 10:18) Paul lays out his
case for the singularity and finality of the representative sacrifice of Jesus Christ – the only means by which man's sins are
taken away, once-and-for-all.

The old covenant, with its sacrificial worship practices,
could not forgive sins (10:4,11); could not cleanse a person's
conscience from the consciousness of sin (9:9,10,13; 10:2);
could not provide access to God, for such was limited to the
high priest once a year (9:7,25); and could not perfect and
sanctify man to function as God intended (7:19; 9:9; 10:1).
The singularly sufficient sacrifice of Jesus Christ, on the other
hand, does effect redemption (9:12,15) and forgiveness of sins
(9:26,28; 10:12,18); does cleanse man's conscience internally
(9:14) so that there is no consciousness of sins (10:2,17); does
provide free access to God, unrestricted, direct, and immediate
(9:12,24; 10:19,20); and does perfect and sanctify the believer
(10:10,14) to be all that God intends man to be.

The finality of Christ's sacrificial death signifies the end of
all animal sacrifices (10:18). His forgiveness of sins is such
that these sins can forever be put out of our remembrance, as
they are from His remembrance (10:17). The inauguration of
the new covenant signifies the complete abrogation of the old
covenant (10:9) – "Christ is the end of the Law" (Rom. 10:4) –
the shadow gives way to the substance (10:1). Christ's victorious access to the Holy of Holies of God's presence evidences
that God cannot be confined to any worship-box in any religion, but has an "open-door policy" for all who will approach
Him through Christ (10:19).

What did this mean for the Hebrew Christians in Jerusalem
to whom Paul was writing? It was a direct warning that to

return to any involvement in the Jewish worship practices would be a denial of Jesus. It would necessarily indicate the apostasy of "standing away from" Jesus, in repudiation of His singular sufficiency. It would be to say that Jesus – His sacrifice, His life – was not enough. Paul will proceed to explain the dire and terrifying consequences of such a rejection.

ENDNOTES

1   Bruce, F.F., *Commentary on the Epistle to the Hebrews.* Series: The New International Commentary on the New Testament. Grand Rapids: Wm. B. Eerdmans Publishing Co. 1992. pg. 196.

2   Fowler, James A., *The Blood of Christ.* Fallbrook: CIY Publishing Co. 1991.

3   Owen, John, *The Death of Death in the Death of Christ.* London: The Banner of Truth Trust. 1963.

4   Bruce, *op. cit.*, pg. 199.

5   Aulén, Gustaf, *Christus Victor: An Historical Study of the Three Main Types of the Idea of the Atonement.* London: Society for Promoting Christian Knowledge. 1934.

JESUS

The Better Way
of Access to God

Hebrews 10:19-39

Jesus, the "better priest" (7:1-28) offered Himself as the "better sacrifice" (9:1–10:18), providing the "better way of access to God" through Himself. This section of the epistle to the Hebrews is the logical conclusion of the argument that Paul has made previously. Paul transitions from instruction to application, from exposition to exhortation, from the didactic to the direct implications.

There are three (3) subsection paragraphs within this direct exhortation. In the first section (19-25) Paul encourages the Christians in Jerusalem to enter the legitimate and certain access that they have to God's presence through the sacrificial death of Jesus Christ, using three (3) appeals to specific action (22,23,24). Warning of divine judgment occupies the second section (26-31), as Paul explains what his readers are in danger of doing, and what the terrifying consequences of apostasy might entail. In the third section (32-39), Paul returns to encouragement by noting the prior hardships that the Hebrew Christians had endured, and prods them to continue to persevere through the trials.

Similarities with Paul's previous encouragement/warning statements (cf. 3:12-14; 6:4-8) are evident.[1] This is to be expected since the historical context of the writing of this letter found the recipients in a very perilous situation. They had previously been ostracized, ridiculed, and publicly humiliated by their Jewish neighbors (cf. I Thess. 2:14), for in becoming Christians they were regarded as traitors to their Jewish heritage and religion. These people had suffered persecution, physical abuse, acts of violence, and the confiscation of their property. Then, these same Jewish countrymen began to woo them, desiring their assistance in the impending conflict of revolution against Roman occupation. There was a strong pressure to capitulate, to join the wave of nationalistic fervor, and to fight for the Jewish faith and homeland. This would have been the "easy way out," to go with the flow of public sentiment, to join the cause of insurrection, and to find some temporary "acceptance" from those around them. But the Hebrew Christians knew that such capitulation would be to deny all they claimed to have in Jesus Christ. To "sell out" in this way would be to "stand away from" Jesus Christ in apostasy ("apostasy" is the transliteration of the Greek word *apostasia*, meaning "to stand away from," though this word is not used in this epistle). To join forces with the Jewish revolutionaries would be to repudiate their Christian faith.

The temptation to give up and apostasize was intense. This is evident in various words that Paul uses throughout the letter. They were "sluggish" (6:12), and in danger of "drifting away" (2:1), of "going astray" (3:10), of "falling away" (3:12; 4:12; 6:6), and of "throwing away" (10:35) all they had in Jesus Christ. Paul could sense that they were "wearying" (12:3), "wavering" (10:23), and "losing heart" (12:3); contemplating the "disobedience" (3:18; 4:6,11) of "shrinking back" (10:38,39) and "hardening their hearts" (3:8) by "neglecting their salvation" (2:3). To do so would be to "come short" of all that God had promised (4:1; 12:15), and to suffer the terrifying consequences of God's judgment.

Perhaps still restricted and restrained by the Roman authorities after being taken as a prisoner from Jerusalem to Rome (Acts 28:17,30), Paul had a heavy heart for his brethren back in Jerusalem. In this last-ditch letter, he employs every means at his disposal to instruct them about the "better things" they have in Jesus Christ, and the superiority of the vital access they have to the heavenly presence of God. Paul reminds them and praises them for their past endurance (10:32-34). He chides them about their seeming lack of maturity and stability (5:12–6:3), and warns them of the precarious position they are in, even threatening the terrifying consequence of everlasting destruction (10:38,39) if they decide to reject and deny Jesus Christ. Like a good lawyer, Paul argues his case from every angle, trying to persuade the Hebrew Christians in Jerusalem to stand firm in their faith in Jesus Christ. "Don't give up! Don't go back! Don't reject Jesus!"

10:19 This long, rambling sentence (typical of Paul – cf. Eph. 1:3-14) comprises the entire paragraph (19-25). It begins with a connective review (19-21) of the previous explanation of Jesus as priest, offering the single and final redemptive sacrifice for sin, which allows for the Christians' unhindered access to God.

"Having, therefore, brothers, certainty unto the access of the Holies by the blood of Jesus...". Jesus is not ashamed to call us "brothers" (2:11), and Paul identifies with his readers by recognizing that they are "brothers" in Christ (3:1,12; 13:22) in the family of God. His objective is to reiterate that by the priesthood of Christ (21) and the sacrifice of Christ (19,20), Christians have legitimate access to the Holy of Holies of God's presence. The verb "having" controls the entire introductory phrase (19-21).

Instead of a subjective "confidence" (35), Paul seems to be referring to the objective "certainty" of the Christian's having legitimate access, a right-of-way of entrance to the heavenly sanctuary. To the Ephesians, Paul wrote, "in Christ Jesus our Lord...we have certainty and confident access through faith" (Eph. 3:11,12), "access in one Spirit to the Father" (Eph.

2:18). Such right of entry to the Holy of Holies was inconceivable to Jewish thought, as they still acted out the religious motions of a temporary and mediated access to God through the high priest in the Jerusalem temple once a year on the Day of Atonement. To have direct and immediate access to God – to have a real personal relationship with God in real face-to-face worship – was beyond their wildest imaginations. Yet, this is what Paul is telling the Hebrew Christians they have by the instrumental means of "the blood of Jesus" (9:12,14; 10:19,29; 12:24; 13:12,20), the representative and sacrificial death of Jesus. Again (9:12,14), there was no magical efficacy in the human blood of Jesus, but by His voluntary death He vicariously and substitutionally assumed the death that was the consequence of mankind's sin, removing the alienation between God and man. "Christ died for sins one for all, the just for the unjust, in order that He might bring us to God" (I Pet. 3:18).

10:20 This certainty of entryway into the Holy presence of God is *"a fresh and living way…"*. The word Paul uses for "fresh" often referred to a freshly-slain animal sacrifice, but Paul's intent was apparently to indicate that the new way of access to God through Jesus Christ was recent, unprecedented, and refreshing. In addition, it was not the old death-dealing way of being held at bay from God, as in the tabernacle/temple exercises, but was a life-giving way that proceeded from death to life in order to open a dynamic interaction with the living God (3:12; 9:14; 10:31; 12:22). Jesus is in Himself, by means of His priesthood and sacrifice, the "way" (John 14:6) of access to God, declaring, "No man comes unto the Father, but by Me" (John 14:6). Having life in Himself (John 5:26; 14:6), Jesus provides a way of access to God that allows a vital relationship of living humanity with the living God. Those, other than the high priest on his annual visit, who entered the Holy chamber of the tabernacle or temple met certain death (Num.

4:20; 17:13). There was no "living way" of access to God in the old covenant.

This new and living way of access to God was the one *"which He has initiated for us, through the curtain, that is,* (through) *His flesh."* The way of access to God was initiated (9:18), inaugurated, dedicated, and made available, when Jesus was willing to go "through the curtain," the veil (6:19; 9:3). The curtain was the means of access to God's presence, but in Jewish thought it was regarded as an obstacle or barrier, representing hiddenness and inaccessibility. The barrier to open access to God was that the death consequences of mankind's sin had to be taken and conquered. Incarnated in the flesh (2:14; 5:7; John 1:14) as the God-man, Jesus was susceptible to death, and "obedient unto death" (Phil. 2:8), to become the sinless representative sacrifice Who could take the death of mankind upon Himself, and open the way to God's presence. "He has now reconciled you in His fleshly body through death, in order to present you before Him holy and blameless and beyond reproach" (Col. 1:22). The "blood of Jesus" (19) and "His flesh" (20) both refer to the instrumental means by which Jesus accepted sacrificial death in order to serve as the forerunner that all Christians can follow directly into intimate relationship and fellowship with God. This was illustrated at the time of Jesus' death by crucifixion when the veil in the temple at Jerusalem was "torn in two from top to bottom" (Matt. 27:51; Mk. 15:38) – which, by the way, indicates that God did it, not man, in order to illustrate His acceptance of Jesus' death, and His open-door policy for all who would come to Him through Jesus Christ.

10:21 The dual basis of our having access to God was because Jesus was willing to be the sacrifice involving "flesh" (20) and "blood" (19), while at the same time serving as the priest Who offered the sacrifice. *"...and* (having) *a great priest over the house of God."* "We have a great high priest

Who has passed through the heavens" (4:14). "A great priest" is just another way of saying "a high priest," and Paul has thoroughly argued that Jesus is the High Priest "according to the order of Melchizedek" (4:14-16; 5:11; 6:19,20; 7:1-28). Jesus' high priesthood "over the house of God" may refer to His eternal priesthood in the heavenly sanctuary of God's presence, or it may refer to the visible and earthly counterpart of such, wherein the community of faith, the church, is regarded as the temple (I Cor. 3:16; II Cor. 6:16) or the "household of God" (Eph. 2:19; I Tim. 3:15). Since Paul referred to "Christ as a Son over His house, whose house we are" (3:6) earlier in the epistle, and nowhere else refers to heaven as the "house of God," the interpretation of "the household of God, which is the church of the living God" (I Tim. 3:15) is preferable. We can be certain that Paul was not referring to the temple in Jerusalem as the "house of God," for his objective is to point out the inadequacy of that house, that priesthood, those sacrifices, and that place of inaccessibility.

10:22 Based on the open access that Christians have to God through the priesthood and sacrifice of Jesus Christ, Paul makes three (3) appeals (22,23,24) using the "we should" or "let us" verb form. Many commentators have noted that within these three encouragements to action there is also the triad of the themes of "faith" (22), "hope" (23), and "love" (24), a triad that Paul seems to have been fond of (6:10-12; I Cor. 13:13; Gal. 5:5,6; I Thess. 1:3; 5:8). One should be cautious, though, of overemphasizing these three topics, lest they diminish the appeals Paul is making.

Appealing to the responsibility that they have as Christians, Paul enjoins, *"Let us draw near* (to God) *with a true heart in full assurance of faith..."*. Earlier Paul had written, "Let us draw near with confidence to the throne of grace" (4:16), for "He is able to save forever those who draw near to God through Him" (7:25). Paul wanted the Judean Christians to utilize their privilege of access and intimacy with God. This approach to God in personal relationship needed to be done with a "true heart" that was genuine, without pretence or divided loyalties (the issue his readers were struggling with). The new covenant in Jesus Christ changes hearts (8:10; 10:16), but a continued loyalty of heart, rather than a "hardness of heart" (3:8,15; 4:7), is still required. Jesus said, "Blessed are the pure in heart, for they shall see God" (Matt. 5:8). Loyalty and purity of heart is evidenced and enacted "in full assurance of faith." Previously, Paul had encouraged his readers to be "diligent to realize full assurance of hope until the end" (6:11). Here, he is encouraging their confident access to God through faith in Christ (Eph. 3:12); faith that is fully persuaded (cf. Rom. 14:5) of what Christ has done.

Access to God is also based on *"having our hearts sprinkled from an evil conscience and our bodies washed with pure water."* In contrast to the external sprinkling of blood (9:13,19,21) by the Jewish priests, Paul is emphasizing the internal cleansing of the conscience (9:14) whereby the Christians is no longer burdened by guilt and consciousness of sins (10:2), but has a subjective sense of pardon and peace in coming before God. Reference to "our bodies washed with pure water" could be a generalized parallel to the sprinkling of the conscience "by the washing of regeneration, and renewing by the Holy Spirit" (Titus 3:6), the "cleansing by the washing of water by the word" (Eph. 5:26; cf. I Cor. 6:11; Rev. 1:5). On the other hand, this may be a reference to the outward expression of such inner cleansing, when their physical bodies were overwhelmed in the water of baptism. Peter refers to baptism as "not just a removal of dirt from the flesh, but an appeal to God for a good conscience" (I Pet. 3:21). The early Christians looked at the event of their water baptism as a decisive public confirmation of their faith in Christ, and Paul is probably reminding the Hebrew Christians of how that event fixed their identification as Christians, especially in the eyes of their Jewish kinsmen.

10:23 Paul's second appeal was, *"Let us hold fast the confession of our hope without wavering, for the One having promised is faithful."* Because the Jerusalem Christians were in danger of letting go of their faith and hope in Christ, Paul repeatedly admonishes them to "hold fast" (3:6,14) their confidence and hope until the end. In like manner, he had encouraged the Corinthians to "hold fast" to the gospel they had received (I Cor. 11:2; 15:2). The "confession of our hope" is not just a verbal formula of a baptismal confession or a creedal recitation, but is inclusive of the Christian's total agreement and concurrence with the Person and work of Jesus Christ, "Who is our hope" (I Tim. 1:1). Subjectively, Paul wants the Hebrew Christians, who have been "born again to a living hope through the resurrection of Jesus Christ from the dead" (I Pet. 1:3), to have a confident expectation in God's continued grace to the very end (3:6; 6:11). His discourse on faith (11:1-40) will begin with the statement, "Faith is the assurance of the things hoped for" (11:1). The reason the Christian can have a hope that does not waver, bend, or vacillate, which can serve as "an anchor for the soul" (6:19), is because there is nothing more stable, steadfast, and unchanging (6:17,18) than the faithfulness of God to His promises. God is faithful (I Cor. 1:9; 10:13; II Cor. 1:18; I Thess. 5:24; II Thess. 3:3), reliable, and trustworthy in every promise He utters (11:11). Our security and hope is founded on God's faithfulness, and every promise finds its fulfillment in Jesus Christ (II Cor. 1:20).

10:24 The third appeal of Paul to the Hebrew Christians pertains to their interactions with one another. *"Let us consider how to incite one another unto love and good works...".* The Jerusalem Christians had cared for one another (33), but Paul wants them to pay attention and be mindful of the need to spur each other on – to prick, to provoke, to "jab," to "needle" (the English word "paroxysm," meaning "intension emotion or excitement" is a transliteration of the word used here) one another about the practicalities of mutual love and good deeds (to be amplified in 12:14 – 13:21). Instead of the "dead works" (6:1; 9:14) of religion, Paul wants His fellow Christians to engage in "love and good works" among themselves. These loving "good works, prepared beforehand that we should walk in them" (Eph. 2:10), and for which we are "equipped" (13:21) by the grace of God, are the outworking (James 2:14,26) of the life and love of Jesus Christ (I Jn. 4:7-21). Paul is advising the Hebrew Christians that they are "in this (Him) together." We need each other. We have a collective responsibility to one another. The isolationism and individualism of "lone ranger" Christians is not compatible with the community of Christ.

10:25 For that reason, because we have a collective responsibility to one another to arouse and stimulate to interactive love and good deeds, we should *"not (be) **forsaking the assembly of ourselves together, as is the pattern of some...".***
Apparently some of the Christians in Jerusalem were withdrawing from Christian fellowship, discontinuing their gathering together, and abandoning or deserting their fellow Christians. Their reasons for so doing are not given. They may have been fearful, and decided to "go underground" in hiding. There might have been personality differences or divisive rivalries. They might have become disappointed by the delay of Christ's victory and second coming. Perhaps they decided to "give up" in apathy or indifference, or worse yet, in contempt and disregard for the things of Christ. Whatever their excuses, Christian love demands that we be there for the other, and any self-centered preoccupation that keeps Christians from such mutual edification in "the upbuilding of the Body of Christ in

love" (Eph. 4:16) is a concern for Paul, for he seems to regard such failure to participate as a perilous prelude to apostasy.

Contrary to such self-oriented withdrawal from fellowship, Paul wants the Christians to be *"encouraging* (one another)*; and all the more, as you see the day drawing near."* Mutual encouragement (3:13) is a foremost purpose of Christian assembly. We gather together for others, not just to selfishly "get fed" with good instruction, or "get high" on the emotional excitement of music or entertainment. The interrelational function of the Body of Christ by the spiritual giftedness of the Holy Spirit allows Christians to serve one another in the new covenant community of faith. We need each other, and the comforting encouragement of the Holy Spirit (John 14:16,26) through other Christians. The intense importance of these relationships was "all the more," because the Hebrew Christians could observe an approaching and impending "day drawing near." The "day" that Paul is referring to might have been "the Day of the Lord" (I Cor. 1:8; 3:13; I Thess. 5:4) when Jesus would "appear a second time" (9:28). More likely, Paul was referring to the "day" that was coming in "a very little while" (37), when the Jews and Romans would meet in mortal conflict. The Christians in Jerusalem could "see" that the winds of war were brewing, the "day was drawing near," the "day" (cf. Matt. 24:36,42; Mk. 13:32) when the Lord would come in judgment through the Roman army, in A.D. 66-70, and destroy Jerusalem, the temple, and the entire Jewish nation and religion. The old covenant would "disappear" (8:13). It was inconceivable to Paul why any of the Jerusalem Christians would be considering a reversion to Judaism.

10:26 Making a direct connection to the foregoing peril of "wavering" (23) and desertion (25), Paul begins this paragraph, *"For sinning deliberately after receiving the full knowledge of the truth, there no longer remains a sacrifice for sins..."*. The previous paragraph (19-25) explained the response that Paul desired from the Christians in Jerusalem, whereas this paragraph (26-31) warns of the unacceptable response and the dire consequences of such.

F.F. Bruce is correct in his observation that "this passage (26-29) was destined to have repercussions in Christian history beyond what our author could have foreseen."[2] Christians with differing theological presuppositions have produced abstract theological arguments about Christian permanency and impermanency in the broad theological systems of Calvinism and Arminianism. Failing to appreciate the dynamic of the living Savior in Christian salvation, such arguments about permanency, security, preservation and perseverance often arrive only at theological dead-ends of static belief-systems. When they approach the text of scripture with the pretext of bolstering their predetermined presuppositions and premises, they find either a proof-text for their position, or engage in bizarre interpretive distortions of the text in order to deny what it states. How tragic when theological commentators seek to protect and preserve their presuppositions, rather than explain the plain teaching of the scripture. They engage in *eisegesis* (bringing ideas into the text), rather than *exegesis* (determining the meaning out of the text).

Paul's warning about "sinning deliberately after receiving the full knowledge of the truth" was made to the Christians in Jerusalem who had received Jesus Christ (cf. John 1:12,13), Who is the Truth (John 14:6), and the full reality of spiritual life. Paul explained to Timothy, "God our Savior desires all men to be saved and to come to the knowledge of the truth" (I Tim. 2:3,4), and the Hebrew Christians had received such by faith. References to the spiritual condition of the Christians in Jerusalem could not be clearer in the immediate context: They had "agreed with the hope that is Jesus Christ" (23); their "hearts had been sprinkled from an evil conscience" (22); and "their bodies had been washed in the water" of baptism (22). They were "enlightened" (32) with the Light of Christ, "sanctified" (29) by the Holy One, and were regarded as "righteous ones" (38).

"Sinning deliberately," whether singularly or repetitively, is not a reference to general (or specific) misrepresentations of God's character in a Christian's behavior. "If we say we have no sin, we are deceiving ourselves" (I John 1:8). Every Christian sinfully misrepresents the character of Christ in their behavior – acting out of character in misrepresentation of their identity as a Christ-one, a Christian, who is spiritually united with Jesus Christ (I Cor. 6:17). Every Christian often does so deliberately and willfully, because sinful expression is a choice of the will. But the Christian knows that "if we confess our sins, He is faithful and just to forgive us our sins" (I Jn. 1:9).

The historical and textual context of Paul's words indicate that by "sinning deliberately," he is referring to the specific and definite sin (or pattern thereof) of deliberately rejecting and denying the Person and work of Jesus Christ. Some of the Hebrew Christians in Jerusalem were on the brink of definitively repudiating and renouncing the efficacy of the life and death of Jesus; of denying and disavowing that Jesus was God's Messiah and Savior; and of regarding Jesus to be of no value. "Standing apart from" Jesus in apostasy, intentional and contemptuous desertion and defection from Christ and the new covenant community of faith, is the particular willful sin that Paul is referring to in this passage, just as it was in 3:12 and 6:4-8.

Such an interpretation of Paul's words admittedly impinges upon the theological presuppositions of some Christians, whose doctrines of "eternal security" and "once saved, always saved" disallow for any secession, defection, desertion, or apostasy. We cannot avoid, however, the obvious assertion that Paul refers to the possibility of a Christian rejecting Jesus Christ in apostasy. Though most genuine Christians find this unfathomable and unthinkable, Paul does posit the possibility of such a terminal repudiation.

When an individual departs from Jesus Christ in apostasy, "there no longer remains a sacrifice for sins." Such defection is irremediable. Once apostasized, always apostasized. There can be no "renewal of repentance" (6:6), because the sacrifice of Jesus Christ for sin is unrepeatable (9:26; 10:18). If one has received Christ and then left Christ, there is nothing left to redeem him. They have rejected and repudiated the only means of forgiveness (18) from sin, and reconciliation with God. There are no options beyond the singularly sufficient sacrifice of Jesus Christ. G.W. Buchanan remarks,

> The once-for-all nature of Christ's sacrifice is like a two-edged sword. On the one hand, it is so effective that it does not need to be repeated (7:27), but, on the other hand, it cannot be repeated, even if needed.[3]

10:27 The only thing the apostate can expect is *"a certain terrifying expectation of judgment, and THE ZEAL OF A FIRE WHICH WILL CONSUME THE ADVERSARIES."* As Paul will declare in the conclusion of this paragraph, "It is a terrifying thing to fall into the hands of the living God" (31). The apostate can only expect the inevitable and inescapable judgment of God, apart from Jesus Christ. In this case (cf. 9:27), the divine assessment and evaluation of judgment has terrifying consequences because God's only solution of eternal life in His Son, Jesus Christ, has been rejected.

Paul quotes from Isaiah in describing God's judgment: "O Lord, Thy hand is lifted up, yet they do not see it. They see Thy zeal for the people and are put to shame; indeed, fire will devour Thine enemies" (Isa. 26:11). Zephaniah also referred to the figure of devouring fire in describing God's judgment: "All the earth will be devoured in the fire of his jealousy" (Zeph. 1:18). "The Lord our God is a consuming fire, a jealous God" (Deut. 4:24), said Moses (quoted by Paul in Hebrews 12:29). God is zealous and jealous to manifest His character, and those who refuse to accept Him through His Son, Jesus Christ (or subsequently reject Him) are necessarily regarded as adversaries. "He who is not for Me, is against Me" (Matt. 12:30; Mk. 9:40; Lk. 9:50; 11:23), Jesus said. Paul is warning the wavering (23) Jerusalem Christians not to become adversaries of God through apostasy, and suffer the irrevocable consequences of God's judgment.

10:28 Arguing from the lesser to the greater (cf. 2:2,3), Paul sets up a comparative argument that contrasts the consequences of apostasy in the old covenant (cf. Deut. 30:15-20) and in the new covenant. *"Anyone setting aside the Law of Moses dies without mercy on* (the evidence of) *two or three witnesses."* On numerous occasions in the old covenant literature the death penalty is assigned for violation or rejection of the Law of Moses. To disregard or disobey the Law concerning idolatry (Deut. 13:8,9; 17:2-7) or murder (Deut. 19:11-13), led to death without pity (Deut. 13:8; 19:13) or appeal. Unintentional violations of Law could be forgiven (Num. 15:27-29), but deliberate and willful (26) defiance of the law (Num. 15:30,31) led to being cast out of the covenant community. The evidence for such required the testimony of "two or three witnesses" (Num. 35:15,20; Deut. 17:6; 19:13,15,21), to avoid vindictive false accusations.

10:29 As Jesus is greater than Moses (3:1-6), the more serious violation of rejecting Jesus Christ leads to a punishment far worse than a physical death penalty. The greater privilege demands a greater punishment. *"How much severer punishment do you think will be deserved for the one having trampled on the Son of God..."*. Paul uses a triad of expressions that explain what apostasy involves. First, it means bringing the One who is Highest to the lowest position, whereby you "walk on Him," and "grind Him in the dirt." With deliberate disdain, contempt, and scorn, such an individual, who had confessed Jesus as the Messianic Savior, now treats the Deity as dirt!

Continuing with his second explanation of apostasy, *"...and has considered as common the blood of the covenant by which he has been sanctified...".* The apostate considers the sacrificial death of Jesus Christ, by which the new covenant was established (20), and by which he was set apart to be the bearer of the holy presence of God, to have no value or significance. The death of Jesus is regarded as "nothing special," just the historical execution of another Jewish troublemaker, another "bloody bore" of Jewish history. To deliberately and defiantly regard the sacred as profane, the Holy as common, the Word of God as worthless, is indicative of the attitude of the apostate.

A third representation of apostasy: *"...and has insulted the Spirit of grace?"* The Holy Spirit, "the Spirit of grace and supplication" (Zech. 12:10), by Whom one has been spiritually born (John 3:1-8), and without Whom one is not a Christian (Rom. 8:9,16), and through Whom the living Lord Jesus is present and actively expressing the grace of God (Acts 2:1-4; II Cor. 3:17), is now arrogantly and contemptuously despised and scorned. Such blasphemy of the Holy Spirit (cf. Matt. 12:31,32; Mk. 3:22-30) is indeed the "sin unto death" (I John 5:16). The apostate has so thoroughly rejected everything that God has done in Jesus Christ, that he now calls good "evil," truth "a lie" (cf. Rom. 1:25), and Deity "demonic." Such full and complete rejection of the things of God is indicative of the apostate, who will not be even slightly concerned with what a "non-existent God" cares about his attitude.

10:30 Judgment of the apostate is certain, *"For we have known Who it was that said, 'VENGEANCE IS MINE, I WILL REPAY.'"* Quoting from Deuteronomy 32:35 (cf. Ps. 94:1,2), Paul reminds the Christians in Jerusalem that God is just in vindicating the righteous and allowing vengeance to be

served upon the wicked. Paul quoted this same statement
(Deut. 32:35) in his epistle to the Romans (12:19), emphasizing there that the enacting of vengeance or judgment is God's
business, and not to be initiated by men, even in the Christian
community.

Continuing the citation from Deuteronomy 32:36, Paul
wrote, *"And again, 'THE LORD WILL JUDGE HIS PEO-
PLE.'"* In Deuteronomy this appears to indicate, "God will
vindicate His people," as in Psalm 135:14, but Paul seems to
be using the text to refer to a punitive judgment upon those
who have been "His people," and have subsequently rejected
Him.

10:31 Paul sums up the paragraph (26-31), *"It is a terrifying
thing to have fallen into the hands of the living God."*
Though this verse has often been used, and abused, as a
heavy-handed warning to non-Christians, Paul's statement is in
the context of a warning to the faltering Christians in
Jerusalem. It does not appear that Paul had "written off" any
of his readers as unsalvageable apostates, but he was still hop-
ing that they would avert the disaster of God's judgment by
drawing near to God (22), holding fast to their confession of
Christ (23), and participating in the community of faith (24).

10:32 In this third paragraph (32-39), Paul seems to cajole the
Jerusalem Christians by reminding them of their previous fellowship and suffering, in order to use that as an incentive to
continued endurance to avoid the dire consequences of defection and apostasy. *"But remember the former days, when,
having been enlightened, you endured a great struggle of
sufferings…"*. Paul wanted his readers in Jerusalem to have a
vivid recollection of the early days after their conversion and
spiritual enlightenment. Some of them had been Christians for
a long time (5:12), perhaps for as long as thirty-five years,
since Pentecost (Acts 2:1-47). Paul was reminding them of the

time when they received Jesus Christ as "the Light of the world" (John 8:12; 12:35), when they "turned from darkness to light" (Acts 26:18), when the light "shone in their hearts to give the light of the knowledge of the glory of God in the face of Christ" (II Cor. 4:6). "Having been enlightened, and having tasted of the heavenly gift, and having been made partakers of the Holy Spirit" (6:4), they had endured a great struggle or striving or contest (the Greek word *athlesis* is the basis of the English word "athletic") of sufferings. The early Christians in Judea suffered persecution at the hands of the Jewish community, who regarded them as traitors. Writing to the Thessalonians, Paul referred to "the churches of God in Christ Jesus that are in Judea who endured suffering at the hands of their own countrymen, …from the Jews, who killed the Lord Jesus and the prophets, and drove us out" (I Thess. 2:14,15). In the Sermon on the Mount, Jesus had said, "Blessed are those who are persecuted for the sake of righteousness, for theirs in the kingdom of heaven. Blessed are you when men revile you, and persecute you, and say all kinds of evil against you falsely, on account of Me. Rejoice, …for your reward in heaven is great" (Matt. 5:10-12). Paul reminds the Christians of Judea of their past faithfulness and suffering in order to encourage them to continue in the present, difficult situation.

10:33 Some of their sufferings are recounted: *"…sometimes being made a public spectacle by defamations and tribulations…"*. It is always difficult to be theatricized (the Greek word is *theatrizomenoi*) as a public spectacle of ridicule, humiliation, and shame. Paul knew what it meant to "become a spectacle to the world,…fools for Christ's sake" (I Cor. 4:9,10). The Christians in Jerusalem had "borne the reproach of Christ" (11:26; 13:13) in denunciation, defamation, and accusation. They had been jeered, mocked, reviled, and ostracized from family and much of society. The pressure was intense as they were afflicted with acts of violence and physical abuse. Paul had explained to the new Christians in Asia Minor, "Through many tribulations we must enter the kingdom of God" (Acts 14:22), and regarded such as "the fellowship of His sufferings" (Phil. 3:10), the "filling up of what is lacking in Christ's affliction" (Col. 1:24).

The sufferings of the Jerusalem Christians were *"at other times, by having become sharers with those being so treated."* They had stood with those who were being mistreated, recognizing the fellowship of being common partners and participants in the Body of Christ. A strong sense of solidarity of identification, association and community was evidenced by this unity of the Church of Jesus Christ. Paul had explained to the Corinthians, "If one member suffers, all the members suffer with it; if one member is honored, all the members rejoice with it" (I Cor. 12:26). "We who are many, are one Body in Christ" (Rom. 12:5).

10:34 Continuing his explanation of their solidarity and suffering: *"For you have sympathized with the prisoners, and have accepted joyfully the confiscation of your property..."*. Jesus explained that a practical expression of righteousness was visiting those in prison, "for to the extent that you do so unto them, you do so unto Me" (Matt. 25:36,40). Paul, himself, may have been a prisoner in Rome when he wrote this epistle (Acts 28:17,30), and could appreciate being visited in prison. Whether the sympathy shown to those incarcerated in chains was to fellow-Christians who had been imprisoned is not indicated, but Paul commends them for such ministry, and encourages them to continue to "remember the prisoners, as though in prison with them" (13:3).

The Christians in Jerusalem had also experienced the seizure and confiscation of their property. Whether this was legal action by the authorities, or the illegal action of pillage, plunder, stealing, looting, or robbery by those opposed to the Christians, we are not told. This may have been a contributing factor to the poverty of some of the Christians in Jerusalem, which prompted Paul to receive contributions for "the poor among the saints in Jerusalem" (Rom. 15:26). Paul commends them for having accepted this joyfully, i.e., without complaint. James, the prior head of the church in Jerusalem, had previously written, "Consider it all joy, my brethren, when you encounter various trials" (James 1:2). His half-brother, Jesus, had taught, "Do not lay up for yourselves treasures upon earth, where moth and rust destroy, and where thieves break in and steal. But lay up for yourselves treasures in heaven, where neither moth nor rust destroys, and where thieves do not break in and steal; for where your treasure is, there will your heart be also" (Matt. 6:19-21). The earliest Christians in Jerusalem had acted on this material detachment, and were "selling their property and possessions, and were sharing with all, as anyone had need" (Acts 2:45).

In accord with Jesus' admonition, the Christians in Jerusalem had suffered, *"knowing themselves to have in themselves a better and abiding possession."* The qualification "in heaven" (KJV) is not in the best Greek manuscripts, and detracts from the immanency of what the Christian has in the indwelling presence of Jesus Christ, but is valid, nonetheless, for the Christian is a "citizen of heaven" (Phil. 3:20), and "seated in the heavenlies" (Eph. 1:3; 2:6). The Christians in Jerusalem knew that the real "treasure" was spiritual, not material; both "an inheritance imperishable and undefiled, reserved in heaven" (I Pet. 1:4), as well as the superior and permanent "treasure" of the indwelling Spirit of Christ (II Cor. 4:7). Such treasure cannot be seized or stolen; but it is often the physical adversities that cause us to focus on, and get a better perspective of, our imperishable spiritual realities, as was apparently the situation with those to whom this letter was written.

10:35 *"Therefore,"* in light of what you have been through, *"you should not throw away your confidence, which has a great reward."* "Don't give up now! Don't let your past suffering count for nothing! Don't jettison your courage and confidence and steadfastness! Don't cast off your faith in Jesus Christ!" "God is a rewarder of those who seek Him" (11:6), Paul will go on to say. Jesus had said, "Blessed are you when men hate you, and ostracize you, and heap insults upon you, and spurn your name as evil, for the sake of Me, ...your reward is great in heaven" (Lk. 6:22,23; Matt. 5:11,12). When salvation (9:28) is consummated in the perfection of life in the heavenly realm, Christians will recognize that "the sufferings of this present realm are not worthy to be compared with the glory that is revealed to us" (Rom. 8:18). Such heavenly reward will not be anything other than, or more than, Jesus Himself, but Christians will glory in the everlasting appreciation and enjoyment of Jesus.

10:36 In order to experience this glorious heavenly reality, Paul admonishes the Jerusalem Christians, *"...you have need of endurance, so that, having done the will of God, you may receive the promise."* Some of the Christians in Jerusalem needed to recognize their responsibility to persevere, to persist, to endure in the midst of the present difficult situation. The Greek word for "endurance" is *hupomene*, meaning "to abide under." Instead of seeking some way to escape or defer the problems they were encountering, the Christians needed to "abide under" the situation, trusting the sufficient grace of God through faith. The "patron saint" of Jerusalem had written, "The testing of your faith produces endurance" (James 1:3). Paul is about to write his extended excursus on faith (11:1-40), which will be followed by the conclusive words, "Therefore, ...let us run with endurance the race set before us" (12:1), in like manner as Jesus "endured the cross, despising the shame, and sat down at the right hand of the throne of God" (12:2).

The Jerusalem Christians could "accomplish the will of God" in their lives if they were willing to be obedient in faith, receptive to the active expression of the character of Christ in every situation – even if that "will of God" meant being "obedient unto death" (10:5-10; Phil. 2:8). By such "endurance" in "doing the will of God," Paul explained, "you shall receive the promise" – the "better promises" (8:6), the "promise of an eternal inheritance" (9:15), the better possession (10:34), "the great reward" (10:35), the "crown of glory" (I Pet. 5:4), "the salvation of your souls" (I Pet. 1:9), the "heavenly city" (12:22; Rev. 21:2,10-27) – the very promises that many heroes of faith sought (11:13,39), and are now ours (realized and yet anticipated) through faith in Jesus Christ (II Cor. 1:20).

10:37 The Old Testament scriptures were lodged in Paul's memory, and he quotes from them again to explain the "need for endurance" (36). *"FOR YET IN A VERY LITTLE WHILE, THE ONE COMING WILL COME, AND WILL NOT DELAY."* Quoting from the Greek Old Testament, the Septuagint (*LXX*), as he does throughout this epistle, Paul allows the words of Habakkuk 2:3 to speak to the situation of the Jerusalem Christians. The delayed consummation of Christ's victory to be revealed in the second advent created an "enigma of the interim" for the early Christians, but Paul uses Habakkuk's words as his words to indicate that "the Coming One," Jesus, will come "in a very little while," very soon, i.e., imminently. This may refer to the "second coming" of the *parousia*, as in Revelation 2:25, "Hold fast until I come." More likely, Paul is referring to the imminent coming of Christ in judgment, when (perhaps within a year after the receipt of this letter) the Romans came against the residents of Palestine from A.D. 66-70, destroying everything and decimating the population. This is the same "coming of the Son of Man" (Matt. 24:27,30,37,42) that Jesus referred to in His Mount of Olives discourse (Matt. 24:3-45). Paul is warning the Hebrew

Christians again that judgment is coming, and everything in
the old covenant will "disappear" (8:13).

10:38 Paul continues to quote from Habakkuk 2:4, though the
two phrases are reversed. ***"BUT THE RIGHTEOUS ONE
WILL LIVE OUT OF FAITH..."***. This is a favorite text of
Paul's, which he quoted in his epistle to the Galatians (3:11),
as well as in the letter to the Romans (1:17). The Jerusalem
Christians are identified as "righteous ones" (Rom. 5:19; I Cor.
1:30; II Cor. 5:21), who needed to continue to "live by faith,"
remaining receptive in faith to the activity of the living Lord
Jesus within them.

   This responsibility of faithfulness is contrasted, ***"AND IF
HE SHOULD DRAW BACK, MY SOUL HAS NO PLEA-
SURE IN HIM."*** Paul uses these words of Habakkuk to continue his warning against defection, desertion, and apostasy.
The word for "draw back" was used in the Greek language as
a nautical term meaning, "to shorten the sail." The Christians
in Jerusalem needed to let the sails of their lives be open and
receptive to the winds of the Spirit of Christ, and if they were
to "shorten sail" in a withdrawal of faith, God would not be
pleased. "Without faith it is impossible to please Him" (11:6).

10:39 Not willing to give up on His Christian brethren in
Judea, Paul identifies himself with them and confidently
asserts, ***"But we are not those who draw back unto destruction, but those who have faith unto the safekeeping of the
soul."*** In a reverse form of encouragement, Paul rallies his
readers to deny that they are defectors and deserters who are
disloyal and draw back from faith in Christ, to suffer the consequence of ruin and everlasting death in "the day of judgment
and destruction of ungodly men" (II Pet. 3:7). Paul draws them
into an identification with "the faithful" who steadfastly
endure in the faith that relies on God whatever the circumstances – which unbeknownst to them would become even

more unpleasant and difficult in the near future. Only in faithful receptivity to the strength and life of the living Lord Jesus would they experience the secure safe-keeping and preservation of their souls in the eternal life of Jesus Christ, and the privilege of enjoying all God's promises (36). "God has not destined us for wrath, but for the safe-keeping (preservation) of salvation through our Lord Jesus Christ" (I Thess. 5:9).

Concluding remarks

A sense of heart-breaking agony can be detected in Paul's words as he expresses his deep-seated desire that the Hebrew Christians might recognize and realize the better way of access to God that they have in Jesus Christ. There is an angst apparent in his appeals to the battered brethren in Jerusalem, to "draw near to God in faith" (22), to "hold fast their confession of hope" (23), and to "incite one another to love" (24).

The real possibility of these Christians lapsing into an irrevocable apostasy has presented a perplexing problem for many Christians throughout the centuries. Some have misused Paul's comments to browbeat fellow Christians into increased performance of piety in order to avoid an alleged ever-present danger of damnation. Others have struggled with, or denied, any possibility of such apostasy, having adopted a static and determinative structure of divine actuation.

Paul always maintains a balanced perspective that takes into account the dialectic of God's sovereign activity and man's responsibility of receptivity. Divine grace and human faith connect for the implementation of God's intent on earth (Eph. 2:8,9). Paul affirms the divine preservation of the Christian: "God...shall confirm you to the end, blameless in the day of our Lord Jesus Christ" (I Cor. 1:4,8). "He Who began a good work in you will perfect it until the day of Christ Jesus" (Phil. 1:6). "I am convinced that He is able to guard what I have entrusted to Him until that day" (II Tim. 1:12).

Simultaneously, Paul explains the necessity of the Christian being faithfully diligent in perseverance and endurance: "He has reconciled you…in order to present you before Him holy and blameless and beyond reproach – if indeed you continue in the faith firmly established and steadfast, and not moved away from the hope of the gospel that you have heard" (Col. 1:22,23). "If we endure, we shall also reign with Him" (II Tim. 2:12). "You have need of endurance, so that when you have done the will of God, you may receive what was promised" (Heb. 10:36). The balanced tension of God's preservation by grace and man's perseverance in faith must always be maintained in the same manner that Paul presents such.

Paul's reference in the final two verses to "the righteous ones living by faith" (38), and "having faith to the safe-keeping of the soul" (39), serve as the transitional springboard for the extended excursus on faith that follows (11:1-40). The survey of the faithful of the old covenant is intended to show the Jerusalem Christians that despite the faith of the Old Testament figures, they "did not receive what was promised" (11:39), whereas Christians, by the "better things" in Christ, "may receive what was promised" (10:36).

ENDNOTES

1   cf. Lane, William L., *Word Biblical Commentary: Hebrews 9-13*. Vol. 47B. Dallas: Word Books. 1991. pgs. 296,297.

2   Bruce, F.F., *Commentary on the Epistle to the Hebrews*. Series: The New International Commentary on the New Testament. Grand Rapids: Wm. B. Eerdmans Publishing Co. 1992. pg. 258.

3   Buchanan, George Wesely, *To the Hebrews*. Series: The Anchor Bible. New York: Doubleday and Co. Inc. 1981. pg. 171.

JESUS

The Better Expectation
of Fulfilled Promises Received by Faith

Hebrews 11:1-40

Long known as "the faith chapter" of the Bible and characterized as "God's Hall of Fame" or "The Westminster Abbey
of Scripture," this excursus on faith has often been extracted
from its historical and textual contexts, disallowing and dis-
torting the emphases that Paul intended when he first penned
this letter to the Hebrew Christians in Jerusalem. Only within
its self-limiting contexts can we properly understand the inter-
twining emphases of promise, fulfillment, faith, hope, and
endurance as they related to the first century Christians of
Palestine, and have meaning by extended application to
Christians of all ages.

It does appear that Paul could have proceeded directly
from 10:39, "We are those who have faith to the safe-keeping
of the soul," to 12:1, "Therefore,...let us run with endurance
the race set before us." Such a transition would have a logical
flow of thought. But Paul takes his transitional "key" from the
quotation of Habakkuk 2:4 in 10:38, "My righteous ones shall
live by faith" (a favorite text of Paul's – Rom. 1:17; Gal.
3:13), and sets out to give a brief description of faith along
with an extended historical review of such faith in the old
covenant. The entirety of 11:1-40 must be interpreted by this
contextual reference to Habakkuk 2:4 in 10:38. Otherwise, the
commentator runs amok by defining faith in accord with
his/her presuppositions and interpreting the text by reading

those biases into the meaning (*eisegesis*) – a false pretext for reading the text outside of its context.

Why does Paul utilize Habakkuk 2:4 to connect with a review of the historical heritage of faith in the old covenant? The revolutionary zealots were demanding that the Hebrew Christians reconnect with their historical Jewish heritage, and join them in their military exploits to oust the Romans from their homeland, thereby allowing the implementation of all the divine promises for the Jewish people. Paul wanted the Judean Christians to recognize that they were already connected with the historic faith of their forefathers by receiving the "better things" in Jesus Christ, that the complete fulfillment of God's promises are in Jesus Christ (10:36; cf. II Cor. 1:20), and that their present need was to respond with a forward-looking faith like that of their Hebrew forebears, anticipating and expecting the ultimate fulfillment of God's promises as they continued to remain faithfully steadfast in their endurance of the present situation.

These exemplars or "heroes" of faith that Paul mentions are intended to provide an exemplary incentive (12:1) for the Jerusalem Christians to respond in like manner. They needed to recognize and receive the better promises of God (6:12; 8:6; 9:15; 10:36; 11:39) that were expectantly anticipated in hope (3:6; 6:11,18,19; 7:19; 10:23; 11:1), but could only be appropriated by a forward-looking faith (4:2; 6:12; 10:38,39; 11:1,6 *et al*; 12:2) that acted in persevering endurance (10:36; 12:1-3,7).

The faith of the old covenant people of God was established on the promises of God and the faithfulness of the One Who had promised (I Cor. 1:9; 10:13; Heb. 10:23; 11:11). Anticipating these promises in hope required their endurance through many obstacles and difficult circumstances, which Paul sets out to review. Jewish eschatology involved a forward-looking faith that sought the promises of God in a hope that was ultimately focused on the coming Messiah. Paul

encourages the Jerusalem Christians to maintain a faith that
continues to be forward-looking to the future fulfillment and
restoration of all things in Jesus Christ, "unto the end" (3:6,14;
6:11). Such a "theology of hope"[1] is a continuing necessity for
Christians, contrary to the assertions of some "full preterists"
who eschew all future expectation of Christian hope. Paul connects Christian faith and hope with its Jewish precedent, but
simultaneously explains that "God has provided something
better for us" (11:40) in the radically new Christocentric object
and dynamic of faith and hope. Christian eschatology begins
by looking back at the historical establishment and basis of
Christian faith and hope in the "finished work" (John 19:30) of
Jesus Christ, when (and where), by the death, resurrection, and
ascension of Jesus, the victory over the counterforce of evil,
sin, death and destruction, the victory of God was won for
eternity. This does not consign Christian eschatology to only
historical categories, but grounds the "last" and final work of
God in Jesus Christ in the historicity of Jesus, allowing
Christian eschatology to develop a dynamic understanding of
faith and hope in the continuous present of the lives of
Christians in all ages. Christians are to have a dynamic expectation of hope in God's continued faithful action in the present
and unto the future. By a dynamic receptivity of the activity of
the living Lord Jesus within, the Christian responds to God in
faith, having the divine dynamic provision of God's grace to
endure and persevere whatever may transpire. There is no
promise in the Christian gospel of exemption or immunity
from the tribulations of life; of escape or deliverance from
problems, hardships, or disease; and no allowance for inertia,
inaction, passivism, resignation or acquiescence. Christians are
responsible to endure and persevere in their faith – the very
point that Paul sought to drive home to the Hebrew Christians
in Jerusalem. The only alternative, in Paul's mind, to such
faithful endurance that expected to receive the promises of

God in Jesus Christ was an abject apostasy that absolutely rejected the Lord Jesus Christ (3:12; 6:4-8; 10:26-31,35-39).

Paul masterfully wove several objectives into the argument that he employed in this passage. [1] He wanted to *connect* the Jewish Christians with their Jewish heritage of faith in a recitative listing of historically attested examples of promise, hope, faith, and endurance. [2] While so doing he would *contrast* the unfulfilled promises (13,39) of the old covenant with the better promises (8:6) of the new covenant in Jesus Christ. He does this by interspersing a commentary of interpretive analysis within the review that posits the better city (10), the better country (16), the better riches (26), the better resurrection (35), and better provision (40) that are eschatologically fulfilled in the new covenant. [3] Throughout, his objective is to *convince* the Hebrew Christians in Jerusalem to endure the trials that were confronting them as the conflict with the Roman army loomed on the horizon.

The entire recitation of the old covenant heroes of faith is distinctively formulated in a context of Jewish Christian thought patterns. The Greeks regarded "faith" in opposition to reason. "Faith" was the response of the simple and uneducated to what could not be explained rationally and logically. Greeks would have conceived of these old covenant characters as "dupes of faith" or "fools of faith," rather than "heroes of faith." They would have been intrigued, if not astonished or appalled, at the willingness of Jews and/or Christians to suffer adversity with an unreasonable certitude in an indemonstrable cause. This makes Paul's comment all the more pertinent when he wrote, "He who comes to God must believe that He is, and that He is a rewarder of those who seek Him" (6).

A structural outline of this chapter is somewhat difficult to formulate, but the following points serve to provide a functional structure:

11:1 Transitioning to continue the theme introduced by the quotation of Habakkuk 2:4 in 10:38, Paul begins, *"Now faith is the substantiation of things being hoped for..."*. Paul is not attempting to formulate a formal definition of faith, but rather to provide a functional description of the faith required by the Jerusalem Christians in the context of the situation confronting them. This is sometimes called a "working definition." The Hebrew Christians needed faith that would endure the pressures and persecutions of their present problems, until such a time that their hopes would be realized in the peaceful fulfillment of the promises of God, whether in this life or beyond. Instead of defining faith as an exact equation of essential equivalence to a particularly defined static idea or concept, Paul is describing faith as the dynamic means of forward-looking action that anticipates the fulfillment of divine promise.

In contrast to the rejection of Christ in apostasy (Greek *apostasis* – "to stand away from"), the Jewish Christians needed a faith that would culminate in the "substantiation" (*hupostasis* – "to stand under") and actualization of all the things they were looking forward to in Jesus Christ. The word Paul uses (*hupostasis*) can be interpreted subjectively as an "understanding" or realization of confidence and assurance (3:14), or objectively as the substantive essence (1:3) that constitutes the underlying foundational support and groundwork of promised expectations. Rather than encouraging an internal and psychological feeling of assurance, it is more likely that Paul is indicating that the faith of the embattled Jerusalem Christians should/would look forward to and lead to an objectively existent and secure fulfillment of everything hoped for in Jesus Christ. This is all the more likely since the Hebrew word for "faith," used in Habakkuk 2:4, from which Paul had just quoted in 10:38, and was using as the springboard for his argument, is *emunah*, which refers to established firmness, solidity and stability. This certainly corresponds with the objective interpretation of faith as forward-looking action that expects the firm foundational substance of the subsequent fulfillment of all Christian hope in the "finished work" of Jesus Christ.

It must be noted, however, that personal faith does not create the substantive reality hoped for. Faith does not give substance to that which does not exist. Christian faith is not "positive thinking" or "possibility thinking" that allegedly brings into being its own object of concern. Rather, Christian faith looks forward with the confident expectation of hope to the substantive actualization and materialization of what God has promised, and what God will faithfully fulfill. It was this objectification of faith that the Greeks could not conceive of with their subjective understanding of faith as "wishful thinking."

Neither could the Greeks have understood faith as the means to proving ***"the certainty of things not seen."*** Again, the word Paul uses, *elengchos*, can be subjectively interpreted as an inner conviction or convincing of certainty, or objectively explained as the evidence, proof, and demonstration that exposes the certainty of that which is looked for, but not seen. The pragmatic (Greek word *pragmaton*) practicalities of the events and realities that were not yet observable with the sense perception of physical sight would be demonstrated and proven by the objective fulfillment of God's promises.

Paul's mention of "things not seen" is not a metaphysical reference to mystical intangibles. Paul is not indicating that faith itself can make invisible things visible in some magical manifestation. Nor is he promising that unseen spiritual realities can be made to seem as real (subjectively) as those observed with physical eyes. The "things not seen" refer to

future promised events and situations, the fulfillment of which
was not yet in sight. Paul was still encouraging the Judean
Christians to a forward-looking faith that could endure the
then present observable situation that appeared quite bleak.
Their enduring faith would lead to an obviating demonstration
of the certainty of all that God had promised in Jesus Christ.
Believing in the certainty of God's faithfulness to His promises would serve to set aside the subjective uncertainty and para-
noia that plagued some of the Christians in Jerusalem. Their
faith would be proven valid in the demonstrable evidence of
events and realities that, though not seen now, would be made
visible and real in the fulfillment of God's promises. Promise
will become reality; hope will become experience; faith will
become sight. In the meantime, faith acts (cf. James
2:14,16,20,26) with a certitude that expects the certainty of
"things not seen" to be made visible in the future in accord
with God's promises. Such enduring action of faith is what
Paul sought to motivate the Jerusalem Christians to maintain.

11:2   Paul commences to connect this "working definition"
of faith with the Jewish forefathers (1:1) who were rightfully
revered by the Jewish Christians. *"For by it the men of old
have received witness."* By their enduring faith that looked
forward to substantive and visible fulfillment of God's promises, the elders (Greek word, *presbuteroi*), the "old ones," the
ancients from earlier generations, the Jewish forefathers whom
Paul will begin to chronologically review in the subsequent
survey (11:4-38), received the witness of God's attestation and
commendation of their faith in the fulfillment of His promises.
The fact that Paul begins (2,4,5) and ends (39) this extended
passage with reference to the divine commendation of faith,
reveals that his intent was to motivate his readers to the
endurance of faith that would receive God's commendation,
"Well done, good and faithful servant" (cf. Matt. 25:21,23).

11:3 Prior to his survey of forward-looking faith in the old covenant people of God, Paul briefly mentions the backward-looking faith that accepts the creative work of God without the benefit of having observed such divine action with the sense perception of physical sight. Mankind was not present to observe most of the creation event. Since the creative acts of God described in Genesis 1 and 2 preceded the first case-study of Abel in Genesis 4, Paul includes faith in the past acts of God's creation as well as the historical acts of God in the lives of the Hebrew faithful.

"By faith we have comprehended the universe to have been ordered by a word of God." God asked Job, "Where were you when I laid the foundation of the earth! Tell Me, if you have understanding" (Job 38:4). Job needed the same kind of enduring faith that the Jerusalem Christians needed, the faith that trusted the acts of God in the past, present and future. Paul explains that it is via faith that we comprehend and understand with our minds (the Greek word for mind is *nous*, and the word for "comprehended" is *nooumen*) the evidence of God's creative acts in the past. Faith is not a blind leap of conjecture or presumption, but is a mental and volitional act based on objective evidence. Looking at the created order, honest searchers after truth can see a power, if not a Person, who brought the universe into being with "intelligent design." Writing to the Romans, Paul explained the natural revelation of God in the universe, "since the creation of the world, His invisible attributes, His eternal power and divine nature, have been clearly seen, being understood through what has been made" (Rom. 1:20).

It is only by means of faith that we understand that the ages, the aeons, the entire space/time context of the universe, was formed, framed, ordered, prepared, and arranged by God. It is interesting that Paul does not use the usual word for "create" (Greek, *ktizō*), but instead uses the word *katartizo*, meaning "to prepare" (10:5), "to equip" (13:21), to form, order, or

arrange. This may have been based on the Hebrew use of *bara*
for "create" (Gen. 1:1,21, 27), and *yatsar* for the forming,
fashioning, framing, and molding of preexisting materials
(Gen. 2:7,8,19). This latter process of formation is explained
in the Genesis account as "God said..." (Gen. 1:3,6,9,11,14,
20,24,26). This speaking things into being in the formation and
arrangement of the creative process seems to be what Paul is
referring to by his reference to the universe having been
ordered "by a word of God." The Psalmist wrote, "By the
word of the Lord the heavens were made, and by the breath of
His mouth all the host. ...For He spoke, and it was done; He
commanded, and it stood fast" (Ps. 33:6,9). Asaph's Psalm
explained, "Thou hast prepared the light and the sun. Thou
hast established all the boundaries of the earth" (Ps. 74:16,17),
obviously referring to the Genesis account, "And God said,
'Let there be light...'" (Gen. 1:3). The universe was formed
and ordered by the utterance of the Creator God bringing
things into being and arrangement out of Himself (*ek autos*).
"Word of God" does not refer to scripture, nor is it a
Christological reference to Jesus as the "Word of God" (John
1:1,14). The word for "word" used in this verse is *rhema*
rather than *logos*. Because of recent misrepresentations of
God's creative acts, it must be noted that God did not create
and fashion the universe by employing some "law of faith" or
speaking a "word of faith," utilizing a proceduralized formula
or technique which can then be exercised by others to create
supernatural phenomenon also. Faith did not create anything –
God created all things! Faith is not predicated of God, but is a
personal responsibility (response-ability) of man – not a God-
given commodity or God-effected response (despite misinter-
pretations of Eph. 2:8,9 and Gal. 2:20) – allowing man to
respond to God by recognizing His past creative acts, His present sufficiency, and His future consummation of all things. Our
faith is not in faith principles, but in God Himself!

The result of comprehending the creative arrangement of the universe spoken into being by God's power is that we then understand *"the things being seen to have been brought into being not out of things appearing."* This phrase might have been a precautionary clarification of the creative process spoken of in the previous phrase, or it might be a transitional statement that links faith in the "things being seen" in creation to faith in "things not seen" (1,7) in future events – the content of the following argument.

If Paul was attempting to clarify by making a parallel restatement or amplification of his comment on God's creative formation of the universe, his words have certainly been interpreted in a morass of ambiguity that is anything but clear. It has been suggested that Paul's statement about "the universe being arranged by God's utterance" could have been misconstrued by Greek philosophy that posited the eternal existence of matter and nature, and regarded this formless, primal matter to have phenomenalized itself into arrangements of various forms by natural processes. Is Paul correcting this naturalistic view of the evolution of rearranging or restructuring material particles into various observable phenomena by stating that the physically observable order was made by that which is not physical material, i.e., that creation points to a Creator, an invisible God who created all things visible? The Greeks explained the origin of everything as *ek phainomenōn*, "out of existent phenomena," and the emphatic part of Paul's statement is that what we see has been brought into being *me ek phainomenōn*, "not out of phenomena." Was Paul emphasizing that visible created objects were not brought into being by created objects, for this leads to the idolatrous worship of the creation (Rom. 1:25)? Was Paul attempting to affirm that the visible creation was brought into being not out of visible material (*ek phainomenōn*), but out of God (*ek Theos*), the invisible, immaterial God Who is Spirit (John 4:24), Who created all things out of His own power and Being (cf. Rom. 11:36; I Cor.

8:6; 11:12). Such a denial of the pre-existence and auto-generation of natural matter would necessarily deny the Greek philosophies, as well as naturalism, radical dualism, monistic pantheism, and a multitude of other pernicious man-made theories of origin and sustenance of the universe. But Medieval theologians were fearful that the idea of creation *ek Theos* would foster a monistic pantheism by failing to differentiate the creation from the Creator if the Creator was thought to have created a phenomenalization that was essentially Himself in visible forms. Failing to recognize that the invisible Creator could (and did) create visible phenomena that were not Himself, the greater creating the lesser, the church theologians used this very phrase to espouse a doctrine of creation *ex nihilo* (Latin phrase, meaning "out of nothing"). To counter the Greek thought of creation *ek phainomenōn*, the traditional explanation of the Christian church has been creation *ex nihilo* – a concept that is not necessarily biblical, even though they have used this verse to document their thesis by interpreting "not appearing" as "not existent," i.e., nothing. The apocryphal account of a mother trying to convince her son "to look at the heaven and the earth and see everything that is in them, and recognize that God did not make them out of things that existed" (II Macc. 7:28) is the only plausible basis for the creation *ex nihilo* doctrine.

In addition to all such theological obfuscation of the process of creation from this phrase, the religious mystics have taken these words out of context to document their convoluted concepts that are often akin to monistic pantheism. "What is visualized is brought into being and created out of the non-phenomenal." "By faith we *noumena* that *phenomena* are but manifested *pneumena*." The Mind-Science advocates and the New Age devotees often interpret this phrase to mean that "visibility is brought into being out of the invisibility of the metaphysical materializing of phenomenality" – whatever that means!

It seems most likely that Paul was using this statement as a connective phrase to return to his main theme of faith that endures to see the fulfillment of God's promised action. These words are best understood as drawing together the fleeting reference to faith in the unseen creative acts of God (3a), to the faith of the Jewish forebears (4-38) who experienced the promised acts of God in their lives, and that with the objective to encourage the Jerusalem Christians to anticipate the unseen acts of God that were yet future in their lives. If the "things not seen" in the working definition of faith in verse 1 referred to events in time which were not yet visible in physical sight (cf. previous comments), an interpretation verified by reference to Noah and "things not yet seen" in the events of the flood (7), then the "things seen" in this phrase (3) are likely to refer to the creative events at the commencement of time, rather than to physical created and visible objects. G.W. Buchanan notes,

> The author's concern for the unseen was not primarily that which was invisible or intangible, but that which was future, that which had not yet happened. It was a concept of time, rather than of substance or essence.[2]

The creative events enacted by God's utterance at the beginning of time were instrumentally and causally brought into being by the non-phenomenal, immaterial, invisible God of the universe. In like manner, the historical events in the lives of the old covenant faithful (which Paul will go on to review) were brought into being by the power of God in fulfillment of His promises. And this was all directed to the Christians of Jerusalem to provide an anticipation of the events yet to come in time which would be brought into being by the God Who is faithful to His promises, as they endured in their receptivity of faith to God's continuing grace activity.

11:4 Paul begins his review of old covenant personages who exemplified faith to one degree or another. These people were not perfect. There are adulterers, murderers, drunkards, prostitutes, and cowards in the list. It has been suggested that this survey of the exemplars of faith could be alternatively viewed as a "rogue's gallery." But these persons exemplified faith in particular situations despite their faults, and Paul considered them worthy of comment on their faithfulness.

"By faith Abel offered to God a better sacrifice than Cain, through which he has received witness to be righteous, God witnessing about his gifts, and through it, having died, yet he speaks." Based on the account in Genesis 4:4-8, Paul comments on Abel, the younger son of Adam and Eve's first two sons. There were a number of interpretive traditions that arose over the ages concerning why Abel's animal sacrifice was better than Cain's produce sacrifice, and how that acceptability was made known to them. Was the difference in the quality of the sacrifice, the manner of the sacrifice, or the attitude of the sacrificers? We can only speculate on the answers to some of these questions. What we do know is that the sacrifice of Cain was regarded as unacceptable (Gen. 4:5), and that he was unwilling to "do right" (Gen. 4:7). Cain's "deeds were evil" because he was deriving "out of the evil one" (I John 3:12), the personified sin who was "crouching at the door" (Gen. 4:7). On the other hand, the sacrifice of Abel God regarded as acceptable (Gen. 4:4), and Abel was commended by God for his righteousness. Jesus referred to Abel as "righteous Abel" (Matt. 23:35), and John writes that Abel's deeds "were righteous" (I John 3:12). The connection of faith and righteousness (10:38; Hab. 2:4) is still on Paul's mind, but he does not divert to explain that new covenant righteousness is only the result of the Righteous One, Jesus Christ (I John 2:1; I Cor. 1:30) manifesting His righteous character in the Christian. Rather, in accord with old covenant criteria of righteousness, God commended Abel's right attitude of faith that

led to right action, and God's testimony of such in Genesis 4:4-8 allows Abel's faith to continue to be a testimony, despite the fact that he was murdered by his brother and became the first martyr to die for doing right. Some have interpreted Abel's continued speaking to be Abel's blood crying from the ground for vindication (Gen. 4:10), and later in the epistle Paul does state that the "blood of Jesus speaks better than the blood of Abel" (12:24), but it seems more likely that Paul is explaining in this context that Abel's faith continues to have a posterity of divine attestation through the approving commendation of God's witness to such in Genesis 4:4-8.

11:5 Paul's second faith-witness is Enoch. *"By faith Enoch was removed not to see death, and he was not found because God removed him, for before his being removed he had received witness to have been pleasing to God."* Enoch is another briefly mentioned figure of the Old Testament, concerning whom there were many traditional additions of interpretive data. In the brief passage of Genesis 5:21-24, the Hebrew text indicates, "Enoch walked with God" (Gen. 5:22,24), whereas the Greek text of the Septuagint (*LXX*) reads, "Enoch was well-pleasing to God" (Gen. 5:22,24). As usual in this epistle, Paul works from the Greek text, and mentions that Enoch had received the divine commendation on his faithfulness as being "well-pleasing to God" prior to his being removed, lifted up, or translated into another realm without seeing death. The details of Enoch's removal without death are sketchy, and many apocryphal accounts were written to fill in the details. Sirach 49:14 states, "No one like Enoch has been created on earth, for he was taken up from the earth." The removal of Enoch without experiencing death was a phenomenon that stood out in the minds of the Jewish people. As they read the narrative of the descendants of Adam in Genesis 5 there was a repetitive statement, "and he died" (Gen. 5:5,8,11,14,17,20,27,31), and the sole exception was Enoch who "was not found because God removed him" (Gen. 5:24 – *LXX*). The majority of people are called upon to endure in faith until they die, but Enoch enjoyed a longevity of being well-pleasing to God in his faithful endurance for 300 years (some of us have a tough time making 30 years), and was apparently miraculously removed from the earth. This should not be construed as a "type" of rapture, or as a mystical representation of Christian death, but merely as the historical reward of his well-pleasing faith. It is clear throughout scripture that God is not pleased by man's "works" of righteousness, but only by faith that allows God to do what He wants to do (cf. Isa. 64:6; Phil. 3:8,9; Gal. 3:11-14), and that the divine commendation is based on such faithful availability.

11:6 Following up on Enoch's being "well-pleasing to God," Paul inserts another statement that explains and describes the forward-looking faith that he was encouraging the Jerusalem Christians to participate in. *"And without faith it is impossible to please* (Him)*, for the one coming before God must have believed that He is, and that He becomes a rewarder of those seeking Him."* Without faith, like that exemplified by Abel (4) and Enoch (5), it is impossible to live righteously or to be well-pleasing to God. Paul wanted his readers to aspire to such righteousness and divine pleasure, looking forward expectantly in faith to the reward of the fulfillment of God's promises, despite what might transpire physically. Abel was martyred. Enoch was translated. Both lived by faith (10:38) and were well-pleasing to God. Whether the Christians in Jerusalem were killed or delivered, martyred or removed in the soon coming conflict, they would still receive their heavenly reward if they would continue to exercise anticipatory and enduring faith, and not reject Jesus Christ. "Without faith it is impossible to please Him," but the ultimate pleasure of God is not in the faith action itself, but in the fact that faith allows God's grace action to manifest His character and work. In his benedictory remarks, Paul prays that the Hebrew Christians will allow God "to equip them in every good thing to do His will, working in them that which is pleasing to His sight, through Jesus Christ, to Whom be the glory forever and ever. Amen" (13:21).

Still attempting to encourage the Hebrew Christians to "draw near to God" (4:16; 7:25; 10:1,22; 12:18,22), Paul notes that "the one coming before God" or approaching God, must believe in the existence of God, that He *is* Who He *is*, and that He is faithful (11) to reward (10:35) those who keep on seeking Him with all the eternal promises (6:12; 9:15; 10:36). Although the words of this verse have been used as an evangelistic call to unbelievers, the context clearly indicates that Paul is referring to Christians who are being encouraged to dynamically approach God and to seek God's action and fulfillment in their lives. Such a relational faith and a forward-looking faith would prove to be the ultimate fulfillment and restoration of the Christians in Jerusalem and the Christians in every age. The words of the psalmist are appropriate: "Those who seek Him will praise the Lord. Let your heart live forever" (Ps. 22:26).

11:7   Noah is selected as the first in a sequence of Old Testament personages whose faith responded to a divine directive. ***"By faith Noah, being warned about things not yet seen, in reverence prepared an ark for the salvation of his household...".*** Though the narrative in Genesis 6:13-22 does not refer to Noah's faith explicitly, Paul surmises such since "Noah found favor (was pleasing) in the eyes of God" (Gen. 6:8) and was regarded as "a righteous man" (Gen. 6:9). Without faith it is impossible to please God (6) and be a righteous man (10:38; Hab. 2:4). Noah was warned by God concerning "things not yet seen" (1,3), events still in the future, i.e., God's coming judgment and destruction in the deluge of the flood. Noah believed in the existence of God (6), that God was in control of history, that God could reveal His intents, and that God would reward (6) those who responded to Him in faith. In the reverence of a godly fear that was attentive to God's direction, Noah prepared an ark according to God's detailed instructions. The ark served as a vehicle of safety for the escape and deliverance of his household, his family members, from the floodwaters. The "salvation" referred to is not the spiritual or regenerative salvation from sin and death that is in Jesus Christ alone, but the ark was the vessel by which they were "made safe" from the destruction of the flood. Peter connects the safety of the ark to the saving significance of Jesus Christ: "In the days of Noah…eight persons were brought safely through the water. And corresponding to that, baptism now saves you" (I Pet. 3:20,21). "God preserved Noah…when He brought a flood upon the world of the ungodly" (II Pet. 2:5).

The consequence of Noah's faith action in constructing the ark was that *"through this he (Noah) condemned the world, and became an heir of the righteousness which is according to faith."* The people surrounding Noah were, in contrast to Noah's faith, condemned in their unbelief. One can only imagine the mockery, scorn and ostracism of those who observed the apparent foolishness of "nutty Noah" building a boat on dry land. Noah's faith endured and prevailed as he expected and experienced the events God had foretold, and it was his detractors who experienced "the vengeance of God because of their wickedness."[3] Though Noah was previously regarded as "a righteous man" (Gen. 6:9), his faith action in building the ark qualified him as "an heir of the righteousness which is according to faith." Noah is commended for his faith obedience to God's revelatory directions concerning future events.

The Jerusalem Christians were being encouraged to have the same kind of enduring faith as that exhibited by Noah. There was a destructive judgment coming against those who would not believe in God's revelation of Himself in His Son,

Jesus Christ. The Christians of Judea needed to prepare for this coming catastrophe by having faith in "things not seen" (1,3,7), despite any scornful opposition around them. Their faith would likewise prove to be a condemnation upon the unbelieving world of their fellow countrymen.

11:8   Paul now commences his extensive coverage of the faith of Abraham (8-19). Approximately one-third of the text of this chapter is devoted to Abraham. This is no doubt because those of Hebrew origin regarded Abraham to be the "father" of the Jewish religion (John 8:33,39). Stephen's defensive review before the Jewish Council began with Abraham (Acts 7:2-8). Paul had previously used Abraham as the springboard for discussion of faith in his letters to the Galatians (Gal. 3:6-18) and to the Romans (Rom. 4:1-23). Even in this epistle, Paul had previously referred to Abraham (2:16; 6:13,14; 7:1-10).

"By faith Abraham, having been called, obeyed to go forth unto a place which he was to receive for an inheritance, and he went out, not knowing where he was going." Abraham responded by believing (Gen. 15:6) in God's promises of a place (8-10; 13-16) and a progeny (11,12; 17-19). God called him to go to an unknown land (Gen. 12:1; 15:7), a destination and destiny "not yet seen" (1,3,7). With forward-looking faith Abraham "listened under" God in obedience (cf. Gen. 26:5), and his faith was put into action as he set out on a journey to the unknown place. Faith is not just theoretical trust, but active advance toward what God has promised. Abraham did not know where he was going. He had no map with an itinerary. He had no advance reservations. A sense of security in our faith is not based on knowing where we are going, but on knowing Him Who called us to go, and being willing and flexible to allow Him to take us through the turns and detours and reversals. The place that Abraham was called to receive as a promised inheritance is referred to as a "land" (9), a "coun-

try" (14), and a "city" (10), even though the ultimate destination was not a geographical place. Abraham was faithful to go to the place of Canaan (Neh. 9:7,8) that was a prefigurative portion of the promised inheritance (Ps. 105:11), but this was not the intended inheritance of God, for Abraham never owned "a foot of ground" (Acts 7:5) in that geographical land. Faith is not sight, and the Christians of Jerusalem needed a similar forward-looking faith that responded to God's calling in obedience, awaiting an eternal place of inheritance which was "not yet seen" (1,3,7) or visible.

11:9 *"By faith he* (Abraham) *sojourned unto a land of promise, as in a foreign land, dwelling in tents with Isaac and Jacob, fellow-heirs of the same promise."* Abraham lived as a pilgrim, a nomad, a transient, a migrant, a temporary resident alien when he lived in various places in Canaan. He was a foreigner in a foreign land, for he did not possess any real estate (Acts 7:5) in Palestine, except for the purchase of a burial plot for his wife (Gen. 23:1-20). Canaan was not the ultimate "land of promise" that fulfilled the promises of God, but was only the "shadow-land" that prefigured the real "promised land." Isaac and Jacob were also migratory wanderers and pilgrims dwelling in tents in a nomadic and impermanent existence. They were all unsettled sojourners (Gen. 23:4; 37:1; 47:4), fellow-heirs of the same promised inheritance, which was not a geographical location, but which could only be fulfilled through Jesus Christ (II Cor. 1:20).

11:10 Consistent with his eschatological understanding throughout his writings, Paul interjects an interpretative explanation to clarify that the objective of Abraham's migration was not to possess a land in the Middle East. *"For he* (Abraham) *had waited expectantly for the city having foundation, of which the designer and builder was God."* Instead of a topographical and geographical place, Abraham was hopefully

345

expecting with a forward-looking faith a community where God's people could have settled communion with God, the "place" that Jesus prepared (John 14:2,3), "near to the heart of God." This "city of God," in contrast to the tent encampments in Canaan, would have permanent and eternal foundation, for its established foundation would be Jesus Christ (I Cor. 3:11). God Himself would be the city planner and city developer of this "city which was to come" (13:14), "the city of the living God, the heavenly Jerusalem" (12:22), "the Jerusalem above" (Gal. 4:26). This "city that God built" would be where God dwells and God reigns eternally in His unshakeable kingdom (12:28). This is the heavenly city that Paul was encouraging the Jerusalem Christians to focus on as the fulfillment of God's promises in Jesus Christ. The religious revolutionaries wanted them to fight for the physical city of Jerusalem, but Paul wanted them to identify with Abraham, Isaac, and Jacob who were sojourning resident aliens in that very land of Palestine. As "citizens of heaven" (Phil. 3:20), the Christians in Jerusalem needed to recognize that they were like sojourning foreign pilgrims who were looking forward in faith to the promised heavenly city, just as their patriarchs Abraham, Isaac and Jacob were.

11:11 Turning from the promise of place to the promise of progeny, Paul continues to note Abraham's faith. ***"By faith, he*** (Abraham) ***received power for the deposit of sperm, even though Sarah herself was barren and beyond the time of age, since he considered Him faithful, the One having promised."*** Many versions have translated this verse to refer to the faith of Sarah. Not only would this be a *non-sequitur* insertion, but there is little evidence of exemplary faith in Sarah who laughed at God's promise (Gen. 18:12) and then lied about having laughed (Gen. 18:15). In addition, and most importantly, this phrase, "the deposit of sperm" (Greek word *spermatos*), was a common Greek phrase for male procreation, referring to the ability to ejaculate semen in order to impregnate a woman and father a child. There is no evidence of its being used of a woman's ability to conceive. The *UBS4 Greek Testament* and several modern English translations (*NIV, NRSV, GNB*) recognize this reference to Abraham's faith for paternity. Abraham believed God's promise of progeny (Gen. 15:6) with a forward-looking faith, despite the fact that Sarah was barren (Gen. 11:30), sterile, and past menopause (Gen. 18:11). Despite every natural indication that childbirth for Sarah was gynecologically impossible, Abraham endured in the faith that "with God nothing is impossible" (Lk. 1:37), and God specializes in the impossible. The reference to being "beyond the time of age" for childbearing may refer only to Sarah or to both Abraham and Sarah, since they were 100 years old and 90 years old respectively at the time of Isaac's birth.

11:12 Continuing his reference to Abraham's faith, Paul wrote, *"and therefore, from one* (man)*, and that one having died, there came into being "AS THE STARS OF HEAVEN IN MULTITUDE, AND COUNTLESS AS THE SAND BY THE SEASHORE."* Through the one man's (Abraham's) faith in God's promise of progeny, a faith that acted to deposit sperm in Sarah, there came into being (were born) many descendants. Abraham's "having died" means that he was impotent, as good as dead when it came to the natural ability of fathering a child. Writing of Abraham's faith in his epistle to the Romans, Paul wrote, "He contemplated his own body, now as good as dead since he was about a hundred years old, and the deadness of Sarah's womb; yet, with respect to the promises of God, he did not waver in unbelief, but grew strong in faith" (Rom. 4:19,20), believing in "God Who gives life to the dead and calls into being that which does not exist" (Rom. 4:17; Heb. 11:3). The promise of God's blessing Abraham with a multiplied progeny (6:14) was reiterated throughout the Old

Testament record. The promises that his descendants would be "as the stars of heaven in multitude" (Greek word *plethei*, root of the word "plethora") is recorded in Gen. 15:5; 22:17; 26:4; Exod 32:13; Deut. 1:10; 10:22; 28:62; I Chron 27:23; Neh. 9:23. The promise of descendants "as countless (Greek word *anarithmetos*, meaning "beyond mathematical computation") as the sand by the seashore" is recorded in Gen. 22:17; I Kings 4:20; Isa. 10:22; Rom. 9:27). The prefiguring of innumerable physical progeny was fulfilled in Israel (cf. Deut. 1:10; I Kings 4:20; II Chron. 1:9; Neh. 9:23), but God's promise of innumerable spiritual progeny through Abraham is fulfilled in all who have faith in Christ (Rom. 4:16; 9:7,8; Gal. 3:7,16,29; 4:28).

11:13 If Paul were just reciting the details of Abraham's faith, he could have proceeded to verse 17. Instead, he gives another (10) interpretive interjection (13-16), an insertion of commentary that explains his eschatological perspective of history. *"All these died in faith, not having received the promises, but seeing and welcoming them from afar, and having confessed that they were strangers and sojourners upon the earth."* Abraham and all of his physical descendants in subsequent generations, particularly Isaac, Jacob, and Joseph (20-22), died with an expectant, forward-looking faith that endured to the end of their lives. They did not receive the intended fulfillment of the divine promises first given to Abraham (Gen. 12,15,17). The descendants of Abraham in the nation of Israel did receive the physical prefiguring of those promises (Josh. 21:45; 23:14; I Kings 8:56), but they did not receive the ultimate spiritual experience and enjoyment of the promises that God had given to the patriarchs. The true and complete fulfillment of the promises to Abraham would only come in Jesus Christ (II Cor. 1:20; Eph. 1:10), leading Jesus to say, "Abraham rejoiced to see My day" (John 8:56). The patriarchs caught a glimpse of the spiritual realities of Christ with the foresight of faith, and greeting those "yet unseen" (1,3,7) Messianic events with an embrace that extended across time. They admitted that they were "strangers and sojourners on the earth" (Gen. 23;4; 47:4,9; I Chron. 29:15), temporary and transient residents of Canaan. They observed the "shadow-land" of Canaan, but looked forward in faith to the deferred "fullness of time" (Gal. 4:4) when the promises would be fulfilled in Jesus Christ.

The Jerusalem Christians need to "hold fast their confession" (4:14; 10:23) that they had already received the fulfillment of the promises in Jesus Christ and were now "citizens of heaven" (Phil. 3:20). At the same time, there was still a yet anticipated experience of the promises in the heavenly realm (6:12; 8:6; 9:15; 10:36) which cast them into a similar situation as their forefathers, as "aliens and strangers" (I Pet. 1:1; 2:11), looking forward to a future fulfillment which likely would require "dying in faith" to fully experience "the city which was to come" (13:14).

11:14 Paul continues his explanation of the faith of the nomadic forefathers. *"For those saying such things make it clear that they seek a fatherland."* Abraham and his descendants, by admitting and stating that they were sojourners, wanderers, pilgrims, nomads, migrants, or transients, make it explicitly plain by their own confession that they are on a forward-looking journey, in transit, on their way to somewhere else, seeking a goal of a homeland where they could feel at home, a fatherland (Greek *patrida*) which would be the land of the Father where they could permanently settle and reside in fellowship with God. They were not seeking real estate on the eastern edge of the Mediterranean Sea, but were journeying toward the "Jerusalem above" (Gal. 4:26), "the city of the living God, the heavenly Jerusalem" (12:22) with permanent and eternal foundations (10).

With a similar faith objective, the Jerusalem Christians of the first century needed to recognize and admit that they were on their way to somewhere else, to the eternal homeland or fatherland of God. The zealots wanted them to join in defending their homeland and fatherland of Palestine against the Romans with nationalistic and patriotic pride, but Paul wanted them to understand that the physical Jerusalem was of no consequence compared to the "heavenly Jerusalem" (12:22) of God's eternal presence.

11:15 Paul clarifies the fatherland that Abraham and his descendants were seeking, first by negation and then by affirmation. *"And indeed if they were thinking of that* (fatherland) *from which they came out, they had time to return."* Abraham did not regard his birthplace in Ur of the Chaldees (Gen. 11:28) in Mesopotamia as his true homeland or fatherland. In fact, he did not even want his son to ever return (Gen. 24:8) to that place of idolatry (Josh. 24:2). The promised fatherland that Abraham sought was not a geographical location in Mesopotamia, or in Canaan or Palestine, but was the place where the divine Father lived.

11:16 Affirmatively Paul explains, *"But as it is, they sought a better* (fatherland)*, that is, a heavenly* (fatherland)*."* With the forward-looking aspiration of hopeful faith, Abraham and his descendants kept their eye on the goal of a better fatherland that would be their permanent homeland. Paul identifies their destination of faith as the heavenly homeland of God, the fulfillment of all the land promises of God to Abraham (Gen. 12:7; 13:4; 15:7,18; 17:8). This "inheritance...reserved in heaven" (I Pet. 1:4), the "heavenly kingdom" (II Tim. 4:18) of the "heavenly Jerusalem" (12:22) was made available and accessible in Jesus Christ.

"Therefore," since Abraham and his descendants desired the place of God, the heavenly fatherland, *"God was not ashamed to be called their God; He prepared a city for them."* God is often referred to as "the God of Abraham, Isaac, and Jacob" (Gen. 28:13; Exod. 3:6,15,16; Matt. 22:32; Lk.

22:37). Because of their faith to seek only a place with Him, God "prepared a city for them." "I go to prepare (same Greek word) a place for you," Jesus told His disciples (John 14:2,3), the "city of God" in the eternal fatherland, the "lasting city" (13:14) with permanent foundations (11:10), the "heavenly Jerusalem" (12:22).

Christians are already "partakers of a heavenly calling" (3:1), "having tasted of the heavenly gift" (6:4), being "seated in the heavenly places" (Eph. 2:6) as "citizens of heaven" (Phil. 3:20), but they still look forward in hope for the perfect and unhindered experience of the heavenly homeland. Paul wanted the Jerusalem Christians to reject all solicitations to fight for the homeland of Palestine and for the physical city of Jerusalem. These geographical locations were not the "promised land." The Hebrew Christians of Jerusalem needed to endure in their faith, unashamed of their pursuit of the presence of God, even willing to die in the certainty of the eventual substantiation (11:1) of the heavenly fatherland and city of God.

11:17 This faith that faces physical death with the hope of resurrection is now illustrated in a subsequent event in the life of Abraham. ***"By faith Abraham, being tested, had offered up Isaac; and the one having received the promises was offering his only-begotten*** (son)...*"*. The Old Testament account of Abraham's binding and offering of Isaac is located in Genesis 22:1-18. Though James wrote that God "does not tempt any one" (James 1:13), the same word, *peirazo*, is used here for God's testing of Abraham, and is used of Jesus' testing of Philip (John 6:6). The intent of the solicitation, whether for evil or for good, is the criteria that must be considered in the differentiation of "tempting" and "testing." God's purpose in "testing" Abraham (Gen. 22:1) was for the good intent of allowing Abraham's faith to be put into action (James 2:21). Abraham, the one who had received the divine promise of progeny and descendancy (Gen. 12:7; 13:15,16; 15:5,18; 17:7,8), and by faith saw this promise materialize physically in the birth of his son, Isaac, then had his faith tested by God's command to sacrifice his "only son" (Gen. 22:2). Yes, Abraham had another son, Ishmael, who was conceived as "a logical alternative to faith" to assist God in the keeping of His promise, but Isaac was the only son begotten according to God's promise and action. Believing that God was faithful to act in accord with His promise, Abraham obeyed despite the seeming irrationality of the request, and "had offered up Abraham" – an act of faith already completed in terms of intent and willingness.

11:18 This was the very son *"concerning which it was spoken that, "IN ISAAC YOUR DESCENDANTS SHALL BE CALLED."* This previous statement of God, recorded in Genesis 21:12, was God's declaration that the "son of promise" for progeny and descendancy was to be fulfilled through Isaac, and not Ishmael. God's promise was "on the line." Why, then, would God ask Abraham to offer this son as a burnt offering (Gen. 22:2)? To test whether Abraham would put his faith in action.

11:19 Abraham's faith was perfected in action (James 2:21). *"He was reckoning that the power of God* (could) *even raise out of death; from which he received him back in a parable."* As Abraham took young Isaac up the mountain, his faith was evident in his statements, "we will worship and return" (Gen. 22:5), "God will provide the lamb for the burnt offering" (Gen. 22:8). Paul goes beyond the details of the text in Genesis and indicates that Abraham was reckoning in faith that even if Isaac, the "son of promise," was killed, the power of God was able to raise him from the dead. Such faith in the resurrection power of God to fulfill His promises was the very kind of faith that Paul was encouraging the Jerusalem Christians to have –

faith that expects that even if they were to die in the approaching war with the Romans, they would see the fulfillment of
God's promise of resurrection life in Jesus Christ.

Abraham received Isaac back, figuratively from the dead,
when God provided a ram for the sacrifice on the mountain
(Gen. 22:13). Paul explained that this was a parable of faith, a
story "thrown alongside" (the meaning of the Greek word
parabole) to illustrate faith. This figurative language should
not be unduly pressed into allegorical typology that projects
Jesus as a child of promise, the only-begotten son, whose life
out of death in resurrection was like unto that of Isaac. The
birth, death and resurrection of Jesus are singularly unique,
and to regard them as an antitype of the type of Isaac is
destructive to the incarnational, redemptive, and restorational
message of the gospel. It is Abraham's faith in the promises
and power of God that is the issue addressed in this passage.

11:20 Paul proceeds to mention the forward-looking faith of
the three immediate generations of Abraham's descendants –
of his son, Isaac; of his grandson, Jacob; and his great-grand-
son, Joseph. ***"By faith Isaac blessed Jacob and Esau concerning things to come."*** Esau and Jacob were the fraternal
twin sons of Abraham. Esau was the firstborn son, and was to
have the priority of parental blessing according to Hebrew cus-
tom. Such parental blessing of the firstborn son was linked to
the lineage of God's promise of descendancy. Isaac's wife,
Rebekah, conspired with Jacob to arrange for the aging and
blind Isaac to give the parental blessing of the firstborn to
Jacob (Gen. 27:5-29). A secondary blessing was subsequently
given to Esau (Gen. 27:39,40). This was all in accord with
God's intent that "the older would serve the younger" (Gen.
25:23; Rom. 9:12), and Jacob was to be the one loved by God
(Mal. 1:2,3; Rom. 9:10-13) in order to serve in the line of
inheritance and blessing of the divine promises (Gen. 28:3,4)
of "the things to come" in the future in Christ.

11:21 Despite his deceit, Jacob was a faithful man of God. ***"By faith Jacob, as he was dying, blessed each of the sons of Joseph, and worshipped*** (leaning) ***on the top of his staff."*** Jacob, who became Israel (Gen. 35:10-12), had twelve sons (Gen. 35:22-26), the paternal heads of the twelve tribes of Israel (Gen. 49:28). Joseph, the favored son of Jacob (Gen. 37:3), had two sons, Manasseh and Ephraim. As Israel was dying, Joseph came before him with his two sons (Gen. 48:8-11). Although Manasseh was the firstborn, Jacob, the grandfather, insisted on giving the foremost blessing to Ephraim instead (Gen. 48:17-20). Quoting from the Greek translation (*LXX*) of the Old Testament, Paul noted that Jacob "worshipped while leaning on the top of his staff" (Gen. 47:31). The Hebrew text indicates, "he bowed at the head of the bed" (Gen. 47:31). What accounts for this difference? The Hebrew consonants *"mth"* could be supplied with differing vowels: *mittah* meaning "bed," or *matteh* meaning "staff." The reference to a "staff" corresponds with the idea of sojourning, journeying, and pilgrimage that has been emphasized in the foregoing theme of a faith that looks forward to a promised land.

11:22 The context of the foregoing reference to Jacob's "worshipping on the head of his staff" was Joseph's swearing to bury the corpse of Jacob outside of Egypt (Gen. 47:29,30). Paul connects this faith in a promised land to Joseph's own forward-looking faith. ***"By faith Joseph, when he was dying, mentioned the exodus of the sons of Israel, and gave orders concerning his bones."*** The final verses of Genesis refer to Joseph's dying words to his descendants. To his dying day he still had faith that looked forward, saying, "God will take care of you, and bring you up to the land which He promised to Abraham, to Isaac, and to Jacob" (Gen. 50:24), a statement that Paul regarded as a prior mention of the Exodus. Joseph made his sons and grandsons promise to take his bones out of Egypt (Gen. 50:25), just as Jacob had requested. Joseph's bones were indeed taken out of Egypt (Exod. 13:19), and buried at Shechem (Josh. 24:32; Acts 7:16). The descendants of Abraham continued to believe in a "promised land", recognizing Canaan as the physical prefiguring of such. Paul wanted the first century Hebrew Christians in Jerusalem, whose heritage was in Abraham, Isaac, Jacob, and Joseph, to have the same kind of resolute faith as their forefathers, believing that despite whatever transpired, even their own death, their final resting place would be in the ultimate and eternal land that God had promised to Abraham.

11:23 Paul's review of the faith of old covenant personages has been from the narratives of Genesis up to this point. Now he begins to draw from the narratives of Exodus, which had been alluded to in the reference to Joseph in the previous verse (22). Whereas Abraham was regarded as the father of the Jewish peoples, Moses was held in high esteem as the deliverer of the Hebrew nation.

"By faith Moses, having been born, was hidden three months by his parents, because they saw he was an attractive child; and they did not fear the decree of the king." This verse does not refer to the faith of Moses directly, but to the faith of his parents, Amram and Jochebed (Exod. 6:20), who were Israelites enslaved in Egypt. When Moses was born, he was hidden for three months in defiance of the Pharaoh's command that, "Every son who is born, you are to cast into the Nile" (Exod. 1:22). The Hebrew text of Exodus 2:2 indicates that this action of hiding the child was undertaken by the mother, but the Greek text (*LXX*) attributes the action to both parents jointly. The explanation of the parent's action of civil disobedience was that they saw that their son was attractive, beautiful, comely, or good-looking (Exod. 2:2). This was surely more than just the common parental pride that causes many parents to think that their child is the most beautiful child ever born. In Stephen's defense before the Council, he explained

that the infant Moses "was lovely in the sight of God" (Acts 7:20), seeming to imply that there was some visible sign of God's favor upon the child signifying that he was destined to be used of God. In that case, Moses' parents had a forward-looking faith that expected the unseen (1,3,7) purposes of God that were yet to transpire in the life of their son. In addition, their faith and love (I John 4:18) was unafraid of the consequences and reprisals that might come from violating the edict of the Pharoah. In faith, they chose to fear God (12:28) rather than the Egyptian Pharaoh.

It was this kind of faith that Paul was encouraging the Jerusalem Christians to exhibit. They needed faith that would stand against what the Jewish authorities were demanding in rebellious action against Rome. The Christians in Jerusalem needed to resist any fear of human reprisal, and be willing to risk their lives for the destined purpose of God in Jesus Christ.

11:24   The faith of Moses himself is now referred to – a faithfulness previously referred to in this epistle (3:2). ***"By faith Moses, having become great, refused to be called the son of Pharaoh's daughter…"***. The reference to Moses' "having become great" could refer to Moses' rise to position and power in the royal household; "educated in all the learning of the Egyptians, he was a man of power in words and deeds" (Acts 7:22). On the other hand, it might refer only to Moses' having "grown up" (Exod. 2:11) to be an adult man. Stephen explained that

> when he was approaching the age of forty, it entered his mind to visit his brethren, the sons of Israel. And when he saw one of them being treated unjustly, he defended him and took vengeance for the oppressed by striking down the Egyptian. And he supposed that his brethren understood that God was granting them deliverance through him; but they did not understand. (Acts 7:23-25)

The faith of Moses was put into action in identification with the Israelite people of God. Moses was willing to renounce the privilege and power of being an adopted son of Pharaoh's daughter reared in the royal palace, and cast his lot with his enslaved and oppressed ethnic Hebrew peoples, even though they did not yet understand that he was destined to be their deliverer.

11:25 By his act of faith, Moses was *"choosing rather to suffer evil-treatment together with the people of God, than to have enjoyment of sin for a time…".* Faith is a choice, a choice to act in a particular manner because one believes in the promises and power of God. Moses knew the promises of God concerning the Jewish people who were identified with God. Instead of selfishly sitting back to enjoy the privilege and comfort of royal advantage, Moses chose to identify with his Hebrew people of God and suffer the persecution that they endured at the hands of the Egyptian Pharaoh (his adoptive-grandfather). To have failed to make that faith-choice would have allowed him temporary enjoyment of royal privilege, but it would also have been a sin-choice to reject and to "stand away from" God and His people in apostasy. "Whatever is not of faith is sin" (Rom. 14:23).

The Hebrew Christians of Jerusalem who received this letter were faced with a very similar choice. Would they take the "easy way out" and possibly "save their own skins" in the self-serving apostasy of standing against Christ and the Christian community – a temporary enjoyment of sin, to be sure, given our hindsight of the devastating decimation of Palestine and its people in the war with the Roman army in A.D. 66-70? Or would they stand firm in their Christian faith and continue to suffer mistreatment with the Christian "people of God"?

11:26 Paul gives His Christian commentary on Moses' faith-choice to identify with God and His people, and suffer the ill-treatment of such identification. In Paul's mind Moses' faith looked forward to the promised Messiah, who would identify with mankind in the incarnation, and by His obedient sufferings (2:9,10; 5:8) endure the hostility and shame of the cross (12:2,3), becoming the real deliverer of mankind, to establish a new "people of God" (8:10) with an eternal heavenly reward (10:35; 11:6). In Paul's words, Moses was *"considering the reproach of Christ greater riches than the treasures in Egypt; for he was looking toward the reward."* Though some detect a reference to the Psalmist's mention of "reproach" (Ps. 69:8-21; 89:50,51), it is more likely that Paul was linking all godly suffering with Christ's suffering, as he commonly did in his writings (cf. Rom. 8:17; 15:3; Phil. 3:10; Col. 1:24). Moses had no more than a glimpse of the Messianic deliverer, but in his faith-choice to be the deliverer of the Hebrew nation and suffer the reproach of such action, his was a faith-action that served as a prototype of the spiritual exodus whereby Jesus Christ would identify with mankind, suffer reproach and death, and deliver mankind from slavery to sin. Paul viewed Moses' faith-action as a typological prefiguring of Jesus Christ. Moses deemed identification and reproach with his people to be of more value than all the royal wealth of Egypt available to him, for he had a forward-looking faith that saw the "yet unseen" (1,2,7) deliverance of the Israelites from slavery in Egypt and their return to the prefigurative "land of promise" in Canaan. The words of Jesus in the Sermon on the Mount retroactively laid down the foundation of Moses' faith: "Blessed are those who have been persecuted for the sake of righteousness, for theirs is the kingdom of heaven" (Matt. 5:10). "Do not lay up for yourselves treasures upon earth, ...but lay up for yourselves treasures in heaven, ...for where your treasure is there will your heart be also" (Matt. 6:19-21).

Paul's commentary in this verse was projecting the exemplary faith-action of Moses, along with the faith-action of Jesus in enduring the shame of the cross (12:2), to the need of the Hebrew Christians in Judea to whom he was writing this terminal letter. They needed to "bear the reproach of Christ" (13:13), to be willing to participate in "the sufferings of Christ" (II Cor. 1:5), recognizing the incomparable value of the riches that were theirs in Christ (Eph. 1:7,18; 2:7), and looking forward to the heavenly reward (10:35; 11:6) of the eternal "promised land."

11:27 Like Abraham, Isaac, and Jacob (9), Moses was a transient sojourner seeking the heavenly homeland of the abiding presence of God. In the context of this recitation of Moses' faith-choices to seek the greater good rather than the lesser personal advantage, Paul wrote, ***"By faith he left Egypt, not fearing the wrath of the king; for he kept on as seeing the unseen** (One)."* The departure of Moses from Egypt has been a subject of debate. Does this refer to Moses' departure from Egypt to Midian (Exod. 2:15) after he realized that his murder of an Egyptian taskmaster had become public knowledge? In that situation it is recorded that "Moses was afraid" (Exod. 2:14), which makes the phrase "not fearing the anger of the king" problematic. Moses' other departure from Egypt was in the exodus, prior to which he fearlessly confronted Pharaoh through the plagues (Exod. 5:1–13:16), and advised the Israelites as they approached the sea, "Do not fear" (Exod. 14:13). The exodus departure solves the problem of the "fear factor," but creates a *non sequitur* in the subsequent reference to the Passover (28). The primary emphasis of the verse, however, is on Moses' enduring vision of the unseen. In synchronous parallel with his "looking toward the reward" (26), Moses had an enduring faith that fixed his eyes (12:2) on God, the Unseen One (John 1:18; Rom. 1:20; Col. 1:15; I Tim. 1:17; I John 4:12,20) and all that He would do in unseen (1,3,7) future events. That was the kind of enduring faith that the Jerusalem Christians needed – faith that was fearless of the reprisals of the authorities, seeing behind the visible threats the

Invisible God at work as they continued to believe in His promises and power.

11:28 In this verse we begin to see the transitional shift from the faith of particular persons to the faith of the nation of Israel (29) and the events evidencing faith in the history of Israel (30-38). *"By faith he* (Moses) *kept the Passover and the sprinkling of blood, in order that the destroying one should not touch their firstborns."* Prior to the exodus Moses participated in the greatest of the evidences of the Unseen God at work (Exod. 11:1–12:32), the plague of death upon all first-born children in Egypt, except for the Hebrew families who sprinkled the blood of a lamb on the doorposts and lintel of their homes (Exod. 12:7). The Hebrews who sprinkled lamb's blood on their doorways were "passed over" (Exod. 12:13,23) when the firstborns were killed. Although some verses in the Exodus narrative seem to indicate that it was the Lord who was destroying the firstborns (Exod. 12:12,13,27,29), others indicate that God allowed or disallowed the "destroying one" (Exod. 12:23) to inflict death on the firstborn. The "destroying angel" (I Chron. 21:15) or "death angel" is often identified as "the one having the power of death, that is, the devil" (Heb. 2:14), the diabolic "destroyer" who destroyed the disobedient in Israel (I Cor. 10:10). Moses had faith that God would cause the death-destroyer to "pass over" the Hebrew firstborns. This became the basis for the Hebrew celebration of the Passover feast (Exod. 12:14-20, 24-28, 42). Later the Passover prefiguring found fulfillment in Jesus as the paschal lamb (John 1:29,36; I Cor. 5:7) whose death allowed for God's "passing over of sins" (Rom. 3:25).

11:29 After the death of the firstborns, Pharaoh agreed to let the Israelite people go (Exod. 12:31,33). *"By faith they went through the Red Sea as through dry* (land); *the Egyptians attempting it were drowned."* In their exodus from Egypt, it often seemed that the Israelites did not have much faith, as they complained about their circumstances and said, "Leave us alone that we might serve the Egyptians. It would have been better to serve the Egyptians than to die in the wilderness" (Exod. 14:12). But when told to "go forward" (Exod. 14:15), they acted in faith and stepped toward the Sea of Reeds (Exod. 15:4,22), and it became dry land (Exod. 14:16,21,22; Ps. 66:6; 106:9; Isa. 51:10). The Hebrew reference to the "Sea of Reeds" (Exod. 13:18; 15:4,22; 23:31) was translated as "Red Sea" in the Greek text (*LXX*). When the Egyptians changed their minds and attempted to follow the Israelites into the sea, they were swallowed up and drowned (Exod. 14:27,28; 15:4; Ps. 106:11).

What were the Jerusalem Christians to learn from this? The Invisible (27) specializes in the impossible! Though their situation may have seemed impossible, they needed faith like the ancient Israelites who stepped into the sea and it turned to dry land. How might God act to protect and preserve them, and take them to the "promised land"?

11:30 Having already referred to the faithlessness of the wilderness generation (3:16-19), Paul passes over the forty-year period of wilderness wanderings and resumes with the faith of the people of Israel as they prepared to enter in to the prefigurative "promised land" at Jericho. In so doing, he moves from the narrative of Exodus to that of Joshua. *"By faith the walls of Jericho fell, having been encircled for seven days."* This is another *non sequitur,* for Rahab's cooper-ation with the Israelites spies (31; Josh. 2:1-21) definitely pre-ceded the fall of the walls of Jericho (Josh. 6:1-21). Despite the seemingly illogical strategy of marching around the walls of Jericho for seven days, the Israelite children of the exodus generation acted in faith at the Lord's bidding (Josh. 6:2-5). It was not the faith-action of the encircling marchers that caused the walls of Jericho to fall. It was the divine action of the God

Who was the object of their faith that caused the massive walls of Jericho to fall, for He had promised, "I will be with you; I will not fail you or forsake you" (Josh. 1:5).

11:31 Prior to the destruction of Jericho two Israelite spies were sent to Jericho and received by a prostitute named Rahab. It is phenomenal that in the patriarchal society of ancient Palestine a woman should be held in high esteem for her faith. In addition, this woman was not an Israelite, and is specifically referred to as a prostitute (Josh. 2:1; 6:17,22,25; James 2:25). In fact, she is included in the genealogy of Jesus Himself (Matt. 1:5).

"By faith Rahab the prostitute did not perish with those disobeying, receiving the spies with peace." Her faith-action was evidenced in concealing the two Israelite spies from the authorities in Jericho who were searching for them (Josh. 2:6,7). Her confession of faith was, "I know that the Lord has given you the land" (Josh. 2:8). The reward of her faith was that she and her family members (Josh. 2:12,13; 6:17,22-25) were preserved from harm and death when Jericho was conquered.

Was there a lesson here for the Jerusalem Christians? Perhaps it was that they needed faith like Rahab that was willing to forsake the security of a walled city (in their case Jerusalem, instead of Jericho), and forsake even the religion of their fathers, in order to find security only in the living God and involvement with His people (8:10). Perhaps they were to recognize that if a sinful prostitute could be praised for forward-looking faith, then they should continue to be faithful to Jesus Christ, and not prostitute themselves in sinful apostasy.

11:32 Paul could not replay all of the Old Testament narratives of the people of faith. So, beginning with a rhetorical question, he asks, *"What more can I say? For time would fail me telling of Gideon, Barak, Samson, Jephthah, and of*

David and Samuel and the prophets." There was not enough time or parchment for Paul to tell all the details of all the Hebrew heroes of faith, so it was necessary to abbreviate and condense his review. The six (6) persons mentioned are not in chronological order; they appear to be in reversed couplets with the greater figure of faith preceding the lesser.

Gideon (Judg. 6:11–8:35) had faith that endured despite the "odds." Not depending on numerical advantage or majority, Gideon pared down his army at God's bidding to 300 men, and the small band then routed the Midianites. It was a battle long remembered in Hebrew history as representative of the power of God (Ps. 83:9; Isa. 9:4; 10:26).

Barak (Judg. 4:1–5:31) was the army general who served Deborah, the judge of Israel, but demanded that she accompany him to war. By faith they triumphed over the chariot army of Sisera.

Samson (Judg. 13:1–16:31) was a strong man with a weakness for Philistine women. Despite his temptation and failure, he had a faith that allowed his weakness to be made strong (34) in the power of the Lord, even unto death.

Jephthah (Judg. 11:1–12:7), the son of a prostitute, rose out of his ostracism to become a judge of Israel. By faith he defeated the sons of Ammon, but in order to keep his rash vow, he was forced to sacrifice his only daughter.

David (I Sam. 16:12–II Sam. 24:5), a man after God's own heart, was the greatest king of Israel. His faith was evidenced in conflict with Goliath, with Saul, with foreign armies, and even with his own son, Absalom. Through Nathan the prophet, God said to David, "When your days are complete and you lie down with your fathers (in death), I will raise up your descendant after you, who will come forth from you, and I will establish the throne of his kingdom forever" (II Sam. 7:12,13). That descendant of David was, of course, Jesus Christ (Matt. 1:1; John 7:42; Rom. 1:3; II Tim. 2:8; Rev. 22:16), "King of Kings and Lord of Lords" (Rev. 22:16).

Samuel (I Sam. 1:19–16:13) was called of God to be a prophet, and became a judge of Israel. He reluctantly appointed Saul to be king over Israel, but had faith that the Lord would not abandon His people (I Sam. 12:22).

Many additional prophets could have been introduced as men of faith, including Elijah, Elisha, Daniel, etc., but time and space did not allow Paul to write of them all.

11:33,34 Paul's generalization of examples of faith moves from named personages to actions of faith. There were untold people *"who by faith conquered kingdoms, administered justice, obtained promises, stopped mouths of lions, quenched the power of fire, escaped the edge of the sword, became powerful out of weakness, became strong in war, and made foreign armies yield."* Barak (Judg. 4:23,24), Gideon (Judg. 8:12), Jephthah (Judg. 11:21,22), and David (II Sam. 8:1-14) all "conquered kingdoms." David, in particular, "administered justice" (II Sam. 8:15; I Chron. 18:14; Ps. 15:2). Those who "obtained promises" are too numerous to mention, but Gideon (Judg. 7:7), Samson (Judg. 13:5), and David (II Sam. 7:9) are noteworthy. Several are recorded who "stopped the mouths of lions," including Samson (Judg. 14:5,6), David (I Sam. 17:34,35), Benaiah (II Sam. 23:20), and Daniel (Dan. 6:22). Daniel's friends, Shadrach, Meshach and Abednego, "quenched the power of fire" (Dan. 3:24-27). David (I Sam. 18:11; 19:10) "escaped the edge of the sword" on many occasion. Samson (Judg. 17:28), David (I Sam. 17:42-46), and Judith (Judith 13:1-10) were all examples of "becoming powerful out of weakness." The leaders of Israel who "became strong in war, and made foreign armies yield" were abundant.

11:35 There were *"women who received their dead out of resurrection."* Elijah raised the son of the widow of Zarephath (I Kgs. 17:8-24). Elisha was used of God to raise the son of the Shunammite woman (II Kgs. 4:18-37).

Paul switched from the successes of faith (33-35a) to the sufferings of faith (35b-38); from the triumphs of faith to the tragedies of faith; from the mighty acts of faith to the martyr-dom of faith. *"Others were tortured, not accepting their release that they might obtain a better resurrection."* Ancient torture tactics were severe and gruesome. Victims were put in stocks or stretched on racks to be beaten and flogged. The Greek word for "torture," *tympanizomai,* meant "to strike, beat, or pound," and is the etymological root for a tympan or kettledrum. Despite such torture, there were men of faith who were offered release if they would renounce their faith and violate their conscience (II Macc. 6:21-30; 7:1-41), but they chose eternal resurrection (by their prospective faith in God's Messianic deliverance) rather than temporal reprieve.

11:36 *"Others received mockings and floggings, and even bonds and imprisonment."* Jeremiah is a good example of a man of faith who was mocked, ridiculed, verbally abused, and made a laughingstock (Jere. 20:7,8; Lam. 3:14). Those who were flogged, whipped, lashed, and scourged for their faith were many, as were those who were bound and imprisoned, including Joseph (Gen. 39:20), Jeremiah (Jere. 20:2; 37:15) and Micaiah (I Kgs. 20:27).

11:37 *"They were stoned..."* like Zechariah (II Chron. 24:20-22). *"They were sawn in two..."* as tradition asserted concern-ing the death of Isaiah upon the edict of King Manasseh. *"They were tempted..."* as were most of the people of God. *"They were put to death by the sword..."* as were many of the prophets (I Kgs. 19:10,14; Jere. 2:30; 26:23). *"They went about in sheepskins, in goatskins, being destitute, afflicted and ill-treated."* The most primitive dress of sheepskins and goatskins indicated an abject poverty so deplorable that such persons were regarded as barely more than animals them-selves. Elijah the Tishbite was one who wore such attire (II

Kgs. 1:8), and was so destitute that he was fed by the ravens (I Kgs. 17:1-7).

11:38 While the world judges men of faith unworthy of their honor and praise, Paul indicates that these were *"men of whom the world was not worthy."* Whereas the world cannot appreciate faithful men, for they regard them as irrational and unproductive, it is the fallen world that is not worthy of having such men of God in their midst.

Once again (9,13) Paul emphasizes the transient and migrant status of the faithful, *"wandering in deserts and mountains and caves and the holes of the earth."* They have no place to call "home" for they are pilgrims seeking the place and presence of God. David certainly dwelt in such places (I Sam. 22:1; 23:14; 24:3), as did the faithful during the time of the Maccabees (I Macc. 2:29,38; II Macc. 5:27; 6:11; 10:6).

11:39 This is the concluding statement of Paul's extended excursus on faith. *"All of these,"* i.e., all of the persons mentioned in this chapter, and perhaps inclusive of all of the "faithful" in the entire old covenant, *"having received witness through their faith,"* the commendation of God for the response of obedient action to the revelation given to them, as attested in Scripture (2,4,5), *"did not receive what was promised…".* God attested to the faith of the old covenant personages in the Old Testament scriptures, indicating His witness of approval and commendation, and Paul will proceed to note that these "faithful" now serve as a "cloud of witnesses surrounding us" (12:1). However, despite their forward-looking faith that sought the promise and power of God, the old covenant personages "did not receive what was promised." As Paul wrote earlier concerning Abraham and his descendants, "All these died in faith, not having received the promises, but seeing and welcoming them from afar, and having confessed that they were strangers and sojourners upon the earth" (13).

The complete and ultimate fulfillment of the promises of God to Abraham and all of the old covenant personages was only made available in Jesus Christ. "As many as may be the promises of God, in Him (Jesus) they are yes (affirmed and fulfilled)" (II Cor. 1:20). From the first Messianic promise to Adam and Eve (Gen. 3:15), to the promises of God to Abraham (Gen. 12-17), to the Davidic promise (II Sam. 7:12,13), to the promises of the prophets (Isa. 9:6,7; Jere. 31:33,34; Micah 5:2), they were all fulfilled in God's revelation of Himself in the Person of the Son, Jesus Christ. Jesus, the "one mediator between God and man" (II Tim. 2:5), was the "last Adam Who became life-giving Spirit" (I Cor. 15:45), the eschatological fulfillment of "the eternal inheritance" (9:15) that effects the salvation and restoration of humanity. The old covenant faithful did not receive the fulfillment of the divine promises during their lifetime, for the historic enactment of redemption and restoration had to be manifested "in the fullness of time" (Gal. 4:4). Jesus Himself said, "Truly I say to you, that many prophets and righteous men desired to see what you see, and did not see it; and to hear what you hear, and did not hear it" (Matt. 13:17).

11:40 Throughout the epistle Paul has been reminding the Hebrew Christians of Jerusalem of the "better things" that have been given to Christians in Jesus Christ. Now he explains that the promises of God remained unfulfilled during the lives of the old covenant faithful, ***"God having foreseen something better concerning us, in order that they should not be perfected without us."*** The "something better" that God has provided personally and historically for "us" (in contrast to those in the old covenant) is, of course, Jesus Christ. Everything provided prior to the historical Jesus was just prefiguring picture, shadow, or type. All the spiritual and theological benefits that Christians enjoy find their essential reality in Jesus Christ. He is our "eternal life" (John 14:6; I John 5:12,13), our righteousness (I Cor. 1:30; II Cor. 5:21), our salvation (II Tim. 2:10; Heb. 2:10), our perfection (Phil. 3:15; Heb. 12:23). He is the King Who constitutes God's kingdom reign (Lk. 17:20,21; Col. 1:13) now and forever. It was Jesus that the old covenant faithful were seeking as fulfillment to God's promises. Since their faith was directed toward the "yet not seen" (11:1) Jesus, and they would not settle for the inadequate physical prefigurings, they are now "made perfect" in solidarity with all Christians. "By one offering He (Jesus) perfected for all time those who are set apart unto holiness" (10:14). All of God's "faithful" are "in Christ" together.

There is a *contrast* between the unfulfilled promises (13,39) of the old covenant and the fulfilled promises of the new covenant (9:15). Paul wanted the Jerusalem Christians to realize that they had received the better fulfillment of the promises of God in the historical and eternal Person and work of Jesus Christ. At the same time, Paul wanted the Christians in Jerusalem to understand that their *connection* with the Hebrew faithful of the old covenant was not in the engagement of physical conflict to preserve and maintain the physical city, temple, and religious practices of Judaism against the Roman occupiers. Rather, their connection with the faithful of the past was in the solidarity and unity of participating in the ultimate and perfect objective of God in Jesus Christ. Paul was seeking to *convince* the brethren in Judea that they needed a forward-looking and hopeful faith like that exhibited by their Hebrew forefathers, willing to endure even unto death.

Concluding Remarks

It is important to recall the context of this lengthy review of faith, lest we lose sight of the flow of Paul's thought and argument.

Paul had quoted Habakkuk 2:4, "My righteous ones shall live by faith" (10:38), and desired that the Jerusalem

Christians "have faith unto the safekeeping of the soul"
(10:39). To encourage such faith, Paul presents a survey of the
forward-looking faith of the Hebrew faithful, beginning with a
"working definition" of faith: [1] faith looks forward to the
substantiation of things expected, [2] faith seeks the certainty
of the fulfillment of events not yet seen, [3] faith draws near to
God, believing that He *is* and that He fulfills His promises.
Such faith is not consistent with escapism that "shrinks back to
destruction" (10:39). Rather, it is faith that faces death boldly,
willing to look beyond death to the eternal reward (6) and
inheritance (9:15) of God. Notice how frequently faith and
death are brought together in these verses (4,13,19,21,22,
35,37), and the references to belief in resurrection to life
beyond death (19,35). Paul was well aware that the Jerusalem
Christians were likely facing physical death at the hands of the
vicious Roman army that was soon to attack the rebellious
Jewish enclave in Palestine (A.D. 66-70). The Jewish Christian
recipients of this letter needed to be prepared for this possibility. The faith that Paul inculcated was for the purpose of their
"running with endurance the race set before them" (12:1) – the
prime example of such endurance of suffering being Jesus
Himself (12:2), and His willingness to die on the cross. The
Jerusalem Christians would likely have to endure the discipline of adversity (12:5-13), and definitely needed the faith
that expected God to provide all that He had promised in Jesus
Christ for eternity.

ENDNOTES

1   Moltmann, Jurgen, *Theology of Hope.* New York: Harper & Row, Publishers. 1975.

2   Buchanan, George Wesley, *To the Hebrews.* Series: The Anchor Bible. Vol. 36, Garden City: Doubleday & Company, Inc. 1981. pg. 184.

3   Josephus, Flavius, *The Works of Josephus: Complete and Unabridged.* "The Antiquities of the Jews." Bk. 1, chpt. 3, para. 8, line 99. Hendrickson Publishers. 1996. pg. 34.

JESUS

The Better Example
and Disciplinary Agent
of Faithful Endurance

Hebrews 12:1-13

The extended excursus surveying the highlights of the faithful people of God in the Old Testament (11:1-40) concluded with the assertion of the failure of the old covenant personages to find complete fulfillment of their expectations of faith. "All of these, having received witness through their faith, did not receive what was promised" (11:39). Paul's continuing discourse to the Jerusalem Christians involves both a continuity of the theme of faithful endurance, as well as a comparative contrast of the superior objective of Christian faith which was stated in the final verse of the foregoing recitation: "God having foreseen something better concerning us, in order that they should not be perfected without us" (11:40).

Continuity is evident because the theme of "faith" is still on Paul's mind. The litany of the examples of forward-looking, persevering faith among the Old Testament faithful is now capped by the surpassing supremacy of the ultimate expression of faith in Jesus Christ. Jesus is set forth as the One to be viewed (2) and considered (3) as the epitome and ultimate "pioneer and perfecter of faith" (2). The Jewish radicals inciting insurrection against Rome could have cited the faith of the Old Testament faithful, and used such as an incentive to encourage the Jewish Christians to remain true to their Jewish heritage of faith by joining the freedom fighters. But the

Jewish restorationists could not and would not have employed
Paul's argument that Jesus Christ was the supreme example
and ultimate expression of faith in God. This is Paul's distinct
argument to encourage the Hebrew Christians of Palestine to
refrain from joining the Jewish fight against Rome, and instead
have faith like that exemplified by Jesus which "endured the
hostility" (3) and "endured the humiliation" (2) to participate
in the exaltation and victory of all that God makes available to
humanity in His Son. The culminating capstone of "faith" has
been modeled in the life of Jesus Christ, and the Christians of
Jerusalem are encouraged to participate in the better provision
(11:40) that is the object of Christian faith.

The Jewish faithful of the old covenant "received witness"
(11:2,4,5,39) of their faithfulness to God in proceeding forward in accord with the revelation given to them. They remain,
Paul states, as a "crowd of witnesses" (1) testifying to the
faithfulness of God. The contrast, however, between the faith
of the Jewish forefathers and those who follow in the faith of
Jesus Christ can be noted in the contrasting pronouns of "they"
and "us" in 11:40, and the continuing emphasis on "we" and
"us" in 12:1. Transitioning from the Old Testament historical
examples (11:1-40), Paul returns to the direct personal encouragement of the Christians in Judea (12:1–13:25) that he had
employed earlier (cf. 10:32-39). Paul appeals to the Jerusalem
Christians to exercise faith like that of Jesus, who endured
(2,3) the hardships to overcome and enact the redemptive victory. Picking up the previous theme of endurance (10:32,36),
Paul adds the element of accepting divine discipline
(5,6,7,8,10,11) in the process of faithful endurance (7), thus
encouraging his embattled Christian brethren in Palestine to
see Jesus as "the better example and disciplinary agent of
faithful endurance."

This contextual paragraph (12:1-13) is introductory to the
concluding practical section of this epistle (12:1–13:23).

Precise sectional divisions are difficult to ascertain and are necessarily arbitrary, but we shall divide them as follows:
- (1) The inevitable discipline of God (12:1-13)
- (2) The unshakable kingdom of God (12:14-29)
- (3) The unchanging Christ (13:1-25)

Three subdivisions can be identified in this initial contextual paragraph:
- (a) The need to focus on Christ in the midst of exertion unto endurance (1-3).
- (b) The inevitable discipline that is part of the process of developing endurance (4-11).
- (c) The consequent responsibility for acting in endurance (12,13).

12:1 Connecting with the previous survey (11:1-40), Paul begins with the conjunction, *"Consequently"* or "therefore," and emphasizes the *"we also,"* identifying himself with the Christians in Jerusalem, as contrasted with the Jewish faithful previously cited (11:1-40). The encouragement to endurance is based on the encircling witness of the old covenant faithful, and the stripping off of extraneous entanglements.

Paul ties his Jewish Christian readers to their Jewish heritage by reminding them of their *"having so great a cloud of witnesses surrounding us...".* The faithful of old are regarded as continuing to serve as a quantitative and qualitative "cloud of witnesses." Both in the Hebrew and Greek languages the word "cloud" was often used as a metaphor for a "crowd" – for a host or multitude of people. The faithful Jewish forebears "received witness" (11:2,4,5,39) of their faithfulness, and are now represented as an encompassing and encircling crowd witnessing the actions of Christians who have the privilege "in Christ" of participating in all that the Jewish believers were expecting in faith. The question might be asked: "Are these prior Jewish faithful circumlocated around the Christians in an historical sense, or in a spiritual and heavenly sense?" Both, though the latter better serves the figurative picture that Paul seems to be drawing. The encompassing "crowd of witnesses" has long been regarded as a metaphor for spectators in a stadium, arena or amphitheater observing an athletic race. As "witnesses" in the heavenly grandstands cheering on the contestants, their "witness" may be regarded as both passive observance, as well as active attestation. As prior participants who have gone before and actively persevered in faith, they now observe and testify to the value of the goal, despite the hardship of the race.

Continuing the metaphor of a race, Paul advises, *"putting off every weight, and the clinging sin..."*. Athletes needed to "strip off" all that might handicap, impede or hinder their run. The "weight" that had to be "put off" may have been excess body weight, but more likely referred to any excess weight, such as training weights, that would impede the runner. Paul is no doubt using "weight" metaphorically, as did the Greek ethicists, to refer to moral vices. Jesus used similar language: "Be on guard, that your hearts may not be *weighted* down with dissipation and drunkenness and the worries of life" (Lk. 21:34). In previous letters Paul had advised the "laying aside" of all "deeds of darkness" (Rom. 13:12), such as "anger, wrath, malice, slander, and abusive speech" (Col. 3:8). Peter (I Pet. 2:1) and James (James 1:21) used similar language. That Paul had such behavioral encumbrances in mind is fortified by his subsequent reference to "clinging sin." First century athletes had to strip off their clinging cloaks, robes and togas in order to run freely. Paul is advising the Hebrew Christians to lay aside their clinging sin patterns – the distractions, diversions, preoccupations, and concerns that "wrap up" and hinder Christian progress. More specifically for the Christians of Judea, this may have included the close-fitting pride of Jewish nationalism, wealth and religion, or the binding concern for self-preservation. The common interpretation of this phrase to putting away "besetting sins" (cf. KJV) and personal strongholds of sin is not illegitimate, but the historical context of Paul's admonition to the Christians in Jerusalem to strip off the excess baggage of closely-held and familiar clinging sin must be the basis of all personal application.

With the incentive of the Jewish forefathers cheering them on, and the laying aside of the impediments of excessive weight and entangling sin, *"we should run with endurance the race lying before us..."*, Paul exhorts the Christians in Judea. This is not a forty yard speed sprint, but more like a long-distance, cross-country marathon that requires stamina, endurance, persistence and perseverance. As noted earlier (10:36), the Greek word for "endurance" is *hupomene*, meaning "to abide under," implying a need to abide under the pain, the exhaustion, and the mental discouragement in maintaining the pace of a faithful Christian life. The race, the course, the contest, the conflict (Greek word *agon*, the root of the English word "agony") that confronted the Christians in Jerusalem was no place for foot-dragging sluggishness (cf. 5:11; 6:12), but required the diligent endurance of forward-looking faith. "Run in such a way that you may win" (I Cor. 9:24), Paul advised the Corinthians. "I run in such a way, not without aim" (I Cor. 9:26). "I have finished the course; I have kept the faith" (II Tim. 4:7), Paul explained to Timothy. The agonizing struggle of the course set before the Christians in Jerusalem would require disentangling themselves from much of what they had cloaked themselves in previously, and running with endurance the course of Christian faithfulness.

12:2 The means by which the Christians in Jerusalem would need to run the race of faith would be by *"looking away from* (everything else) *unto Jesus, the pioneer and perfecter of faith..."*. The beleaguered Christians in Jerusalem were not to concentrate on their trials or their difficulties. They were not to set their attention on the insurrectionists or the imminent portent of war. These distractions would not facilitate faithfulness. Instead, they were encouraged to focus on Jesus – the ultimate model of faithful endurance. How did Jesus live the life that He lived as man on earth? He did so as a human choosing creature, responding to God the Father in complete receptivity to God's activity, putting His "trust in Him" (2:13) and allowing God the Father to speak (cf. John 5:30; 8:28; 12:49; 14:10) and act (John 5:19,30; 14:10) at every moment in time through Him. Jesus lived the life that He lived by faith. His perfect exercise of faith established Him as "the pioneer and perfecter of faith." The superiority of Jesus' faith, compared to the old covenant faithful (11:1-40), is beyond all qualitative comparison. Jesus is the trail-blazer, the pioneer of faith. The Greek word *archegon* (cf. 2:10) can mean "founder, originator, initiator, leader," etc. – the principal or chief who leads the way. Jesus is the archetype of Christian faith. He is the One Who perfected the "obedience of faith" (Rom. 1:5; 16:26) by being "obedient unto death" (Phil. 2:8), and was perfected thereby (2:10; 5:9; 7:28). He took human faith to the end objective (Greek word *teleiotes*, derived from *telos*, meaning "end") that God intended, finishing (John 17:4; 19:30), accomplishing and achieving God's redemptive and restorative purpose. The believers in Jerusalem were encouraged to focus on the faith exemplified by Jesus, "the pioneer and perfecter of faith," the initiator and implementer of faith, the founder and finisher of faith, the archetype and achiever of faith. Jesus is indeed the "faithful witness" (Rev. 1:5) revealing God's intent for man to respond and choose dependence upon Him. Of course, the historical Jesus is also the living Lord Jesus of the Spirit, and the call to focus on Jesus is not just a call to view Jesus' faith as an historical example, but is inclusive of our gazing on the risen and ascended Christ Who empowers Christian action (John 15:5) and perfects us (cf. Phil. 1:6), but the emphasis in this particular context is on Jesus' historical exhibition of faith, as the subsequent statements indicate. It must also be noted that reference to Jesus as "the author and finisher of faith" does not allow for the Calvinistic concept that faith is given to the Christian or enacted within the Christian by God, for consistent interpretation of scripture recognizes that faith is man's response to choose dependency upon and derivation from God in "the receptivity of His activity."

Paul documents how the historical faith of "the man Christ Jesus" (Acts 2:22; I Tim. 2:5) was the original and ultimate objective of God, by explaining that Jesus, *"Who for the joy lying before Him endured the cross, despising the shame..."*. Was "the joy lying before Him" the memory that Jesus had of the pre-existent bliss and glory of heavenly function? Was "the joy lying before Him" the expectancy of exaltation sitting at the right hand of the throne of God? Was "the joy lying before Him" the incentive of redemptive efficacy that looked forward to the restoration of functional humanity united with Him? Or, since the Greek preposition *anti* (meaning "against" or "opposed to") is used, instead of the more common preposition translated "for" or "because of" (Greek *gar*), could this be a statement of substitution? If he was employing the primary meaning of *anti*, was Paul indicating that Jesus "instead of, in place of, or against the joy lying before Him" of avoiding the cross (cf. Matt. 26:38,39; Mk. 14:34-36; Lk. 22:42; Heb. 5:7) "did not please Himself" (Rom. 15:3) by seeking the fame and accolades of man in the world's way of victory? Whether His action was based on a memory, an expectancy, an incentive, or a substitution, Jesus faithfully endured the cross, voluntarily choosing the obedience, "even death on a cross" (Phil. 2:8), to effect the "will of God" (Heb. 10:9) and God's way of victory. This faithful endurance of Jesus, even unto death, was the exemplary model (cf. I Pet. 2:21-23) that Paul wanted his brethren in Judea to focus on, for they could well be required to endure and face death in the near future as the Romans descended upon Palestine.

The particular death that Jesus endured in faith, the horrendous execution of crucifixion, was regarded as especially shameful, degrading and contemptuous. This form of execution was often reserved for slaves, foreigners, and the worst of criminals. The public scorn of crucifixion was regarded as despicable and ignominious by Roman citizens, while the Jews regarded such a form of death as a curse (Gal. 3:13; Deut. 21:23). Jesus, however, was willing to submit to such humiliation (Phil. 2:8), "despising the shame," disdaining the disgrace of such a death, for He knew in faith that this was God's means of victory over sin and death. Paul is reminding his readers of how Jesus "despised the shame" in the midst of faith endurance that led to execution, because they, too, were likely being subjected to public shame for not being true and loyal to their Jewish heritage, and joining the revolt against the Romans. In the midst of such scorn and contempt, the Jewish Christians in Jerusalem needed to disregard the shame and endure in their faith in Jesus Christ, perhaps unto death. They needed a forward-looking faith that looked beyond the present humiliation to the heavenly exaltation.

The humiliating death of Jesus Christ on the cross led to His being highly exalted (cf. Phil. 2:8-11) as the risen and ascended Lord and Saviour. Having endured the cross, Jesus *"has sat down at the right hand of the throne of God."* Paul had used this theme of the enthronement of the exalted Son of God numerous times in this epistle (1:3,13; 8:1; 10:12). The seated posture represents the completion of his work. He "accomplished the work which the Father gave Him to do" (John 17:4), having exclaimed from the cross, "It is finished!" (John 19:30). Permanent and eternal victory was achieved in Jesus submitting to death in order to overcome "the one having the power of death, that is, the devil" (2:14). Jesus has assumed His exalted place (7:26) of royal honor and authority "at the right hand of the throne of God," having become our

378

High Priestly intercessor (7:25) with "all authority given to Him in heaven and on earth" (Matt. 28:18).

The assaulted Christians in Jerusalem needed to look beyond all the present circumstances and focus on Jesus, the ultimate exemplar of forward-looking faith. They needed to run the race of life with faithful endurance, willing to despise the disgrace and endure even unto death, as Jesus did. Just as Jesus progressed from humiliation to exaltation, Paul encourages these Christians to accept and submit to God's way of victory, which often means that "the way to win is to lose" (Matt. 10:39; 16:25). What appears to be loss or defeat by the world's standards is often the means of God's eternal victory.

12:3   As his readers were in apparent danger of discouragement, disheartenment and despair, Paul encourages his Hebrew brethren to ***"Consider again the One having endured such hostility under the sinners unto Himself...".*** "Take another long look at the enduring faith of Jesus," Paul is saying. Using a banking term, he encourages his readers to "calculate" and "take inventory" of how Jesus endured such an intensity of dispute (6:16; 7:7), antagonism, cruelty, and violence under the hands of sinners. Who were these "sinners" who mistreated Jesus with hostile intent? For the most part the instigators were His own Jewish people. Jesus had told His disciples that "the Son of Man is being betrayed into the hands of sinners" (Matt. 26:45; Mk. 14:41) just prior to His arrest by the Jewish chief priests and their henchmen. Who was it that was engaging the Jerusalem Christians in hostile opposition and "conflict of suffering" (10:32-34)? Their own countrymen, the zealots of the Jewish religion, were once again the "sinners" countering and contradicting God's action in His people. The Christians of Jerusalem needed to see that they were following in the footsteps of their Saviour, and needed to endure such with the same kind of faithfulness as Jesus did.

Although most modern translations indicate that this "hostility under sinners" was "against Himself" as the recipient of the antagonism, some of the oldest Greek manuscripts indicate that the hostility of the sinful persecutors was "against themselves." In this case, Jesus' sinful oppressors were acting to their own detriment, ruin and harm, in the ironic situation of self-destruction (cf. Prov. 8:36; Heb. 6:6).

The objective of Paul's words encouraging the Jerusalem Christians to "run with endurance the race set before them by focusing and reflecting on Jesus" was ***"in order that you should not grow weary in your souls, being faint."*** The course or race (1) of the Christian life requires a certain resolve and stamina to "go the distance." The terms that Paul employs are words that were used of athletes who collapsed in exhaustion or fatigue and could not finish the contest. Paul did not want the struggling saints in Jerusalem to have a weakened resolve or a breakdown in endurance. Such would indicate that they had "given up," relapsed, and apostatized. To the Galatians, Paul had written, "Let us not lose heart in doing good, for in due time we shall reap, if we do not grow weary" (Gal. 6:9). The apostle John later penned the words of Jesus to the church at Ephesus: "You have perseverance and have endured for My name's sake, and have not grown weary" (Rev. 2:3). Paul was doing everything he could to coach the Christians in Jerusalem to continue in their faith without fainting.

12:4 Despite their having endured hostile opposition (10:32-34; 13:3), Paul reminds the Jewish Christians in Jerusalem, ***"You have not yet resisted to the point of blood shedding*** (in your) ***struggling against sin."*** They had resisted the taunts and the ostracism of the Jewish religionists and revolutionaries who regarded them as traitors for having received Jesus as the Messiah, but this resistance was not "until blood." This phrase could be a metaphor meaning "to the uttermost," but even so, the ultimate sacrifice would be resistance unto death. Jesus "endured the cross" (2), execution by crucifixion, in His faithful resistance, and the Jerusalem Christians had not yet been called upon to resist to the point of martyrdom. Compared to Jesus, their sufferings were not yet as severe, and Paul is encouraging them to remain faithful in their present situation which involved a lesser degree of hostility than that of Jesus, at least "to this point." It must not be minimized, however, that they were "struggling against sin." Some have noted that the athletic metaphor of a race (1-3) seems to have changed to a different kind of contest (1), the resistance and struggling of a pugilistic boxing match (cf. I Cor. 9:26) or a wrestling contest. There is no doubt that the recipients of this letter were involved in the conflict of an antagonistic (the Greek word for "struggling" is *antagonizomenoi*) fight against determined opponents. Their "struggling against sin" was not so much against personal "clinging sin" (1) as it was against the "hostile sinners" (3), who were of that same category of Jewish religionists who had crucified Jesus.

12:5 In the midst of the onslaught of religious "sinners" (3), while suffering hostility (3) and shame (2), it is often difficult to remember and recognize that God remains in sovereign control of the situation, especially when those causing the pain claim to be serving as God's instruments. The pain and unpleasantness of the conflict can be so discouraging, distressing, disturbing, and unsettling. There is always a temptation to question why God allows such suffering, hardship and adversity. In theological language, this is the issue of theodicy – the attempt to determine an explanation for evil and suffering. We must avoid a direct attribution of all affliction and adversity upon God, for such can impinge upon His character and be a denial of the fact that God "does not tempt any one" to evil (James 1:13), for He cannot act contrary to Who He is – His own Being. Persecution and suffering often have a primary cause in the hearts of, and at the hands of, evil doers and "sinners" (3) who act out of the character of the diabolic Evil One (cf. John 8:44; I John 3:8,12). The same situations of suffering can, however, become positive disciplinary training as God uses them as a means of good in the lives of His people. "God causes all things to work together for good to those who love God, to those who are called according to His purpose" (Rom. 8:28). In God's sovereignty, those who inflict suffering on His people cannot thwart His purposes. After all that Job had suffered, he confessed, "I know that Thou canst do all things, and that no purpose of Thine can be thwarted" (Job 42:2). "Shall we accept good from God and not accept adversity?" (Job 2:10), asked Job. We must recognize that adversity has a purpose, that there is significance in our sufferings. The unpleasant experiences of our existence are not to be viewed as random events of "bad luck" under which we have the misfortune of being victims. God is a heavenly Father Who loves His children, and therefore He does not protect them from all problems, but perfects them in the midst of distressing situations, and brings them through as "overcomers." This is what Paul was encouraging the Jerusalem Christians to understand.

"Have you forgotten the encouragement He speaks to you as sons?" Paul asks. Though these words could be an indicative statement of accusation ("You have forgotten..."), they can also be translated as an interrogative question ("Have you forgotten...?"). The latter of these alternatives seems preferable. Paul is asking his readers if they have forgotten the encouraging words of exhortation that God spoke through the wisdom literature of scripture in Proverbs 3:11,12, which he then quotes. He applies these words directly to the Jewish Christians, indicating that they are addressed "to you as sons." In so doing, Paul is introducing the filial family relationship which is the context for understanding God's disciplinary purposes in the unsettling circumstances of life. Christians are "sons of God through faith in Christ Jesus" (Gal. 3:26), and

the intent of God in Christ is to "bring many sons to glory" (Heb. 2:10). The process of doing so means that God loves us enough to seek our highest good through disciplinary training by His grace.

Quoting from Proverbs 3:11, Paul writes, *"MY SON, DO NOT REGARD LIGHTLY THE DISCIPLINE OF THE LORD, NOR FAINT WHEN YOU ARE BEING REPROVED...".* Paul had cautioned the Christians in Jerusalem against "fainting" (3), and this was undoubtedly the connection in Paul's mind to the admonition against fainting here in Proverbs 3:11. The book of Proverbs is, in large part, a parental manual advising fathers in the upbringing of their sons, and thus provides a comparative connection to God's Fatherly concern for His Christian sons. In these particular verses (Prov. 3:11,12), personified Father Wisdom is advising the sons of God not to despise, disregard, or "regard lightly" the Lord's disciplinary action, by failing to appreciate what God is doing in the circumstances of life. The Jerusalem Christians, in the midst of their persecutive trials, were apparently in danger of "regarding lightly" and failing to appreciate the discipline of the Lord.

When people hear or read the phrase "the discipline of the Lord," different meanings and connotations come to their minds. Many people equate discipline with punishment. Depending on their own experiences as the recipients of parental discipline, they may view discipline as primarily a punitive process. There are several Greek words for "punishment" (cf. *dike, kolazomai, timoreo*), but the word "discipline" in these verses should not be interpreted as "punishment." The fact that the KJV uses the translation of "chastisement" or "chastening," meaning "to punish, castigate, or censure," does not facilitate an accurate understanding of Paul's intent. The word for "discipline" (Greek *paideia*) in this passage (5-11) is etymologically rooted in the word for "child" (*pais*) or "little child" (*paidion*). Discipline is the process of bringing up a child, the nurturing (cf. Eph. 6:4) process of child-training (cf. II Tim. 3:16). This process will involve corrective, instructive, and directive action to bring the child to the maturation of responsible adulthood. The English word "discipline" is derived from the Latin *disciplina*, meaning "teaching" or "learning." From the same Latin root of *discipulus*, meaning "learner" or "follower," we derive the English word "disciple." The Lord's discipline in the new covenant context is the process of developing a disciple of Jesus Christ, the corrective, instructive and directive process of training a "child of God" unto the mature recognition of God's sovereignty and the faithful expression of His character.

The experiences and trials of life are "common to man" (I Cor. 10:13). We have an extended vocabulary of words to describe these circumstances: problems, difficulties, troubles, tribulations, tragedy, hardships, adversity, affliction, attacks, persecution, pressures, pain, suffering, etc. on and on. Though God is the essential cause of all things as the Sovereign Creator God, He is not the blameworthy cause of evil which is contrary to His character. We cannot, therefore, claim that God purposes, causes, or orchestrates all events, especially such evil-doing as rape, murder, torture, or disease, without imping- ing on God's absolute character of goodness. What we can indicate, though, is that God tests (John 6:6; Heb. 11:17) and examines His people in the midst of all situations, employing His corrective, instructive, and directive purposes of discipline, and soliciting us to allow His character of perfect godliness to be manifested in our behavior in response to, and in the midst of, the situation that confronts us. Moses explained to the Israelites that during their forty years of wandering in the wilderness, "The Lord was disciplining you, just as a man dis- ciplines a son" (Deut. 8:5). Eliphaz advised Job in the midst of his sufferings, "Do not despise the discipline of the Almighty" (Job 5:17). The Psalmist admits, "It was good for me that I was afflicted, that I might learn Thy statutes" (Ps. 119:71). The

Lord Jesus Christ "learned obedience" (Heb. 5:8) and was perfected (Heb. 2:10) "through suffering." In like manner, God's
children are made perfect (cf. Phil. 1:6; Col. 1:28) in the maturation of being "conformed to the image of the Son" (Rom.
8:29). God the Father is committed to the child-training and
disciplining that develops persons into the divine intent of evidencing and exhibiting His character in their behavior to the
glory of God. This developmental process of "bringing many
sons to glory" (Heb. 2:10) may involve,

> if necessary, being distressed by various trials, that the proof of your
> faith...even though tested by fire, may be found to result in praise and
> glory and honor at the revelation of Jesus Christ; and...believing in
> Him, you may rejoice with joy inexpressible and full of glory, obtain-
> ing as the outcome of your faith the salvation of your souls. (I Pet. 1:6-
> 9)

Understanding the positive purpose of divine discipline in
this way allows us to avoid "regarding it lightly," and rather to
appreciate and respect what God is doing in the midst of the
circumstances of life. Thus we do not "faint," give up, or
relapse into unbelief even when God's discipline involves the
corrective element of exposing our weaknesses, inadequacies
and inabilities; of convincing and convicting us of our selfish
preoccupation with self-preservation; or of reproving or rebuk-
ing us for thinking that we can solve all of our own problems
by employing self-discipline and self-control. As the risen
Lord Jesus says to the Laodiceans, "Those whom I love, I
reprove and discipline; be zealous therefore, and repent" (Rev.
3:19). The reproving action of divine discipline is necessary to
negate the selfish tendencies of personal action and reaction in
order to allow the positive expression of God's character in the
situation. This corrective discipline of reproof is sometimes
represented as the refining and purifying (cf. Ps. 66:10; Isa.
48:10; Mal. 3:3) action of being "tested by fire" (I Pet. 1:7) so
that the dross (Isa. 1:25) of imperfections can be removed, and

the "gold" of Christ's character (Job 23:10; I Pet. 1:7) can be exhibited. Corrective reproof is an essential part of being "disciplined by the Lord, that we should not be condemned along with the world" (I Cor. 11:32).

12:6 Paul continues to cite the quotation from Proverbs 3:12 from the Greek Septuagint translation (*LXX*): *"FOR THOSE WHOM THE LORD LOVES HE DISCIPLINES, AND HE SCOURGES EVERY SON WHOM HE RECEIVES."* The motivational context of God's discipline is always His absolute character of love. "God is love" (I John 4:8,16). God's love always seeks the highest good of the other. In order to do so, it must often be expressed as "tough love" – love that cares enough to confront. God's love is not sentimental, indulgent permissiveness that allows us to do as we selfishly please. Neither is His love a heavy-handed coercive force that castigates until we capitulate. God disciplines in love so that His children may become disciples who will "listen under" Him in the dependence of the "obedience of faith." This often involves the corrective element of exposing our inadequacies and inabilities, and bringing us "to the end of ourselves." God's love takes the risk that the individual might blame Him for the problems and pressures, doubt His love, reject Him altogether, and rebel in sinful self-orientation. That is the risk God takes in disciplining those He loves.

Proverbs 3:12 goes on to indicate that "God scourges every son whom He receives." In the analogy with parental discipline, the word "scourge" often refers to the corporeal discipline of spanking, whipping, or flogging. As the root word of *mastigoi* is *masso*, meaning "to squeeze," a more general interpretation might be that in the midst of His discipline, God often "puts the squeeze on" or "puts the pressure on" those who are His spiritual children. In the new covenant God's sons are those who have received Jesus Christ and have become "sons of God through faith in Christ Jesus" (Gal. 3:26). God has received such persons into Himself, into union with Himself, into a dynamic relationship with Himself as a son in the family of God. This is not a future reception into heaven, but a present reception into relationalism with the Triune God, Father, Son, and Holy Spirit. In the midst of such spiritual relationalism the Persons of the Trinity allow the disciplinary pressures of life to prepare us for the unique expression of divine life and character in us.

The Christians in Jerusalem may have been at their wits end after years of harassment by their Jewish brethren. The pressure to question the Christian hope, to revert to their Jewish religious heritage, and to espouse the cause of the Jewish independence movement was no doubt intense. In the midst of their trials, hardships and adversities they were likely tempted to think that God had abandoned them – that there did not seem to be any future in remaining a minority remnant of believers in the seemingly forsaken Jerusalem outpost of the Christian faith. Paul knew that they needed to be reminded that God loved them and was at work in the midst of their situation to mold them into what He wanted them to be, and to prepare them for what they were to encounter in the days to come.

12:7 Commenting on the meaning of the words from Proverbs, Paul writes, ***"Endure** (in response) **to discipline."*** The brevity of Paul's three words in the Greek text allow for different translations and meanings. The verb can be understood as either an indicative statement ("The response to discipline is to endure.") or as an imperative command ("Endure in response to discipline."). Another Greek manuscript variation (*ei* instead of *eis*) allows for the reading, "If you endure discipline...." (KJV), but this is not the better attested manuscript reading.

Throughout the epistle Paul has been calling upon the embattled Jerusalem Christians to "endure" (10:36,39; 12:1,2,3), to "abide under" the trials and situations they were encountering. Now, he encourages them not to capitulate, not to "cave in," not to attempt to escape their problems, but rather to regard their trials as part of God's child-training process of divine discipline.

"God is dealing with you as with sons," Paul explains. Then he asks, *"For who is a son whom a father does not discipline?"* Divine discipline can only be properly understood in the context of relationship. William Lane writes, "There is a necessary and integral relationship between disciplinary sufferings and sonship."[1] "Paternal discipline is an integral part of family life."[2] In the Hebrew culture, fathers were held responsible for parental discipline that led to the child's respect for and obedience to God. Note these admonitions in the parental manual of the Proverbs:

> He who loves his son disciplines him diligently. (Prov. 13:24)
> Discipline your son while there is still hope. (Prov. 19:18)
> Foolishness is bound up in the heart of a child; the rod of discipline will remove it far from him. (Prov. 22:15)
> Do not hold back discipline from the child. (Prov. 23:13)
> Correct your son, and he will give you comfort; he will delight your soul. (Prov. 29:17)

To the Ephesian Christians Paul had advised that the fathers should "bring up their children in the discipline and instruction of the Lord" (Eph. 6:4). Despite Dr. Spock's disastrous doctrines of permissive parenting that have resulted in "dead-beat dads" who deny and shirk their responsibility of parenting, God has always indicated that responsible fathers will discipline their children. Paul's argument to the Christians in Jerusalem is that their disciplinary difficulties are proof that God is their Father, and that He is responsibly working in their lives and dealing with them as sons.

12:8 Paul restates his general principle of relational discipline in the hypothetical negative. *"But if you are without dis-*

cipline, of which you have all become partakers, then you are illegitimate children and not sons." The absence of discipline would indicate parental rejection and abandonment. The exercise of parental discipline, however, evidences the legitimacy of relational sonship. "That is why you can correctly surmise that you are legitimate sons of God," Paul is explaining to his readers in Jerusalem. We have all, in common with all legitimate Christians, become children of God (John 1:12,13), and in the midst of that relationship "have become partakers" and participants who share together in the disciplinary child-training of our loving Father. "As many as are led by the Spirit of God, these are the sons of God" (Rom. 8:14) The directive discipline of God confirms our relational sonship.

Roman law (unfair as this might be to the unmarried mothers and their children) placed illegitimate children outside of any legal paternal responsibility and protection. Illegitimate children, "bastards" (KJV), were not required to (and usually did not) receive the discipline of the one who fathered them. They were not regarded as real or genuine sons of the one who fathered them – just accidents that occurred along the way, for whom the mothers were henceforth responsible.

Paul's concern, however, is to cast this rationale of legitimacy and genuineness into the relationalism that a Christian has with God the Father. Christians and non-Christians alike encounter experiential events of trial, adversity and suffering. The unregenerate, who are not "sons of God through faith in Christ Jesus" (Gal. 3:26), are unrelated to God (Gal. 4:8; Eph. 2:12;4:18; Col. 1:21), and must face the circumstances of life in a non-relational context that cannot experience and appreciate God's disciplinary child-training of His spiritual children, though this does not imply that they are outside of His general providential care. The problematic situations of life are often viewed by the unregenerate as irritating and frustrating obstacles which are attacked with blame and anger toward the perpetuators (if there are such, and they can be identified) or toward God. Reacting with such fight (anger, blame), fright (fear, anxiety), and flight (escape, compromise, take the easy way out), those who are non-relational with God seek to regain control of the situation (to whatever extent is possible). The best explanatory "spin" they have for such hardships is that they "build character" and "make one stronger" for dealing with the next difficulty.

Christians, on the other hand, are not exempt from the same kinds of trials and adversities of life. These are "common to man" (I Cor. 10:13). In the relational context of sonship, in connective union with the Son, Jesus Christ, the Christian can view these difficulties from the perspective of God's loving, disciplinary child-training. Christians take comfort in the knowledge that God is in sovereign control of the entire situation confronting them, as well as their future destiny. Christians are encouraged in the recognition that God is using the circumstances, however difficult and painful, and "causing them to work together for good to those who love Him and are called according to His purpose" (Rom. 8:28). Accepting the sufficiency of His grace in the midst of the situations, Christians can remain faithfully receptive to His activity and endure through the situation to experience God's outcome. James writes,

> Consider it all joy, my brethren, when you encounter various trials, knowing that the testing of your faith produces endurance. And let endurance have its perfect result, that you may be perfect and complete, lacking in nothing. (James 1:2-4)

It is the relational context of God's corrective, instructive and directive disciplinary action that assures Christians of the legitimacy and genuineness of their relationship with God through Christ. God is a loving Father, who will not reject or abandon His children. Christians must trust God's ways, even though they may not be able to determine God's specific purposes and

objectives in the particular circumstances of life. "Since the
Lord is directing our steps, why try to understand everything
that happens along the way?" (Prov. 20:24 -LB). By faith,
Christians accept and endure the situations of life, assured that
God's directive discipline evidences the legitimacy of their
sonship relationship with God in Christ.

12:9 Continuing to connect physical paternal discipline with
divine discipline, Paul writes, *"Furthermore, we had fathers
of the flesh as disciplinarians, and we respected them..."*.
Paul presumes that his Jewish Christian readers, with their
Hebrew heritage, had natural, human fathers who disciplined
them, serving as correctors, instructors, and directors of their
lives as children. As a result of such proper parental discipline,
children are taught to "honor their father and mother" (Exod.
20:12; Eph. 6:2,3), and to respect and submit to the authority
of parents, other leaders, and God. Some have questioned
whether Paul's assumptions of parental discipline were more
appropriate to his ancient Hebrew culture than to modern
Western culture. Modern psychologies of parenting often
oppose many forms of direct discipline of a child on the misguided premises that such methods of child-training result in a
self-image of shame, accompanied by a disrespect for parents
that blames them for abuse. Granted, there are (and have
always been) selfish, irresponsible, unjust, unloving, and abusive parents that are hardly worthy of respect, but the arranged
order of the divinely ordained parent/child relationship still
demands that "children be obedient to their parents" (Col.
3:20; Eph. 6:1; Prov. 6:20), and respect their parents as the
God-ordained means of "training up a child" (Prov. 22:6).
    Based on the basic familial principle of children being sub-
ject to their parents, Paul then transfers to divine discipline,
asking, *"shall we not much more be made subject to the
Father of spirits, and we will live?"* In that we should have
greater respect for God's authority than for parental authority,

and recognize that our spiritual benefit is of higher importance than the physical benefits of child-rearing, Paul challenges the Jerusalem Christians to accept their subjection to divine discipline in the midst of their trials.

Identifying God as "the Father of all spirits" may refer to His spiritual authority over all created beings, angelic and human, who are able to relate to Him on a spiritual level. However, since God is referred to as "the God of the spirits of all flesh" (Num. 16:22; 27:16), and humanity in particular are those in whom God has "formed their spirit" (Zech. 12:1) and breathed the spirit of His life (Gen. 2:7; Job 33:4), it is more likely that Paul has the divine/human relationship in mind. Even more specifically, the Jerusalem Christians, who have received God's spiritual life in Christ Jesus, are being encouraged to accept disciplinary subjection under their spiritual Father in order to experience the spiritual life that God intends to its fullest. Jesus said, "I came that you might have life, and have it more abundantly" (John 10:10). In the midst of the pressures and problems of life it is often difficult to see and appreciate the abundant fullness of Christ's indwelling life and sufficiency, but Paul frames his question in such a way as to expect an affirmative answer: "Yes, we should submit to, and accept being made subject to, our spiritual Father in order to 'live by faith' (10:38), both now and forever."

12:10 The comparison of physical parental discipline and divine discipline continues. ***"For they*** ("our fathers of the flesh") ***disciplined us for a limited period of time according to what they deemed proper."*** The parental discipline of our physical fathers was for a relatively short period of time, until we came of age and achieved adulthood. The Greek text reads "a few days," figuratively indicating a brief and limited period of time. Our earthly fathers administered their discipline "according to what they deemed proper," "according to their way of thinking," "as seemed best to them." Many parents, fully cognizant that they were not "perfect parents," have found a sense of consolation in these words of Paul. Parental perception and training is fallible – full of uncertainties and often expressing "the deeds of the flesh" (Gal. 5:19-21). Human parents often discipline in exasperated "outbursts of anger," capricious unfairness, or rejective favoritism. Parents will indeed be held accountable before God for the character expressed in the disciplining of their children, but Paul recognizes that conscientious parents with the best of intentions still have to discipline their children in accord with their best personal discretion, which is still human and finite, rather than divine and infinite. The translation of the Authorized Version (KJV), that parents discipline "after their own pleasure," must not be understood as "for their own amusement."

Paul draws the contrast to human parenting by writing, *"but He"* (God the Father) disciplines us (the verb and object are drawn from the previous phrase) *"for the ultimate advantage, that we partake of His holiness."* God's love always seeks our highest good and acts for our eternal benefit and profit. His disciplinary purposes are always directed at the fulfillment of His creative and redemptive objectives that mankind should function by being receptive to the expression of His own glorious character. The holy character of God sets Him apart from all others. Mankind can never "possess" or even "share" the holy character of God. He does not give His glory to another (Isa. 42:8; 48:11). The only means by which we can "be holy as He is holy" (I Pet. 1:15,16) is to receive, partake of, and allow Him to manifest His holy character in our behavior. Such participation in the divine life of the Trinity sanctifies the Christian and sets him apart to function as intended by allowing the holy character of God to be expressed in Christian behavior. This holy disciplinary objective of the Father God supersedes the temporal discretionary discipline of earthly parents for it is directed at the permanent and eternal participatory expression of God's holy character in humanity.

12:11 Paul's next words form a truism that may have seemed like an extreme understatement to the beleaguered Christians in Jerusalem. *"All discipline for the moment does not seem to be joy, but grief...".* Although this statement is true both of human and divine discipline, it is surely the latter that was on the mind of Paul and his readers. The surface evaluation of what was transpiring in the lives of the Jerusalem saints could not deem their persecution and harassment to be joyful. Discipline usually impinges on our status quo and infringes on our "comfort zone." The circumstances are often unpleasant, painful, grievous and sorrowful. Such trials are not something we enjoy, but are called to endure. James' statement, "Consider it all joy when you encounter various trials" (James 1:2) must be interpreted within its context, which is not that we are to seek out and enjoy the trials and the discipline, but rather to anticipate joyously the result of God's perfect and completing (James 1:4) work in our lives.

This result of God's disciplinary action is what Paul proceeds to refer to: *"...but later it* (God's discipline) *gives back the peaceful fruit of righteousness to those having been trained through it* (God's discipline)." In contrast to the momentary discomfort of the difficulties, the resultant disciplinary benefits can only be evaluated "later" from the perspective of 20/20 hindsight. God's disciplinary activity allows the Christian to "partake of His holy character" (10), and it yields "the peaceful fruit of righteousness." Righteousness, along with holiness (10), is the exclusive character of God. Paul is not referring here to the forensic imputation of justification/righteousness, but to God's intent to express His character of righteousness in Christian behavior. Such righteousness cannot be generated or produced by man (cf. Isa. 64:6; Phil. 3:9; Gal. 2:21), but is exclusively the result of Jesus

Christ, the Righteous One (cf. Acts 3:14; 7:52; 22:14; I John 2:1) dwelling within the Christian and being allowed to manifest His character fruit (Gal. 5:22,23) in the behavior of the Christian by faith (Phil. 3:9). The Christian bears the fruit of Christ's character (John 15:1-8), the "fruit of righteousness which comes through Jesus Christ, to the glory and praise of God" (Phil. 1:11). "Walk as children of light," Paul advises the Ephesians, "for the fruit of light consists in all goodness and righteousness and truth" (Eph. 5:8,9). The resultant harvest of God's discipling child-training in the trials of life is the "fruit of righteousness" (cf. James 3:18), as Christians participate in the kingdom living of "righteousness and peace and joy in the Holy Spirit" (Rom. 14:17).

God's righteous character expressed in man's behavior, individually and collectively, is the result of "having been trained through" God's discipline. Paul returns to the athletic metaphor of the "training exercise" required for victory in the course or context (1) of life. The Greek verb Paul uses for "having been trained" (*gumnazo* - cf. I Tim. 4:7) is the source of the English words "gymnasium" and "gymnastics." God's discipline of the Christian is the "training exercise," the "time in the gym," the process that must be endured if we are to be the victors God intends us to be. "No pain, no gain" is a common training slogan, but we must remember that we do not seek the pain, and the gain is not something acquired or achieved through self-effort, but the gain of the expression of His godly character in Christian behavior. God puts us through the exercises, and God supplies the results.

12:12 Verses 12 and 13 are transitional. They contain imperative verbs which address a collective responsibility within the Christian community, as is prevalent throughout the remainder of the epistle. At the same time these verses are tied to the foregoing verses by the connective and conclusive conjunction "therefore". The athletic metaphor of God's discipline as a "training exercise" seems to be summed up in some final directions about preparing to run the race. "Get ready, get set, go!" For this reason, it seems best to maintain the connection of verses 12 and 13 with 1-11.

"Therefore, flex the hands having become limp and the knees having become loose...". The imperative verbs indicate a definite sense of responsibility on the part of the Jerusalem Christians, not only to accept God's discipline, but to ready themselves for the race (1). This preparation will involve flexing and "stretching" limp and listless hands, as well as weak and wobbly knees. These figures of atrophied attitude and droopy discouragement again evidence the apparent sluggishness (5:11; 6:12) of the readers. In accord with the prophet Isaiah, Paul is attempting to "encourage the slack hands and strengthen the tottering knees" (Isa. 35:3) so that "the lame will leap like a deer" (Isa. 35:6) in the fulfillment of the new covenant in Jesus Christ.

12:13 Using another imperative verb, Paul admonishes the Jerusalem Christians to *"make straight paths for your feet...".* In that the shortest distance to the goal is a straight line, Paul encourages his Christian brethren to make straight-forward progress in the Christian race, directly pursuing the goal of God's intent, the unique teleological objective in their lives. There is no time for mindless meandering or swerving off course. As the proverb says, "Turn not aside to the right hand or to the left, but turn away your foot from an evil way,...and He will make thy ways straight, and will guide your steps in peace" (Prov. 4:26,27 - *LXX*).

Paul's objective in admonishing the Christians in Jerusalem to get ready and be prepared is *"in order that the lame should not be turned out, but rather be healed."* Who are the "lame" that Paul refers to? Are they particular persons in the Jerusalem fellowship who are gimpy, limpy, crippled or maimed, and not walking very well in their Christian lives?

Or, are all the Christians in Jerusalem identified as "lame" due to their "sluggishness" (5:11; 6:12) and tendency to "drift away" (2:1)? Paul is concerned that the lame not be "turned out." Physically this would mean that the legs of the lame should not be dislocated or "put out of joint," but Paul's figurative usage is to dissuade the Jerusalem Christians from "turning out" in apostasy and rejection of Jesus Christ. Paul's other usages of this same Greek verb pertain to those who "*turn aside* to fruitless discussion" (I Tim. 1:6), "*turn aside* to myths" (II Tim. 4:4), and "*turn aside* to follow Satan" (I Tim. 5:15). Paul's deep concern for his brethren in Jerusalem was that they should not "turn aside" and drop out of the race, but rather be restored to a healthy Christian walk. His desire was for their spiritual healing whereby they would participate in the new covenant realities of the "lame walking" (Matt. 11:5) and "leaping like a deer" (Isa. 35:5) in the joy of reaching the goal of God in their lives.

Concluding remarks:

We must keep in mind the *sitz im leben*, the "setting in life," of the Jewish Christians of Judea to whom this letter was written. Having accepted Jesus as the expected Messiah, they were ostracized and persecuted by their Jewish kinsmen. Some of them had experienced the seizure of their property (10:34). Some had been subjected to imprisonment (10:34; 13:3) and mistreatment (13:34), although none had apparently experienced the death of martyrdom (12:4). Their economic suppression was so severe that Paul had sought contributions from among the Gentile Christians for "the poor among the saints in Jerusalem" (Rom. 15:26; I Cor. 16:2,3). Paul himself was constantly "dogged" by the Judaizers from Judea wherever he went, and had asked for prayers that he "might be delivered from those who are disobedient in Judea" (Rom. 15:31).

With the revolutionary uprising against Rome coming to a fever pitch in the seventh decade of the first century, the Judean Christians were subjected to increased pressure to join the cause to oust the Roman oppressors. Christians who would not participate in the insurrection were regarded as unpatriotic traitors unwilling to fight for what the Jewish militants regarded as their God-given right to a Jewish nation-state. They were already regarded as irreligious for refusing to participate in the Jewish temple practices, but when the Christians would not take a stand for restoring the Judaic high priesthood, they were despised as those who had divorced themselves from their Jewish heritage.

The "cost of discipleship" was high for the Christians in Jerusalem when this letter was written. To recognize the divine discipline unto deeper discipleship in the midst of their difficulties was not an easy perception to develop. Yet Paul, who was very familiar "with insults, with distresses, with persecutions, with difficulties for Christ's sake" (II Cor. 12:10), having been "afflicted, ...perplexed, ...persecuted, ...struck down, ...and delivered over to death for Jesus' sake" (II Cor. 12:10), by being "imprisoned, beaten, stoned," etc. (II Cor. 11:22-27), and while likely still imprisoned in Rome for his Christian faith, writes to encourage the Christians in Judea to endure in their faith. He lifts up Jesus as the prime example of One Who endured humiliation (2) and hostility (3) as the "pioneer and perfecter of faith" (2) to experience God's ultimate exaltation. From the Proverbs, Paul draws the analogy of a father's relational child-training of his sons, which must be endured to achieve God's intended results. To view their tribulations as situations that God was using in His disciplining process would not doubt have been difficult for the hard-hit Christians in Jerusalem. The easy way out would have been to seek a way of escape, rather than the endurance of faith – to "drift away" (2:1), to "shrink back" (10:39), to "fall away" (6:6). Paul uses every argument he can think of to encourage his fellow Jewish believers that they have "everything better" in Jesus Christ. Here his argument is that Jesus is "the better example and disciplinary agent of faithful endurance." This does not diminish the need, however, for responsible action on the part of the Christians in being receptive to God's grace (15) in the process of sanctification (14) unto holiness (10) and righteousness (11), and in the kingdom expression of worship, as Paul will proceed to address.

ENDNOTES

1   Lane, William L.,*Word Biblical Commentary*. Hebrews 9-13. Vol. 47B. Dallas, Tx: Word Books. 1991. pg. 407.
2   *Ibid.* pg. 422.

JESUS

The Better New Covenant Basis of Holiness and Worship

Hebrews 12:14-29

Consistent with his typical epistolary style, Paul concludes this letter, like his others, with practical admonitions and directives. In the conclusive hortatory section (12:14–13:25), Paul employs imperative statements to exhort the Jerusalem Christians of their individual and collective responsibility to recognize their new covenant blessings (12:22-24), to respond with peace and holiness (12:14) and the obedience of worship (12:28), and to refuse to defect in apostasy (12:15-17, 25-27). The theme of enduring in faith (12:1-3) via God's discipline (12:5-12), now gives way to the practicalities of living holy lives in peaceful Christian community (14) while listening to God in obedience (25) and engaging in genuine kingdom worship (28).

Connection with the previous paragraph is evident. The result of God's discipline, Paul had explained, would be "the *peaceful* fruit of righteousness" (11) and "partaking of His *holiness*" (10). The practical and necessary pursuit of communal peace and holiness are Paul's initial admonitions in this paragraph (14).

Paul, the apostle of grace, begins and ends this contextual section (14-29) of his letter with mention of "grace" (15,28). The grace dynamic of God's action is required for peaceful and sanctified behavior (14), as well as for listening to God in worship (25-28).

401

Within this contextual section (14-29) are three (3) subdivisions or paragraphs. The first paragraph (14-17) connects to the previous section (as noted above), and encourages the Hebrew Christians to avoid apostasy by engaging in peaceful community and personal holiness. The second paragraph (18-24) provides the central foundations of Paul's exhortations by establishing the superiority of the new covenant over the old covenant in the imagery of the unapproachability and terror of Mt. Sinai (18-21) contrasted with the immediate presence and festivity for Christians at Mt. Zion (22-24). The summary of eschatological realities provides the basis of the privileged status that the Christian readers have in Jesus Christ. The third paragraph (25-29) has a connective link to the second paragraph in the privilege of listening to the voice of God, and worshipping in the unshakeable kingdom of Jesus Christ.

When summarized, Paul seems to be advising the Christians in Jerusalem that "Jesus is the better new covenant basis of holiness and worship." The new covenant realities of being drawn into the immediate presence of God with angels and other Christians allows the Christian to manifest the peaceful, faithful, and holy character of God by His grace, rather than attempting to be "holy" by law-based performance. New covenant union with Christ allows the Christian to listen to the voice of God without fear and terror, and express the worth-ship of God's character in worship, rather than in law-based worship forms of prescribed procedures in particular locations (such as the temple that still stood in Jerusalem). Paul continues to encourage the Jerusalem Christians that they have "everything better" in Jesus Christ.

12:14 Perhaps Paul had received word that there was dissension among the Christians in the congregation at Jerusalem. His imperative admonition is to *"pursue peace with all."* Paul is not advocating the pursuit of a subjective peace of inner tranquility by withdrawal into a cerebral or emotional spirituality. Rather, he is encouraging a visible social harmony and community solidarity in the local Body of Christ in Jerusalem. Although Paul advises the Romans, "If possible, ...be at peace with all men" (Rom. 12:18) universally, the "all" referred to here seems contextually to be "all" the saints in the Christian community. Later, in the context of the interpersonal relationship of the kingdom, Paul exhorted the Romans, "So then, let us pursue the things which make for peace and the building up of one another" (Rom. 14:19), which is more akin to what he was writing to the Hebrews in this context. Paul's pastoral advice to Timothy was to "pursue righteousness, faith, love, and peace, with those who call on the Lord from a pure heart" (II Tim. 2:22). Both Paul and his readers, being thoroughly grounded in the Old Testament scriptures, might have remembered the words of the Psalmist, "Seek peace, and pursue it" (Ps. 34:14), but the particular emphasis of this admonition to the Hebrew Christians was to implement new covenant social interactions in their local Body of Christ that were indicative of the peaceful interrelations of the Triune God.

The same imperative verb provides the admonishment of responsibility to "pursue" both peace *"and the holiness without which no one will see the Lord."* Paul had just explained that the purpose of God's discipline in the trials of life was "for the ultimate advantage, that we partake of His holiness" (10). The manifestation of God's holy character in the behavior of the Jerusalem Christians would obviously facilitate the social implications of a peaceful community. The sanctification or holiness that Paul is demanding is not the objective or positional imputation of being set apart and "sanctified through the offering of the body of Jesus Christ (10:10; 13:12), "through faith in Christ" (Acts 26:18), but is a command that the sanctified saints of Jerusalem should allow for the behavioral manifestation of the holy character of God. Already regarded as "saints" (13:24) and "holy ones" (3:1) by the presence of Jesus Christ, the Holy One (Acts 3:14) in them, the

Jerusalem Christians needed to be involved in the process of expressing the holy character of God in present-tense salvation. Such sanctification holiness is not by ethical achievement or external conformity, but by the process of deriving from God's holiness.

Such progressive holiness in Christian behavior is imperative and indispensable, for "without it no one will see the Lord." Sanctification is not a static experience or event in the life of a Christian, but is the dynamic receipt and expression of God's holiness, initially and continually. The absence of progress in Christian holiness is necessarily regress, and Paul's concern for the Hebrew Christians was that such regress would result in apostasy. To the Thessalonians, he had written, "This is the will of God, your sanctification" (I Thess. 4:3). Paul wanted the Christians in Jerusalem to understand the importance of progress in the process of holy living, for only holiness can come into the holy presence of God. His concern for the Jerusalem saints was that the holy character of God so permeate their being that they would in no way be disqualified from the future and eternal seeing of the Lord (cf. I Cor. 13:12; I John 3:2; Rev. 22:14).

12:15 Using another imperative verb, Paul exhorts, ***"See to it that no one comes short of the grace of God…"***. With a vigilance that senses the true peril, Paul wants them to "watch out" and "observe carefully" that none of their fellow Christians should "come short of the grace of God." Earlier Paul had addressed his concern that they not "come short" of entering God's rest (4:1). To the Romans, Paul had used the same word in writing of how sin caused all to "come short of the glory of God" (Rom. 3:23). Paul's concern was that the Christians in Judea not renounce or repudiate the power of God's grace to preserve them, and thus fail to attain and forfeit all that God had for them by "shrinking back to destruction" (10:39) in apostasy (cf. 2:1-3; 3:12,15; 4:1; 6:4-6; 10:29-31,39).

Previously Paul had mentioned the possibility of "insulting the Spirit of grace" (10:29). He intimated that some of the Galatians had "fallen from grace" (Gal. 5:4), and urged the Corinthians "not to receive the grace of God in vain" (II Cor. 6:1). The preserving grace of God is the divine dynamic that energizes and enables all Christian activity. "He Who began a good work in us will perfect it until the day of Christ Jesus" (Phil. 1:6), so that we can "do all things through Him Who strengthens us" (Phil. 4:13). But we must "grow in the grace and knowledge of our Lord and Savior Jesus Christ" (II Pet. 3:18), drawing on such grace by faith, and must avoid despising, repudiating and thus forfeiting the grace of God. We have a mutual responsibility as Christians (cf. 3:12,13; 4:1; 10:24,25) to encourage one another to receive the grace provision of God, rather than "coming short" by disinterest or lack of faith.

Paul's exhortation of the mutual responsibility of "seeing to it" or "watching out" for one another has several subordinate clauses: See to it [1] that no one comes short of the grace of God, [2] that no root of bitterness causes trouble, and [3] that no one sells out their birthright, like Esau.

The second of the sequence of admonished observations is to see to it *"that no root of bitterness springing up should cause trouble, and through it many be defiled..."*. There may have been some within the Jerusalem fellowship who were speaking despairingly of the Christian endeavor and of the preserving power of God's grace, perhaps even advocating they should give up on being Christian "hold-outs" and join the league of Jewish defense against Rome. Paul uses the figure of a poisonous root or shoot that produces bitter fruit and causes corruption or defilement for those associated with it. This was a figure that was used in the Old Testament when the Israelites were in the wilderness at Moab, and Moses warned them about the possibility of there being "a man or woman, or family or tribe, whose heart turns away from the Lord our God...; lest

there be among you a root bearing poisonous fruit and worm-
wood. ...the anger of the Lord and His jealousy shall burn
against that man, and every curse that is written in this book
shall rest on him, and the Lord shall blot out his name from
under heaven" (Deut. 29:18-20). In other letters Paul warned,
"a little leaven leavens the whole lump" (I Cor. 5:6; Gal. 5:9).
Today we might say, "A bad apple spoils the whole bushel."
Whatever the metaphor, Paul is concerned that the malignancy
of a few might affect the health of the whole Body. If there
were some who had an "evil, unbelieving heart" (3:12), and
had already determined to defect and apostatize from their
Christian faith, their vexation could become contagious and
cause many others to be corrupted and defiled by following
their example of defection. Paul warns the community of
Christians in Jerusalem that they have a mutual responsibility
to disallow this kind of pervasive damage from within the
Body.

12:16 The third of the subordinate clauses is a warning to
watch out *"that* (there be) *no mercenary or desecrator, like
Esau, who in the place of one meal gave up his birthright."*
Paul was inculcating the mutual responsibility of the
Christians in Jerusalem to be on guard for those who might
contemptuously despise their spiritual birthright as a Christian
and sell out to other causes for temporal gratification. The narrative concerning Jacob and Esau can be found in Genesis
25:29-34. There is no reference in the narrative of Esau being
sexually immoral or a whoremonger, which is the direct meaning of the Greek *pornos* (from which we get English words
like "pornography") used here. To avoid such undocumented
reference to Esau, some translations (ex. KJV and NIV) have
added a comma after *pornos* and made a separate and additional subordinate clause warning "that there be no immoral
person" in their midst. Grammatically, it seems better to retain
the word as referent to Esau and interpret the word in a figura-

tive sense of a mercenary willingness to pay for the services of self-gratification. Esau is also represented as a coarse, profane and irreverent person to whom God's blessings meant little, and therefore he was willing to contemptuously desecrate his inheritance rights by selling his birthright privileges for the temporal self-gratification of a solitary meal of bread and stew in his moment of hunger. Paul is warning against such persons who would "despise their birthright" (Gen. 25:34) and sell out their spiritual blessings and inheritance in Christ. "God has blessed us with every spiritual blessing in the heavenly places in Christ" (Eph. 1:3). Christians have "the promise of an eternal inheritance" (Heb. 9:15), "an inheritance which is imperishable and undefiled and will not fade away, reserved in heaven" (I Pet. 1:4). Any Christian who would contemptuously despise the fullness of God's blessing and inheritance, and be willing to desecrate such, willing to yield and hand it over, selling out for the mercenary pleasures of temporal self-gratification, is obviously apostate and must be cautioned against.

12:17 This statement may be parenthetical, but serves nonetheless as a warning comment on the consequence of such apostasy as that represented by Esau. Concerning the contemptuous action of Esau, Paul writes, ***"For you know that indeed afterwards, desiring to inherit the blessing, he was rejected, for he did not find a place of repentance, though seeking it with tears."*** Though he despised his birthright (Gen. 25:34), Esau still wanted to receive the paternal blessing of the first-born son as his father was dying. His mercenary motives never diminished. Since no one can "pull the wool over the eyes" of God, and God knew that Esau had disqualified himself from His covenant dealings, God had rejected him (cf. Rom. 9:12,13). The narrative in Genesis 27:1-40 mentions nothing about any repentance on the part of Esau, but only an attitude of murderous revenge against his younger brother, Jacob. Paul does not indicate that Esau was repentant either, only that "he did not find a place of repentance," meaning that there was no possibility of repentance for Esau, having experienced the irretrievable loss of having been rejected by God after his apostasy. No change of mind by Esau could have led to a change of action whereby God would work in Esau again. This is entirely consistent with what Paul had written earlier in 6:4-6:

> For those having been once enlightened, those having once tasted of the heavenly gift, those having been once made partakers of the Holy Spirit, those having once tasted the good word of God, those having once tasted the powers of the coming age, and having fallen away, it is impossible to renew them again to repentance, since they recrucify again to themselves the Son of God, and put Him to open shame.

Again in 10:26,27 Paul wrote:

> For sinning deliberately after receiving the full knowledge of the truth, there no longer remains a sacrifice for sins, but a certain terrifying expectation of judgment, and 'the zeal of a fire which will consume the adversaries'.

Repentance is not possible after a willful rejection of God in apostasy. Though the Genesis text indicates that Esau "cried out with an exceedingly great and bitter cry" (Gen. 27:34), which appears to be the anguish of failing to get what he wanted in his mercenary drive, it does not refer to Esau's seeking anything "with tears." What he sought in his anguish, which may have included tears, was not repentance, and certainly not God. He sought only the privilege of the paternal blessing which was part of the old covenant agreement, and this he could not have for he had repudiated the covenant arrangement of God by despising his birthright in apostasy, and was thereafter fixed in his condition of being rejected by God. Paul's intent in including this commentary on Esau's reaction was to warn the Jerusalem Christians that there is a point in the renouncing of God's privileges beyond which there is no possibility of repentance, but only a fixed state of rejection by

God. That is why they needed to "watch out" (15) and take notice of their mutual responsibility to "encourage one another" (10:25) in the avoidance of selling out their Christian faith.

12:18 This central paragraph (18-24) of the contextual passage (14-29) provides the theological and eschatological foundation for the imperative exhortations that precede and follow it. In fact, this paragraph (18-24) can legitimately be regarded as the eschatological climax of the entire epistle to the Hebrews, summarizing, as it does, the privileged eschatological blessings that Christians have in Jesus Christ.

Paul provides a connective foundation for the pursuits (14) and perusals (15-17) that he has advised for his Hebrew brethren in Jerusalem. He does so by contrasting the old covenant symbol of Mt. Sinai (18-21) with the new covenant symbol of Mt. Zion (22-24), and carrying over the judgment motif mentioned in his comments about Esau (17). He reminds the Jerusalem Christians, *"For you have not come near to* (a mountain) *being touched and having been burned by fire, and to darkness and gloom and tempest..."*. The Hebrew Christian readers would have known well the details of the inauguration of the old covenant at Mt. Sinai (Exod. 19,20; Deut. 4,5). Though the earliest Greek manuscripts of this epistle do not include reference to "a mountain" in this sentence, the mention of "mountain" in verse 20, and the contrast of having "come to Mt. Zion" in verse 22, make it obvious that this is the intent, and for this reason some scribes inserted the word "mountain" in this verse in later manuscripts. Moses ascended Mt. Sinai (Exod. 19:3) and came back to tell the Israelite people "not to go up on the mountain or touch the border of it" (Exod. 19:12). In Paul's mind the mountain and all that occurred at that location were representative of the inauguration and implementation of the old covenant. He mentions seven features that were indicative of the theophany of God at Mt. Sinai:

(1) forbidden touch
(2) burning fire
(3) darkness
(4) gloom
(5) tempest
(6) trumpet blast, and
(7) sound of words

Together these illustrate that the old covenant was a figure of external sensory phenomena and observation, all of which present God as a visual and auditory threat that made Him unapproachable. When God did come down on Mt. Sinai in fire (cf. Exod. 19:18; 20:18; Deut. 4:11,24; 5:22,23,25), and darkness (Deut. 5:23), and gloom (Deut. 5:22), and tempest (cf. Exod. 19:18), the reaction of the people was fear and uncertainty that led to dread and terror.

12:19 Continuing the list of the sensory phenomena experienced by the Hebrew people at the inauguration of the old covenant at Mt. Sinai, Paul mentions, *"and to a blast of a trumpet, and to a sound of words, which those hearing begged that not a word be added."* The trumpet blast (cf. Exod. 19:16,19; 20:18) is common imagery to announce the presence of God (cf. Matt. 24:31; I Thess. 4:16; Rev. 11:15). The "sound of words" was such that the Hebrew people in the wilderness "saw no form, but heard a voice" (Deut. 4:12) as God declared His covenant in the Ten Commandments. God's voice from the midst of the darkness (Deut. 5:23) was a shuddering reverberation of His awesome power, and the Israelites were afraid that if they heard the voice any longer they would die (Exod. 20:19; Deut. 5:25; 18:16). They begged and pleaded with Moses to be the mediator who would listen to God and then relay God's message to them indirectly (Exod. 10:19; Deut. 5:27). All of the external phenomena associated with God's presence at the beginning of the old covenant caused the people to be terrified in fear and repelled from God's presence.

They did not want to draw near to God, but backed off to a distance of twelve miles according to Jewish tradition, regarding God as inaccessible and unapproachable.

12:20 *"For they could not bear being threatened, 'IF EVEN A BEAST TOUCHES THE MOUNTAIN, IT WILL BE STONED'."* The narrative in Exodus 19:12,13 does not include the explicit threat that Paul quotes, but it does record that bounds were to be set, so that people did not go up to the mountain or touch the border of it. In consequence of such action, "whoever touches the mountain shall surely be put to death" (Exod. 19:12). The offender was not to be touched, but "he shall surely be stoned or shot through; whether beast or man, he shall not live" (Exod. 19:13). It is not difficult to see why some later manuscripts of this epistle extended the quotation to read, "or shot through with a dart" in accordance with the Exodus text, which was followed in the English translation of the Authorized Version (KJV). The threat of possible execution for merely touching the mountain where God was revealing His covenant was more than the Israelite people could bear. God's holy character was so "set apart" from His people that they were repelled by His annihilating judgment.

12:21 *"And so terrifying was the spectacle being displayed, Moses said, 'I AM EXCEEDINGLY FEARFUL AND TREMBLING'."* The Exodus narrative records that the Israelite people "trembled" (Exod. 19:16; 20:18), but there is no reference in the Pentateuch to Moses being afraid and trembling, other than his being afraid of God's anger concerning the golden calf (Deut. 9:19). Moses' fear at the inauguration of the old covenant at Mt. Sinai was included in the literature of Jewish tradition, however, and Paul may have been quoting from these sources. Paul's objective was to impress upon the Jerusalem Christians, who were in danger of reverting back to Judaism, the inadequacies of the entire old covenant as inaugurated at Mt. Sinai. The law-based performance standards of the old covenant necessarily produced a fear-based religion, which bred dread and terror, gloom and doom. God was regarded as inaccessible and unapproachable (cf. 9:1-10; 10:1-2,11), distanced from any real relationship with people.

12:22 In contrast to the old covenant inaugurated at Mt. Sinai, Paul reminds the Jerusalem Christians of the "better things" that are theirs in Jesus Christ via the new covenant inaugurated at Mt. Zion. ***"But you have come near to Mt. Zion, even to the city of the living God, the heavenly Jerusalem..."***. Having mentioned seven features of God's presence at Mt. Sinai (18,19), Paul now identifies seven features of the new covenant blessings associated with Mt. Zion:

(1) Mt. Zion, city of the living God, heavenly Jerusalem (22)
(2) myriads of angels in festive gathering (22)
(3) the church of the first-born ones having been enrolled in heaven (23)
(4) God, the judge of all (23)
(5) the spirits of righteous ones made perfect (23)
(6) Jesus, the mediator of a new covenant (24)
(7) the sprinkled blood (24)

Together, these sum up the inaugurated and realized eschatological hopes of the people of God in the new covenant.

Whereas they had "not come near" (18) to God at Mt. Sinai when the old covenant was established, Paul now emphasizes in contrast that Christians have "come near" to God and are able to approach him in direct and immediate access through Jesus Christ in the new covenant. They can "draw near" (cf. 4:16; 7:19,25; 10:19,22) to God in the intimate spiritual communion of immediate personal relationship. Paul uses a perfect tense verb to indicate that the Hebrew

Christian readers have definitively "drawn near" to God and the consequences of such closeness remain to the present. The immediate access "already" enjoyed will be balanced later with the "not yet" of the "lasting city which is to come" (13:14).

In a triad of synonyms (cf. Ps. 48:1,2; 51:18; 102:21; Joel 2:32), Paul explains to the Jerusalem Christians that they "have come near" to God in "Mt. Zion, the city of the living God, the heavenly Jerusalem." The mountain "stronghold of Zion" was originally conquered by David and used as the location of his residence (II Sam. 5:7-10; I Chron. 11:5,7). When Solomon constructed the temple there later, God was identified as the One "Who dwells in Zion" (Ps. 9:11). The entire city of Jerusalem was often identified as "Mt. Zion, the city of God, the holy mountain, the city of the great King" (Ps. 48:1,2; 76:2). King David's mountain was prophesied to be the place where the Messiah would be "installed as King upon Zion, the holy mountain" (Ps. 2:6; 110:2). As the expected Messiah, Jesus' reign is figuratively (but no longer geographically or topographically) located on Mt. Zion (cf. Rev. 14:1), representing the presence and dwelling place of God. This symbolic place is further identified as "even the city of the living God," which would be the city that Abraham sought in faith, "the city having foundations, of which the designer and builder is God" (11:10). The "city of the living God" is the completed community of God's people who live in God's presence through Jesus Christ. The third designation identifies this as "the heavenly Jerusalem." This removed the "city of peace" from all reference to a mound in Palestine, a walled city, or a temple mount – from all external tangibility and localized phenomena – for it is now equivalent to the "heavenly fatherland" (11:16) that Abraham sought. As "citizens of heaven" (Phil. 3:2), "partakers of a heavenly calling" (Heb. 3:1), "seated in heavenly places" (Eph. 2:6), Christians have come to the place that Jesus prepared (John 14:3), "near to the heart of God." "The

Jerusalem above" (Gal. 4:26) is the city of peace where Christians dwell with immediate access to God, while at the same time looking forward to the consummation in "the new Jerusalem" (Rev. 3:12; 21:2).

The Christians to whom Paul was writing were residing in the earthly Jerusalem where the Judaic religion had its centralized headquarters at the temple. They were being pressured by their Jewish kinsmen to militarily defend the physical Jerusalem with their lives, having no idea that it was soon to be destroyed by the superior Roman armies. Paul is advising them to recognize and appreciate the spiritual presence of God, the perfect heavenly place where Christians dwell with the living God, in the heavenly Jerusalem. The heavenly Jerusalem is far superior to the earthly Jerusalem, and allows access to God wherever the Christian might be at any time.

The second feature of the new covenant blessings to which Christians have "drawn near" is ***"to myriads of angels in festive gathering…"***. The presence of God is often represented as accompanied by and surrounded with angels (cf. Jude 14; Rev. 5:11). Even at the inauguration of the old covenant at Mt. Sinai angels were present (Deut. 33:2; Acts 7:38), and Paul had previously compared "the word spoken through angels" (Heb. 2:2) at Mt. Sinai with the Word revealed in Jesus Christ (cf. John 1:1). In the new covenant, Christians have the privilege of approaching God together with the angels, who serve as "ministering spirits, rendering service to those who inherit salvation" (1:14). These myriads (literally "ten thousands," but figuratively "countless" and "innumerable" – cf. Dan. 7:10-14) of angels join with Christians in "festive gathering." This is the only usage of this Greek word, *panegurei*, in the New Testament, but in other Greek literature it referred to a festive crowd or assembly gathered for joyful celebration. Christians and angels celebrate all that God has done in the triumph of His Son, Jesus Christ, and the angels rejoice whenever a sinner repents (Lk. 15:10) and joins the festivities. This celebratory festivity is certainly antithetical to the terror experienced at Mt. Sinai, and Paul wanted the Jerusalem Christians to see the contrast. It was not that the Jewish people did not enjoy festivals and feasts, but all of the old covenant festivals pictorially pointed to Jesus Christ, and their fulfillment is in the festive gathering of joy that Christians and angels have in Christ.

The grammatical variation of different English translations is influenced by how one translates the word for "festive gathering." Some translations miss the linguistic meaning, and translate the word as "general assembly," attaching it to the third phrase of "the church of the first-borns" (cf. KJV, NASB, NEB). Those translations (cf. RSV, NIV, LB) that recognize the Greek usage as "festive gathering," also take into consideration that the conjunction *kai* occurs at the beginning of the "church" phrase and not prior to "festal gathering." This latter punctuation and translation is preferable.

12:23 The third subordinate clause signifying the new covenant benefits to which the Hebrew Christians "have come near" and entered into is ***the church of the first-born ones having been enrolled in heaven...".*** The church is comprised of the "called out ones" (Greek *ekklesia*), Christians who have been called out of their sin, selfishness and individualism into the assembled gathering of Christian community, the Body of Christ (Col. 1:18,24). For this reason, they are not "to forsake their assembling together,...but to encourage one another" (10:25). The church is not an organization or institutional entity, but is the Christian assembly of the praising community wherein Christ sings God's praise in the midst of the congregation (2:12). The communal oneness of the church of Jesus Christ was an identification with community that was far deeper and more lasting than the commitment to the Jewish community that the Christians in Jerusalem were being pressured to defend.

There is no apparent reference in the designation of "first-borns" back to Esau (16,17) who sought the blessing of the first-born son. Jesus, however, is often referred to as "the first-born" (1:6), and "the first-born from the dead" (Col. 1:18; Rev. 1:5) by virtue of His resurrection. To the Romans, Paul explained that Jesus was "the first-born among many brethren" (Rom. 8:29), those who would be spiritually "born again" (John 3:3,6) and given divine life by the indwelling of the Spirit of the living Lord Jesus. Being "born again to a living hope through the resurrection of Jesus Christ from the dead" (I Pet. 1:3), Christians have the full blessing of His birthright and are "fellow-heirs with Christ" (Rom. 8:17). To be a first-born son physically was an important privilege and blessing in Hebrew culture. Paul wanted the Jerusalem Christians to recognize that they were all spiritual "first-borns" in identification and union with Jesus Christ, the "first-born."

The "first-born ones" (note the plural), the Christians who comprise the church of Jesus Christ, "have been enrolled in heaven." Having received the heavenly life of God in Christ, "every spiritual blessing in heavenly places" (Eph. 1:3, and become "partakers of a heavenly calling" (3:1), Christians are enrolled, recorded, and registered in heaven. Jesus told the seventy to "rejoice that your names are recorded in heaven" (Lk. 10:20), and there are numerous New Testament references to Christians' names being inscribed in the book of life (cf. Phil. 4:3; Rev. 3:5; 13:8; 20:12; 21:27). Though the Christians in Jerusalem were registered and enrolled as citizens of Judea, Paul wants them to realize their superior "enrollment in heaven" as "citizens of heaven" (Phil. 3:20), already participating in "the heavenly Jerusalem" (22).

As the fourth feature of new covenant privilege, Paul explains to the Christians in Jerusalem that they have come near *"to God, the Judge of all..."*. At Mt. Sinai, the Israelite people of the old covenant did not draw near to God. They cowered in fear and were repelled by the awesomeness of

God's revealed presence, as well as what they perceived to be the judgmental consequences of violating God's commands. At Mt. Zion, representing the new covenant, Christians have drawn near to God in the direct access of personal relationship. The new covenant concept of God as judge is no longer that of a condemnatory magistrate in a legal context meting out punishment for improper performance. God as judge is the One Who lovingly ordained and predestined that divine approval would be granted to all persons in Jesus Christ. All divine determinations or judgments are made referent to and in conjunction with Jesus Christ. That is why Jesus explained, as recorded in John's gospel:

> God did not send the Son into the world to judge the world, but that the world should be saved through Him. He who believes in Him is not judged; he who does not believe has been judged already, because he has not believed in the name of the only begotten Son of God. And this is the judgment, that the light has come into the world, and men loved the darkness rather than the light. (John 3:17-19)

God is "the judge of all" men universally, because God determined to love the world of mankind and "send His only begotten Son, so that those who believe in Him should not perish, but have eternal life" (John 3:16). Christians, who have received Jesus Christ by faith, therefore need not have any fear of being judged by God in the sense of being punished, condemned, or damned. Acceptance (Rom. 15:7; Eph. 1:6 - KJV) and approval (I Cor. 11:17) are the judgment of God for all believers. Unbelief, however, including those who apostatize, will bring the judgment of God's condemnation (2:3; 10:26-31). Paul wanted the Hebrew Christians in Jerusalem to rest assured that God's judgment of all was historically enacted in Jesus Christ, and those who receive Him by faith are approved and secure in a dynamic relationship with Him. At the same time, Paul warns them of the possibility of apostatizing in unbelief.

417

Continuing his panorama of new covenant benefits, Paul advises the Jerusalem Christians that they have drawn near *"to the spirits of righteous ones having been made perfect...".* Previously Paul referred to God as "the Father of spirits" (12:9), and it was noted that God is "the God of the spirits of all flesh" (Num. 16:22; 27:16), with particular reference to human persons capable of receiving His Spirit in their spirit. The Hebrew Christians of Jerusalem had been drawn into the fellowship of the faithful of humanity. Despite the opinions of many commentators who have attempted to identify "the spirits of righteous ones made perfect" as persons who have previously died, whether the Old Testament faithful (11:3-38), or deceased Christians, or Christian martyrs, there is no reason to limit or confine this designation to the dead. Paul's whole point is to emphasize the involvement of Christians in the divine dynamic of the eternal present. Christians have been joined together with the entire community of faithful people throughout all time. Human spirits have become "righteous ones" through faith (cf. Hab. 2:4; Rom. 1:17; Heb. 10:38). "Through the obedience of the One (Jesus Christ), the many (who receive Him) are made righteous" (Rom. 5:19), becoming "the righteousness of God in Him" (II Cor. 5:21). The indwelling presence of "the Righteous One" (Acts 3:14; 7:52; 22:14; I John 2:1) creates a spiritual identity of righteousness for all Christians. They are also made perfect by the spiritual presence of the Perfect One, Jesus Christ. Earlier in this letter, Paul wrote that Jesus "has perfected unto perpetuity those being sanctified" (10:14), and to the Philippians he referred to Christians as those who "are perfect" (Phil. 3:15). The Jerusalem Christians needed to be aware that religious exercises of prescribed "righteous actions" make no one righteous or perfect (cf. Isa. 64:6; Phil. 3:6-8) in spiritual condition, but as Christians they are drawn near in fellowship with "the spirits of righteous ones having been made perfect" in Jesus Christ.

12:24 All of the realities that Paul identifies are encompassed in the Jerusalem Christians having drawn near in intimate union *"to Jesus, the mediator of a new covenant...".* In eschatological fulfillment of the prophecies of old (Jere. 31:31-34; Ezek. 37:26,27), Jesus came as "the one mediator between God and man" (I Tim. 2:5), "the mediator of a new covenant" (8:6; 9:15). The old Sinaitic covenant, the Mosaic covenant, the law covenant, kept people distanced and removed from God. Through the intermediary action of Jesus Christ in His death on the cross, the "eternal covenant" (13:20) was enacted to draw Christians into intimate communion with God, and provide every spiritual blessing in Christ (cf. Eph. 1:3). Paul wanted to emphasize the superiority of the new covenant arrangement of God and His people, for he was aware that his Hebrew Christian brethren in Judea were being tempted to revert back to the defense of the old covenant religious expectations and practices, even though the old covenant was obsolete, antiquated, abrogated, and near to disappearing (8:13). (See extensive comments on "covenant" in 8:1-13).

The "blood of the covenant" was sprinkled on the people at the inauguration of the old covenant (Exod. 24:8), but the blood of animals had only a temporal effect for the people of God (Heb. 9:11-22). Paul emphasizes again to the Christians in Jerusalem that Jesus "through His own blood" (9:12), "offered Himself without blemish" (9:14), as "the mediator of a new covenant" (9:15), and "the blood of the covenant" (10:29) has "sprinkled our hearts clean" (10:22). In the seventh of the glorious eschatological realities of the new covenant, Paul reminds the readers that they have drawn near *"to the sprinkled blood, speaking better things than that of Abel."* The "sprinkled blood" is a euphemism for the redemptive efficacy of the sacrificial death of Jesus Christ on the cross at Mt. Zion. No Hebrew Christian would have missed the connection of the sprinkling of blood as the seal of the old covenant, and how the death of Jesus by crucifixion was the establishment and seal of the new covenant. The Hebraic terminology of the Christian being "sprinkled with His blood" (I Peter 1:2) was recognized as the redemptive action of forgiveness whereby the Christian could draw near to the presence of God "by the blood of Jesus" (10:19). Christians remember such every time they partake of the Lord's Supper and hear Jesus' words, "This cup is the new covenant in My blood" (Matt. 26:28; Lk. 22:20; I Cor. 11:25).

Paul adds a comment that "the blood of Jesus speaks better than that of Abel." This may appear at first to be off the subject, but we must attempt to discover how these were connected by contrast in Paul's mind. The account of Cain and Abel (Gen. 4:1-15) records how Cain murdered his brother Abel in anger, and the Lord told Cain, Tthe voice of your brother's blood is crying to Me from the ground" (Gen. 4:10). Both the death of Abel and the death of Jesus were the deaths of innocent persons. Abel's blood cried out for vengeance and justice. Jesus' blood declares the gospel message of forgiveness and reconciliation. Abel's blood led to the imposition of a curse (Gen. 4:11,12). The blood of Jesus secures the redemptive blessing of the new covenant. Abel's blood testified only of death, whereas the blood of Jesus testifies of divine life restored because of the vicarious death of Jesus for all men. It is not difficult to understand why Paul thought "the blood of Jesus speaks better than the blood of Abel." The thrust of Paul's argument throughout this letter is to emphasize to the Jerusalem Christians that everything is "better" and more effective in Jesus Christ.

It is important to note, however, that Paul refers to the blood of Jesus "speaking" in a present tense. The death of Jesus is more than just an historical event or statement. Because Jesus died and rose again, the crucified and risen Lord Jesus continues by the Spirit to proclaim the "good news" that spiritual death has been taken for all men in His death, in order that His life might be restored to mankind when received by faith. This eschatological message of the new covenant restoration of humanity in Jesus Christ is certainly a better message than that of Abel.

12:25 This third paragraph (25-29) of this contextual passage (14-29) has a connective link to the present tense "speaking" of Jesus' blood in the previous verse. *"See to it that you do not refuse the One speaking,"* Paul exhorts with another imperative verb. The One speaking is God in Christ by the Spirit. God's revelatory "speaking" did not cease at the death, resurrection, or ascension of Jesus, nor at the conclusion of writing or the canonization of scripture. Such concepts of "cessationism" set up various forms of deism with a detached deity who can no longer interact and reveal Himself to His creation. God in Christ "is speaking," and "those who are being led by the Spirit of God are sons of God" (Rom. 8:14). Christian obedience is "listening under" (Greek *hupakouo*) the speaking and direction of God. Paul wanted the Jerusalem Christians to recognize their ongoing responsibility of listening to the voice of God in obedience. He did not want them to disregard, reject, or refuse what God was saying to their hearts. His warnings against rejecting Jesus Christ in apostasy continue to reveal his heart of concern for the brethren in Jerusalem.

In a comparative warning similar to what he expressed earlier in 2:2,3, Paul cautions the readers in Jerusalem: *"For if those did not escape having refused the One warning on the earth, much rather, we* (shall not escape), *those turning away* (from the One speaking) *from heaven."* If, as was the case, the Israelites, as the prefiguring people of God, refused, rejected, and "begged off" (19) of having to face God, and distantly "stood away" from God when He warned them through the visual and auditory phenomena of His presence at Mt. Sinai (18,19), and they did not escape the consequences of their unbelief (3:19), then the greater blessing of the new covenant implies a greater responsibility with severer consequences. The same God spoke in both covenants, but He spoke "on earth" in the old covenant, while He speaks "from heaven" in the new covenant. Christians have the superior privilege of God's speaking to them and revealing Himself to them "from heaven," and "for this reason we must pay much closer attention to what we have heard, lest we drift away from it" (2:1). Paul is making an argument from the lesser to the greater. The "we" of the second phrase, signifying Christians, is emphatically juxtapositioned against the "those" of the first phrase, signifying the Israelites. "If the word spoken through angels (to the Israelites) proved unalterable, and every transgression and disobedience received a just recompense, how shall we escape so great a salvation?" (2:2,3). The divine voice of God in Christ by the Spirit speaks to the hearts of Christians, for as Jesus said, "My sheep hear My voice" (John 10:27; cf. 10:1-17). The superior revelation of God to Christians demands a greater responsibility to be faithful and avoid "turning away" from God in unbelief and apostasy.

12:26 The contrast of old covenant and new covenant continues: ***"His voice shook the earth then...".*** Paul explains, referring to the inauguration of the old covenant at Mt. Sinai. The Exodus narrative records, "the whole mountain quaked violently" (Exod. 19:18). Reiterating the occasion, Deborah and Barak lyrically recall, "The mountains quaked at the presence of the Lord, this Sinai, at the presence of the Lord, the God of Israel" (Judges 4:5). The Psalmist, David, likewise explained in song, "The earth quaked,...Sinai itself quaked at the presence of God, the God of Israel" (Ps. 68:8; cf. 77:18). The earth was shaken when God revealed Himself at Mt. Sinai, and the people recognized the awesome power of God.

Contrasting the "then" of the old covenant with the "now" of the new covenant, Paul writes, ***"But now He has promised, saying, 'YET ONCE I WILL SHAKE NOT ONLY THE EARTH, BUT ALSO THE HEAVEN'."*** Paul quotes from the prophecies of Haggai (Hag. 2:6,21; cf. Isa. 13:13), which referred to the coming eschatological shaking that was to occur at the inauguration of the new covenant. Jewish interpreters in the Talmud regarded these prophecies of Haggai to be Messianic. The prophet Joel also foresaw that "the earth shakes, the heavens tremble" (Joel 2:10), and there will be "wonders in the sky and on the earth" (2:30-32), which Peter explicitly indicated were figuratively fulfilled at Pentecost (Acts 2:16-21) in the implementation of the new covenant. What was still future at the time of Haggai and Joel was fulfilled in the cosmic shaking of all things in the advent and work of Jesus Christ, allowing for the unshakeable realities of the new covenant for Christians "now." The shaking of the earth at the time of Jesus' death and resurrection (Matt. 27:51-54; 28:2) was but the preliminary to the cataclysmic phenomena that affected heaven and earth at the inauguration of the new covenant in Jesus Christ.

Other interpretations have been made of Paul's quotation of Haggai's prophecy: (1) that Paul was referring to the specific "now" of Jerusalem Christians being "shaken" by their persecution and suffering at the hands of their fellow Jewish countrymen. (2) that Paul was referring to the "shaking" that was soon to occur in A.D. 66-70 when the Roman armies would destroy Jerusalem (cf. Matt. 24:29; Lk. 21:26). (3) that Paul was referring to a yet future "shaking" of earth and heaven that will result in a "new heaven and a new earth" (II Pet. 3:10-13). The first two of these interpretations fail to give adequate import to the shaking of "heaven" as well as earth, and the third fails to address the "now" contrast that Paul is drawing with the old covenant. It is preferable, therefore, to recognize that Paul is using Haggai's prophecy to refer to the metaphorical impact of the inauguration of the new covenant.

12:27 Paul proceeds to give his commentary on Haggai's prophecy. *"So the* (phrase *'YET ONCE,' indicates the*

423

removal of those things being shaken, those things having been made...". The word "yet" denotes a contrast with the shaking at Mt. Sinai. "Once" indicates the singularity and finality of Christ's action. Paul has used this word (Greek *hapax*) and its derivatives throughout this epistle to explain the singularity and completeness of the redemptive activity of Jesus Christ (7:27; 9:12,28; 10:10) in the establishment of the new covenant. Consistently, Paul refers to how the work of Christ was the shaking of heaven and earth that removed (cf. 11:5) and displaced the external, physical, material, perishable, and temporal things that could be shaken and removed. The externalities of the old covenant community and its religious practices have been shaken, have fallen, have been destroyed, and have been removed in the sense of having any significance before God. The physical city of Jerusalem and its temple were still standing, but were soon to disappear (8:13).

The tangible and temporal things of the old covenant were removed by the work of Christ, *"in order that the things not being shaken might remain."* The contrast is between the physical and created things of the old covenant which have been shaken and removed, and the spiritual, heavenly, and eternal realities of the new covenant which cannot be shaken and remain forever. This coincides with the contrast between perishing and permanency that Paul drew from Ps. 102:25,26 in the introduction to this epistle (1:10-12). The uncreated spiritual and heavenly realities of the new covenant that find their substance in the eternality of Christ Himself are unshakeable. They remain and abide as unchangeable, permanent, and eternal for they are comprised of God's Being in action in the living Lord Jesus. Jesus "abides forever, and holds His priesthood permanently" (7:3,24), and that is why Christians have the "abiding possession" (10:34) of a heavenly inheritance in the "heavenly Jerusalem" (22).

Paul continues to emphasize to the Christians in Jerusalem the necessity of recognizing all that they have in Jesus Christ in the new covenant. Only if they accept the permanency and sufficiency of the new covenant grace of God in Jesus Christ will they respond with fidelity and endurance. Paul does not want his physical and spiritual brethren in Jerusalem to be shaken by the Jewish and Roman hostilities, nor does he want them to capitulate and stand against Jesus in apostasy.

12:28 In consequence of God's having shaken heaven and earth in the implementation of the new covenant, and removed the externalities of the old covenant which were never meant to be permanent – its religious practices, its physical connections, its legal impositions, its political kingdom, etc. – Paul concludes, ***"Therefore, receiving an unshakeable kingdom, we may have grace, through which we may serve God well-pleasingly, with reverence and awe...".*** The unshakeable realities of the new covenant in Christ (27) are summed up in the Christian's receipt of and participation in an unshakeable kingdom. This is a spiritual kingdom not based on might and power (Zech 4:6; I Cor. 2:4), but on the reign of the living Christ by the Spirit in Christian individuals and the Christian community. Paul uses a present participle to explain that Christians are presently "receiving" this dynamic reign of Christ. The unshakeable new covenant kingdom is a process that involves the dialectic of "already" and "not yet." God has "delivered us from the domain of darkness, and transferred us into the kingdom of His beloved Son" (Col. 1:13). Jesus Himself said, "The kingdom of God is within your midst" or "within you" (Lk. 17:21). The kingdom reign of Christ as the indwelling Lord of His people is already a reality. God has "made us to be a kingdom, priests unto God" (Rev. 1:6; 5:10), for "kingdom" is the dynamic reality of the Lordship reign of Christ in His people and His church. God is presently "calling us into the kingdom and glory of Himself" (I Thess. 2:12), and His kingdom involves "righteousness and peace and joy in the Holy Spirit" (Rom. 14:17). All the while Christians are looking forward to the ultimate and unhindered expression of "the eternal kingdom" (II Pet. 1:11) at Christ's appearing in the future (II Tim. 4:1).

The Zealot insurrectionists were pressuring the Jerusalem Christians to join the fight to restore the physical and political Jewish kingdom in Palestine by ousting the hated Roman oppressors. Paul was advising the Jerusalem Christians that the political Jewish kingdom was one of those old covenant realities that was shakable and had been removed – displaced and replaced by the unshakeable spiritual kingdom wherein Christ reigns as "Lord of Lords and King of Kings" (Rev. 19:16). The "heavenly kingdom" (II Tim. 4:18), the "eternal kingdom" (II Pet. 1:11) is permanent and unshakeable, and Christians "reign in life" (Rom. 5:17) as Christ reigns as Lord in them.

Since Christians are receiving the kingdom reign of Christ, "we may have grace, through which we may serve God well-pleasingly, with reverence and awe." The grace-dynamic of God's Being in action expressing His character and activity is operative in the Christian who is participating in the kingdom reign of the risen Lord Jesus. Paul uses the same word (Greek *charis*) that he used in verse 15 when he cautioned the readers about "coming short of the *grace* of God" (15). When this word is translated in its primary sense, recognizing that "God is able to make all *grace* abound to you, that always having all sufficiency in everything, you may have an abundance for every good deed" (II Cor. 9:8), then it follows that through this grace-dynamic the Christian may worship God acceptably. As Paul will later write, "God equips you in every good thing to do His will, working in us that which is *well-pleasing* in His sight through Jesus Christ" (13:20,21). Paul had exhorted the Romans to "present your bodies a living and holy sacrifice, *well-pleasing* to God, which is your spiritual service of worship" (Rom. 12:1). The word Paul uses for "serving" God (Greek *latreuo*) was used by the Jews to refer to temple service and worship (8:5; 9:1,6,9; 10:2; 13:10), but Paul transforms the word in the new covenant to refer to the Christian's "service of worship" in the heavenly temple wherein Christ "cleansed our consciences from dead works to *serve* the living God" (9:14). It is only by the grace-dynamic of God that Christians, in the priesthood of all believers, can worship God acceptably and well-pleasingly, reverently recognizing His good authority in awesome fear, and expressing the worth-ship of His character. If the word *charis* is translated with its secondary meaning of "gratitude" (cf. Lk. 17:9; I Tim. 1:12; II Tim. 1:3), then Christians' "service of worship" is prompted by thanksgiving (Greek *eucharisteo* – cf. Eph. 5:20; Col. 3:17; I Thess. 5:18) that recognizes God's "good grace." The danger of using the secondary meaning, "gratitude," instead of the primary meaning, "grace," is that is can be misunderstood as the grateful and thankful incentive that causes Christians to attempt by works of self-effort to offer acceptable service of worship to God, while failing to recognize that genuine Christian service of worship is only through, and by means of, the grace-dynamic of God's activity (cf. Fowler, *Christocentric Worship*). Hermeneutic principles call for the primary meaning of the word *charis* as the preferable choice of translation of this verse.

12:29 Although this concluding phrase, ***"For indeed our God is a consuming fire,"*** may seem abrupt, the conjunctive "for" provides a connective link to the service of worship that stands in awe and fearful reverence at the character of God (28). Paul wanted to advise the Hebrew Christians that God holds Christians accountable for functioning in His kingdom by His grace (15,28). Because He created mankind as choosing creatures, they are responsible for the choices of receptivity by which they live.

The God of the old covenant at Mt. Sinai is the same God of the new covenant at Mt. Zion. His character is not altered in the new arrangement of the new covenant. At the inauguration of the old covenant, "the appearance of the glory of the Lord was like a *consuming fire* on the mountain top" (Exod. 24:17). Moses told the Israelites, "The Lord your God is a *consuming fire*, a jealous God" (Deut. 4:24). Paul repeats this figurative designation of God to explain the accountability of Christians in the new covenant to recognize that there are determinative consequences to their choices: "For indeed our God is a *consuming fire*." The fire of God's passion for absolute purity must eventually consume all that is not consistent with His character. It will be burned up like "wood, hay, and straw" (I Cor. 3:12-15). God's absoluteness demands that everything that is not His Being at work in His creation unto His glory be removed, so that His perfect purity of Being can be expressed in His eternality.

The difference between the old covenant and the new covenant is that the Israelites committed themselves (Exod. 24:7) to performance that attempted to measure up to God's character, and they failed miserably because the endeavor was impossible (Rom. 3:20; Gal. 2:16; 3:11). In the new covenant Christians are responsible to believe in the performance of the One God sent, His Son, and to be receptive in faith to the grace of God whereby God will generate and express His own character in sanctification (14) and worship (28). The basis of God's determinative judgment is belief in Jesus Christ. "He who does not believe has been judged already, because he has not believed in the name of the only begotten Son of God" (John 3:18). Those who revert to unbelief in apostasy and rejection of Jesus Christ are likewise judged by the single criteria of belief in Jesus Christ. For this reason Paul emphasizes to the Jerusalem Christians that "our God is a consuming fire," and "it is a terrifying thing to fall into the hands of the living God" (10:31). The determined consequences of God's judgment referent to belief in Jesus Christ are not inconsistent with God's love (I John 4:8,16). The other side of God's love is the "tough love" that demands that man function as God intended by deriving all from Him, or be accountable for the consequences of God's consuming fire.

Concluding remarks:

As Paul prepares to draw his epistle to the Hebrew Christians to a close, he continues to make repeated reference to their historical heritage. He mentions Esau (Gen. 25:29-34; 27:1-40), the terrifying fear at Mt. Sinai (Exod. 19,20; Deut. 4,5), and the blood of Abel (Gen. 4:1-15). In addition, he alludes to the shaking of the earth at the inauguration of the old covenant (Exod. 19:18; Judges 4:5; Ps. 68:8), Haggai's prophecy of the shaking of earth and heaven (Hag. 2:6,21), and reiterates that "our God is a consuming fire" (Deut. 4:24). The Jewish Christians in Jerusalem were facing the militant Zealots who wanted them to join the insurrection and revolt against Rome. They were being accused of being traitors who were divorcing themselves from their Jewish heritage. Paul, on the other hand, emphasizes that they are intimately connected with their Hebrew heritage, having received the better and intended fulfillment of all the Hebrew prefiguring in Jesus Christ. In the "better things" of Christ Jesus, they have realized all of the eschatological hopes of Israel.

Many of the major themes that Paul has used throughout the epistle are drawn together in this contextual passage (14-29). These include the contrast of the old and new covenants (8:5-13; 9:11-23; 10:15-18), and the contrast between separation from God and access to God (4:15,16; 9:1-14; 10:1-25). The danger of "coming short" (2:1-3; 3:12-15; 4:1) is reiterated, alongside the warning against apostasy (3:12; 6:4-8; 10:26-31), and God's judgment (2:2,3; 6:8; 10:29-31).

Paul was very concerned that the Christians in Jerusalem should not forfeit all they had received in Jesus Christ. He wanted them to recognize that in Jesus Christ they had "the better new covenant basis of holiness and worship." In the remainder of the letter he provides practical admonishment of how this Christian holiness and worship is worked out in the situations of life.

JESUS

The Better Practical Expression
of God at Work

Hebrews 13:1-25

This epistle has been predominantly theological in content.
Paul has been laying the theological and eschatological foundations of the supremacy of the new covenant realities in Jesus
Christ. His objective was to convince the Hebrew Christians in
Jerusalem that the spiritual relationship they had with Jesus
Christ was far better than the old covenant Judaic religion that
surrounded them, and to which they were being pressured to
revert. Even in the midst of Paul's theological arguments, his
pastoral heart of concern for his brethren causes him to inter-
sperse his instruction with practical behavioral admonitions.
For example, he has exhorted them to "encourage one another"
(3:13), to "enter God's rest" (4:9-13), to be "diligent to realize
the full assurance of hope" (6:11), to "incite one another unto
love and good works" (10:24), to "not forsake assembling
together" (10:25), to "endure" (10:36), to accept discipline
(12:3-11), and to "pursue peace and holiness" (12:14). Here at
the end of this epistle, Paul employs his typical style (cf. Eph.
5:1–6:9; I Thess. 4:1-12) of using imperative verbs (1,2,3,7,9,
17,18) to admonish practical behavioral action. Paul understood that the theology and the theory had to issue forth in the
practicum and praxis of behavior consistent with the character
of Christ.

Some commentators have questioned the coherence of this
final chapter with the rest of the epistle, regarding the content
of these latter admonitions to be a loose collection of brief eth-

431

ical exhortations disconnected from what precedes them. On the contrary, it is not difficult to observe the natural flow of theme and vocabulary that draws this final section into the integral whole of the epistle at large. Paul's encouragement to "pursue the holiness without which no man shall see the Lord" (12:14) is certainly amplified in the practical situations of brotherly love, hospitality, visiting prisoners, respecting marriage, and avoiding materialism (13:1-6). This expression of God's holy character in Christian behavior is also essential to the "well-pleasing service of worship" that is to be evidenced in the "unshakeable kingdom of Christ" (12:28). "*Well-pleasing* service of worship" finds practical expression, therefore, in the entirety of the admonitions of chapter 13, but more specifically in verses 7-21 where the Christian readers are advised to worship "outside the camp" of religion (13), offering a sacrifice of praise (15) and sacrifices of doing good and sharing with which God is *well-pleased* (16), all of which God works in the Christian and thus causes to be "*well-pleasing* in His sight" (21). The "*well-pleasing* service of worship" (12:28) involves the entirety of our lifestyle and behavior as we allow God to work in us and express the worth-ship of His character in every situation. Paul was explaining to the Jerusalem Christians that "Jesus is the better practical expression of God at work," expressing His character of holiness in a lifestyle of worship – so much better than the rituals of religious worship that were still taking place in the temple at Jerusalem.

13:1   This first paragraph (1-6) addresses a particular expressive feature of God's holy character – love. "God is love" (I John 4:8,16). The practical expression of God's holy character in lifestyle worship will involve seeking the highest good of others in love. Such love will be expressed to the brethren of the Christian community (1), to strangers in hospitality (2), to prisoners and those mistreated (3), as well as in respect for marriage (4), but not toward material things (5,6). God's love through us (cf. Rom. 5:5) is toward people, not things! Let it be noted that in Paul's thought the practicum of Christianity does not allow for a sacred vs. secular dichotomy. When Christ is our life (Col. 3:4), everything in life is invested with the sacredness of His character expression. All of life is to be marked with holiness and worship, and in particular the practical areas that Paul proceeds to mention.

"Let love of the brethren continue." Apparently the Jerusalem Christians had a healthy community of love. Earlier Paul had mentioned "the love which you have shown toward His name, in having ministered and in still ministering to the saints" (6:10), and urged them to "pursue peace with all" their brethren (12:14). This brotherly love (Greek *philadelphia*, from which the "City of Brotherly Love" is named – cf. Rev. 3:7-13) for the "brethren" (cf. 3:1,12; 10:19; 13:22) of the Christian community is encouraged and commended throughout the New Testament writings (cf. Matt. 23:8; John 13:35; 15:12,17; Rom. 12:10; I Thess. 4:9; I Pet. 1:22; I John 4:14-17). "Love of the brethren," our spiritual brothers and sisters in the family of God, is more than a polite handshake on Sunday morning, with a standardized questioning, "How are you?" and the token response, "Fine!" Rather, "love of the brethren" is based on the deeper spiritual commonality of Christians whereby they are interdependent upon one another in the Body of Christ (cf. I Cor. 12:12-26). Christians are integrally linked and united because the living Christ dwells in each Christian, and they are thereby invested in each other's lives. The conception of a "lone-ranger" Christian "doing his own thing" without connection to the Body is alien to Christian thought. Paul was encouraging and exhorting the Christians in Jerusalem to abide, remain, and continue in their expression of God's love for one another in the Christian community.

13:2 Expressing God's love to those in our local Christian community is expanded to include strangers. ***"Do not neglect to show hospitality to strangers, for through this some have entertained angels unknowingly."*** As a practical expression of God's worthy character of holiness and love, Paul exhorts the Jerusalem Christians to "not neglect, forget, or disregard" showing hospitality to strangers. Who are these "strangers" or "foreigners" (Greek *philoxenias* – "love of strangers") that Paul mentions? The context of the "love of the brethren" in the previous sentence (1) makes it likely that Paul is referring to Christian brethren who were outside of their fellowship, and from another city. Practicing this kind of hospitality by receiving Christians from others places as guests in their homes was an important expression of love among Christians in the first century. Paul had encouraged the Roman Christians to "practice hospitality" (Rom. 12:13), and suggested that it be a criteria for elders of the church (I Tim. 3:2; Titus 1:8). Peter also advised Christians to "be hospitable to one another without complaint" (I Pet. 4:8,9). In the *Didache*, a collection of early Christian teachings, it is written, "Let everyone who comes in the name of the Lord be received. If he comes as a traveler, help him as much as you can" (*Didache* 12:1,2).[1] The Roman Emperor, Julian, is reported to have objected that the Christians' kindness toward strangers was a chief means of propagating their atheism. (Christians were often charged with "atheism" because they did not have a god who was identified with a particular temple, with a particular person, such as the emperor, or with a particular idol object.) The importance of Christian hospitality in the early church was based largely on the unavailability of acceptable lodging facilities. The inns that were available were notoriously immoral, akin to brothels. Loving hospitality to strangers became an identifying practice of Christians who wanted to maintain a holy expression of the character of Christ. Paul recommended persons for hospitable reception: Phoebe (Rom. 16:1,2), Timothy and Epaphroditus (Phil. 2:19-30, and sought such for himself (Philemon 22).

Either as incentive or explanation, Paul notes that through the practice of hospitality to strangers, "some have entertained angels unknowingly." Old Testament examples of receiving angelic messengers from God includes Abraham and Sarah's reception of three messengers (Gen. 18:1-15), the two angels who visited Lot in Sodom (Gen. 19:1-26), and the angel who came to Gideon (Judges 6:11-24). Jesus' comments to His disciples expands the concept of entertaining angels to entertaining the Lord Jesus Himself,

> "For I was hungry and you gave Me something to eat; I was thirsty, and you gave Me drink; I was a stranger, and you invited Me in; naked, and you clothed Me; I was sick, and you visited Me; I was in prison, and you came to Me.' The righteous will answer Him, saying, 'Lord, when did we see You hungry, and feed You, or thirsty, and give You drink? And when did we see You a stranger, and invite You in, or naked, and clothe You? And when did we see You sick or in prison and come to You?' And the King will answer and say to them, 'Truly, I say to you, to the extent that you did it to one of these brothers of Mine, even the least of them, you did it unto Me'." (Matt. 25:35-40)

In the hospitable reception and entertaining of strangers we are often unaware of what God is doing. God often ministers through the messengers, and many a host has declared that they received the greater blessing than the visitor.

In contemporary society there are an abundance of motels and hotels for lodging. Christians are often wary of strangers, protective of their personal privacy, and isolationistic about their homes. The legitimacy of Paul's admonition remains, however, for Christian love takes the risk to open our doors to our Christian brethren.

13:3 "Love of the brethren" will also "remember" or ***"Be mindful of the prisoners as having been bound together with them..."***. These prisoners (literally "bound ones") that Paul

refers to were probably fellow-Christians who were imprisoned for their faith. Paul had previously commended the
Hebrew Christians for "sharing sympathy to the prisoners"
(10:34), and is now encouraging them to continue this practical expression of holy love. The issue of remembering the
prisoners was particularly close to Paul's heart, for he was frequently imprisoned for his Christian faith, and may have been
imprisoned in Rome while he was writing this epistle.
"Remember my imprisonment" (Col. 4:18), he wrote to the
Colossians. Later in this chapter he will tell the Hebrew
Christians to "take notice that our brother Timothy has been
released" (13:23) from prison. Incarceration in Roman prisons
often involved harsh and brutal conditions of being chained
within dungeons and caverns. The meals provided were mea-
ger and not nutritional. Christian prisoners often depended on
their brethren for food, fellowship, and personal needs, even
though the guards often expected bribes to allow such visita-
tions.

Paul's exhortation to "remember" or "be mindful" of the
prisoners is not simply a call for cognitive recollection of cerebral memory, but is an admonishment to let love be put into
action in the expression of God's holy character for others.
This will include not only prayer, but also active visitation and
provision for needs. "What kind of faith is that," asked James,
"if a brother or sister is without clothing and in need of daily
food, and one of you says, 'Go in peace, be warmed and be
filled,' and yet you do not give them what is necessary for
their body, what use is that? Faith, if it has no works, is dead"
(James 2:14-17). Faith and love are never passive, but always
active!

Paul's rationale for his call to "remember the prisoners" is
"as having been bound together with them." Some have interpreted this as a hypothetical identification "*as if* you were fel-
low-prisoners" or "*as though* you were in prison with them." A
more meaningful interpretation is to recognize this as an actual

solidarity wherein Christians are bound together in Christ, and thus bound with one another in the unity of the Body of Christ. Such spiritual solidarity and oneness includes being bound together in hardship. To the Corinthians, Paul wrote, "If one member suffers, all the members suffer with it" (I Cor. 12:26). Jesus' words can again be quoted, "When I was in prison you came to Me... When did we see you in prison and come to You? ...To the extent that you did it to one of these brothers of Mine, even the least of them, you did it to Me." The union solidarity of every Christian with Christ and all other Christians seems to be the primary incentive of Paul's admonition.

Attaching another subordinate phrase to the imperative verb, Paul wrote, *"and* (be mindful of) *those being mistreated, as also yourselves being in the body."* Though most who were imprisoned were also ill-treated and often injured, this phrase does broaden the practical admonition to love all those who are abused, treated cruelly, persecuted with violence, etc.

Paul's explanation is again more than just a hypothetical identification, "as if you yourselves were in their body." Instead, the explanatory phrase, "as also yourselves being in the body," may refer to the shared vulnerability that all Christians have, liable and subject to such mistreatment as long as they remain in their physical bodies. Previously Paul had referred to the "defamation and tribulation" experienced by the Hebrew Christians, and how they "had become sharers with those being so treated" (10:33). The solidarity of suffering (I Cor. 12:26) that Christians experience with one another involves feeling the pain of another in a form of empathy that goes far beyond emotional identification, but becomes a genuine spiritual participation in the pathos of another. That is what Jesus did for us "in the body," when He partook of humanity, temptation, and death (cf. Heb. 2:14,17,18), participating in our human pathos of mistreatment to counter it all with His redemption. Jesus continues to participate and experience the mistreatment of mankind, for "inasmuch as you have done it unto the least of these, you have done it unto Me" (Matt. 25:40). Though some commentators have interpreted the word "body" in this phrase to refer to the Body of Christ (Col. 1:18,24), the context of physical mistreatment and suffering seems to indicate that Paul was referring to the physical body.

13:4 Practical expression of faithful marital love is another important expression of God's holy character. Whether Paul's inclusion of this particular area of practical Christian behavior was a reactive response to a problem of immortality in first century Hebrew society (as some have suggested), we do not know. Whatever his motivational intent, Paul makes a clear call for the honor and sanctity of marriage.

In the absence of a verb to dictate the action, some translators have made this into a statement, "Marriage (is) honorable in all" (KJV). The context of practical imperative exhortations (1,2,3,5,7,9) suggests that these phrases should also be understood in an imperative sense. "(Let) *marriage* (be held) *honorable in all.*" Jesus spoke concerning marriage,

> He who created them from the beginning 'made them male and female' (Gen. 1:27), and said, 'For this cause a man shall leave his father and mother, and shall cleave to his wife, and the two shall become one flesh' (Gen. 2:24). Consequently, they are no more two, but one flesh. What therefore God has joined together, let no man separate. (Matt. 19:4-6)

Early in church history there were some who disparaged marriage as an inferior state, prompting Paul to mention those false teachers who "forbid marriage…, which God has created to be gratefully shared in by those who believe and know the truth" (I Tim. 4:3). Some think that Paul himself had an adverse view of marriage also (cf. I Cor. 7:1-17). The new covenant scriptures do not exalt celibacy as a higher form of spirituality, either for church leaders or for Christians in general. "Let marriage be held honorable in all," Paul writes. The covenant union of one man and one woman (the only form of marriage union the Bible allows) is honorable and to be respected. Marriage is to be regarded as a precious (Greek word *timios* – cf. I Pet. 1:19; Rev. 18:12,16, 21) treasure, the highest and most glorious relationship between persons here on earth, and likened by analogy to the intimacy of union between Christ and the Christian (Eph. 5:23-33). Such a marriage relationship should be honorable "in all," states Paul, which can be interpreted as "in all respects," or "in all persons" or "among everyone," all of which are legitimate.

Paul continues the theme of marriage in another phrase that has no verb, but should probably also be translated as an imperative, *"and* (let) *the* (marriage) *bed* (be) *undefiled...".* The "marriage bed" is a euphemism for sexual activity (Rom. 13:13) that may lead to conception (Rom. 9:10). The Greek word is *koite* from which we get the English word "coitus" meaning "sexual intercourse." The bible is very explicit about human sexuality, and has more references to sex than to prayer. God created human beings "male and female" (Gen. 1:27). The Latin word *sexus*, the origin of the English word "sex," meant "to divide" between male and female. The sexual expression of husband and wife in marriage is in accord with God's creative intent. One entire book of the bible, the *Song of Solomon*, deals with the theme of sexual expression in marriage.

Only as God's holy character of unity, purity, and fidelity is expressed in the marriage act of sexual intercourse is the sanctity, honor, and preciousness of God's intent for marriage preserved. Otherwise, marital sexual expression is defiled (cf. Gen. 49:4; 35:22) or contaminated, which is what Paul goes on to warn his readers about. How can the sexual intimacy of marriage be defiled? On a physical level, the sexuality of marriage can be defiled by "being joined" (cf. I Cor. 6:16) in sexual relations with another person other than one's husband or wife, which is the reason Paul goes on to address the infidelity, immorality, and adultery that God will judge. Defilement of the sexual act might also occur on a psychological level. Paul explained to Titus, "To the pure all things are pure; but to those who are defiled and unbelieving, nothing is pure, but both their minds and their consciences are defiled" (Titus 1:15). The "marriage bed" can be defiled by selfishness that fails to express love for the other person without thought of self-concern. The sexual expression of husband and wife can be defiled by deep-seated bitterness and resentment that wrongfully uses sexual intercourse as a bargaining chip, a means of manipulation, a method of bribery, or a form of punishment. The "act of marriage" can be defiled when marriage partners fail to focus on one another in love, and are fantasizing or visualizing impure involvement with someone else. Marital sexual activity can be defiled when the emphasis is placed on quantity or frequency, procedures or positions, rather than on the quality of love expression between husband and wife.

In consequence of the defilement of the purity of marital sexuality, Paul explains, *"but sexually immoral persons and adulterers God will judge."* The word Paul used for "sexually immoral persons" is the Greek word *pornous* from which we get the English prefix and subsequent noun "porn" (as in "pornography" or "porn star"). Although the word has often been translated as "fornicators," and applied to those who engaged in premarital sexual activity, more recent linguistic scholarship has recognized that the word includes all sexual activity outside of the loving context of marriage that God intended. "Sexually immoral persons" is thus the better English translation (cf. I Cor. 5:1; 6:18; Eph. 5:5; I Tim. 1:10). The word "adulterers" refers to those who are unfaithful to their vows of marriage in sexual infidelity, and serves as a synonymous parallel to "sexually immoral persons" in this context. The seventh commandment stated explicitly, "You shall not commit adultery" (Exod. 20:14; Deut. 5:18), and was based on the recognition of the faithful character of God that was to be exhibited in the behavior of His people. Violation of God's character of faithfulness in the act of adultery merited the extreme punitive judgment of death in the old covenant (Lev. 20:10; Deut. 22:20-23). In the new covenant there are still consequences, both present and future, for violating God's character of holiness, and for failing to be receptive in faith to God's character of fidelity and purity. The difference in the new covenant judgment of God is that God has determined all things in reference to man's believing reception of Jesus Christ in faith (cf. 12:23). When Christians are receptive to Christ's manifestation of His character of love and purity and fidelity in their marriages, they will not defile the beauty of God-ordained marriage in sexual immorality and adultery, and God's judgment will be, "Well done, good and faithful servant" (Matt. 25:21,23).

13:5 Perhaps Paul's mind flowed in typical Hebrew fashion from the seventh commandment, "You shall not commit adultery," to the eighth commandment, "You shall not steal," or the tenth commandment, "You shall not covet." Whatever his train of thought, Paul follows his admonitions for brotherly love toward strangers, prisoners, and the mistreated, and his exhortation to the honor of a faithful and loving marriage, with a call to resist the "love of money" and materialistic greed. The imperative verb must again be supplied, *"(Let your) manner of life (have) no love of money, being content with the things being present...".* The manner and means of conducting your life (Greek *tropos*, origin of English word "trope") should not be characterized by greed and avarice for the acquisition and accumulation of money. Money is not an evil in itself, for it is but a medium of exchange, serving as legal tender for the purchase of items or payment for services rendered. But when a person develops an inordinate desire and concern for money

and the material things it can buy, such personal aspiration (cf.
I John 2:16) can become a selfish greed that amounts to idolatry (cf. Col. 3:5). In the Sermon on the Mount, Jesus said,

> Do not lay up for yourselves treasures upon earth, where moth and rust
> destroy, and where thieves break in and steal. But lay up for yourselves
> treasures in heaven, where neither moth nor rust destroys, and where
> thieves do not break in and steal. ... No one can serve two masters, for
> either he will hate the one and love the other, or he will hold to the
> one, and despise the other. You cannot serve God and mammon (rich-
> es). (Matt. 6:20-24)

Luke's gospel adds that the Pharisees scoffed at Jesus when
He spoke those words, because they were "lovers of money"
(Lk. 16:14). When Paul wrote to Timothy, he addressed this
same theme,

> If we have food and covering, with these we should be content. But
> those who want to get rich fall into temptation and a snare and many
> foolish and harmful desires which plunge men into ruin and destruc-
> tion. For the love of money is a root of all sorts of evil, and some by
> longing for it have wandered away from the faith, and pierced them-
> selves with many a pang. (I Tim. 6:8-10)

Paul also advised that the elders of the church should be "free
from the love of money" (I Tim. 3:3), and warned that "in the
last days...men will be lovers of self and lovers of money" (II
Tim. 3:2). When the focus of a person's life is on the acquisition of money and material things, there will be an inevitable
discontent. How much is enough? "Just a little more than I
presently have," was the response of John D. Rockefeller. The
materialist is never content with what he has.

Paul warned the Jerusalem Christians to avoid coveting
and to be content with their present resources. F.F. Bruce
wrote, "The greedy man can never be a happy man; but the
opposite of covetousness is contentment."[2] Contentment and
satisfaction with the sufficiency of what we have is not neces-

sarily a resignation to the status quo. Paul is dealing with the issue of inordinate focus and improper priority toward material things that allows them to become an idolatrous pursuit that can never produce contentment. To the Philippians, Paul wrote, "I do not speak from want; for I have learned to be *content* in whatever situation I am" (Phil. 4:11). To Timothy he advised, "Godliness is a means of great gain, when accompanied by *contentment*. For we have brought nothing into the world, so we cannot take anything out of it either. And if we have food and covering, with these we should be *content*" (I Tim. 6:6-8). Failure to find contentment in what God has provided, and seeking to find security in material things, leads only to anxiety. Trust in wealth evidences distrust in God's care and provision.

The security of trusting in God's ever-present provision is what Paul proceeds to document, explaining, **"for He has said, 'I WILL NEVER ABANDON YOU, NOR WILL I EVER FORSAKE YOU'…".** This was a particularly important reminder to the Hebrew Christians in Jerusalem, for God's promise of provisional care was constantly reiterated throughout the old covenant literature. Moses' final counsel to the people of God was, "The Lord your God is the One Who goes with you. He will not fail you or forsake you" (Deut. 31:6,8). When Joshua assumed leadership after Moses, God said, "Just as I have been with Moses, I will be with you; I will not fail you or forsake you" (Josh. 1:5). The Jewish Christians in Jerusalem needed to remember God's promise of His unfailing presence and provision. Jesus had reiterated the promise that God would take care of every need, saying,

> Do not be anxious for your life, as to what you shall eat, or what you shall drink; nor for your body, as to what you shall put on. …Your heavenly Father knows that you need all these things. Seek first His kingdom and His righteousness, and all these things shall be added to you. (Matt. 6:25-33)

In his letter to Timothy, Paul had advised, "Instruct those who are rich in this present world, not to be conceited or to fix their hope on the uncertainty or riches, but on God who richly supplies us with all things to enjoy" (I Tim. 6:17). The "riches of His grace" (Eph. 1:7; 2:7) are sufficient, and we need not fear that He will abandon or forsake us, even if the bottom drops out of the economic system that our society operates by and relies on.

It should be noted that this verse, with its citation of the Old Testament promise of God, has often been wrested from its context and used as a proof-text to bolster a particular theological system of salvation security, i.e., the doctrine of eternal security. This is entirely illegitimate, for the text within its context deals with the security and contentment of God's provision of necessary physical and material provisions, and not with the permanency or security of a static concept of salvation.

13:6   As a consequence of God's promise of adequate provision, the Christian can respond in faith. *"So that we may confidently say, 'THE LORD IS MY HELPER, I WILL NOT BE AFRAID. WHAT SHALL MAN DO TO ME?'"* The quotation Paul uses is likely from the Passover Psalm 118, "The Lord is for me; I will not fear. What can man do to me?" (Ps. 118:6). It is similar to another, "In God I have put my trust, I shall not be afraid. What can man do to me?" (Ps. 56:11). When our trust and confidence is in God, we need not fear the outward circumstances (economical or otherwise), or what men might do to us by way of deprivation, injustice, litigation, etc. All such circumstances of economic decline, lowered standard of living, job loss, theft, unfair laws, or litigated deprivation, are of no consequence when considered in reference to the eternal life that the Christian has in Jesus Christ (cf. Matt. 10:28-33). If we are tempted to be fearful, we need only remember that the antidote to fear is faith (cf. Matt. 14:27;

Mk. 5:36; Lk. 8:50). "If God is for us, who (of any consequence) can be against us?" (Rom. 8:31).

Some have objected to the idea of viewing God as our
"Helper." Humanistic concepts such as "God helps those who
help themselves," and "Do your best, and God will help you
do the rest," have polluted the proper biblical concept of God
as Helper. There is no hint here of God's assisting our performance and works to meet His expectations by some form of
"infused grace" booster-shot. On the other hand, the recognition of God as Helper by His grace maintains the necessary
distinction of God and man that avoids a pantheistic overem-
phasis on immanence and oneness.

13:7 The second paragraph (7-17) of this final section of the
epistle begins and ends with references to the leaders of the
church fellowship in Jerusalem (7,17). In between these leadership references Paul reverts to his theological mindset to differentiate the old covenant and new covenant realities again
(10-14).

With another imperative admonition, Paul writes,
***"Remember those leading you, who have spoken the word of
God to you..."***. Many commentators assume that Paul is referring to leaders of the church who had previously died, which
would include James, the brother of the Lord, who had been
the leader of the Jerusalem church (Acts 12:17; 21:18; Gal.
1:19; 2:12), and had been stoned to death. There is no com-
pelling reason, however, to regard these leaders in the historical past. Paul exhorts the Jerusalem Christians to remember
"those leading you," using a present participle. "Those leading
you" (the same present leaders referred to in 17 and 24) are
those who "have spoken the word of God to you." The aorist
tense "have spoken" indicates previous teaching, preaching,
and proclamation by the present leaders. These leaders are
identified quite generally (cf. Lk. 22:26; Acts 15:22), without
any allusion to a particular title, position, or office in the

church. They may, or may not, have been elders who engaged in teaching and preaching (I Tim. 5:17). The content of their verbal sharing was "the word of God." This was not just Bible information, but must be understood Christologically. The gospel message of salvation (cf. 2:3) is not a collection of static information to be assented to as a belief-system, but is the sharing of the dynamic life of Jesus Christ, Who as the risen Lord functions continually as Savior and Lord in Christians.

Being mindful of the present leaders was for the purpose of *"observing the outcome of their conduct,"* and subsequently to *"imitate their faith."* Although elders are exhorted to be "examples to the flock" (I Pet. 5:3), Paul is not simply encouraging the Jerusalem Christians to imitate the exemplary behavior of their leaders. He advises the Hebrew Christians to observe, behold, or examine the outcome or "out-walking" of the conduct (cf. 13:18) and behavior of their leaders. Such observation should allow them to perceive and discern that the "walking out" of the leaders' behavior was the manifestation of the life of Jesus Christ, as they were receptive to the activity of the living Lord Jesus in them. The command to "imitate their faith," was not a call to emulate the behavioral example of the leaders. Christians are not called to mimic the external actions of others, not even the behavioral activity of Jesus Himself, by attempting to be "like Jesus" or to question, "What would Jesus do?" The Christian life is not an imitation, but the manifestation of the life of the living Lord Jesus (II Cor. 4:10,11). Paul's exhortation to "imitate the faith" of the leaders is not a call to reproduce their behavior, but to function in like manner as the leaders were functioning (cf. 6:12), by the faith-receptivity of the activity of Christ Himself. The imperative is to "imitate their faith," not their behavior!

13:8 Having instructed the Jerusalem Christians to function by the same faith as their leaders, allowing for the receptivity of the activity of the life of Jesus Christ in them, Paul proceeds to write, *"**Jesus Christ** (is) **the same yesterday, and today, and forever."** There is a constancy and consistency of divine character whenever Jesus Christ manifests Himself, whether in His historical ministry on earth or in the lives of prior saints in the past, in present manifestation of Christian behavior, or "unto the ages." The past, present, and future expression of Christ's life will evidence the absolute and timeless character of God. This does not mean that there will be an identical behavior expression in every Christian, but the character of Christ exemplified in the "fruit of the Spirit" (Gal. 5:22,23) will be consistent when the life of Christ is lived out uniquely in each Christian.

An alternative interpretation suggested by some commentators is that human leaders come and go, and their conduct may vary, even in the expression of failures, misrepresentations, and sin, but Jesus Christ is the ultimate and supreme leader of the church, Who will always be present, yesterday, today, and forever, and will never fail. Another interpretation regards this verse as a statement of the unchangeableness of the gospel message, the fixed doctrine and theology of Christology, the "word of God" spoke by the leaders (7), which must not be varied, for it is "the same yesterday, today, and forever." Those seeking to justify charismatic manifestations have misused this verse in their attempt to explain that Jesus functions in the same way, "yesterday, today, and forever," in the performing of miracles, healings, and speaking in tongues.

Perhaps the greatest misuse of these words has been when they are extracted from their context and made a proof-text for the doctrine of God's immutability or changelessness. God does declare to Malachi, "I, the Lord, do not change" (Mal. 3:6), and this is in the context of His response to sinful oppression. Earlier in this epistle to the Hebrews, Paul quoted the Psalmist, "Thou art the same" (Heb. 1:12; Ps. 102:27). There is truth in the recognition that God is not capricious and fickle.

His character never changes. But we must not assume that
God's *modus operandi* never changes. Some theologians seem
to think that they have God and His ways of action figured
out, despite the fact that "His ways are past finding out" (Rom.
11:33). This is particularly evident in Reformed theological
thought, as they stress a restrictive continuity of God's
immutable action. Attempting to fit God into man-made patterns of how He has acted and must continue to act is a pre-
scriptive form of handcuffing God, tying His hands, and putting Him into a performance straightjacket. It is an attempt to
put God in an ideological box wherein He must act with a static and identical mode of operation throughout all historical
time. God cannot be thus restricted. God's mode of action
changed from the old covenant to the new covenant, when the
actuating incentive changed from law to grace. The scripture
narrative indicates that God changed His mind; He "repented"
(Gen. 6:6; I Sam. 15:35; Amos 7:3,6; Jonah 3:10). God's character never changes, but His actions are unlimited in scope and
variance as they remain consistent with His character and
over-all purposes. God always *does* what He *does* because He
is Who He *is*.

Paul was not advocating a doctrine of immutably prescribed divine action when He wrote, "Jesus Christ is the same
yesterday, and today, and forever." Having mentioned the
Christocentric proclamation of the "word of God" (7a), and the
conduct of the out-lived manifestation of the life of Jesus in
the leaders, and the faith that is the receptivity of Christ's
activity, Paul logically asserts the constancy and consistency of
Christ's character in all of His manifestations, past, present,
and future.

13:9   With another imperative verb, Paul urges the Jerusalem
Christians, ***"Do not be carried away by various and strange
teachings, for*** (it is) ***good to be sustained by grace, not by
foods, by which those walking have not been benefitted."***

Whether Paul was intending to contrast "various and strange teachings" with the "word of God spoken by the leaders" (7) is questionable. There is no doubt, though, that Paul remained concerned about the steadfastness of the Hebrew Christians in Jerusalem, concerned that they might "drift away" (2:1), "fall away" (3:12), "come short" (4:1), and "throw away their confidence" (10:35) by an apostatizing reversion to Judaism. Paul had urged a maturity for the Ephesian Christians to avoid being "*carried away* by every wind of doctrine, by the trickery of men, by craftiness in deceitful scheming" (Eph. 4:14). Here, he uses the same word to exhort the Jerusalem Christian "not to be *carried away* by varied, divergent, strange teachings which are alien to new covenant teaching." In this context it is not novelty that marks these teachings, but the attached traditions of Judaism concerning various food laws. Paul did not want the Christians in Jerusalem to revert back to putting their faith in, and seeking God's blessing through, the Judaic teachings about food. They were, no doubt, being pressured by their Hebrew kinsmen to keep all the ceremonial and customary food laws of Judaism. The rabbinic interpretations were many and varied concerning what was or was not permissible or kosher. Jewish religion had always focused on food, with strict dietary regulations (cf. Lev. 11), and food being central to their festivities. How they prepared and ate their food was regarded as having value in their relationship with God.

The Psalmist wrote, "Wine makes man's heart glad,...and food sustains man's heart" (Ps. 104:15). This verse had become a standard statement of blessing before every Jewish meal. Jewish people ate and drank to make them happy and to praise God. Paul responds by writing, "It is good for the heart to be sustained by grace, not by foods...". He is countering the inordinate emphasis that Judaism placed on food by noting that such teachings are alien to the new covenant understanding of God's grace. Previously in the epistle, Paul had mentioned "food and drink and various washings, regulations for the body until a time of reformation" (9:10), emphasizing the temporary and preliminary nature of all Jewish food regulations. In a very different context Paul had issued a general statement, "The kingdom of God is not eating and drinking, but righteousness and peace and joy in the Holy Spirit" (Rom. 14:17). Similarly, he had written, "Food will not commend us to God; we are neither the worse if we do not eat, nor the better if we do eat" (I Cor. 8:8). Under very different circumstances, but with correlative instruction, Paul wrote,

> Therefore, let no one act as your judge in regard to food or drink, …things which are a shadow…; but the substance belongs to Christ. …If you have died with Christ, …why do you submit to decrees, such as, "Do not handle, do not taste, do not touch?" …These are matters which have, to be sure, the appearance of wisdom in self-made religion and self-abasement and severe treatment of the body, but are of no value against fleshly indulgence. (Col. 2:16-23)

Though the historical contexts differ, Paul was consistent in his insistence that the externalities of religious food laws were of no spiritual benefit for new covenant Christians. That Paul's comment here in the epistle to the Hebrew Christians is contra Judaic food laws (rather than eucharistic abuses or Gentile dietary regulations as some have suggested) seems to be verified by *The Epistle of Ignatius to the Magnesians* written late in the first century or early in the second century, which seems to provide an interpretation of this verse,

> Be not deceived with strange teachings, nor with old fables, which are unprofitable. If we go on observing Judaism, we acknowledge that we never received grace.[3]

Foods may enervate and provide energy to the "outer man," to the physical body of man, but they do not have spiritual benefit. It serves God's good purposes, Paul explains, "for the heart" of man, the "inner man" (II Cor. 4:16), the spirit and soul of a person, to be sustained, strengthened, and supported by the grace of God. God's grace is the divine dynamic of His activity through Jesus Christ, for "grace and truth were realized through Jesus Christ" (John 1:17). In the new covenant the heart of the Christian is sustained by the Christic grace of God, and "renewed day by day" (II Cor. 4:16).

To further dissuade the Jerusalem Christians from going back to the external legalism of the Jewish food laws, Paul explains that those "walking," following the Jewish course of action, and conducting their lives by the Jewish meal customs, have not been benefitted or profited in their relationship with God by so doing. Just as "the word the Israelites heard did not profit them" (4:2), neither did their meticulous dietary concerns. "It is the Spirit Who gives life; the flesh profits nothing" (John 6:63), Jesus said. Paul wanted the Christians in Jerusalem to understand that there was no benefit before God in reverting to the varied Jewish customs and traditions concerning food. Gladness and joy are not found in food, but in Jesus. The heart of a Christian is not sustained by food, but by the grace of God in Jesus Christ.

13:10 Despite Paul's pastoral concerns for practical expressions of the Christian life, his mental orientation was theological. In verses 10-13 he reverts to the foundational contrast between the old covenant and the new covenant, between Judaism and the Christian faith, the theme that he has been emphasizing to the Hebrew Christians of Jerusalem throughout this epistle. The connective link of thought was the mention of the Jewish food laws in verse 9. From the idea of 'foods" (9), Paul proceeds to address that which Christians "eat" that those associated with Judaism cannot "eat."

"We have an altar, from which those serving the tent do not have authority to eat." Notice the contrast: *"We* have ... *they* do not have." Paul has repeatedly emphasized the "better things" that "we have" as Christians. *"We have* hope as an anchor for the soul" (6:19). *"We have* a high priest Who has

passed through the heavens" (4:14), Who is "seated with the Majesty in the heavens" (8:1), and Who allows us to draw near to God (10:19-22). Now Paul asserts, *"we have* an altar...". Jewish religion had a sacrificial altar in their worship center of the tabernacle and the temple. What does Paul mean in declaring that Christians have an altar? Early Christians were charged with being "atheists" and not having a "real religion" because they did not have visible, tangible, material sacred sites or objects – no temples, altars, idols, or priests. Paul's statement, "We have an altar," must obviously be interpreted figuratively, for the early Christians did not have a physical structure of an altar made of wood or stones. This would also preclude any reference in this text to a Eucharistic altar of the Lord's Supper table, or an altar rail at the front of the sanctuary or auditorium. Historically, the cross is where Jesus made the sacrificial offering of His own life for mankind. Based on that historical sacrifice, Paul has argued that we have direct and immediate access into the heavenly sanctuary of the Holy of Holies of God's presence (9:24; 10:19-21) where the living Lord Jesus serves as High Priest. The Christian altar, then, is best understood metaphorically as the spiritual altar in the heavenly sanctuary of God's presence, where Christians are "seated in the heavenlies" with Christ (Eph. 1:20; 2:6), offering up "sacrifices of praise to God" (15), while being "sustained by grace" (9).

From such a heavenly altar, "those serving the tent have no authority to eat." Those "serving the tent," the old covenant worship place of tabernacle and temple, includes not only the Judaic priests, but by extension all Jewish participants who sought to worship God in that place via the cultic rituals of that religion. Thinking that they were sustained in their relationship with God by food laws, they have no right to partake from the heavenly altar where Christians are "sustained by grace" (9), having partaken of Jesus Christ. The Jews were aghast when Jesus said,

Unless you eat the flesh of the Son of Man, and drink His blood, you
have no life in yourselves. He who eats My flesh and drinks My blood
has eternal life; and I will raise him up on the last day. For My flesh is
true food, and My blood is true drink. He who eats My flesh and
drinks My blood abides in Me, and I in him. (John 6:53-56)

With their meticulous food regulations and literalistic
legalisms, the Jews would never consider eating human flesh
or blood, but they failed to recognize that Jesus was speaking
figuratively of partaking of Himself. Likewise, Paul speaks
figuratively when he refers to Christians having "tasted the
good word of God" (6:5), and of Jewish adherents having no
right to "eat" from the heavenly altar. Judaic participants, who
still placed their faith in Jewish food laws, instead of Jesus
Christ alone, could not partake ("eat") and be "sustained by
the grace" of God in Jesus Christ at the heavenly altar. Those
who persisted in the "shadows" (cf. Col. 2:17; Heb. 8:5; 10:1)
of old covenant rituals were precluded from participation in
the new covenant substance and spiritual reality of Jesus
Christ. To the Corinthians, Paul wrote, "Those who eat the
sacrifices are sharers in the altar" (I Cor. 10:18), indicating
that participation involves identification. In this letter Paul is
advising the Hebrew Christians of Jerusalem that participation
in Jewish practices identifies them with the Jewish altar rather
than the heavenly Christian altar, where Christians partake of
Christ and are "sustained by grace." There is a complete
antithesis between the two, an either/or dichotomy that allows
no merging or mixing of Judaism and Christianity. Paul was
warning the Jerusalem Christians that to revert and seek solace
or security in the Jewish practices of worship or food regulations was to forfeit Christian identification and participation in
the new covenant relationship with God in Christ. The truism,
"What you take, takes you," is valid nutritionally and in spiritual metaphor.

13:11 Paul returns again to the parallels and contrasts of Christ's sacrifice with the sacrifices that were made on the Day of Atonement in Judaism. *"For the bodies of those living animals whose blood is brought into the holy place by the high priests concerning sin, those are burned outside the camp."* Every Hebrew person was thoroughly indoctrinated with the details of what transpired on the Day of Atonement. Drawing from Leviticus 16:1-28, Paul summarizes how the blood of a bull and a goat (not the scapegoat) were placed on the altar in the Holy of Holies of the tabernacle or temple as a sin-offering for the priest and the Israelite people. These annual animal sacrifices signified the covering of the people's sins for the year. The carcasses of these animals were afterwards taken "outside the camp" (Lev. 16:27) and burned. They were not allowed to be eaten, as were some of the other Jewish sacrifices. The regulations for the disposal of the carcasses of these sacrificed animals "outside the camp" illustrated the traditional practice of removing things and people regarded to be impure, unclean, polluted, profane, sinful or unacceptable outside of the boundaries of the camp or city where God's people lived and worshipped. The Day of Atonement was still being enacted at the temple in Jerusalem when Paul wrote this letter. Note that he uses present tense verbs: "the blood of those animals *is brought* into the holy place," and "the bodies *are burned* outside the camp." In the practice of first century Judaism, the bodies of the sin-offering animals were taken outside of the gates and walls of the city of Jerusalem to be burned on the Day of Atonement.

13:12 Comparing the old covenant animal sacrifices with the new covenant atoning sacrifice of Jesus Christ, Paul explains, *"Therefore Jesus also, in order that He might sanctify the people through His own blood, suffered outside the gate."* The death of Jesus on the cross was the once and for all sacrifice that removed sin permanently for the people of faith, and

454

set them apart unto God's holy purposes. "Through His own blood" (cf. 9:12,14,22), signifying the sacrificial death that Jesus suffered (cf. 2:10; 9:26) on the cross, Jesus fulfilled the type of the High Priest (7:27; 8:1-3; 9:11-15,24-26; 10:9-11), making His sin-offering of His own life in the Holy of Holies of God's heavenly presence. In so doing, He "sanctified the people" (cf. 10:10,14), setting them apart for direct and intimate access to the Holy God, that He might indwell them and make them "holy ones" (Rom. 1:7; I Cor. 1:2; Eph. 1:1; 4:12; Heb. 6:10) who would express His holy character behaviorally within His creation. In his letter to Titus, Paul wrote, "Christ Jesus...gave Himself for us...that He might...purify for Himself a people for His own possession, zealous for good deeds" (Titus 2:14).

There is both parallelism and contrast as Paul compares the animal sacrifices of the old covenant with the sacrificial death of Jesus Christ. As the High Priest and the sin-offering, Jesus fulfills the prefiguring prototype of the old covenant atonement sacrifices, providing a connective association and junction of the new with the old. At the same time, His execution by crucifixion "outside the gate" of the city reveals a fracturing of the old covenant prototypical picture, creating a disconnection, disassociation, and disjuncture with Judaism.

Jesus "suffered" death on the cross, "despising the shame" (12:2) of being crucified as a common criminal "outside the gate" of the city of Jerusalem. Golgotha, "the place of the skull" (Matt. 27:33; Mk. 15:22; Lk. 23:33; John 19:17), was "near the city" (John 19:20) of Jerusalem, but "outside the gate." The Jewish leaders regarded Jesus as profane and contrary to all their Messianic expectations. They wanted Him removed, expelled, cast out – killed in a most unacceptable manner, by crucifixion, regarded as a "curse" (Gal. 3:13). His execution on a cross "outside the gate" of their sacrosanct temple and city represented their attempt to get rid of the carcass of the troublesome Jesus. In the process of their rejection and repudiation of Jesus, and the facilitation of His death in consort with the Romans, there was enacted a complete rupture and dichotomy with Judaism. In the same events of Jesus' death there was both a fulfillment of old covenant prefiguring as well as a complete fracturing that forever separated Judaism and Christianity.

13:13 *"So then,"* as a consequence of Jesus' suffering "outside the gate" (12), *"let us go out towards Him outside the camp, bearing His reproach."* Paul calls on the Jerusalem Christians to act in identification with Jesus and to go where He is "outside the camp." Jesus is obviously "outside the camp" of Judaism, the religion of unbelieving Israel, so Paul is encouraging the Hebrew Christians of Jerusalem to make a clean break from the Judaic religion, disassociating with the religious culture and practices that they were being pressured to adopt. This has been a major thrust of his counsel to the Jerusalem Christians throughout this epistle. But there may be more import in the advice that Paul gives to his readers. The call to "go outside the camp" is certainly [1] an urging to go outside the strictures of Judaism with all its prefiguring shadows and legalistic regulations, and to seek the new covenant substance of Jesus Christ Himself, being "sustained by grace" (9). By extension [2], this could be understood as an admonition to "go outside the camp" of all religion which binds people in devotion and ritual. Another alternative interpretation [3] is that Paul is advising them to "go outside of the camp" of earthly attachments of the here and now (14), such as food (9) and money (5) and the security of physical families; to "go out of the camp" as Abraham went out (11:8), seeking the intangible unknown of the heavenly altar (10). This should not be construed, however, as escapism or withdrawal from the world, for Jesus made it clear that Christians are "in the world" (John 17:11,18), but "not of the world" (John 17:14,16). There may be [4] a somewhat cryptic or prophetic encouragement that Paul is delivering to the Christians of Jerusalem, advising them to "go outside the camp" of the city of Jerusalem. Sensing that the old covenant and everything associated with it was "near to disappearing" (8:13), and knowing that the Jewish resistance movement was no match for the powerful and ruthless Roman army, Paul might have subtly indicated that the Christians in Jerusalem should "get out of town." This interpretation has textual validity since "outside the camp" (11) meant "outside the city gates" (12) in the Jewish practice of the first century, and Paul proceeds immediately to indicate that Christians do not have a lasting, abiding, geographical city (14). All of these interpretations, the theological, religious, sociological, and geographical, may have some validity, but they must be understood in correlation with Paul's contextual words that to "go outside the camp" is to "go towards Jesus," bearing His reproach."

It has been noted that when the old covenant people of God rejected God in the golden calf incident (Exod. 32:1-20), Moses called the people out of the camp (Exod. 32:26) and pitched the tabernacled presence of God "outside of the camp". "Everyone who sought the Lord would go out to the tent of meeting which was outside the camp" (Exod. 33:7). In like manner, the Jewish people had rejected God's Messiah, Jesus Christ, and Paul may have been indicating that God's presence was no longer in the camp of Judaism and in the city of Jerusalem, but "outside the camp," to be approached through Jesus alone at the heavenly altar (10). To choose to stay inside the Judaic religion with its temple altar and legalistic ritual, and to choose earthly attachments of family and heritage inside the city of Jerusalem, would be to lose everything, spiritually and physically. To go "outside the camp" where Jesus went to His death (John 19:20), and where Jesus continues to be in His heavenly ministry, was to participate in the heavenly realities of Christ's high priesthood in the presence of God at the heavenly altar (10) in the heavenly Jerusalem

(12:22) where Christians rest (4:1-11) in their sanctification (2:11; 10:10,14; 12:14) and are "sustained by grace" (9).

To do so, however, would involve the identification of "bearing His reproach." As Jesus was condemned to an accursed death (Deut. 21:23; Gal. 3:13) of disgrace (12:2) outside of the city (John 19:20), in correspondence with Jewish contempt for the carcasses of sacrificial animals (11), so the Jerusalem Christians were to follow Him out of the camp of Judaism and religion, and out of the doomed city of Jerusalem (Matt. 24:2), willing to "bear His reproach." The Hebrew Christians in Jerusalem had already borne His reproach in ostracism, persecution, denunciation, and humiliation (10:33). But if they were to denounce Judaism entirely and leave Jerusalem at this very time when they were being solicited to fight the Romans, they would not doubt "bear His reproach" in increasing contempt and hostility, suffering reviling defamation and the alienating stigma of being cowardly traitors who were repudiating their heritage and religion. The price of being "sustained by grace" (9) is to suffer the disgrace of religious repudiation and contempt. Jesus made the cost clear when He said,

> If anyone wishes to come after Me, let him deny himself, and take up his cross, and follow Me. For whoever wishes to save his life shall lose it; and whoever loses his life for My sake and the gospel's shall save it. For what does it profit a man to gain the whole world, and forfeit his soul? For what shall a man give in exchange for his soul? For whoever is ashamed of Me and My words in this adulterous and sinful generation, the Son of Man will also be ashamed of him when he comes in the glory of His Father. (Mk. 8:34-38; cf. Lk. 14:27)

Jesus also forewarned, "In this world you will have tribulation" (John 16:33). "You will be hated by all on account of My name" (Matt. 10:16-42).

13:14 To provide the rationale and motivation for "going out-side the camp" of Judaism and Jerusalem, Paul continues, *"For here we do not have an abiding city, but we seek that which is coming."* "Here," in this world on earth, we, as new covenant Christians, do not have an abiding, enduring, lasting city in which we might settle down and make our abode, and practice Christian religion. Many religions have sacred cities with permanent precincts and tangible temples for religious rituals. The sacred city of Judaism was Jerusalem where the recipients of this letter resided, and where they were tempted to adapt to the Jewish religious regulations and rituals. Paul is advising them not to put their trust in physical Jerusalem, and everything associated with it. Even Jerusalem, representing the whole of Judaism, was not a permanent city, for it was doomed (Matt. 24:2) to be destroyed in a few years, in A.D. 70.

Christians do not have a temporal, tangible, geographical city to settle down and make their abode in. Rather, Paul explains, "We seek that (city) which is coming." This is not necessarily a reference to a future residence that is yet to come. Paul does not use a future tense verb, "will come," but a present participle, "is coming," which indicates that this is in the process of being realized. The dialectic of "already" and "not yet" must be maintained. In the progressive pilgrimage of the Christian life, we seek, as Abraham sought (11:14), a "heavenly country" (11:16), a "fatherland" (11:14), "the city whose architect and builder is God" (11:10). This "age to come" (6:5) has already been inaugurated and realized for Christians who "have come...to the city of the living God, the heavenly Jerusalem" (12:22), and "are receiving an unshake-able kingdom" (12:28). Christians recognize that their "citizen-ship is in heaven" (Phil. 3:20) *already* as they await the com-plete fulfillment of the promise of the "holy city, Jerusalem, which is coming down out of heaven from God" (Rev. 22:10-27; cf. 21:2) and *not yet* realized in full.

459

The spiritual and heavenly intangibility of Christianity is often difficult for Christians who still exist in the space/time context of this world, and tend to think in more concrete spatial and temporal terms. The church of Jesus Christ is a spiritual society "called out" to live and worship in a transcendent heavenly city. The sacred space and place (cf. Jn. 14:2) where the Christian lives is in the Holy Place of God's presence, "near to the heart of God." This is the permanent *polis* of eternal security, which the Jerusalem Christians would never find by reverting to participation in the religious practices of Jewish Jerusalem.

13:15 Having gone "outside the camp" (13), seeking all that is coming (14), ***"Through Him then, let us offer through all things a sacrifice of praise to God, that is, the fruit of lips confessing His name."*** Advising the Jerusalem Christians to "go outside of the camp" of Judaism and "towards Jesus" (13), "through Him then" they are challenged to offer continuously, unceasingly, and in all circumstances "a sacrifice of praise to God." It is not through the old covenant sacrifices of the Jewish priests at the temple that they are to offer their praise to God. Neither is praise offered only in gratitude for the sacrificial death of Jesus on the cross. Rather, through the living Lord Jesus, on the basis of the dynamic of His resurrected life, Christians offer their sacrifice of praise to God. Every manifestation of the Christian life is "through Him," for the behavior and worship of the Christian life is the living Jesus in action. Jesus is the pray-er, the worshipper, the Christian life.

Historically, Jesus offered His own life as the once and for all (9:26,28; 10:10) death sacrifice for the sins of the human race, acting as High Priest in the Holy of Holies of God's presence, that we might have access to God (10:19,20) in the holy place. It is there that "we have an altar" (10) with unlimited opportunity (not just annually on the Day of Atonement) to offer to God an acceptable and well-pleasing service of worship (12:28). Christian sacrifice is not the sacrifice of animals, but the presentation of praise to God in adulation and adoration of His person and work. This should never be reversed in such a way that praise to God becomes a "law" or a "force" that causes God to act, as if a so-called "power of praise" could become a mantra that leverages God's action. Christian sacrifice is an availability to be the useful vessels through which God is praised. Writing to the Romans, Paul urged the brethren "by the mercies of God, to present their bodies as a living and holy *sacrifice, well-pleasing* to God, as their *spiritual service of worship*" (Romans 12:1). Peter explained that Christians collectively are "living stones, being built up as a spiritual house for a holy priesthood, to offer up spiritual *sacrifices well-pleasing* to God *through Jesus Christ*" (I Pet. 2:5).

Paul provides an interpretive comment to explain "a sacrifice of praise to God," "that is, the fruit of lips confessing to His name." The phrase "fruit of our lips" is used in Isa. 57:19 and Hosea 14:2 (*LXX*). It is a figurative expression that refers to the manifestation of verbal or auditory speech. Christian worship will involve confessing, agreeing, and concurring that God is who He has revealed Himself to be. His "name" is an expression of His character, as names were so often employed in Hebraic culture. Such confessing and praising God for Who He is is always "through Jesus," for Paul quoted earlier from Psalm 22:22 indicating that Jesus "proclaims God's name to His brethren, and in the midst of the congregation sings God's praise" (2:12).

13:16 Continuing to explain the worship sacrifices that God desires of Christians, Paul writes, ***"But do not neglect doing good and sharing, for with such sacrifices God is well-pleased."*** The verbal "sacrifice of praise" must be translated into practical behavior. It is not enough to sit around with our hands in the air praising God, and fail to act in loving ways toward those in need. When this happens we are like those

whom God spoke of through Isaiah, "This people draw near
with their words, and honor Me with their lip-service, but they
remove their hearts far from Me" (Isa. 29:13). Not only are we
to "love the Lord," but also we are to "love our neighbor as
ourselves" (Matt. 22:37-40; Mk. 12:30-33; Lk. 10:27; Rom.
13:8-10; Gal. 5:14; James 2:8). Our love must be expressed
"in word and deed" (Col. 3:17; I John 3:16-18). Paul, therefore, advises the Jerusalem Christians not to forget, disregard,
or neglect "doing good and sharing." Jesus "went about doing
good" (Acts 10:38), and what would we expect as He now
lives in us, but that God would "equip us with every *good
thing* to do His will, working in us that which is *well-pleasing*
in His sight, *through Jesus Christ*" (13:21)? The general
expression of "doing good" is particularized in the admonition
to share and contribute generously with those who are in need
(cf. Acts 4:32-34). God is well-pleased (12:28; 13:21; cf. Rom.
12:1; Eph. 5:10; Phil. 4:18) with the Christian sacrifice of
practical worship that expresses the worth-ship of His character in Christian behavior.

13:17 Another expression of Christian worship in holiness is
to *"have confidence in those leading you, and defer* (to
them)*; for they are vigilant on behalf of your souls, as those
who will give an account. They should do this with joy and
not groaning, for this would be disadvantageous to you."* Just
as Paul began this section (7) with reference to "those presently leading" the Christians in the church at Jerusalem, he again
mentions the necessity to be persuaded of the advisability of
respecting and cooperating with those leading them. Similarly,
Paul encouraged the Thessalonians to "appreciate those who
diligently labor among you, and have charge over you in the
Lord and give you instruction" (I Thess. 5:12). Holy Christian
behavior will defer, yield, adapt, and submit to those designated as leaders, willing to work together with them in compliant
cooperation. Paul is not advocating a mandated subordination

or subjugation to a hierarchical structure of authoritarian leadership. Jesus said, "All authority has been given to Me in heaven and on earth" (Matt. 28:18), and Christians must beware of those who would claim "spiritual authority" or "pastoral authority" to "lord it over" (I Pet. 5:3) others as false shepherds with dictatorial control. Paul is simply advising the Jerusalem Christians to respect and have confidence in their leaders, willing to lovingly interact in collective cooperation, without engaging in critical challenge or antagonistic rebellion.

Those given the responsibility of leadership, Paul explained, "...are vigilant on behalf of your souls, as those who will give an account." The word "vigilant" is translated from a Greek word that etymologically meant, "to not sleep," but linguistically referred to vigilance and alertness in "keeping watch." Paul had told the elders of the church in Ephesus to "be on the alert" (a variation of the same word used here), as those who "shepherd the church of God" (Acts 20:28-31). Those who are entrusted to lead in the church must be diligent (Rom. 12:8), as they are accountable to God for their leadership service, having a "stricter accountability" (James 3:1) because of their influence over the souls of God's people.

Leaders should be able to do this service of vigilant leadership with the joy of serving as God's selected vessels, rather than with the groaning and sighing of a burdensome grief of having to battle uncooperative and unruly people. It is most unfortunate when Christian leaders are challenged, criticized, and second-guessed, losing sleep in anguish and frustration over the souls entrusted to their care. "This is disadvantageous and unprofitable for you," Paul advises the Jerusalem Christians. The purpose of the leadership of the church is that the body might be "built up in love" and "grow in all respects into Him, Who is the head, even Christ" (Eph. 4:11-16). When Christians are uncooperative and recalcitrant with their leaders, this does not serve God's end objective to manifest His holy and loving character by allowing the Christ-life to be lived out in Christian behavior within a loving community that is to represent the Triune interaction of the Godhead.

The Jerusalem Christians, whether within Jerusalem or outside of Jerusalem, were to worship God at the heavenly altar (10) with a verbal "sacrifice of praise" (15), in practical sharing with those in need (16), and by deference to their leaders (17). In such holy behavior (12:14) and worship, God would be well-pleased (12:28; 13:16,21). Paul wanted the Hebrew Christians in Jerusalem to understand that Christian worship was not constituted by the ritual and regulations of the Jewish religion, but by a practical lifestyle of worship that expressed the worth-ship of God's character in all situations.

13:18 Within the final contextual section (18-25), Paul shares some personal concluding comments that reveal his heart-felt affection for his Hebrew kinsmen in Jerusalem. He solicits their prayers for himself and his colleagues (18,19), expresses a prayer for the readers (20,21), encourages the readers to accept what he has written as intended (22), advises them of Timothy's release and his desire to visit them (23), exchanges greetings (24), and concludes by entrusting them to God's grace (25).

"Pray for us, for we are persuaded that we have a good conscience, desiring to conduct (ourselves) *well in all things."* Paul was not too proud to solicit the prayers of others. He often requests prayer in his epistles (Rom. 15:30,31; Eph. 6:19; Col. 4:3,4; I Thess. 5:25; II Thess. 3:1). The present tense verb can be translated, "Keep praying for us," indicating an awareness or assurance that the Christians in Jerusalem were already doing so. The plural pronouns, "us" and "we," could be editorial accommodation, but probably refer to Paul and his colleagues in Rome. Some have interpreted this to mean Paul's inclusion of himself with other apostles or other leaders (17) of the church.

Paul considered himself and his colleagues as worthy of the supportive prayers of his readers in Jerusalem, being "persuaded" and "convinced" that he and those with him had done what God willed in their lives, by being and doing what God wanted to be and do in them. Previously in this letter Paul had mentioned the cleansing of the conscience at regeneration (9:9,14; 10:2,22), but here he appeals to the inner perception of peace in having been faithfully and behaviorally available to do what God wanted. On several occasions in his writings Paul expressed his assurance of integrity based on a good conscience. In Jerusalem before the Jewish Council, Paul stated, "I have lived my life with a perfectly *good conscience* before God up to this day" (Acts 23:1). Before Felix, Paul said, "I do my best to maintain always a *blameless conscience* before God and before men" (Acts 24:16). These statements were made just prior to his state-sponsored transport to Rome (Acts 27:1). Writings to the Corinthians, Paul explained, "I am *conscious* of nothing against myself, but the One Who examines me is the Lord" (I Cor. 4:4), and later, "For our confidence is this, the testimony of our *conscience*, that in holiness and godly sincerity, not in fleshly wisdom but in the grace of God, we have conducted ourselves in the world, and especially toward you" (II Cor. 1:12). The apostle John wrote, "If our heart does not condemn us, we have confidence before God" (I John 3:21).

Continuing to include his colleagues, Paul indicated that they were "desiring to conduct themselves well in all things." They wanted their behavior to be good and exemplary, a faultless and irreproachable (cf. I Tim. 3:2; Titus 1:6) expression of God's holiness (12:14) in all situations and among all people.

Many commentators have speculated that Paul was attempting to justify his own behavior in explaining why he was worthy of the readers' prayers. Was there resentment or alienation between Paul and the Jerusalem Christians? Paul, as the "Apostle to the Gentiles" (cf. Acts 26:17), may well have been regarded with some suspicion and skepticism by the

Hebrew Christians.[4] Perhaps Paul feared that this letter, this "word of exhortation" (22) might not be well received by the Jerusalem Christians since he advocated such a definitive dichotomy between the old covenant and the new covenant, between Judaism and Christianity, with a rejection, repudiation, and severance from all Judaic religious traditions in order to participate in the "better things" in Jesus Christ.

13:19 There does not seem to be any apparent alienation in Paul's continued urging of the Jerusalem Christians to pray for him. *"And I entreat you especially to do this, that I may be reunited with you sooner."* Paul appeals to the Jerusalem Christians, beseeching, entreating, and encouraging them to pray for him. The word he uses can also be translated as "exhort" (22) or "counsel," but these have more of a demanding connotation. Paul wanted them to pray "especially" (cf. II Cor. 1:12; 2:4) and more specifically, that he might be reunited with them in a personal visit very soon. His desired reunion with the Jerusalem Christians can be understood as both the *content* of the prayer that he encourages, as well as the *consequence* of such prayer. Paul had been with the Jerusalem church on several occasions previously (Acts 9:26-30; 15:1-29; 21:15–23:22), and wanted to be with them again as soon as possible, "before long" (I Tim. 3:14), shortly, in order to speak with them face-to-face. The question that must be asked is: Was Paul hindered from such a reunion visit because he was incarcerated in Rome, and would have to be released from custody in order to return? There is inadequate information to answer that question, but in another epistle written from prison in Rome, Paul stated, "I hope that through your prayers I shall be given up to you" (Philemon 22).

13:20 Having sought their prayers, Paul turns around and expresses in writing a benedictory and doxological prayer for the Jerusalem Christians. Paul's prayer is heavily weighted theologically, but what would we expect from one whose mind was so oriented to theological intricacies?

"Now the God of peace, the One having brought out of a corpse the great Shepherd of the sheep in the blood of the eternal covenant, (even) *Jesus our Lord...".* These words simply establish the subject of the sentence, and the One to Whom the prayer is addressed. The designation of God as "the God of peace" was a common way to refer to God, and one that Paul used often (Rom. 15:33; 16:20; II Cor. 13:11; Phil. 4:9; I Thess. 5:23). God is the source of inner and outer peace – spiritual peace, psychological peace, and social peace.

The Son of God, the "Prince of Peace" (Isa. 9:6), is "the great Shepherd of the sheep." Jesus identified Himself as the "good shepherd who lays His life down for the sheep" (John 10:11,14), indicating that the Shepherd would be struck down (Matt. 26:31). Peter referred to Jesus as "the Shepherd and Guardian of our souls" (I Pet. 2:25), the "Chief Shepherd" (I Pet. 5:4) of the church. The "*great* Shepherd" is the "*great* High Priest" (4:14; 10:21). The Shepherd gave His life for the sheep. The High Priest offered Himself as the sacrifice for sin.

"Through the blood" (13:12) of the sacrificial death of Jesus on the cross, the "eternal covenant" was established extending "eternal salvation" (5:9), "eternal redemption" (9:12), and "eternal inheritance" (9:15) to those united with Him. The prophets had foretold of this new "eternal covenant" (Isa. 55:3; 61:8; Jere. 31:33; 32:40; 50:5; Ezek. 16:60; 37:26). Whereas the old covenant was designed as provisional and temporary with planned obsolescence (13:8), the new covenant in Jesus Christ would be final and permanent, never to be superseded. At the Last Supper, Jesus spoke to His disciples, "This is the blood of the covenant, which is to be shed on behalf of many" (Matt. 26:28) for the sins of all time (10:12), establishing the eternal new covenant for all ages between God and mankind.

God the Father "brought up" the crucified Jesus "out of a corpse," raising Him from the dead to be the "great Shepherd of the sheep" and the Lord of the church. The implications of the resurrection of Jesus were (and are) the foremost message of the Christian gospel. We are "born again to a living hope through the *resurrection* of Jesus Christ from the dead" (I Pet. 1:3). Christians are "those who believe in *Him Who raised Jesus from the dead*" (Rom. 4:24; I Pet. 1:21). Paul advised the Colossian Christians, "You were raised up with Him through faith in the working of *God, Who raised Him from the dead*" (Col. 2:12). The dynamic of the Christian life is the indwelling resurrection-life of Jesus. "If the Spirit of *Him Who raised Jesus from the dead* dwells in you, *He Who raised Christ Jesus from the dead* will also give life to your mortal bodies through His Spirit Who indwells you" (Rom. 8:11). Paul prayed for the Ephesians that they would "know the surpassing greatness of His power...in accordance with the working of the strength of His might which He brought about in Christ, when *He raised Him from the dead*" (Eph. 1:19,20). The divine dynamic of the Christian life is the grace provision of the resurrection-life of Jesus by the activity of the Holy Spirit. In the midst of that "newness of life" (Rom. 6:4) wherein we are "united in the likeness of His resurrection" (Rom. 6:5), we anticipate that *"He Who raised Jesus from the dead* will raise us also with Jesus" (II Cor. 4:14) in the future bodily resurrection (cf. I Cor. 15:12-28).

Jesus "was declared the Son of God with power *by the resurrection from the dead*, according to the Spirit of holiness, Jesus Christ our Lord" (Rom. 1:4). The resurrection of Jesus is the empowering basis of the Lordship of Jesus Christ, reigning and ruling in the lives of individual Christians and collectively in the church. The simplest affirmation of the early Christians, and Christians through the ages, has been, "Jesus is Lord" (I Cor. 12:3). Christians are to "set apart Christ as Lord in their hearts,...and keep a good conscience so that...those who revile their good behavior may be put to shame" (I Pet. 3:15,16).

13:21 Paul's prayer first established the subject, "the God of peace," and explained His historical action through His Son of crucifixion, resurrection, and the establishment of the eternal covenant community wherein the living Christ serves as "the great Shepherd of the sheep" and the Lord of the church (20). Having stated in prayer what God has done, he then prays for God's continuing action in the lives of the Jerusalem Christians. Paul's prayer is that God will *"equip you in every-thing good to do His will, doing in us that which is well-pleasing in His sight, through Jesus Christ, to Whom be the glory unto the ages. Amen."* Of all the new covenant writers of scripture, Paul seems to be most clearly cognizant that the Christian life can only be lived by the grace of God. He prays that God will prepare (cf. 10:5; 11:3), equip, and supply the Jerusalem Christians to be complete (II Cor. 13:11) and perfect (I Pet. 5:10) by His provision of grace, in order to be function-ally operative to manifest His goodness in accordance with His will. The Christian life is the "supplied life"[5] wherein the Christian is fully equipped by the dynamic power of God's grace for all good. Some manuscripts and translations read, "in every good *work*" (KJV), whereas the oldest manuscript (P^{46}) simply refers to being equipped "in good." The "fruit of the Spirit" includes "goodness" (Gal. 5:22,23), and the apostle John explained that "the one doing *good* derives what he does out of God" (III John 11). God equips the Christian to express His character of goodness in every good expression and good deed of the Christian life. "We are His workmanship, created in Christ Jesus for *good works*, which God prepared before-hand that we should walk in them" (Eph. 2:10). "God is able to make all grace abound to you, that always having all suffi-ciency in everything, you may have an abundance for every *good deed*" (II Cor. 9:8).

Equipped by His grace to express His goodness, we are prepared "to do His will." As Paul wrote to the Philippians, 'I can *do* all things through Him Who strengthens me" (Phil. 4:13). We can "do the will of God" only because He is the cause of His own character expression. That which God wills, He works! That which God desires, He does! Earlier Paul had put the words of the Psalmist (Ps. 40:7,8) into the mouth of Jesus, "I have come to do Thy *will*, O God" (Heb. 10:7,9). Jesus accomplished the will of God as "the Father abiding in Him did His works" (John 14:10), and we "do the will of God" (cf. 10:36) as the indwelling Christ expresses His life and character in and through us. Expressed succinctly, we can state that "the will of God is Jesus" expressing Himself in our behavior.

The "God of peace" is "doing in us that which is well-pleasing in His sight, through Jesus Christ...". God is the dynamic of His own demands, the cause of His own effects, the working of His own will. Nothing in the Christian life is generated or produced by human effort or "works," but it is all accomplished by God's grace. Paul's duplication of verbs is not always apparent in English translations, for Paul prays that, "God equip you *to do* His will, *doing in us* what is pleasing in His sight." This is similar to Paul's words to the Philippians, advising them to "*work out* your own salvation, for *God is at work* in you *to work* for His good pleasure" (Phil. 2:12,13). Based on His having "put His laws into our minds, and written them upon our hearts" (8:10; 10:16; cf. Jere. 31:33), by the indwelling presence of Jesus (cf. John 14:20; 17:23; Rom. 8:9,10; II Cor. 13:5; Gal. 2:20; Eph. 3:17; Col. 1:27; Heb. 3:14), God's internal dynamic of grace in the living Lord Jesus supplies everything necessary to live a Christian life pleasing to God. During His incarnation on earth, Jesus "always did the things that were *pleasing* to the Father" (John 8:29). It is only "through Jesus Christ" (cf. 15), His life expressed through us, that our behavior can be *well-pleasing* in

470

His sight" (cf. 12:28; 13:16). Every legitimate expression of the Christian life is "through Jesus Christ" (cf. Phil. 4:13). Christianity is Christ.[6]

God is glorified unto the ages by His own action, by His own all-glorious character expressed within His creation. Therefore, Paul's prayer is that as God equips the Christians in goodness to do His will, and does in the Christians what is pleasing in His sight, through Jesus Christ, the "God of peace" (and by extension, Jesus Christ as God) "might be glorified unto the ages" (cf. Gal. 1:5; II Tim. 4:18). God created all things (cf. Ps. 19:1) and all persons (cf. Isa. 43:7) for His own glory, but He "does not give His glory to another" (Isa. 42:8; 48:11). God's glory is in His own Self-expression through His Son, Jesus Christ, for godliness is exclusively the expression of God's own character, and God is glorified only by the manifestation of His own absolute and all-glorious character in the manifestation of the life of Jesus Christ. The extended phrase, "unto the ages *of the ages*," or "forever *and ever*," is an apparent addition not contained in the earliest manuscripts.

"So be it," "let it be," "Amen," Paul concludes his written prayer. He prays, believing that God will accomplish what he has prayed for.

13:22 Some have regarded the remaining words of this epistle to be an addendum or an attached postscript, but they seem to be an integral part of Paul's personal conclusion. ***"But I exhort you, brothers, bear with this word of exhortation, for I have written to you through a few words."*** Paul urges (cf. Rom. 12:1; 15:30; 16:17), entreats, beseeches, appeals, counsels, encourages, or exhorts the Hebrew Christians of Jerusalem to give due consideration to this letter he has written to them. The same word was translated "entreat" in verse 19, but to make the Greek word-play more obvious we have here translated it, "I *exhort* you...to bear with this word of *exhortation*...". This may overstate a sense of demanding harshness

not intended by Paul, but he is certainly appealing to the
Christians in Jerusalem to "bear with" (cf. Eph. 4:2; Col.
3:13), endure (II Tim. 4:3), or to "hold on to" the "word of
exhortation" (cf. Acts 13:15) supplied by this epistle, which
was meant to be a "word of encouragement" (10:25) of the
"better things" that Christians have in Jesus Christ. Some commentators have speculated that Paul was making a courteous
apology for the forthright and direct manner of his expressing
the dichotomy between Judaism and Christianity, thereby
attempt to soften the blow for the Hebrew Christian readers.
Paul was surely unapologetic about the stand he had taken in
the content of this letter, and was more likely urging them to
cling tightly to the message of all "better things" provided in
Jesus Christ alone. The only apology may have been for the
length of the epistle, since he proceeds to explain, "I have
written to you through a few words." This may be a classic
example of understatement, as Paul recognized that the epistle
was rather lengthy. On several occasions throughout the letter
Paul indicated that he had "much to say" (5:11; 11:32) and
could not "go into detail" (9:5) on every point, but given the
breadth of the subject of comparing the old covenant with the
new covenant, he had indeed written briefly "through a few
words."

13:23 Concerning his understudy and colleague, Paul wrote,
*"Be advised that brother Timothy has been released, with
whom, if he comes soon, I will see you."* Timothy was Paul's
student and traveling companion (cf. II Cor. 1:1; Phil. 1:1; Col.
1:1; I Thess. 1:1; II Thess. 1:1; I Tim. 1:2; II Tim. 1:2), and the
Christians in Jerusalem would have been well aware of that
relationship. On Paul's last trip to Jerusalem, Timothy was
accompanying him (Acts 20:4), and likely visited the church in
Jerusalem at that time. Timothy's "release" probably refers to
his being set free from custody or incarceration in prison, even
though we do not have any direct scriptural statement of his

being imprisoned. We do know that Timothy was with Paul in Rome when Paul wrote some of his prison epistles (Phil. 1:1; Col. 1:1; Philemon 1:1). Paul informs the Jerusalem Christians to "be advised, take notice, know" that Timothy has been released – information they would surely be glad to hear.

The briefly stated travel plans are rather ambiguous. Did Paul expect Timothy to come to Rome so they could travel together to Jerusalem, provided Paul was free to go? Or did Paul expect Timothy to travel to Jerusalem where Paul antici-pated that he could see and visit with Timothy and the Jerusalem Christians? We do not know the details of the pro-jected travel plans, but Paul obviously hoped to visit with the Christians in Jerusalem and with Timothy.

13:24 As was customary in ancient letters (cf. Phil. 4:21; I Thess. 5:26; III John 14), Paul sends concluding greetings. ***"Greet all those leading you and all the saints."*** There may have been several house churches in Jerusalem, each having leaders. If so, the "saints" and their leaders probably kept touch with the other church groups in a network of contact. The exhortation was to convey Paul's greetings to all the pres-ent leaders (7,14) and all the Christian saints.

In addition to his own conveyance of greetings, Paul adds, ***"Those from Italy greet you."*** The likely meaning of these words is that the Christians with whom Paul associated in Italy also sent their greetings to the Christians in Jerusalem. Several early sources and manuscripts of this epistle indicate that this letter was written by Paul "from Rome," so Paul was express-ing greetings on behalf of his fellow saints in Italy. Many speculations have been proffered whether this phrase refers to displaced or non-resident Italians living at either the place of origin or the destination of the epistle, but such adumbrations lead to no substantial conclusions.

13:25 In typical Pauline form (Phil. 4:23; Col. 4:18; I Thess. 5:28; II Thess. 3:18; I Tim. 6:21; II Tim. 4:22; Titus 3:15), Paul, the "Apostle of Grace," concludes the letter, *"Grace be with you all."* This is more than a casual and customary sign-off. Throughout this epistle Paul has returned to reference to God's grace. "Let us draw near with confidence to the throne of *grace*" (4:16). "See to it that no one comes short of the *grace* of God" (12:15). "It is good for the heart to be sustained by *grace*" (13:9). In Paul's mind, grace was the divine dynamic by which the entirety of Christian life was expressed, the free-flow of God's activity consistent with His character manifested by the risen Lord Jesus. Paul's final words to the Christians in Jerusalem were to express his desire that they live by God's grace, received by faith.

Concluding Remarks:

Despite his propensity for definitive theological precision and documentation, Paul concludes this letter to the Hebrew Christians in Jerusalem with a personal touch of pastoral concern. He allows his loving heart to be expressed through his pen in exhorting the readers to practical loving interactions. He seeks the prayers of his Jewish Christian brethren, and expresses his desire and intent to visit them soon.

The first paragraph (1-6) of this final section (13:1-25) is a series of imperatival exhortations to allow for the manifestation of God's love toward one another (1), strangers (2), prisoners (3), the mistreated (3), and toward their spouses in the sexual intimacy of marriage (4). Money and material things, on the other hand, are not to be loved, but Christians are to rest in the security of God's sufficient provision (5,6).

The practicum of love is carried over into the second paragraph (7-17) in the admonition to respect and cooperate with present church leaders (7,17,24). Sandwiched between these references to leaders, Paul reverts to a theological argument of how Christians are "sustained by grace" (9) because they par-take ("eat") from a heavenly altar (10) that is "outside the camp" (11,12,13) in a heavenly city (14), where they worship God in verbal praise (15), in generous sharing with others (16), and by deference for their leaders (17).

In his concluding comments (18-25), Paul solicits the prayers of his readers (18,19), and inscribes a prayer for them (20,21) that expects God to provide the sufficiency of His grace action by the indwelling presence of the Spirit of Christ in order to do God's will and glorify Him. Exhorting them to endure his exhortation (22), Paul then advises them of Timothy's release (23), explains his intent to visit them in Jerusalem (23), sends greeting to all, including greetings from those with him in Italy (24), and bids them to live in God's grace (25).

This final section (13:1-25) continues the theme of the "better things" in Christ Jesus, by emphasizing that the risen and living Lord Jesus provides the "Better Practical Expression of God at Work," in love and worship and prayer. As this may be the last extant epistle of the Pauline corpus of literature, it is most fitting and consistent that Paul should con-clude by emphasizing the divine dynamic of God's grace as He energizes and enacts all that is Christian. God is "doing in us that which is pleasing in His sight, through Jesus Christ" (21).

ENDNOTES

1　Goodspeed, Edgar J., *The Apostolic Fathers, An American Translation*. New York: Harper and Brothers. 1950. pg. 17.
2　Bruce, F.F., *The Epistle to the Hebrews*. Series: The New International Commentary on the New Testament. Grand Rapids: Wm. B. Eerdmans Pub. Co. 1972. pg. 394.
3　Roberts, Alexander and Donaldson, James, *The Ante-Nicene Fathers: Translations of the Writings of the Fathers down to AD 325*. Vol. I. Grand Rapids: Wm. B. Eerdmans Pub. Co. 1985. pg. 62.
4　Eusebius, *Ecclesiastical History*. VI,1,2. *A Select Library of Nicene and Post-Nicene Fathers of the Christian Church*. Second Series. Grand Rapids: Wm. B. Eerdmans Pub. Co. 1982. pg. 261.
5　Freeman, Bill, *The Supplied Life: A Daily Devotional*. Scottsdale: Ministry Publications. 1995.
6　Fowler, James A., *Christianity is Christ*. Fallbrook: CIY Publishing. 1996.